Arctic Sun on My Path

AN EXPLORERS CLUB BOOK

Arctic Sun on My Path

THE TRUE STORY OF AMERICA'S LAST GREAT POLAR EXPLORER

Willie Knutsen and Will C. Knutsen

Foreword by William W. Fitzhugh,
Director of the Smithsonian Institution's Arctic Studies Center

THE LYONS PRESS
Guilford, Connecticut
AN IMPRINT OF THE GLOBE PEQUOT PRESS

10 9 8 7 6 5 4 3 2 1

Printed in the United States of America.

Excerpt from "Air Force School for Survival" by General Curtis LeMay (National Geographic, 1953), reprinted by permission.

Library of Congress Cataloging-in-Publication Data is available on file.

Knutsen, Willie, d. 1992
  Arctic sun on my path: the true story of America's last great polar explorer/(Willie Knutsen, as recorded by) Will Knutsen.
    p.cm.
  ISBN 1-59228-672-0 (trade paper)
  1. Knutsen, Willie, d. 1992. 2. Explorers—Arctic regions—Biography. 3. Explorers—United States—Biography. 4. Arctic regions—Discovery and exploration—American. I. Knutsen, Will C., 1945-II. Title.
G635.K58A3 2005

910'.911'3—dc22

This book is dedicated to explorers everywhere, whether of the physical kind or intellectual. I want to particularly thank The Explorers Club for their all-important help in getting this almost forgotten story out to the public. A special thanks also goes to my editor, Holly Rubino, and others at The Lyons Press who labored in order that this special story could come to the public in the form it deserved. The responsibility for any mistakes missed in the rather complicated contents of this book falls on my offending shoulders.

—Will C. Knutsen

Contents

Foreword

To the average person who experiences the exploits of others from a safe distance, the lives of explorers—particularly arctic explorers—seem reckless and driven. What is it that compels people to throw their fate to the winds, to leave secure lives and loved ones behind for months or years, and to embark on dangerous enterprises of uncertain outcome? What is it that sends a purple gallinule to Goose Bay, Labrador, from the Gulf of Mexico, or a Ross's gull to Plum Island, Massachusetts, from Siberia? What sets a caribou out over the frozen Laptev Sea in search of an arctic island hundreds of miles offshore, or a Robert E. Peary or Matthew Henson north to the Pole? Biologists, psychologists, and historians can debate the particulars, but probably to one degree or another all are simply responding to the same elemental force recognized simply as Sir Edmund Hillary's "because it's there."

So it was also with Willie Knutsen. Knutsen is not a name that comes to mind when most people think of arctic exploration. He was not a glory-seeking Peary or a Richard Byrd trying to attain an ultimate geographical point. He was not adding continents and new worlds to a half-known globe like a Columbus or a Leif Eriksson. He was not immortalized in Viking sagas, and his statue does not stand in any national capitol plaza. He wrote little, although he did author two articles in *National Geographic*, and was written about even less. And since he was not a scientist, his reputation is not secured by academic tomes or the names of high-altitude radiation belts or new animal species—although some of his expeditions made contributions in all of these areas. If he was not known for what typically makes explorers famous, we have to ask: Who is this Willie Knutsen, and why is he one of America's last great arctic explorers?

One does not think of the 1930s as a great time for arctic exploration, certainly not in depression-saddled America. It was not a time of grand arctic ventures for North America. Most of the great ship-based expeditions like Nansen's or Amundsen's were long past, and the technological frontier had shifted to feats of arctic air passage. Even so, Norwegians, with more than one thousand years of voyaging in arctic waters, were continuing to play a major role in northern exploration of all forms. With changing technology and transport, the goals of arctic research had also shifted. No longer were expeditions venturing forth primarily for geographic discovery; rather, they were increasingly motivated by economic or scientific goals. It was a time of connecting the dots, of detailing the smaller elements of arctic lands discovered centuries, a generation, or several decades earlier. And it was handy, in this business, to be Norwegian!

Knutsen's father had been a master ship mechanic who had moved to Brooklyn, New York, a major Norwegian community in the days when Norwegians controlled much of the North Atlantic shipping business. Willie was born there, an American citizen, but soon moved back to Norway where he spent his youth sailing and banging around the coast between Oslo and Tromsø, where many of his relatives lived, and from where arctic vessels large and small routinely sailed, heading for exploration and adventure. His relatives and ancestors came from a long line of arctic mariners, one of whom had traded chart making for hunting rights in the Barents Sea from the Russian czar, while others had discovered Barents's death camp on Novaya Zemlya, returning with artifacts documenting the lost expedition. The arctic sun had indeed shined on Willie's path long before he set out on his first expedition to Northeast Greenland as an apprentice aboard an expedition financed by a wealthy Frenchman, Count Gaston Micard. Their ship was none other than Ernest Shackleton's *Quest*, on which the famous explorer had died in 1922. By the time Micard's second expedition was launched, Knutsen, who had proposed and planned the expedition, had been appointed its leader — an unusual turn of events for a young Norwegian-American trained as an artist and an architect!

To many, especially those in the fields of science or academic work, Knutsen is an unknown figure. He did not keep extensive diaries or write about his polar explorations. He was not scientifically trained, and made few scholarly contributions to polar studies, nor was he the subject of heroic tales, movies, or feature articles, except for a brief period when he became recognized as the most famous explorer in Norway in 1939. During this explosive early phase of his career in Northeast Greenland, from 1936 to 1939, his expeditions and discoveries secured him a place among the last great arctic explorers. (Also quite strangely during this time, he found himself owning personal title to Germania Land, which he later sold to Norway when he needed the cash.)

Knutsen spent the rest of his career employed by the U.S. government as an arctic expert in various defense-related capacities. He played a role in establishing U.S. air bases in Goose Bay, Labrador, and Crystal Two in Frobisher Bay, supporting Crimson Route airlifts to and from Europe in World War II. He led air rescue teams in Labrador and developed arctic survival training schools that served some twenty thousand men, and he helped establish the DEW Line early warning stations across the Canadian Arctic. In 1957, Knutsen commanded the U.S. science effort on Fletcher's Ice Island (known as T3) in the Arctic Ocean. Most of the latter exploits are the stuff of barroom sagas that never reach the printed page. Mercifully, in this case, they have survived through the efforts of Willie and his son, who for five years in the 1990s tape-recorded his father's vivid recollections and stories, and later, for this English-language edition, supplemented these recollections from other sources.

As a result, we have an unabashedly enthusiastic memoir of a man whose life straddled the transition from the heroic age of arctic exploration to an age dominated by science and technology in the service of national purpose—winning the Cold War. In the former capacity he was known to all of the great arctic explorers of his day—Vilhjalmur Stefansson, Helge Ingstad, Paul-Emil Victor, Robert Bartlett, and many others; while during the latter period he played a less visible role, maintaining the arctic infrastructure of the U.S. defense system. In both phases he was well known to his colleagues, if not to the general public; hence, the importance of this book.

Willie was above all else a doer, an actor, a storyteller—not a diarist, analyst, or essayist. This book includes many vivid, thoughtful passages, like his gripping account of being caught in a small tent during a five-day Northeast Greenland blizzard; his descriptions of the luminous qualities of arctic light; his reveries about the changing North and his role in it; and a clear-eyed insight into the condition of the Inuit as they moved from the Stone Age to the modern world. At the heart of Knutsen's story, however, is the straightforward, unabashed tale of a "polar man" forever gripped by an arctic fever that wouldn't subside. From the moment he began his trek across Lapland at the age of nineteen until the day he died, the North was his passion, and he had little interest or time for anything else. We owe an immense debt of gratitude to Willie and his son for rescuing—at virtually the last minute—Willie's colorful life for posterity.

While many arctic explorers have waxed eloquent about the land, its animals, and its vastness, in a very self-conscious and frequently romantic style,
Willie's book is really about the relationships he shared with the people he met
and served with in the Arctic. In these pages, his old friends from Germania
Land, Thule, Goose Bay, and elsewhere are always turning up in the most improbable places! Knutsen was a gifted people person and raconteur, and he
made friends quickly and easily, talking himself onto expeditions and making
the first radio "phone call" from Greenland to Norway. It seems he could not arrive in any new place—say, New York—before finding himself lecturing at The
Explorers Club or making a pitch to the Pentagon. With all this talk, its flavor
and verve amply captured here, comes some real explorer's swagger—like when
he recalls giving a certain "tip" to Helge Ingstad. Knutsen believes his information led to this other most-famous Norwegian discovering the L'Anse aux Meadows Viking site at the northern tip of Newfoundland. Helge did look there, and
discovered what is probably Leif Eriksson's Vinland camp. If perhaps Willie
takes too much credit for the discovery, he does so with humor!

Willie Knutsen was a generous person who was keenly interested in advancing scientific knowledge. His Northeast Greenland explorations were organized as scientific enterprises, and he learned much from the scientists
involved. His Norwegian-French Germania Land Expedition of 1938 to 1939
made important scientific discoveries about the aurora borealis, weather, ice-
leads, natural history, and electromagnetism. He saw science as the legitimate
goal of the new philosophy of exploration, and having had some early experience with archaeology, made a number of original contributions in this area too.

While archaeologists today would not approve of his undocumented and
somewhat cavalier "excavations" of Thule houses and grave sites in Greenland
(where he dug at Deadman's and Dove Bays, excavated by pioneering Danish
archaeologist Helge Larsen in 1932 to 1934), he was always careful to inform
specialists of his finds, and he deposited his collections in museums. One of
the sites Knutsen discovered was on the Sylvia Grinnell River near the modern
village of Iqaluit. After his initial excavations, Henry Collins, my predecessor at
the Smithsonian, was invited to conduct excavations there, and discovered a
large Dorset site below Knutsen's Thule village level. A number of Knutsen's

collections from Greenland, the Canadian Arctic, and Labrador are among the holdings of the National Museum in Ottawa, the Smithsonian, and other museums.

When I arrived at the Smithsonian as curator of North American archaeology, I first heard of Knutsen through Henry Collins. Their acquaintance resulted in Willie donating some archaeological collections he had obtained from a Moravian missionary in Nain, Labrador. After Collins retired, I was hired in 1970 to take his place as arctic archaeologist. I was beginning a major archaeological research program in Labrador at the time, and wasn't familiar with the collection, so Collins thought I should take a look at it. Ten minutes later I was up in the old attic of the Natural History Museum. It was indeed a Dorset Culture collection that Willie had donated in 1949, just after he returned from his air rescue work in Goose Bay. The records include no details other than the fact it was "obtained from the missionary in Nain, Labrador." Knowing the region and having excavated Dorset materials around Nain, seeing the collection was like being transported back two thousand years. This is just one example of how Willie Knutsen contributed to Northern science.

Reading Willie's book thirty-five years later, his story does much more than fill the information void about how the Knutsen Collection arrived at the Smithsonian; it also paints a vivid portrait of the exciting life of a twentieth-century arctic explorer who committed his life to the exploration and study of the Arctic.

WILLIAM W. FITZHUGH, DIRECTOR
Arctic Studies Center
National Museum of Natural History
Smithsonian Institution
23 February 2005

PART ONE

CHAPTER ONE

The Dream

D uring four stormy days and nights in 1936, the most famous arctic ship in the world plowed through the Norwegian Sea, heading for the northeast coast of Greenland. I was twenty-four years old, had recently graduated from university as an architect and artist, and was heading for my first arctic expedition. I was on board *Quest* as the guest of the French count, Gaston Micard, a millionaire whose grandfather, Ferdinand de Lesseps, had built the Suez Canal. Count Micard had chartered *Quest* for an entire year just so that he could contemplate life in the stillness of the Arctic. The "Micard Expedition" would over-winter, the first such expedition in decades.

As I stood on the wooden deck of the noble ship, the wind slowed to a stiff breeze and the air felt as if we had crossed some invisible geological frontier. The rough, tough Norwegian veteran of the Arctic, Captain Schjelderup (pronounced *Shell-der-up*), climbed the mast to the crow's nest, and soon shouted, "Ice-blink! Northwest!" With my heart pounding, I went starboard with the rest of the crew. At the horizon we could see a massive white, phantasmagorical light—a mirage caused by light reflecting off of the vast fields of ice floes far out of sight. My heart thumping in my chest, I thought, *This was the real Arctic, and what I had dreamt of visiting since I was eight years old.*

The *Quest* steamed for six hours before we actually met that arctic welcoming committee, the pack ice. At first we furrowed through it easily enough. It was like going through slush. But soon the stout oaken prow of the ship came toward a massive, flat hunk of ice the size of ten football fields. Captain Schjelderup slowed the ship until we gently nosed against it. Then, with engines going full bore, *Quest* began to spin the block out of our way. As the floe rotated, it created a current that pushed other slabs away, and we slipped inside and around them. Schjelderup really knew his stuff. He sent his most experienced men, one at a time at hour-long intervals, to the crow's nest to watch for the easiest routes. Gradually we wormed our way deep into the pack, only to enter the eerie, low-hanging fog that often hangs over ice floes in summer. The fog did not quite cover the top of the mast, so the crow's nest sailed in the sun, while we on deck in the gray gloom could only listen as *Quest* noisily bumped and ground its way through the ice. It was more than a bit unnerving.

Hours later the fog cleared enough so that we could see about us. We were surrounded by thousands of small icebergs. All hands were put on alert. We were heading directly toward larger bergs, and within a half hour we found ourselves among enormous, sculpted icebergs of every conceivable shape and contortion. Today, through television and other forms of mass media, icebergs seem almost common sights, but in reality, it is still rare to see them. In the thirties, not only was spotting icebergs a relatively rare event, but seeing them in person was like visiting another planet.

We were on a coal-fired wooden ship far out of radio contact with any other vessel, and all around us were gargantuan ice sphinxes, gargoyles, and trolls with ice arches for gaping mouths. There were pyramids and Pentagon-size hunks, Picassos, and even ice formations resembling a kind of stylized pornography. Anything the human mind had designed, ice, wind, and sun had beaten us to it by millenniums, and nature churned the designs out by the hundreds . . . every year! A berg a hundred feet high and a thousand feet long sailed past us, dreamlike yet dangerous. Our boat was like a tiny speck in an infinite field of hunks of moving, yet frozen, energy. The air really did have a peculiar charge to it, and light careened crazily off the facets of millions of airborne ice crystals. That strange light bounced off the bergs, rebounded off water and distant fog, and mixed with other light that had reflected off the pack ice behind us—the effect creating an altogether unreal, mind-dazzling light-world, albeit an extremely treacherous one.

The fog grew around us again, but not down to deck level. We could see a hundred yards in front of us, where tremendous hunks of ice floated together, some actually touching and forming a huge moving wall. There was nothing to do but wait for this "roadblock" to sail past. Still, in order to make progress westward, most of the time we had to squeeze our way through the bergs like a microbe through a complex barrier. This was the only way to reach the northeast coast of Greenland. It was easy to see why, even by 1936, this area had hardly been explored.

After hours of this slow going, we came out of the fog—as if through a sky-high curtain—into total sunshine, with a clear, cloudless blue sky above it. Just fifteen miles away loomed enormous mountain peaks. Greenland! We could see for miles, up and down the forbidding coast. Behind the peaks shone the white of the massive ice cap, the vast top of which was even higher than the mountains. No one needed to shout, "Land ho!" Captain Schjelderup, who was not one to waste time on beautiful views, brusquely remarked that, concerning the ice floes and deadly bergs, it was the least ice he had ever seen in the region, and that we had come through relatively easily. I was flabbergasted.

On the sixth day since leaving Tromsø, in northern Norway, we sailed into the relatively protected waters of Gael Hampke's Bay. As we came closer in, at the far end of the bay on its southern shore, nearly vertical alps loomed ever higher. They were the peaks we had seen from sea. Ice capped their frozen peaks, and narrow glaciers spilled over and hung down through nearly perpendicular valleys like tongues from tired dogs. What a sight! After four years and three missed chances, I had finally made it! It was the beginning of thirty-three years of work in the Arctic. But I had had a hell of a time getting there.

I was lucky to be gripped by fate early in life and steered unerringly to my life's work. The Arctic had shouted to me ever since my childhood, and there was not much I could do but follow the call. I was born in Brooklyn, New York, on April 13, 1912, the night before the *Titanic* sunk. My parents were from Norway and had friends and relatives aboard that unlucky ship. My father later said about my obsession with the Arctic that "It must have been because all you ever heard about for your first days on Earth was icebergs!"

Father had been a ship mechanic and had traveled all over the world. He spoke Chinese and Japanese. When I was born, he was considered a master mechanic and was stationed in Brooklyn with a large Norwegian shipping firm. He liked America so much that when his employers were going to send him to Oslo, he instead took a job fixing printing presses for a Norwegian newspaper in Brooklyn. You have to understand that Brooklyn was a Norwegian colony in those days, with four newspapers in Norwegian. The famous "Brooklyn-ese" way of talking probably came about from Norwegians teaching even newer immigrants than themselves their version of English! At any rate, after two years on the presses, father reluctantly took his family—my mother, Joanna, my older sister, Signy, and me—back to Norway, thus sealing my fate in the direction of the Arctic.

My parents were both born and raised in Tromsø, which at two hundred miles north of the Arctic Circle, or near 70 degrees north, was used in those days as a jumping-off point by more arctic expeditions to the unknown than any place in the world. It was the Cape Canaveral of its time. Tromsø was also where ships bound for seal and walrus hunting took on supplies. We visited Tromsø every other year in the summer to see friends and relatives, so I often witnessed the dockside excitement of polar preparations, and the triumphant returns of brave men from adventurous journeys. Wagons filled with ships' supplies were in those days pulled by horses. With the sound of hoofs clattering on the docks and the air filled with the shouts of men loading preparations for arctic travel — think how that infected a young boy's imagination!

My ancestors had lived in Tromsø for decades, and had a long record of arctic travel. My maternal grandfather had started a shipping business there in the 1860s, and my mother's uncle, Jacob Krane, had obtained a concession from Czar Nicolas to map northern Russia along the coast of the Barents Sea in exchange for fishing, sealing, walrus hunting, and trading rights. The Krane family became ambassadors for Norwegian interests in Russia, and still serves in that role today. My father's uncle, Elling Carlsen, was a well-traveled arctic man. He was the first to circumnavigate the Arctic island of Spitsbergen. In 1871, Carlsen, circumnavigating for the first time the massive but little-explored Russian Arctic island of Nova Zemlya (later used by Soviet Russia for nuclear bomb tests), found the hut and belongings of the ill-fated Dutch expedition of Willem Barents, which had disappeared in 1597. The Barents Sea, north of Norway and eastern Arctic Russia, is named after Willem.

When Carlsen brought these exciting findings back to Tromsø, it created a sensation. A visiting English gentleman suggested that Carlsen donate these important historical artifacts to the Dutch. Carlsen, a man who knew how to hold on to every øre — the Norse equivalent of a penny — and to whom every sailing trip was a business venture, said he'd sell the collection to them instead! The British subject, no doubt aghast at such mercantile crassness, bought them from my great-uncle, and donated them free of charge to the Dutch nation. Thanks to this upstanding citizen, these findings can be seen at the Dutch National Museum to this day. However, since the wonderful Arctic Museum in Tromsø also has a good collection of artifacts from Barents's camp, obviously my cagey ancestor held quite a bit back from the Englishman.

The illustrious names on our family tree were not all daring, tough seagoers. Though she had little to do with the Arctic, we were proud that the late, great

Norwegian actress Joanna Dybwad—a family member, on my mother's side—was the only woman the nation honored with a statue outside the National Theatre in Oslo. Only the playwrights, Ibsen and Bjørnsen, were given the same honor.

Obviously, my young mind was filled with these family stories of arctic adventure. And of course, the urge to travel and explore is rife in Norwegian culture. Norwegians are world-famous as sea rovers, shipping geniuses, and lovers of adventure. The Viking inheritance is much more than a mere saying: I rarely saw my father, due to his profession at sea, but when I did, he always encouraged my interest in the Polar Regions, thus helping to continue a family and national tradition of exploration.

When I was born, polar explorers had already probed the Arctic for three centuries, but still not much was known about the icy region that comprises a huge part of the earth's surface. Just two decades before my birth, there was still so little known about the Arctic that some people had theories that an advanced civilization—an Atlantis—existed at its frozen heart, hidden from the prying eyes of mere humans. Several serious Christian religious thinkers of the day thought God might have an earthly kingdom hidden in the Arctic's "impenetrable" heart.

In 1888, one of the "scientific" missions that constituted the first crossing of the Greenland ice cap by the Norwegian Fridtjof Nansen was to see *if* indeed a super-civilization existed there. Nansen apparently did not believe anything of the sort, but was willing to take donations from anyone who offered. And besides, though the idea of hidden worlds may seem unscientific today, who in those days could be sure? After all, discovering the unknown is what exploration is all about, and in 1888, the Arctic was a great unknown. That some people thought the Arctic was where God lived may explain why a large arctic city in Russia was named Archangel, the guardian of heaven.

During the days of my youth, polar exploration had greatly enlightened man since 1888, but the vast Arctic still had the questioning eyes of the world riveted to it, and polar explorers were among the greatest of heroes. And this, of course, was why so many young people of that time dreamed of becoming daring "polar men"; it was like wanting to be an astronaut. It was my good fortune, out of the thousands who shared similar visions of polar adventure, to be one of the few who realized his goal.

In my teens, the biographies of great explorers were best-sellers, and I had read and collected many. The adventures of Nansen, Amundsen, Robert Peary,

Sir Ernest Shackleton, Vilhjalmur Stefansson, and the great English explorer, Robert Falcon Scott, were favorites of mine. And new adventures were being carried out yearly. The Australian explorer and pilot, Sir Hubert Wilkins, who had begun his arctic work with the Canadian-born Stefansson in 1913, and who had been with Shackleton to Antarctica, had made daring flights over much of the Canadian Arctic during the 1920s. He had even attempted to reach the North Pole from Norway by submarine in 1931. The exploits of these great men, however, had still not shed much light on the unknown Arctic.

The famous Norwegian polar explorer, Roald Amundsen, called the early forays—including his own—into the vast, unknown lands "stunts" and "Arctic dashes." Among his other great contributions to exploring the Polar Regions, he was the first to "dash" to the South Pole. These "firsts" captured the public's imagination, but did little to enhance deep scientific understanding. A dash by a sled or plane to the North or South Pole obviously could not unravel the secrets of the Arctic or Antarctic Oceans. When I first arrived in Greenland in 1936, the world's largest island—larger in area than Mexico—was still barely explored, especially the ice-locked northeast coast, which I would eventually help to reveal to the public.

My first real encounter with polar explorers came in 1925, when I was thirteen. That year, Roald Amundsen, along with the American, Lincoln Ellsworth, had made an attempt to fly to the North Pole with two Dornier Wal amphibious airplanes (Dornier was the manufacturer, and *wal* means whale in Dutch). When the planes were reported missing, the whole world waited anxiously for news of their fate, as if waiting for news of a member of their own family. This tension went on for almost a month. Hope was gone. Then, like a movie with a happy ending, the explorers reappeared. And, yes, they had had a rough time. They had almost perished.

Amundsen's Dornier Wal was later flown back, and was parked out in Oslo's harbor. I rowed my ten-foot dinghy out to the floatplane, circled it with awe, then got up the nerve to row up next to it and touch it. When I returned to the dock, there was a crowd of office workers who had quit working early to come see the famous plane. Seeing me in my boat, some men offered me the equivalent of a dollar each to row them out so they could get a closer look. Not only was I happy to do it, but they insisted on rowing! And so it went. All day I ferried passengers to and from Amundsen's plane. At the end of the day, my hero had unwittingly helped me to become a well-off thirteen-year-old.

A year later, in 1926, Roald Amundsen and Lincoln Ellsworth were at Spitsbergen preparing for what the press called, "A race to be the first to fly over the North Pole." They were awaiting the arrival of the Italian, Umberto Nobile, with his huge dirigible. Richard Byrd, of the United States, was also there with his pilot Floyd Bennett. They had a Fokker plane with a Ford tri-motor, and hoped to beat Amundsen's team. The race was on.

I actually saw the dirigible when it arrived in Oslo on its way North. It came floating over the mountains, and it was a bit eerie. Dirigibles were even rarer than planes, and it was nearly as exciting and strange to see the thing as it would have been to see a flying saucer.

Although Byrd's plane eventually claimed victory, Amundsen flew not just to the Pole, but beyond it, and all the way to Alaska, an incredible feat for the time. Both reported that they saw no hidden civilization. The next year, Charles Lindbergh became the first in a race to fly nonstop over the Atlantic. There were other planes that landed relatively soon after him, though they have since been forgotten. Richard Byrd was among those who made the crossing safely. His pilots were the American, Acosta, and a young Norwegian named Bernt Balchen, who had been a member of Amundsen's crew on Spitsbergen the year before.

Bernt was to become a lifelong friend of mine, as well as an Arctic co-traveler. We would know each other for decades before we found out we were distant cousins! In 1929, for the first time in history, Bernt Balchen, as pilot for Richard Byrd, flew the American team over the South Pole. The American financial backers for this expedition had insisted on an all-American team, so Congress voted by a unanimous show of hands to make Bernt an instant American citizen. When the team returned in triumph, New York City gave them a ticker-tape parade. It was a huge event. The whole world celebrated, and Byrd became a household name, as did Bernt. These polar flights captured worldwide headlines, and kept my imagination fired, though I was getting worried there would be nothing left for me to explore. If I had known then what I know now, I should not have been troubled.

My teen years were spent, like so many Norwegians, in athletics and rugged outdoor activities. A week's cross-country skiing expedition with a heavy backpack and blizzards en route was a normal way to spend one's free time from school in winter. And this went for the girls as well. Summers spent sailing the fjords and the rough waters on Norway's south coast was also part of the lifestyle that prepared me well for later polar life. These were just routine activities in Norway. Plus, I was a member of The Sea Scouts, which meant that I learned how to sail tall-masted ships in my teens. To top it off, a kayak was given to me by my parents for my fifteenth birthday. This wonderful craft was actually made by the great shipbuilder, Jensen, who had been the foreman in the building of Amundsen's famed Arctic vessel, *Maud*. When he made my kayak, Jensen created a work of art. It floated like a swan, and made me very popular with the girls. (Coincidentally, while I was working with the Canadian and American Arctic Survival Training Schools in 1951, I would visit the remains of *Maud* in Canada's arctic waters near Victoria Island.)

My first real chance for Arctic exploration came in the summer of 1932. I had taken a break from my job as an apprentice bricklayer. I was studying to be an architect, and such an apprenticeship was required before going to university. For my summer vacation I planned to walk across the wilderness of Lapland, also called Finnmark in those days, and now officially called Sapmi, or Sámi Land. Starting from the north Norwegian coast at the little town of Alta, I planned to walk seventy miles southeast to the inland town of Kautokeino, then another fifty miles south to Karesuando, in Sweden.

It was a little scary. There were no roads, few people, and trillions of mosquitoes. It would be mostly through arctic swamps; the maps showed not even one hiking trail! None of my friends would join me, and thought I was out of my mind. And my girlfriend, Inger, thought I was being very irresponsible, putting myself in harm's way like that. They wanted to sail the fjord and have picnics, but I had done that with them since we were ten. And the year before, a friend and I had sailed his boat to Sweden. It was getting old and repetitious. I had to see something new. So I made plans to go with my sister, Signy, to see family in Tromsø, and from there I would travel alone to Alta, the only "town" of any size on the Lappish coast.

On my way northward to Tromsø on board the still-famous coastal ship *Hurtigruten*, or "Fast Route," I met the man who would change my life. He was Count Gaston Micard. It was fate. There is no doubt about that. We were immediately drawn to each other even though he was a middle-aged man. He looked eccentric, especially since he carried an exotic, brightly colored parasol; he stood out like a sunset on the deck, but he carried himself with dignity, parasol notwithstanding. He was accompanied by his equally charming sister, Madame Smet, and they kindly invited Signy and me to join them as they sat on the deck.

Count Micard, along with Madame Smet, was planning a summer practice expedition on Greenland's east coast to prepare a team he had hired for the following season's year-and-a-half expedition to a place as far north as anyone had gone to make a winter scientific camp. I could not help bragging a bit about my planned walk across Lapland, and Signy told them, in her rather imperious manner, that our great-uncle was *the* Elling Carlsen, who had found the explorer Barents's last camp. The count suggested we all meet later at his table for dinner. That evening, over a delicious meal of cod served with a fine white wine, the count told me in all earnestness that I had the right spirit for arctic work, and promised that when we got to Tromsø he would check with the captain of the ship he had chartered to see if I could go to Greenland with them. I nearly fainted. The main problem, he told me, was that by law, the expedition had to bring enough provisions for each person for at least a year. They were planning to spend just two, maybe three months, but still, by law, they had to be prepared in case the infamous ice pack from the East Greenland current trapped them in for the year. So, said the count, a year's provisions for an extra person on such short notice was asking a lot of the skipper. I tried not to get my hopes up too high.

The expedition was to sail on the aforementioned *Quest*. Made in Norway, the *Quest* had often been the England-based exploration ship of Sir Ernest Shackleton. The *Quest* had been to both the Arctic and Antarctic. In 1909, Sir Shackleton had almost sledded to the South Pole, coming within ninety miles. Roald Amundsen would reach the pole two years later, but Shackleton's getting to within ninety miles of it is close enough in my mind. Shackleton's voyages and adventures in endurance and survival in impossible conditions became legendary, and in the 1920s *Quest* was known worldwide. Sir Ernest had died onboard the boat in 1922, near South Georgia Island, on his way to study Enderby Land. By 1932, *Quest* was back in Norwegian hands, owned by Captain Ludolf Schjelderup, the gruff old sea dog from Bodø. I had a book in my collection called *Shackleton's Last Voyage: The Story of the* Quest. It had a detailed diagram of the interior of the ship, so I felt I already knew the ship inside and out. I was delirious with anticipation.

In Tromsø, we discovered what Count Micard had feared: The ship could not take on another expedition member on such short notice. Micard told me, "Willie, I want you on my expedition next year. I promise you that!" The next morning, I stood on the dock where I had seen so many ships head out for arctic expeditions. As the *Quest* sailed off to Greenland for high adventure, I watched until the ship had gone out of sight around one of the islands between Tromsø and open arctic waters. But I was not too disappointed—Lapland called. And I had Count Micard's promise for the Greenland expedition the next year.

CHAPTER TWO

Lapland: Slogging Through an Arctic Swamp

To get to the then very remote Alta, I hitched rides on small fishing boats. The Lapp trading center at Alta, which today is a town, was then mostly a temporary summer camp of Lapp tents. There was a small hotel of sorts, Wiiks Hotel, and there I met, very briefly, an Englishman about my age named Tom Manning. We got to talking because my parents had just moved to Newcastle-upon-Tyne in northern England, where my father had been made head of the Norwegian Seamen's Home. Plus, I had recently been accepted to attend architecture classes in Newcastle-upon-Tyne, England, at Rutherford College.

Manning wanted to see the Arctic more than anything he could dream of, so he was going to Nord Kapp, the northernmost point in Europe, 350 miles above the Arctic Circle. (Nord Kapp is as far north as Point Barrow, Alaska, the northernmost point of the United States.) Tom would eventually go into polar work in Canada, and we would meet again more than ten years later on Baffin Island. (Such meetings and subsequent reacquaintance with people like us in the most unlikely places throughout the Arctic continued over my thirty-odd-year career as an "arctic rat." There just were not that many of us in the Arctic, involved in arctic work. We were bound to bump into each other again and again.)

Lapland in the early 1930s was a land that, although inhabited by the Lapps for thousands of years, was sparsely populated, to say the least. There was no industrialization. The human population of Norwegians and Lapps in the sixty thousand square miles of Norwegian Lapland was just forty thousand, and more than half of this population lived along the coast. Some archaeologists have linked the oldest-known Scandinavian Stone Age culture, the so-called *Komsa* culture by the Arctic Sea, to the ancestors of the Sámi (the true name of the Lapps). This culture from around 9,000 B.C. had been researched by one of my professors at Oslo University, the world-famous Gudthorm Gjessing—and there he was, kneeling in the moss just off the road!

"Good day, Professor Gjessing," I said, expecting him to be amazed to find me way out there, but he simply looked up and said, "You know, I have just discovered a new species of insect!" He was quite engrossed, and added, "Well, I have to get this back to camp. Sorry I cannot chat." And off he went. I had hoped to pump him for information about the ancient Lapp culture; it was a good thing I had read one of his books.

Gjessing had a theory that some early Lapps may have migrated by ice all the way to America. At any rate, the Sámi had lived happily on this coast for thousands of years, fishing and herding reindeer. The area was still pretty primitive, but Alta actually had a beat-up old Chevy that passed as a taxi, and the driver tried to persuade me to have him take me out the long way to the infamous trail across the interior.

"I am walking, not riding across Lapland!" I told him a bit snobbishly. In truth, I hadn't the money for such luxuries. And I would have missed having dinner with all the Lapp girls and old ladies who invited me to eat with them at their camp of tepee-like tents. Luckily for me, all the men were with the reindeer. I had one of the older women take a photo of the rest of us. In that photo I look like a "Peer Gynt" type with a harem of Lapp women.

The next morning I began the long trek on the road the taxi would have taken. This "road" was actually a grass-covered rut. Just outside of the camp, I caught sight of a Lapp sprawled absolutely still on the ground. I thought he was dead. There were no mosquitoes around his exposed face, and since they swarmed around mine, I thought perhaps they didn't bother with dead people. Stooping over him to see if he was breathing, I had to jerk my head back from the powerful fumes emanating from his mouth. It was Sterno, or "canned heat." He was drunk on the stuff! No wonder the insects wouldn't go anywhere near him! I took a photo for posterity.

After three days of bug-plagued walking along the one and only dirt road in the whole territory, I spent the night in a hiker's cabin where the road ended. There was a guest register in the cabin, intended partially for safety reasons. If a hiker had signed the register and never showed up at the next trail hut, at least his next of kin would know where he had been last. I read some of the entries, and came across this rather disturbing one: "We came here with a keen interest to study the Lapps and their wonderful, wild land. We made it a few kilometers from here. The mosquitoes took over . . . we surrender . . . are returning to Oslo tomorrow!" I thought, *My God, do they mean the mosquitoes get worse?!* I was having some doubts as to the wisdom of walking alone. Nobody did that. But I would soon find out that I did not have to endure a solo crossing of Lapland.

Over a breakfast of bread and cheese in the bug-free safety of the cabin, I heard the coughing sound of the old Chevy. Looking out, I saw one passenger step out. The taxi turned around and headed back the long, lonely route to Alta. This new companion, Erik Normann, was a young Swedish man about my age, who was also planning to walk Lapland alone. Upon meeting me, he immediately suggested we join forces to keep each other from going crazy from the bugs. Even though I had some doubts about a guy who would begin his cross-Lapland walk in a taxi, Erik had a good point about the bugs, and soon we were headed out into the wilderness together.

It was a beautiful, sunny day. Except for the piercing buzz of the insects, we were in the grip of the wonderful solitude that nature extends to those who leave cities and the bustle of civilization behind. As we walked, there was no wind. The bugs loved this, for with no effort they could stay pressed tightly to us. The wisdom of having a Lapp hat, topped with its long tassels, became painfully apparent. As one walked, the bouncing tassels shooed the mosquitoes away from the face. We would have killed for one of those hats! After three hours of hiking we stopped to eat. We dug out some bread and dried reindeer meat. The meat was hard and tough and had to be held in the mouth for awhile to soften it up enough so that it could be chewed, and its wonderful, invigorating flavor released. We had some butter, but the moment we spread some on a hunk of bread, the gnats and mosquitoes covered it thickly, and were impossible to remove. Hungry as we were, we could not bring ourselves to eat that black gunk.

Erik, in desperation, came up with a solution. He had a piece of tarpaulin, about six feet by six. Taking pieces of the small, finger-thick tundra birch, he used them to stake down the tarp to the ground. We wriggled like snakes to get under this shelter. It was tight quarters, but it worked! We had a bug-free lunch, and bug-free butter. After we had eaten and wriggled our way out, Erik lit his pipe, hoping to keep the bugs away. But there were so many of them (the cloud was several feet thick above our heads) that the ones caught in the pipe smoke were shoved down by the ones flying above them, until they actually clogged the pipe!

We continued our journey over typical tundra dotted with small lakes. Some of the lakes and ponds were noisily draining off recent rains, and though the sound from one was minute, the combined symphony of hundreds of small ponds was musically thunderous. The tundra was like a Japanese garden, with lichen-covered rocks splayed with hues of orange, green, and blue set among miniature flowers. These flowers, when you bent down closely to observe them, were delicately intricate, and the effect was truly enchanting. All the mirror-like ponds and lakes drained off noisily into bogs that led to lively rivulets, which in turn led to rushing streams that led at last to the Kautokeino River. Though in summer there are twenty-four hours of daylight, toward midnight we could see the nearly setting sun hovering near the horizon. It shot red rays through the many white-skinned branches of the miles and miles of small birches, creating an eerie light one could almost feel. This effect was most moving, of course, when a breeze scattered the bugs just enough so that their thick cloud did not dim the unearthly light.

At the cabin station of Masi, we took a ride upriver with two Sámi postmen, Klement Mortensen and Morten Klementsen—these were not their true Sámi names, but names they created for contact with the "outside world." The postal service boat was a sort of canoe made of wooden planks. The old craft was equipped with a tiny, rickety-looking Evinrude outboard motor. I had hardly expected to see any motor out there in the wilderness, but Erik agreed with me that traveling by this crude boat was not cheating on our "walk." We rationalized that it was part of the true Lapland experience. The boat generally had to be propelled through the rapids by the man using two short oars sitting in the bow, so the motor was not used much, anyway. With energetic movements, he would ease us through rocks and boulders in the river. Long oars would have been useless. Meanwhile, the man in the stern used a stout pole to help push and guide the craft, particularly so the swift downward current would not swing the bow around. Whenever we came upon flat, quiet stretches of water, the Evinrude would be started up, and we would "zip" along at 5 mph.

Later that night—while the sun still shone—we sat around a fire munching delicious, freshly caught trout. We had camped by a roaring waterfall so that the spray would keep the bugs at bay, and I was able to clear the exhausting, mosquito-filled days of walking from my mind. I was busy instead looking around at the scene: the two Lapps with calm, strong faces, dressed in their native clothes; the falls; the woods, and the open sky above. The same scene could have taken place hundreds of years ago. I was in the quiet heart of Lapland. All my plans had come true. This land had called to me since my youth, and I had finally come to see why. Nearby, I found the remains of many old "dugouts," the semi-subterranean dwellings of the old-time Lapps. There were enough ruins covered by carpets of moss to hint that this had once been an important settlement, maybe hundreds of years before, though moss can cover anything in two years. I was itching to do some archaeological work, but of course, there was no time for it.

After a total of about fifty hard-earned miles from Masi, we reached Kautokeino, the principal settlement in Norwegian Lapland. Today one can drive to Kautokeino, but then it was in the middle of a vast wilderness. Low, tree-covered hills surrounded the village, and on the lower slope of one of them, a small church first drew one's attention. Perhaps some few hundred people lived in Kautokeino. Some, probably visiting herdsmen, actually still lived in tepees of reindeer hide, or the usual canvas. There were *Lappegamme*, huts made of sod and moss piled up around a tepee-like structure of birch poles. Smoke circled from the holes in the tops of both types of dwellings. But neat log huts were home to most.

Throughout the village were upright posts that had fulcrum poles and buckets attached indicating where the wells were. There were no streets or gas-powered vehicles, no streetlights or power poles. Still, it was a community, complete with a log cabin for the elderly. We watched in amazement as two nurses chased an old man who was heading for the woods. A local resident explained that the old Sámi refused to take his jacket off. He believed it was magic, and that he would die if it were taken off. He hadn't taken it off for weeks, and the result was quite smelly. The nurses tried daily to strip him of the offending garment, but he'd hightail it for the woods every time.

Looking for a place to sleep, Erik and I went as directed to the only two-storied house in town. It stuck out like the Eiffel Tower, and belonged to Issak Hetta, the richest man in town, perhaps in all of Lapland. We had been told he would rent us rooms. He did, and also lost no time in telling us he had made the bulk of his money in, of all places, Alaska!

He had been sent to Alaska to be a herder for reindeer imported by Alaska from Lapland to establish a new source of food for the Eskimos, since their herds of caribou were being depleted. In Alaska he had lived on reindeer meat, fish,

wild berries, and whatever else he get could harvest from the land, thereby saving all his money for when he retired. He told us with a wink that it had not hurt
to have panned for some gold as well. Before he retired, he trained others to take
his place. (It's one of those many remarkable coincidences that I would later
meet Harry Strong, one of these men Issak had trained, in Arctic Canada!)

As we left Kautokeino and the river to head across land to Karesuando, a village in the Swedish Lapp country, the land quickly became uninhabitable tundra pocked with vast bogs that were spattered by tufts of scraggly trees. Once again
we were surrounded by miles of moss-covered land dotted by never-ending
mounds of moss-covered, rotting birch branches and logs. There were millions of
puddles brewing mosquito larvae. Patches of small, feathery evergreens were surrounded by bushes of red cranberries and blueberries. Everywhere were the dramatic displays of those lichen-covered rocks, and the triumphant flowers, and the
cloud-like meadows of downy "arctic cotton." We rarely saw birds, or heard their
song, and though it may not have been the season for them, I was sure it was the
gnats and mosquitoes that had driven the birds into exile! Once we saw some
dead ducks. Not surprisingly, their mouths were filled with mosquitoes.

After a few days of the same terrain, we came to an awesome, intimidating
sight: Ahead of us lay a vast swampy area that even the Sámi rarely bothered
going into. There was supposed to be a trail, but an old woman some miles back
had told us with a cackling laugh that it was not very well marked. How could
it have been? We were looking at slime-covered water out of which stuck small,
mossy mounds with a scrub-birch or two sticking out of them. There was nothing else we could do but leap from mound to mound. Our heavy packs, and the
spongy ground of the mounds, made our leaps precarious. We took turns grab-
bing onto each other to save ourselves from a dunking in the swamp water,
which had the consistency of a thin, brown pudding with a slimy-green topping.
The smell of rot and decay was heavy in the air, but that did not deter the gnats
and mosquitoes one bit. On and on we went, leaping from mound to mound.
Our boots were soaked, sweat from the exertion made our bodies soggy from the
inside out, and then it began to rain! For three days the rain was ceaseless. The
swamp rose, and the bugs' relentless attacks got even worse. Our rain gear made
us sweat even more profusely than before. Our packs caught on branches. Our
legs turned to rubber. We set up camp wherever and whenever exhaustion dictated, the two of us squeezing uncomfortably into my one-man tent.

We had no real idea if we were still going in the right direction, because the few signs of the trail had vanished. Certainly we must have made a few circles on our slog through the swamp. Finally, we stumbled upon an ancient sod lean-to, a Lappegamme, set up on a larger-than-usual island-mound of moss, and so we assumed we had hit upon the "trail" by luck. The hut dripped a bit inside, but at least we were out of the torrential downpour. Utterly spent, we stayed there for a day and a half to recover our strength. The rain was still coming down in a wet, gray blanket when we headed out again with teeth gritted. We slogged, and leapt. It was hardly a "walk" across Lapland!

Interestingly, we soon came upon some tracks made by automobiles. We knew they had to be from the Citroen Expedition of 1930, which had used "caterpillar" tracks over the tires for traction. The marks still looked fresh. We followed this trail wherever we could, knowing that the expedition had headed for Karesuando. The tracks on the wheels had helped prevent the cars from sinking in the mucky ground, but every once in a while we would see one of the vehicle's tracks end at a rather deep and ominous-looking waterhole in the bog, and we wondered if a vehicle was at the bottom of it.

We tramped along in the gray, wet air for days. All around us were the endless wisps of pale green trees on those damn mossy mounds. Our world was an eternal sound of rain, rising swamp, and our sloshing footsteps and leaps. This went on for two days; then, suddenly, like a curtain rising on a play, the swamp opened up onto a good-sized lake. We knew it had to be *Siilijarvi* or "Deep Lake," and that meant we were near our destination. Five minutes later we actually found a trail, the first we'd seen in a week. Erik and I looked at each other. We were quite stunned. Then we broke out with grins. We had made it though the swamp, and right on course! We threw our heads back and laughed out loud. We did a little dance. Then we pretended we were quite untouched by the whole rough adventure. Affecting proper British accents, we spoke calmly in English: "Nice stroll, old chap!" "Yas. Lovely. Let's do it again sometime soon." Then we broke into a maniacal jig, accompanied by similarly maniacal laughter. It was a good thing we had no audience.

We had been in absolute wilderness for weeks. Arriving at Karesuando, we walked through the bustling "metropolis" of a small hostel, a café, a real street (albeit a dirt one), and a row of frame homes. It was as though we'd never seen civilization before. And it *was* civilization. It even had a telephone. Erik called his father in Sweden, and then told me in his fake British accent that a car and chauffeur were on the way. I thought my new friend had a good sense of humor. We lounged around town for a day and a half, until, sure enough, a large, chauffeur-driven Cadillac—I think—pulled into the quiet town in a cloud of dust. It turned out my hiking partner's father was the manager of the famous iron mine at Kiruna, in Northern Sweden.

We found ourselves magically transported, as if on a magic carpet, through the still fairly wild forests. Occasionally, the limousine had to go through the indignity of having to cross rivers by ancient ferries made of logs, which were hauled from one bank to the other by stout cables. We shared such ferries with old horses and their carts. Erik and I enjoyed the joke of the two young explorers suddenly pampered by such luxury.

Erik's home was a stately one set among graceful birches and a well-tended yard. The interior was a model of upper-middle-class orderliness, yet very homey and bright, and held a fine library. When the Normanns heard that I had a strong interest in Arctic exploration, Erik's father smilingly directed me to a book by the Greenland explorer, Knud Rasmussen. Pulling the book from the shelf, I found it was signed by the author himself, and included a handwritten note from Rasmussen to Erik's family. I read his note, which ended with these words:

If you make plans, and stick to them,
the sun will always be on your path!

I immediately took this for my own motto.

CHAPTER THREE

The Teasing Hand of Fate

Not long after my adventure in Lapland, I found myself at Rutherford Technical School in Newcastle, England, where I studied art and architecture before transferring to Durham University at Newcastle, now called Newcastle University. As I said earlier, my mother and father had moved to Newcastle where Father had been given a position as head of the Norwegian Seamen's Home. They would stay there fifteen years. Previous to this position, my father had been a top salesman for a Swedish company that made hydraulic equipment, and Father was thus able to afford sending me to university. Not bad for a man who, as a young boy in Tromsø, had been told he had no chance of a higher education, so it was best he learned to do something "useful," like repairing shoes. Not only did he learn to speak Chinese and Japanese, and earn a master mechanic's certificate early in his career, but he was also a poet and a well-read man. So much for the *experts'* opinion of my father's intelligence.

I knuckled down to my studies. The promised expedition to Greenland with Count Micard had never materialized. I constantly read bulletins announcing arctic expeditions, but his name never turned up. I was too busy at classes—and socializing!—to be terribly disappointed. Even so, I did wonder what became of the count. By sheer luck, my art instructor was the famous sculptor, Herbert Maryon, who also taught me archaeology. Professor Maryon later became head of the much-publicized Sutton Hoo dig, the treasure-filled find of an early Saxon chieftain ship burial. Professor Maryon and I became good friends. We often went out to do digs along Hadrian's Wall, and there he taught me the finer points of archaeological work—that is to say, unhurried, meticulous attention to detail. His example would be put to use during my many years of arctic work. He also admonished me to "Never stop painting!" And I have not. Even years after I graduated we kept in touch by mail.

At the end of my first year of university in 1933, my father told me it was time to decide which citizenship to take: U.S. or Norwegian. He suggested I become a U.S. citizen. "You'll always be thought of as a Norwegian at home, so why not have the best of two worlds?" I was convinced. But there was a slight problem. I would have to step on United States soil to get my citizenship, and the journey would be expensive. Father had it all worked out. He had a connection with a shipping firm which owned a small cargo ship soon sailing to America from southern England, and it was arranged that I could sail on it as a "fireman" in the boiler room. This meant that I would have to shovel coal the whole way! On top of that, the crew was made up of American convicts just released from English prisons where they had each spent time for various offenses. They had been released on the condition that they would work on board for free. They were a rough bunch, and we were not long into the voyage before I was thinking I should have stayed in Lapland. What a way to return to the land of my birth, a land in the middle of the Great Depression.

Staying with family friends in Brooklyn, and having proudly just gotten my formal U.S. citizenship, one day I was reading a Norwegian newspaper and was shocked to read: "Count Gaston Micard to explore little-known interior of Labrador. Will sail from Quebec." Micard, coming to North America! I hoped he still remembered me, and immediately sent him a wire in France. My whole world got brighter when I received his reply—"Of course I remember you"— and that I should meet him in Montreal. I wired my father with the wonderful news, as well as to ask for money. He wired back that the money would be waiting at the Bank of Montreal.

With what few dollars I had, I bought a rucksack, a one-man tent, and a sleeping bag at an Army-Navy Surplus store, then purchased a ticket to Albany, New York. I hoped to save some money, and see some of the country, by hitchhiking the rest of the way to the Canadian border. It was not as easy as I had thought. It seemed like everyone in America was hitchhiking, searching for work. I passed over the border and arrived at the Canadian passport control office with just a dollar left. The customs agents would not let me into Canada. I told them that once I reached Montreal I would have money waiting for me at the Bank of Montreal, and that I was going on an expedition with the great French arctic explorer, Count Gaston Micard. I did not speak French, and if they spoke English, they did not show it, but they managed to make it clear that, as for French counts, arctic expeditions, and money in banks, they had "heard it all before from bums like me." I was summarily deported!

I had my money wired to me at Rouses Point, on the American side of Lake Champlain, but the deportation paperwork would take more time than would allow for me to reach Micard before his departure date. Micard wired his condolences, and once again promised, "You'll be on the next expedition!"

Back in Newcastle, I resumed my studies. Soon after my second year of school ended, I read a newspaper article about an arctic expedition to Greenland, which included Sir Ernest Shackleton's son, Edward, and Professor Wordie, the well-known head of the Scott Polar Research Institute at Cambridge. A Norwegian arctic sealer and crew chartered from Tromsø had left with the expedition members from London, and were due in five days' time to make an unscheduled stop in Aberdeen, Scotland. In a fevered pitch, I decided on the spot to go to Aberdeen. One of my good friends from Tromsø, Johan Hagerup, had come to live with us while he studied and worked at a shipping office. His family had been in the shipping business for generations and were old friends of my family. Johan and I took our bicycles, rucksacks, and little else, and by morning we were off to Aberdeen, hoping to get on the expedition.

It rains a lot in the month of May on that northeast coast of Great Britain. We pedaled through the cold rain and against a stiff northwest wind for five days. It was uphill most of the way, but we were determined to get on that expedition. At night we usually crammed into my one-man tent. We cycled madly against time toward our goal.

When we arrived at last in Aberdeen, we headed straight for the piers. We saw a crowd of people, including reporters, on the quay. The expedition ship was coming in to dock. We had just made it.

Johan called out loudly to one of the crew, "Hey, boys! How's the herring fishing in Tromsø?" It turned out that Johan knew most of the crew, including the captain. It was heartening to find that some of them knew my family as well, and one said he knew me when I was "this big," holding his hand out to waist level. Johan and I were sure we would have a place on the expedition. Bottles were pulled out, and greetings and news exchanged. I met Professor Wordie, and the young Shackleton, who was about my age.

I told Edward Shackleton how I had almost gone on his father's old ship to Greenland, and he said he hoped I could come on this voyage.* But in the end we were told by the captain the now-familiar story—that the expedition did not have time to get the extra legal amount of supplies for two more crew members, as the ship was leaving in a few hours. This time the blow was even greater. I was getting the feeling that I was never going on an arctic expedition. Instead, I took a job for a few weeks shoveling coal on a ship bound for Senegal to fetch a load of peanuts for buyers in Bordeaux. At least I got to see some of the world!

Finding the summer soon over, I plunged into my architectural studies and artwork at university, but did not forget my dream of arctic exploration. I spent as much time on arctic research as I did on my university courses. Maybe more! One particular article I read in the September 1934 issue of *National Geographic* magazine, sent to me by friends in America, was of Charles and Anne Lindbergh's 1933 flight, and few days' stay in Greenland. The Lindberghs were surveying the best routes for possible intercontinental flights. In the article, I saw some of the first aerial photos ever taken of Greenland. They had met with the Danish explorer, Lauge Koch, whom I had heard so much about over the years. Their plane had accompanied his to the northeast coast at Clavering Island where he had a small station called Eskimonaes.

Since this was the area that interested Count Micard so much, and where his expedition had gone, I was astonished and worried to see aerial photographs of the place. Perhaps there would be nothing left there to explore. But the article also said that on their flight south from Clavering, the Lindberghs saw an uncharted range of mountains with one peak over twelve thousand feet high. So, there was unexplored land—thank Thor for that! Also, simply knowing that the infamous icebergs coming down the east coast had kept explorers out of that area reassured me there was still something left for me. (Of course, I did not know then that I would be playing an important role in the development of the northern air route pioneered by the Lindberghs and others.)

---

* Author's Note: In 1990, I received a letter from Sir Edward Shackleton. Lord Shackleton wrote to explain the amusing reason they had had to make the unscheduled stop in Aberdeen: "We put into Aberdeen to collect the chronometer watches which cleverly I left in the hall of the RGS [Royal Geographic Society]! We also bought a cat in Aberdeen."

Also in the Lindbergh article was an aerial photograph taken near Scoresby Sound of the *Pourquoi Pas?*, the ship of the French polar explorer Dr. Jean-Baptiste Charcot. It was strange to think that those of us who read the article in the comfort of our homes, far away from the action, had a better view of his position in that remote, hard-to-reach place than Charcot did himself. Even though the world saw the photo, the expedition had no way of knowing they had been photographed from the air. This was how fast technology was changing the world.

I received my architect's and art degrees in June 1936, and was offered a job with the Platou architectural firm in Oslo. With diplomas and a few art awards in hand, I went back to Norway to begin my professional career. The prospect of adventure in the Arctic seemed very remote, and understandably, I had some sense of personal failure.

I was a month into my job at the architectural firm, I had become engaged to be married to Inger, and was settling into the routine of Oslo life, when, once again, I read a newspaper article announcing an arctic expedition headed by Count Gaston Micard. It was to leave soon from Tromsø. I fired off a telegram to him at the hotel in Tromsø, where I expected him to be staying, giving the Platou building as my return address. Going to work the next morning, I had not sat down at my drafting desk for more than five minutes when the superintendent handed me a telegram. It said simply, "COME. — MICARD."

Mr. Platou was away, so with hands trembling and heart pounding, I went immediately to the head architect. I told him I was grateful for the opportunity they had given me, but I had to resign. I just told him there was an arctic expedition I would miss if I did not leave immediately. Being a Norwegian, he understood completely, and without any lectures about my impulsive behavior, or lack of concern for a secure future, he signed my resignation papers.

I would have to catch that night's train to Trondheim in order to board the *Hurtigruten* in time to catch Micard in Tromsø before he left for Greenland. His cable to me had arrived on July 31 — and the *Quest* was due to sail August 5! Considering all my last-minute disappointments in the past, I was understandably desperate. Phoning my sister at her job at city hall, I told her the news. She left work immediately to go to my studio to help me pack. I gathered up my drafting equipment, said good-bye to my fellow architects and my job, and then dashed out into the street.

My main concern, of all things, was to obtain art materials. I figured I could get arctic gear in Tromsø. Going to the biggest art-supply store in Oslo, I went to the manager of the store and explained my situation. "But I cannot pay for materials now," I said. No problem. He packed up a roll of canvas, selected a respectable array of oil paints and brushes, gave me the whole lot, and I was off to the train station. I didn't even have time to say good-bye to my fiancée, who was away for the summer. The best I could do was to ask Signy to send Inger some flowers when she returned to Oslo. Considering her usual attitude about my habit of "irresponsibly putting myself in harm's way," I should have known that flowers would not be enough to secure Inger's undying love through the whole year and more that I would be away. I left, and that was the end of any chance at further communication with her. There was no way to send or receive letters from Greenland—not where we were anyway!

With great relief I managed to catch the *Hurtigruten* to Tromsø. Today, the journey is internationally recognized as "the world's most beautiful voyage," but I only wished the bloody boat would go faster and not make so many damn stops. After something like forty hours and too many stops, I was standing on the deck at Harstad, awash with impatience, when a passenger just a little older than myself, who had just come aboard, said hello. We got to talking, and he told me he was going to Greenland. I said, "So am I!" and asked him on what ship.

"The *Quest*," he replied.

"So am I!" I said. And that was how I met Karl Nicholaisen. Karl went by the nickname, "Kalle." He had been sealing since age fifteen at Spitsbergen, where he had learned trapping and hunting. The previous year he had wintered there. He had sea captain papers, but had signed on the *Quest* as a trapper. He would winter on a remote trap line, give the captain a percentage, and keep the rest of the profits. He invited me to be his partner. "Of course," he said, "with only a small part of the profits. But at least you won't be stuck on board ship all winter with that bastard, Captain Schjelderup!" I readily agreed to his plan, especially after Kalle told me some gossip about our soon-to-be skipper, the master of the *Quest*.

It seems Schjelderup was something of an arctic buccaneer, helping himself to supplies from depots left by trappers who had gone back to Norway. His motto was, "Better that I get it, than the polar bears!" This might seem reasonable, Kalle said, except for the fact that these depots included building supplies and fuel, and that the supplies had been left for the next trappers to arrive. My new friend told me that the captain was a notorious skinflint, as well as a man who did not think conservation laws regarding hunting applied to him. Kalle added, "But he has the best arctic ship on the polar seas!"

Count Micard met the ship in Tromsø. It had been four years since I had last seen him. We had a grand reunion. "I promised you!" he said with a laugh. He seemed genuinely aggrieved, however, as I told him some of the details of my string of past disappointments in trying to link up with him. He bought me a fine dinner to make up for it, and we drank very good champagne. He thought it a good idea that Kalle and I had linked up and said, "Staying on the ship would soon bore a young fellow like you. I however plan to stay on the ship all winter. You, Willie, will be my guest on this expedition, but by law you have to have an official capacity, and architect—or artist—is not on the approved list! Also, you must understand that Schjelderup is your boss."

I was issued a hunter's permit so that I could have official status on the expedition. I'd never shot anything in my life except for a single quail, and that had been rather traumatic for me. The next morning I got to meet the impressive captain. He did not really approve of taking a "city boy" along, he told me gruffly, but since Micard was paying, he'd put up with me. I was, however, he warned, to think of him as my boss. Kalle and I then got our first assignment: to pick up a dog. This dog was to become our friend and protector on two expeditions, but the beginning of our relationship with him was not very promising.

Kalle told me the dog's history. The owner was doing a little time in jail in Alesund for having helped himself to other trappers' skins and pelts on a previous hunting expedition. I had not known there were so many arctic buccaneers! This man also owed Captain Schjelderup some money, and since he was in no position to pay up, had offered the use of his dog as payment. *Labban*, or "Big paw," was a large, white, long-haired animal, and had recently been pampered by an old aunt of its shady owner. We went to her cozy home to fetch Labb. As we watched, the old lady hand-fed him cream cakes and sugar cookies, and made a big fuss over the dog, petting him, and talking sweetly to his drooling face.

Kalle finally "ahemed" and said we had to be getting back to the ship with the dog. She said kindly, "Yes, I suppose you must." She paused, her eyes narrowed, her face got serious, and then she launched into a whole list of do's and don'ts regarding the treatment of Labb. We listened with disbelief as she listed the way the dog was to be treated, "or else!" Finally, nodding politely, and not daring to disagree with her on anything, we backed out the front door with the spoiled, pampered pet. We had to hurry since the ship was soon sailing, and it was with a shock that I realized I had not had time to buy arctic clothing! Kalle told me not to worry; it was summer time! I could make my own arctic gear later and save the money. He said it so casually I actually figured he was right.

The *Quest* was bustling with activity. We were hand-loading her, using only ropes to lower into the hold the heavy barrels that contained everything from flour to nails, and cases of everything from blocks of margarine to beer. At last the ship was ready. The whole crew, the trappers, and the dogs were aboard. The first mate and ice pilot was the famous John Anton Ness; he had been a high school classmate of my father's. His second mate was Ruben Goldman. Ruben's family had fled Russia in 1917 when the Bolsheviks took over. Schjelderup's aide was named August Jackobsen. Meyer Olsen, a dour-looking Lapplander, was ship's carpenter. The cook was Karl Skauguoll, though Count Micard had brought his own chef, a Norwegian named Lockert, who was trained in French cooking.

I can't for the life of me remember the name of the old chap in charge of the engines, but his fireman was George Eriksen. Then there was the expedition's official photographer, Eigil Halvorsen, my age, who had just returned from a year spent photographing the ravages of the Spanish Civil War. Also on board, paid for by the government, was Captain Brun, an army man who was going to attempt the first-ever solo crossing of the Greenland Ice Cap. We had not yet left the dock, but crew members were betting Brun would never make it, even though they did not say it to his face. Everyone was having a wonderful time making toasts with shots of whiskey to the success of the expedition.

The harbormaster, Helmer Hansen, who was making his share of toasts, was on deck making sure everything was shipshape, that the ship was not overloaded, nor under-equipped for the dangerous expedition. Hansen had been on the first crossing of the Northwest Passage with Amundsen, and had been head dog-driver on Amundsen's victorious dash to the South Pole in 1911. I had known Helmer Hansen by sight since my childhood days in Tromsø where he was a local hero, and there I was, on board an arctic ship with him. Talk about a heady feeling! I watched as Helmer took a cursory glance at our waterline, noticed we were "a bit" overloaded, took another shot of whiskey, and pretended he hadn't noticed.

There was also a doctor from town going around the ship making sure everyone was healthy enough to make the long, tough expedition. He too drank his share of whiskey as he did his job. The doctor came up from below and told Captain Schjelderup that all the men seemed fit except for the engineer. Kalle had told me about the engineer, who was in his late sixties and liked his drink. Kalle said that Schjelderup, a man noted for his thrift, had not wanted to hire an expensive engineer for a sea crossing that would last only a week. After that, the ship would soon be frozen in for the winter, and the engineer would have nothing much to do until spring. The doctor told Schjelderup the engineer would never make it.

"Want to bet?!" roared Schjelderup. A bottle of whiskey was wagered on the spot.

The engineer, bleary-eyed and blissfully ignorant of the wager being made, stuck his head up from down below to tell the captain the engines were ready to go. Helmer Hansen and the doctor, having astutely done their duty, went ashore. I was a bit nervous, wondering what might go wrong at the last minute to prevent my going, and was only able to relax once the ropes had been cast off, and the ship pulled away from the pier. On the dock, newspaper reporters from everywhere snapped last-minute photos, people cheered, and ships lining the quay blasted their foghorns in a salute that sent a shiver of excitement up my spine. I'd heard that sound since I was a kid. Now it was my turn! The *Quest's* foghorn blasted in return salute, and we on deck felt the pride of knowing we were headed out for a very special journey. Looking about me, I could see the members of the expedition were standing a little straighter than usual, their heads slightly tilted skyward. I was soaring inside, remembering the words of Knud Rasmussen:

If you make plans, and stick to them,
the sun will always be on your path!

CHAPTER FOUR

The Glint of Ice

We did not have an auspicious beginning. After just forty miles or so through the coastal islands, and with a storm having hit suddenly, the ship abruptly lost power. We found the old engineer in the engine room nearly passed out drunk. George, the fireman, shrugged his shoulders helplessly. Schjelderup cursed and shouted, "Does anyone know how to run these damn engines?" I hesitatingly said I had shoveled coal on board a ship to America four years earlier. "Good enough! Besides, your father's a ship's mechanic. Something must have rubbed off, even if you are just an architect. Get down there and help George!"

My short, three-week stint as a fireman when I went to America had not taught me how to run the boilers without blowing up the ship. But with the semi-coherent engineer hanging over a bench in a reclining position, waving his arms, pointing to this valve and that as they needed opening or closing, George and I did as he mumbled us to do, and thereby we made quite a team. In this way we steamed through rough waves for four or five hours until free of the coastal storm. By then the engineer had sobered up a bit, and we settled down for the crossing to Greenland. We sailed for four marvelous days and nights, hit the ice floes, ran the gauntlet of those massive bergs, and there I was, in Greenland, at long bloody last. This was the same place where Count Micard had come in 1932, the first time I had not been able to accompany him. It really was quite astounding that I had made it.

We sailed out of the ice-choked sea into the relatively less ice-choked Gael Hampke's Bay. We sailed up the bay, heading for Wordie Glacier, which hovered massively at the bay's terminus, over thirty miles away. Captain Brun had to be dropped off at the base of the glacier as soon as possible, since time was against him in his plan to cross the ice cap.

On our right, or to the north, lay Clavering Island, its western end nearly reaching the glacier. Midway along Clavering's southern shore, lay the tiny, year-round Danish weather station, Eskimonaes, but had no time to stop to visit. Besides, the views were thrilling company enough.

Wordie Glacier swept gracefully down from the ice cap to the sea. Along the bay's south coast were those startling alps we had seen from sea. And the scenery was more magnificent than I had imagined it would be. The low land along the bay was clear of snow. Vibrant patches of colors marked profuse tundra plant life. Flocks of arctic terns wheeled and landed along the distant shoreline. All the while, at the end of the fjord, that colossal glacier loomed more and more impressively as we came nearer.

Suddenly, the name of the glacier hit me. It had been named for Professor Wordie, who had been on the expedition I had tried to join in Aberdeen! Well, well. Here I was, four years later. I was amazed. And it was all so magnificent! The wall of mountains seemed steadily more massive, rising straight up for thousands of feet. At the end of the alpine "dog tongues" of glacial ice, steep alluvial fans spread out and down, gradually flattening out to form the long, gravelly beach at the bay's edge. The mountains were at first layered with multiple hues of reds and oranges. As the light changed, stripes of yellows, tans, and pinks were graced by belts of green. The midnight sun was making the colors burst into life, and they made an astounding, beautiful contrast to the bright, white glacier, shimmering with tones of blues and greens. We were immersed in color.

These mountains are called Henry Hudson Land, after the seventeenth-century explorer who had only seen these peaks from way out at sea due to the infamous pack ice. The intrepid explorer had come seeking the fabled Northwest Passage. He was a determined fellow, as proven by the places named for him: Henry Hudson Land here in Greenland; Hudson's Bay in Canada; and, of course, the Hudson River in New York. The passage would prove elusive until 1907 when Amundsen wound his tiny ship, the *Gjoa*, through a nightmare maze of islands and ice to reach the Pacific at Alaska. Amundsen proved the passage was there all right, but highly impractical for shipping.

Though the sun shone brightly, the air was frigid, and, just in case the glaciers and temperature had not made it clear we were in the Arctic, suddenly a polar bear with her two large cubs were seen on a large piece of floating ice. A great shout went up from the hunters. Schjelderup came with a rifle, took quick aim, and shot all three. It was my first experience of real hunting. It did no good to feel sorry for the cubs and their mother. We were there to hunt and trap, and we needed food. The mores and morals of cities with well-stocked store shelves did not fit those of the Arctic in those days.

Schjelderup, Kalle, and I went down the rope ladder to a rowboat, rowed to the ice floe, and jumped onto it where the bears lay dead. I learned by watching Kalle, and we quickly gutted the animals. Then a rope hauled the carcasses aboard to be skinned as we continued sailing. It was quite a rough initiation into arctic realities. While the bears were being skinned, Schjelderup told the story of Tutein, a Danish hunter and artist, who had run a trap line near the coast we were sailing past, the same coast where Kalle and I would winter alone. Tutein had been painting the view to the sea from a cliff's promontory, when a polar bear had snuck up behind him and struck him dead with one blow. His brother, an author, had watched horrified from a distance as the bear came closer and closer to his brother, but was too far away for his warning shouts to be heard. Schjelderup ended his story by saying, "Take your rifle with you wherever you go!" He was looking directly at me, the only neophyte in the group. He had convinced me. I was now a believer. I was, however, so damn happy to be there that I was not too worried about bears.

The *Quest* was anchored near the mainland, just past Clavering Island, at Jordan Hill, which was an eight-hundred-foot wonder capped by a small glacier. We landed at Cape Else, one of the few landing sites near the Wordie Glacier. Here was another alluvial fan created by the melting ice. We set up our base camp, which consisted of a small tent supported by the whaler's oars. We were comically diminutive under the massive glacier. The roar of glacial melt and calving icebergs filled the air, leaving barely enough room for thought. So I sketched the scene instead.

It was decided by Schjelderup that I should help Captain Brun lug his equipment up to the top of the ice cap. No one could do that alone, and then cross the cap. The worst part was this climb, as the cap itself was flat. Once reached, the going—barring any unforeseen weather issues—should theoretically have been easy. To film the historic event—the start of the first solo crossing of the ice cap—the photographer Eigil Halvorsen would accompany us. First, he filmed Micard, Brun, and Schjelderup together on the ship. The usually rough Schjelderup put on a coat and tie to look his best. No one else bothered. (Later, back in Oslo when the film was developed, it was discovered that Halvorsen had "cut off" most of their heads—he was new to that kind of camera.)

With the filming done, I rowed the three of us to shore in a rowboat full of Brun's supplies, which included a *pulk*—a narrow, rounded, covered Lapp sled one pulled behind as one skied over snow. However, going over ice creased by gullies, dips, and crevasses was another thing, and so Brun had added a small universal joint from an automobile drive shaft so that his pull line would not get twisted up, and also so that the pulk could flop around behind him if necessary. This invention is still used today, and I will bet no one knows the inventor was Brun. He was also, by the way, the inventor of the "netted" thermal underwear now used by skiers and winter sports enthusiasts the world over.

So far north in the "Arctic wastes," colorful dwarf poppies bloomed, shimmering yellow like bright beacons amongst the gray shale pebbles. There were also dwarfish pinkish-purple lousewort growing here and there, showing off their fine-haired leaves, and relieving the land from an otherwise drab backdrop. Small whitish, fluffy *Erigon (daisies)* grew in clusters in alluvial sand; shell-white *Arenaria* showed off its five-pointed asters in prosperous colonies. In this setting we shouldered backpacks and rifles, took the pulk in tow, and began the steep climb. We climbed up the slopes of Jordan Hill just edging the glacier until we were above the glacier's calving, crevasse-laced face. About a mile inland, at an elevation of about five hundred feet, we stepped out onto the glacier.

It was a sunny day, and of course, with twenty-four hours of sun, the slope of Wordie was absorbing a lot of heat. Countless small rivulets of melted water joined to make glacial creeks. Where the water raced over the ice, it cut deep, rounded, curvaceous, super-slick slides, like flooded, Olympic bobsled runs. These rivers plummeted almost lightning-like, and in places would disappear down a yawning hole in the glacier as if down a drain. Sometimes a creek would not reappear for hundreds of feet, but would then pop up a ways before disappearing again. One of these creeks didn't reappear until it had reached the foot of the glacier. Beneath the thousands of tons of glacial ice, it blasted out into the fjord as if from a hydroelectric dam. We knew that to slip into such rushing water would mean the end.

After fifteen tortuous and torturing miles, we had to say good-bye to the courageous Captain Brun. He put on a brave show but was clearly having some misgivings. Eigil filmed him as he headed for the top of the ice cap, which seemed to be no more than a few miles away, and relatively easy to reach on skis. His pulk clattered and swung crazily behind him as it rolled around the dips and gullies, but his invention seemed to be working as planned.

We turned back, and from our remarkable vantage point we could see for miles. We were probably the second group of humans, at least non-Inuit, who had ever climbed this glacier. In 1932, a Dane, T. Johansen, and three others had come partway up this glacier by sled, and then cut over to come down at Besselfjord. Even the ancient, long-vanished Inuit would have had no reason to make this climb—certainly not to hunt. We had climbed the highest up its impressive slope, for all that was worth historically, but the view was certainly worth the climb.

We could see across part of Henry Hudson Land, out the fjord along Clavering Island, and across to the peaks of Manley Land, ten miles to the east. We had a clear view all the way to the open sea. I made sketches of some of the scenes, including one of a mountain peak rising a few hundred feet out of the glacier. These types of glacier-locked "islands" are called *Nunatak* by the Inuit. I could survey the whole lonely coast along the southern side of the bay that was to be Kalle's and my trap line. For most of the next winter we would be the only two inhabitants along that sixty-mile-long coast.

When the World Was "Krogness"

The *Quest* sailed back along the bay to drop Kalle and me off at our main cabin. Another ship lay at anchor there. It was the *Polarbjorn* (Polar Bear), and would take two trappers who had spent the last two years at the cabin back to Norway. The trappers could be seen hauling their things out to the shore by the ship. We disembarked to check out our new home, which sat on a wide, open coastal plain. In the distance behind it rose high mesas with perpendicular cliffs dropping to the plain.

Cabin? It was a shack—and a joke at that. Insulating sod from the tundra covered what we presumed was the hut. Only two small windows indicated that it was meant for human habitation. Otherwise, it looked like a large, melting chocolate cake that had been dropped there long before from a great height. Junk was lying all about on the ground, and a dangerous-looking dog tied up to a pole snarled at our approach. One of the trappers came up and said with a laugh that we could have the dog, free of charge.

"So you won't mind if I shoot it?" asked Kalle, wearing a sardonic grin. "I can tell a mutt that's gone crazy when I see one."

The trapper smiled. He asked our names. His was Sivertsen, the same as my mother's family, and upon finding out who I was, he cried out, "Christ! I went to school with your father!" This was an excuse for celebration. The trappers produced some bottles of what was quite powerful booze. After a half hour of hard drinking, and just before they finally departed, the second trapper, Johan Johansen, came up to me and Kalle. Misty-eyed with solemn ceremony, he said, "I make a gift to you boys. Take good care of it. Inside the hut you will find our best friend for two years. Boys, I give you our still!"

Finally the trappers were gone, and then the *Quest* also departed. It sailed across the bay to visit Eskimonaes before entering the long fjord off Gael Hampke's Bay (called Loch Fyne) for the winter. Schjelderup, having agreed with Kalle that the savage black dog left to us was useless, had decided Labb could be our sled dog, so he was left with us.

"Great!" Kalle said to me with disgust. "A spoiled, scared, overgrown pet!" Kalle, Labb, and I watched from shore as our link to civilization sailed off. We then walked into what would be our home for over a year, and just laughed.

The hut was as crude as could be imagined. And it stank. The old trappers were probably too soused most of the time to notice or care. A table in the center of the twenty-by-ten-foot hut tilted ridiculously as it conformed to the slope of the floor. The hut had stood up to the severe winters, but the summers had softened the permafrost foundation at the south end, causing the sloping. Against the east and west walls, two cots made of wood looked like castoffs from a medieval dungeon. The walls were papered with pages from old *National Geographic* magazines of the 1920s. Kalle told me with a smile that the pages were plastered there to keep out winter blasts carrying very fine grains of sand-like snow, not for educational purposes.

The name of this place, he informed me, was "Krogness." It was the "monument" named for Dr. Krogness, the meteorologist who had made possible the expedition that erected the crude hut in 1924. Hearing the name, I realized with astonishment that I had once seen an aerial photo of the hut and its surroundings in a book. It was a wonderful coincidence that I had come to live here. And what a setting it was!

There was a gradual, tundra-plant-loaded incline leading past a small, shallow pond to a promontory called Cape Stosch, overlooking Clavering Fjord. It took me a half hour to reach the lookout. From there one could see Clavering Island clearly, as it was only about nine miles away. Cape Stosch was an ideal observatory of the area, and others before me had known that. Ancient stone tent rings were everywhere. Knowing I could do some archaeological work on the Eskimo ruins located there provided the icing on a perfect cake. But more important tasks awaited me at the hut.

"Our first order of business," Kalle said grimly, "is to get the damn liquor still out of the cabin. Stills can explode. Last winter when I was at Svalbard, two trappers got killed when their still blew up and set the cabin on fire. One trapper got out, but only in his underwear. He was found frozen in the outhouse where he had tried to take shelter. His partner was found burned beyond recognition, and locked in an ice coffin. The fire had melted the snow, which then froze over him," Kalle said. We lugged the still outside, only to be greeted by the eerie snarls of the dog the trappers had left behind. Kalle calmly got his rifle, walked up to it, and shot it in the head.

Kalle turned to me, shook his head sadly, and said, "He was cracked. Beyond help. He might have killed Labb, and taken our hands off if we tried to be helpful. I've seen it before. Beyond help. It's a tough business, Willie. Get used to it." Kalle, whom I had quickly learned was a kindhearted person, and gentle with dogs, must have known what he was talking about. I had faith in his decisions in matters I then knew nothing about.

Kalle told me that the most important survival item was not food, but heat. He looked around at the broken bags of coal scattered about and muttered, "Those two only survived because God loves drunks and little children." We re-bagged the coal, picking up every scrap laying about on the tundra surface. The bags were set next to the door. We had of course brought our own coal, and these heavy bags we set in the lee of the hut—so snow would not pile up over them—and covered them with wooden pallets, which were then weighed down with large rocks—"or else the bags will blow away in a storm," my new partner explained. I thought he was pulling my leg, and he must have read my mind because he added with a mysterious grin, "No, I am not kidding you." He did this mind-reading thing so often it got a bit spooky, but in time I learned his secret: experience.

With coal at the ready, the next order of business was the paraffin used to start the coal burning. Under a small trapdoor in the floor of the cabin, we set a case of the small bottles of the highly flammable stuff in a hole we had dug in the tundra, and set a large flat stone over it. Kalle took loose bottles and stashed them in the outbuilding used to hang fox pelts. We would use these, he explained, until we could not get out of the hut because of snow. He had not said *if* we could not get out; I involuntarily cringed. We then scoured the land around the hut for every scrap of wood, no matter how small. It was amazing what a big pile we gathered. We went out at least a hundred yards in every direction to pick up wood blown away by the horrific winds I was being warned repeatedly to expect.

We next gathered every piece of metal, from nails to old buckles. We found metal files and wood rasps, bullet cartridges and wire. There was an amazing variety of useful objects, many of which I had never seen before, and had no clue as to their purpose. "Bunch of wastrel slobs!" my well-organized buddy said about the newly departed hunters.

A few days later the hut was up to Kalle's strict standards, and we set out in an old skiff, a whaler with an old Evinrude outboard motor, to get the lay of the land. We had to learn where the trap line's huts were, and, if necessary, to repair them. We headed east toward the hut named *Knoph-hytta*, or Knoph's Hut.

The outboard proved to be in need of service itself, so we did a lot of rowing on the way, and believe me, whalers are heavy boats. The huts were scattered over sixty miles of coastline, so tuning the motor was essential if we did not want to kill ourselves rowing. This my clever partner did while I, the new kid on the block, did the hard work. As I was quickly finding out, Kalle was pretty good at just about everything, and he had that motor tuned up and running smoothly after about an hour, though it felt more like ten at the time.

The hut was set near high cliffs which eventually ended at the sea, thus barring further access to the coast by land. Above the cliffs directly behind the hut site was Spathe's Plateau, home to trap lines of some Danish hunters who were not there that year. It was also the area in which the polar bear had snuck up and killed Tutein a few years before. Knowing this reminded me to take my rifle with me everywhere I went.

At Knoph's Hut we were greeted by more of the old trappers' slovenliness. Fortunately, the trap line huts were even smaller than Krogness, and it did not take long to re-sod where necessary, and make minor repairs, followed by the annoying gathering of coal, wood, and metal. Labb ran around, afraid of his own shadow. He did chase a few lemmings, the tiny mice-like tundra rodents, but even they could startle him with their sudden movements! I had to admit that it looked like we were stuck with a "Ferdinand" among dogs. Kalle cursed Captain Schjelderup as a cheap bastard who would not provide a proper sled dog. He was also disgusted by the shoddy workmanship of the fox traps left behind by the trappers.

"Should be ashamed of themselves!" he said with disgust. He consoled himself by first baking bread while I made some sketches with colored chalk. He made half a dozen loaves and stored them in the bread box, to be ready for the next time we returned. "In case we arrive starving in a blizzard," he explained with a cheerful grin, as if relishing the thought. It was true the bread would freeze, making it fine to eat when thawed, but it was such good weather apart from a cold snap, I did not think he should jinx it by conjuring up images of deadly storms.

The traps we made were the "deadfall" kind: A wooden frame, weighted with heavy stones, was propped up by pieces of wood set in a "figure-four" shape. These pieces were notched, and held together by the weight of the stones. A baited piece of the "four," when yanked on by a fox, would collapse the "four," and the stone-weighted trap would of course then drop on the animal.

The frame—in fact, all of the wood—came from the Siberian forests halfway around the world from us. The currents of the high Arctic Sea brought logs washed down from Siberian rivers across the roof of the world, then down Greenland's east coast. So salt-laden were they after the long journey, they were like iron, but could be split into pieces usable for traps. For thousands of years, the Inuit of this coast got all their wood from Russia. They made kayak frames from this wood, as well as paddles, and there was an unending supply to tap. Since they had never seen a tree, the bountiful, useful flotsam on their coasts must have seemed a gift from the spirits. Indeed, they carved mystical masks from wood, and made representatives of their spirit world—*tupilaks*—from them.

The traps we worked so industrously on would not be baited until winter, when the foxes' fur was full and glistening. Summer pelts, shedding and dull, were worthless on the market, but we had brought bait anyway. Kalle knew a lot of tricks of the trade. Up in Spitsbergen he had had a large box of rancid margarine, so he left it outside where the foxes could get at it. The pelts they got in that area were the glossiest and fullest of all their trap lines! We were to use the same cosmetic trick. The fatty stuff got foxes used to coming along our trap line.

The trap line to the east of Krogness all the way to Knoph Hut was more or less beneath the mesa-like mountains of Spathe's Plateau. When the sun struck, the steep cliffs looked like colossal Hindu temples shimmering in stratified colors. The third day there, we were walking about a half hour from the hut while admiring the deepening colors of the "temples." In the distance, we suddenly saw an almost dream-like moving form silhouetted against the cliff base. It had come out of a steep, narrow valley, and was slowly moving in our direction. It would disappear beneath a knoll, and then pop up again. It looked like a walking blanket. We peered at it quizzically, then recognized its shaggy form: It was a musk ox! The prehistoric-looking creature slowly shuffled along, all alone. Though we had seen hordes of lemmings and clouds of birds, including migrating geese, we had seen no large land animal in the vast wilderness, so the musk ox was an awe-inspiring sight. But the awe left us suddenly when we both said simultaneously, "That's meat!" Labb seemed to understand, and did no barking, nor even whining, but he was scared. Kalle grabbed his old Krag-Jorgensen rifle, knelt on one knee, took aim, and dropped the musk ox from a well over a hundred yards away. He was a hell of a shot! And that was the first of many musk oxen we hunted.

As we gutted and skinned the ox, Kalle told me that if we had bowls we could save the blood as well as the meat. "Good vitamins. Everything is going to count. You'll see."

Eager for our first taste of musk ox, we chewed into the meat. It was hard, tough, and worthy of the arctic environment. We could not make a dent in it. The old bull had probably been driven from the herd by a younger one, but he was having the last laugh on us young hunters. We got the meat back to the hut and had to boil chunks for two hours before it was palatable. While we were trying to eat the damn thing, we saw a small motor-driven launch come up to our shore. The two men who arrived, smiling happily to see other humans, were Danish scientists from Eskimonaes.

One was Dr. Eigil Nielsen, who introduced himself as a zoo-paleontologist, and the other was Harvey Jensen, his assistant. Nielsen was about my age and wore a sparse beard. Wearing a hooded parka made him look like a Tibetan monk. We invited them to eat with us. The Danish government frowned on the killing of musk oxen, but Nielsen and Jensen had some anyway. Nielsen gently castigated us for "killing one of the rare beasts." Kalle and I held back our laughter when we heard him mutter, "Especially one that is this old!"

Nielsen and Jensen were collecting fossilized fish and plants, their specialty, and they planned to climb amid the colorful, stratified layers of the cliffs.

Paleontologists worldwide were trying to find fossil proof of a "missing link" between fish and four-legged creatures—anything to further Darwin's theory of evolution. The Devonian Period was where such a find was predicted, and Greenland had the most exposed Devonian outcrops in the world. Nielsen, besides being a competent scientist, was a good teacher. He instilled in both of us what would become a lifelong interest in the fossilized archives of life from millions of years ago. Nielsen would later be involved in the research which followed the dramatic discovery of the "living fossil," the *coelacanth*, off east Africa.

It was only the day after these great researchers had returned to Eskimonaes that we took the whaleboat out to the pack ice. The sea was like glass, with not a ripple. One would have thought we were on a lake. The sky was brilliantly blue, and the sun hurt our eyes. I kept turning back to look at our kingdom from this new perspective. It was a very, very large land we two occupied. And Spathe's Plateau dwarfed our trap line on the strip of coast beneath it. Suddenly, Kalle shut the engine off and pointed to a black spot on the ice. It had to be a seal. We muffled the oarlocks with our scarves and then rowed quietly, trying not to make any noise with the water dripping from our oars. It seemed to take forever, but the black spot eventually became a blob, and then a real form with flippers. When we were within an easy shot, Kalle put a bullet in its head. He crawled onto the pack ice, tied a rope around the flippers, and then crawled back to the boat. We dragged the seal to us and flipped it into the boat. While we still rocked a bit crazily in those dangerously cold waters, Kalle put the kettle we always had for making coffee under the seal to catch the blood, and I immediately started the motor.

Just as we landed on the gravelly beach near Knoph Hut, a flock of geese rose from where they had been protectively camouflaged not fifty feet from us. They had to run to get airborne, and we both grabbed and fired our shotguns at the same time. Several geese fell from just above the ground. This was a stroke of luck for us. This group was composed of stragglers from the big flocks that had already headed south for the winter.

We pulled our heavy whaler high up onto the gravel beach, then set to flaying the seal, and preparing the ducks. We stripped the skin, feathers and all, from the birds: "Indigestible," Kalle said of the skin with its thick layer of fat. I told him the thought of eating goose skin and fat had never crossed my mind. He chuckled, saying, "We'll keep the guts. Good vitamins."

Later in the hut, Kalle cooked up the entrails. Reluctantly, I ate them, but they turned out to be damned good, and the bread was as well. We then settled in for some much needed sleep. We awoke to the sounds of heavy wind and rain. Looking down to the bay, to our horror we saw huge swells lifting the heavy cover of pack ice, and then sloshing up the beach all the way to the boat, which was slowly being dragged out to sea! Running down the slope, we were able to save it. But we were shocked that swells could have penetrated the wide, protective belt of pack ice, and still have retained such powerful energy. The storm continued for three days. We could not go outdoors. Often the wind howled and beat against the hut as if with massive fists. This outrage against sanity kept up for hours. A day after the tumult calmed, we saw the *Quest's* whaler motoring into the bay.

Schjelderup had come to check on us after the storm, and not finding us at Krogness, had begun a search. He told us they had learned over the radio that the incredible storm had caused havoc all over the North Sea. The great French explorer, Charcot, and all but one of his crew had gone down with his ship *Pourquoi Pas?*, off the coast of Iceland! What a shock. What a loss. Over his years of exploration, Charcot, a friend of Count Micard's, had gathered an experienced group of scientists. Now all of them were lost except for a teenaged cabin boy. The name *Pourquoi Pas?* had rolled so often and so easily off the tongues of so many who studied the Arctic. For all of us, the loss of the ship and crew was a personal one.

Schjelderup had another piece of unfortunate news. Captain Brun had found the journey to the ice cap too difficult. What had looked like level going had been a two-hundred-mile incline. We had left him a "bit" far below the level top. The pulk had started to splinter and break up from the abrasion caused by the hard, icy surface. Defeated before he reached the ice cap, he had been forced to turn back. He made camp along the shore by Jordan Hill. Schjelderup, as planned, had gone to check on Brun after eight days, and had picked him up. Brun had caught the *Polarbjorn* just before it had sailed back to Norway. The Arctic was taking its toll. And it was not yet winter.

It was not long before the center of our world became Krogness. We went out from it in all directions on hunting trips, exploratory ventures, and trap-line searches. Within the first ten days we had sufficient fresh meat, mostly musk oxen, to last a long while, and our huts were secure. Kalle contented himself with baking and puttering around the cabin. He had an unshakable good humor, and smiled most of the time. I found it strange, though, that he seemed not to notice the awesome beauty around us, and he never "waxed philosophical" as I did. Conversely, I was astounded by the Arctic, by its vast openness, and did not particularly enjoy being in and around the confines of the cabin. He knew one song, and he sang that damn thing over and over:

My wife is far from slim,
She has every kind of fault;
She has large hands and feet,
She hasn't got her teeth —
But she is mine.

It sounded better in Norwegian, and he had a really good voice, but the repetition got to me. After a few days of that torture, I started to hum a jazz tune I had picked up in England. On my tenth cycle of it, Kalle said he'd stop singing if I ended that "damn jazz nonsense!"

While Kalle cheerfully puttered, Labb and I began to do some archaeological work at the Eskimo ruins at Cape Stosch. This must have been a summer camping spot, as winter winds would have made the place a nightmare to live year-round. There were six circular remains. The tent-huts made from skins had typically been created by first digging a subterranean floor. Then whalebones or driftwood, or both, were used as frames over which walrus skins were laid. Sod was often piled around the skins, and the huts had flagstone floors. I began digging where someone had begun a few years before, but had given up because of the permafrost. The "archaeologist" could have been one of the trappers, inspired by the work of the Norwegian, Helge Larsen, who had done digs on Clavering from 1931 to 1934. At any rate, the sun had softened the area exposed by the digging, and so I had an easier time of it than my predecessor did.

The Eskimos' early culture had been much more specialized than was generally believed, with each man having his own area of expertise. The first house I unearthed was obviously that of a jeweler-craftsman. I found finely crafted ornaments made of walrus-tusk ivory, and some made of the hard, black shale found in the area. There were also implements and tools made of walrus-tusk ivory. I found harpoon heads and even rare sewing needles. These needles had been perfectly crafted with fine eyes, and I found them only in that house.

The biggest house had probably belonged to the best hunter, often the closest thing the Inuit had to a chief. I found a large space presumed to be a kind of freezer for storing meat next to that house. All the huts had such freezers dug into the permafrost, but this was by far the largest. I found dehydrated, mummy-like meat scraps and a variety of bones from walrus to hare. Though I found the remains of caribou, seal, and other animals all over the settlement, there was nothing relating to the musk ox, except one, old, worn-out tooth. Since the disappearance of these people, and the caribou, the musk oxen had arrived in greater numbers.

A book Count Micard had on board the *Quest* that I had read on the sea journey over to Greenland explained that this region had suffered a few years of rainy periods. The wet ground then froze solid, making it impossible for caribou to paw down to their food, resulting in a great extinction of many of their numbers. Some of the caribou herds may have migrated to the west coast, but they would have had to cross the ice cap. There are Inuit stories of just such an occurrence in modern times.

The old settlement at Cape Stosch was not just intelligently situated because of its good hunting views of the sea and land, but also because of the beauty of the place. To my amazement, nearby stood a natural basalt and granite formation that slightly resembled a miniature Stonehenge. Set in a rough circle, some of the stones looked like chairs. There were ancient trails leading to it from all directions. Very likely it could have been a meeting site, a place to gather for drum dances and other festivities of a religious, socially binding nature. I discovered a pile of flint by one of the chairs. It was a silent, stone record that a man once wielded his special craft there, perhaps to give his arrow and spearheads magical power, or perhaps just so he could take in the view.

I sat in a reverie for a long time, and then began to hear ghostly laughter. I had thought that I didn't have a superstitious bone in my body, but the hairs stood up on my neck. Labb got up from his sitting position, with his head cocked—he'd heard it too! Maybe it was just the wind. But then it came again: a lilting laugh, as though children played nearby. I knew the Inuit believed that if a child dies, he joins other dead children in the sky to play, creating the northern lights—the beautiful dance of midwinter lights called the aurora borealis. But this was broad daylight, and not yet winter. I tried to be scientific.

The laughter grew louder, drawing near, and I followed Labb toward the cliff edge from where the sound seemed to be coming. Peering over we saw two young Inuit men running along, laughing and pointing to the ground. There, lemmings ran in shallow tunnels just beneath the tundra surface, and as they ran, the thin cover of moss undulated like a snake. It really was funny to watch. The tunnels would change direction sharply, forcing the Inuit to make sudden, darting motions to follow them. From my vantage point I had fun watching both the undulating ground motions, and the antics of the two happy men chasing about like madmen. They finally heard Labb's barks, looked up in astonishment, saw us, and began laughing good-naturedly at themselves. They called up in good Danish that they were sled drivers from Eskimonaes, and were out for a day of fun with their kayaks. They waved and went back to their fragile crafts.

From the Eskimo Stonehenge I could see far west to the entrance of Loch Fyne, the fjord where the *Quest* was being prepared for the winter freeze-in at its far end. The "loch," or fjord, offered safety from the crushing pressure of moving ice as happens in more open waters. The next day, Kalle and I set out for this inlet to Loch Fyne in arrangement with Schjelderup. Kalle wanted to build a new hut in a good trapping area currently devoid of any shelter for us near Wordie Glacier, and the captain was to bring us building material.

At the trapper hut *Villaen*, or "the Villa," by the churning water of the narrow inlet to Loch Fyne, we did repair work while waiting for Schjelderup. He arrived with the inboard motor launch, along with two of the crew, including Halvorsen and his movie camera. Besides building materials for our new hut, they had brought fishing nets. On the far side of Loch Fyne, and near its mouth, were inland lakes that held freshwater trout. There was a small inlet that led upstream to a creek that drained from a lake, and we were able to motor up it.

The lakes we fished were nestled along the base of the gravelly foothills of the alps of Henry Hudson Land. Flat to sloping terrain stretched for miles to the west and held more lakes, though they were not connected by creeks to those we fished. It is not an exaggeration to say the land beneath the cold, towering mountains was enormously empty. It had that effect on the mind, and Halvorsen said he'd like to try to capture the effect on film. He needed a human subject in the film to show the proper dimensions, so I strode back and forth like an idiot to give perspective to the immensity of the gravel base against the more immense height and grandeur of the alps. On the fifth stroll, I'd had it, and threw my hands up like a pampered film star, shouting, "Enough takes, for crying out loud!" He left the gesture in the silent film.

At the end of two days, we had all the trout we could handle, literally barrels full. No one had ever fished there, of course, except for the occasional trapper. We putt-putted back to the fjord, and left the barrels by the fjord's edge after filling them with seawater. They would be picked up later, and by more boats. The fish would later be gutted and salted to be used mostly for dog food, though the ship personnel would use them in case of emergency. After all, such salted fish is an expensive treat in many lands.

Schjelderup towed us twelve miles west along Gael Hampke's Bay to where Kalle had scouted a good spot for the hut. During the whole trip, a Nansen burner sat on the bottom of the boat making a constant supply of hot water for coffee. Scandinavians drink a lot of coffee. I have heard that the further north one goes, the more coffee people drink. The Lapps surely drank it like water, even though coffee was expensive that far north. We drank coffee, usually in silence, the whole way along the cold coast. It was interesting that we could travel for hours without needing to say a word. Norwegian men, especially from the northern parts, are pretty much self-contained.

When we arrived, musk oxen were grazing near the shore. The men fanned out silently like wolves following ancient instincts. Labb trembled with fear again, and cowered near the boat, but one of the captain's dogs was let loose and it shot like a demonized arrow straight for the herd. Immediately the oxen went into their protective circle where they made easy targets. We shot a few to use for food, but Schjelderup kept shooting until they were all dead. It was obvious we could never clean and butcher all the carcasses and still get the hut built in the time Schjelderup had allotted. One of the creatures was simply dumped into a ravine. Kalle said philosophically, "It will draw foxes." The weight of the skins and heavy heads of the musk oxen nearly had the ocean spilling over the gunwales into the boat, and I was glad Kalle and I were not returning with the others. They later told us they had to bail the whole way, but the miserly captain was not going to lose one øre by lightening the load.

The exterior of the hut had been nearly finished by the time the rest had left to help prepare the *Quest* for her winter freeze-up in Loch Fyne, so we only had to fix the interior as we wanted it. It had room for one cot, and one man could sleep on the floor. Like the other huts, the entranceway could store food, guns, and, in an emergency, another man could sleep there. The entranceway required a step up into the hut, which allowed cold air to settle there instead of entering the hut. One also stepped up from the outside into the entranceway. This step allowed space for drift snow to accumulate without building up in front of the door. I named the hut *Kallehytta*.

The next morning Kalle and I hiked up a long, narrow valley leading to the left and southward, between Wordie and the alps. Protected from the drafts blasting down the face of Wordie, it must have been lush tundra terrain in the summer, although at that time of year the dwarf bushes were anything but verdant. Instead, the red, gold, and yellow of fall spread like an award-winning quilt as far as we could see. It was like a beautiful dream, and I felt privileged to be there. I cursed myself for not bringing along my art materials. Because we were on a natural migration path for herd animals, we understandably came across hundreds of caribou antlers. It was eerie to see the valleys now empty of any of those animals. One thing was clear: The arctic cold had the awesome power to change lands, and to alter the behavior of animals and people.

We hiked up the valley for two days. Obviously this was the fabled "Valley That Goes on Forever" that the two trappers who had preceded us had told us about, though they had never bothered to explore it. Rounding a hill, we came upon an immense, broad, fertile plain. It swept before us toward the northwest, then made a wide turn to the west and continued out of sight. I knew from looking at aerial maps made by Lauge Koch that the valley eventually went south for miles over to Musk Ox Fjord and the great Walterhausen Glacier near Franz Josef Fjord. The wind shook the thousands of short bushes which rustled mournfully in this valley that had once been the home of the great herds and the people who had followed them out of Asia. When the herds of this valley had left, did the Inuit leave as well? We could not tell for sure, but had a feeling they had died out by disease. We found skeletons in some Eskimo huts, and Inuit did not normally leave their dead in houses. Perhaps there was no one left alive to remove them. Tools made of caribou antler were everywhere, testimony to a vanished people.

With not much to do on the trap lines until the really cold weather fell, we decided to visit the Danish station at Eskimonaes, and then go see Micard on board the *Quest*. We crossed to Clavering Island in rough water, bailing the whole way. Winds from the glacier and ice cap really whipped up the sea. The sound of the waves slapping on the side of the boat was deafening, and it took three rough, ear-aching, finger-numbing hours to make the nine-mile trip through the "friendly Arctic."

We learned from the Danes at the station that the first white men to visit Clavering Island were Douglas Clavering, captain of the HMS *Griper*, and his crew in 1823. Clavering found twelve Eskimos at a summer settlement, and for some dumb reason he allowed them to fire his firearms. They then disappeared, and no one ever saw Inuit settlements in the area again! But that frightening experience could not be the only reason for their total demise. Helge Larsen had done archaeological work near there in 1934, and called it "Deadman's Bay" because of the skeletons he found inside rock houses. Since, as I've mentioned, the Inuit are not in the habit of leaving their dead in houses, the skeletons signaled another problem: Clavering may have brought disease with him as well as firearms. The double blow of the caribou migration and the sicknesses of white men probably was a cataclysmic moment in their ancient history on this coast.

At the Danish site at Eskimonaes, none of the animosity displayed in the Norwegian and Danish press over the subject of who owned northern Greenland was ever evident among the men who actually lived and worked there. The case was in The International Court at The Hague at the time, but none of us actually present in the disputed territory worried much about it. The leader of the station was Niels-Ove Jensen, the radio operator and "weather buster." Later he would become a leader of Greenland's legendary World War II "Sled Patrol." Niels-Ove spoke good English from having jumped ship in New York as a fifteen-year-old. He was taken in by an American couple for a few years before he returned to Denmark.

I was also reintroduced to the two paleontologists, Dr. Eigil Nielsen and Harvey Jensen. They had collected a great deal of fantastic fossils many hundreds of millions of years old. I shared their enthusiasm, and so luckily they shared some of their collections, items which I later donated to the Oslo Geological Museum. These fossils would tell an astounded world that frigid Greenland had once been tropical. The world today takes this for granted, but it was mind-boggling in those days before the theory of continental drift had become universally accepted.

Also on hand were two other paleontologists, Dr. Fisher and Dr. Mainck from the University at Bern in Switzerland, but they specialized in tropical trees and fruit. Dr. Nielsen told Kalle and me of his previous work there with Dr. Lauge Koch. It had been an international effort. Two Swiss geologists had found gold during the expedition near Deadman's Bay, but further digging proved the site to be unprofitable. Hearing all this, I realized that the only expedition to the area not funded by large institutions was ours. Micard was paying a small fortune just to be able to experience Greenland. And the *Quest* was the only ship spending the winter.

A few days later Kalle and I headed for Loch Fyne in high winds to visit the *Quest*. We motored into the narrow entranceway to Loch Fyne. The water always churned with tremendous turbulence, but this day it was particularly so. Drifting hunks of ice spun crazily and threatened the small boat. Before we knew it, we were caught in the whirling current. We were in a true maelstrom, a whirlpool capable of upsetting the boat and even pulling us down into its swirling vortex. The whaler went around like a spinning top, with hunks of ice crashing into us—and then our motor died!

We pulled the oars with all our strength, the sound of the maelstrom fueling our efforts. It was terrifying, but I also felt it would be silly to die that way. We would make a little progress, but then be pulled back. This happened over and over, and our arms were not getting any stronger. Suddenly the swirling slowed just a bit, for just a moment, and we were able to slowly work our way out and make it to the rocky cliff of the far shore. We tied the boat up, and then laid ourselves down on the ground. We were totally exhausted. The wind was strong and cold, and when we got some strength back we had to build a little windbreak of stone. Nestled behind that, we went into a deep sleep.

Kalle and I reached the ship the next day just as two of the crew were leaving to hunt for ptarmigan. Out among the dwarf plants, ptarmigan seemed then as plentiful as mosquitoes had been in summer (mercifully the latter had retreated for the winter). Blue-black crowberries, and red partridgeberries (a type of cranberry) were ripe, and many of the tundra plants had gone to seed, so there was plenty of bird food. Dwarf bushes, never more than a foot high, showed the colors of fall: blazing reds, brilliant oranges, and powerful yellows. All spring, ptarmigan had particularly enjoyed the thick buds of arctic willows. By fall, the fat birds were easy to bring down.

Boarding the ship to good-natured jibes about our ragged appearance, I saw Micard was sitting on the deck holding his Ethiopian umbrella to block the rather strong sunlight. I went over to my patron, and we shook hands warmly. He got to asking me how I liked life alone in the wilderness, and I told him in detail what made it so great. He was very pleased, but admitted he did not go off the ship much.

"I just came here to contemplate, you know. Did the same in Kashmir once. This umbrella came in handy there, I can assure you," he said.

I asked about the umbrella's history. "Oh, I inherited it from my grandfather," Micard said. "Not only did he build the Suez Canal, but the Ethiopian railway as well. Yes, he was awarded the Ethiopian title for count, and this is the official symbol of that office." He laughed, then added, "I take it wherever I go, whether to palaces or huts. I've eaten at the finest hotels the world over, and have always carried it with me, even to the table! I had it with me when I had an appointment with the Pope. Of course my late uncle had been Pope Pius IX, so that gave me certain privileges." He smiled like a Hindu sage, a sage with a pope for an uncle. My benefactor was full of surprises. For the whole year, whenever he came on deck or went to shore, Micard always carried his colorful, silk parasol, and made an odd but interesting spectacle. The rough-and-tumble crew and trappers had nothing but respect for this refined, contemplative gentleman in their midst.

We talked more about the history of French exploration on this coast. Far to the north, off the coast of Peary Land, lay the barren, relatively recently discovered Ile de France. It was Micard's hope to be able to get further north the following year, to winter where no expedition had yet gone, perhaps as far as Peary Land. "You are of course invited!" he said, and added that he was serious. I assured him nothing could stop my going with him.

After our visit, Kalle and I headed back to Kallehytta to set more traps. With that hard, cold task finished, on our way back to the hut we saw a herd of musk oxen grazing peacefully. Even though it was obvious they had seen us, they seemed unperturbed, which was rather unsettling. It was more reassuring when they spooked and ran away, their typical reaction. Perhaps because their calves had grown and were now strong, they felt less threatened. Nonetheless, we kept our rifles handy and our eyes on the powerful beasts.

We were heading back to Krogness, going along the coast of Gael Hampke's Bay, when our outboard gave out again. Nothing we did could get it to start, so we began to row the many miles back to the hut. We crawled along, not seeming to get anywhere. In our exhaustion we maintained enough of our sense of humor to call the beach "The Beach that Goes on Forever!" We had one diversion along the way—we bagged a large seal. We must have been delirious! It easily weighed three hundred pounds. Why did we want to further tire ourselves by pulling a heavy seal into the boat, and then have an extra load to row? What fools we were! What would normally have taken us four hours with a motor took us all day and part of the night to row.

Nights had begun to have a period of dusk, which signaled the approach of winter. By the time we reached the hut, the moon was full, bathing the landscape in a beautiful gloom. The sun at the horizon, its red rays glowing in the distance in the north, created something supernatural when combined with the moon's effect. A couple of weirdly shaped icebergs floated silently past, glowing eerily. The shallow water lapping gently at the beach had a strange sheen.

Kalle and I pulled the seal onto the beach, gutted it, and then headed up to the cabin for a cup of coffee before we tackled the job of flaying the animal. When we returned, we saw strange movement in the shallows where the seal's blood and some blubber oil had run. Forms moved like apparitions in the strangely lit water. Then the forms began to wriggle up on land to get to the seal. They were Greenland sharks! There were two of them, each about ten feet long. Wasting no time, we grabbed long-poled hooks, and simply hauled the sharks the rest of the way up on land, where we quickly dispatched them.

Although the liver of the Arctic shark is poisonous (and often, the meat as well), the dried flesh makes good dog food and bait for traps, as drying removes the toxicity. I have heard that the toxin is akin to that of the "magic" mushroom, *Amanita muscaria*, rumored to have been a favorite of some Vikings. *Amanita* is also poisonous, but much less so when dried, just like the shark flesh. The fact that the same phenomena occurs in both a land plant and an ocean animal is a remarkable coincidence. I am no biologist, but I have heard that the toxicity of the sharks is possibly caused by the toxic algae that often infect shellfish such as mussels during what are called "red tides." Isn't life wonderful?

We headed back to the cabin for another cup of coffee. We barely reached the cabin when we heard the most god-awful screeches and growls and yelps coming from the beach. Running to investigate, we saw a Great Snowy Owl, wings spread and talons stretched out in front to do battle with a large white fox for possession of the carcasses. They danced like pale, berserk demons, the owl hovering in the air, and the fox leaping up at it. The wings of the owl snapped the air like whips, and its sharp-taloned legs shot out at the face of the fox, while the fox dodged and ducked, and made high, acrobatic lunges into the air with bared teeth and snapping jaws! We drove them off by running at them and shouting. Then we had to laugh. All that food, and they were fighting like there was nothing but a tiny scrap. Had they quietly gorged themselves, we would not have known about it until the next day. The image that fight created stuck with me my whole life, until in 1984 I finally painted the scene.

CHAPTER FIVE

Winter!

T he darkness lengthened and brought the deep cold. The first signs of deep freeze signaled that it would soon be time to set and bait the traps as the foxes' fur would be getting full and smooth. The first snow fell on September 9, and inspired a bit of creative woodwork. Using driftwood and sides of wooden boxes, we carved pieces for a small, crude dogsled for Labb to pull that would hold food and supplies. From strips of seal-skin we fashioned a harness. We made shoulder pads from musk ox hairs, so the hide would not chafe Labb. We boiled the hairs first, releasing the glutinous protein inside, and then matted them together to form the pads. When cooled, the hairs stuck together to form a felt-like material. During this entire creative endeavor we must have drunk three pots of what to us seemed like extremely good coffee. After that it was time for me to do some sewing.

Kalle kidded me about coming to the Arctic "in hiking shorts," but the fact that I had not been able to purchase arctic gear in Tromsø was becoming no joking matter. Luckily my cousin in Tromsø had given me a good pair of arctic boots made from reindeer hide, the kind the Lapps wore. When stuffed with sedge grass for insulation, they made for excellent, durable footwear. I set to making my own arctic gear with what materials were on hand. I sewed my pants and parka from sealskins. I used Kalle's heavy sail-making needles, and the all-important metal-palmed glove used to push the needles through the heavy material. I lined the finished product with layers of cloth I found laying about—it was a lining of many colors and textures.

For insulated innerwear to be worn between my normal insulated underwear and the outer garments, I used some fashionable coffee sacks. When I wore them, I had SAN SALVADOR emblazoned in big red letters on my chest. This colorful clothing provided the all-important "dead" airspace needed for insulation, and also kept the hard, hide outer garment from chafing me, or sticking to me when I perspired. Rabbit fur was sewn around the edge of my parka to insulate the skin from icy blasts, and to prevent fine, powdered snow from blowing inside the hood. The fur also prevented the rough edge of the sealskin from rubbing me raw.

My mittens were fashioned from sealskin cured in the traditional Inuit way—by soaking them in buckets of urine. We kept the buckets of urine in holes dug in the permafrost under the floor of the cabin. The strong acids of urine penetrate tough hide as efficiently as the strongest industrial solvents, making the material supple and rot-resistant. If we wanted the hair still on the hide, we soaked it for eight days; if we wanted a hairless hide, fourteen days. Rabbit fur lined the mittens for the same reason as the parka hood, but also served a very practical purpose when the cold weather got one's nose running. Kalle showed me how to sew a pleat in the palm of the mitten, at the ball of the thumb, so that it was more flexible when doing chores.

When the long chore of hand-tailoring was completed, I did not cut a very trim figure wearing the outfit, but I was certainly warm. It was actually quite an achievement for a young man who had only a month before been sitting at an architect's drawing board, dressed in a suit and tie. And there was the meas-ure of personal pride for my handiwork that I would not have felt had I simply purchased arctic gear. Still, it had been a close call. I had learned the hard way not to be so lackadaisical about going to the Arctic.

When it was time to bait our traps, we harnessed Labb to the sled and loaded it with bait pins. He barked excitedly, anxious to go. What a picture we made: our crude, one-dog sled team, and me in my Neanderthal outfit. We three ragtag kings took off to tour our vast people-less kingdom with Labb on the sled, and us on our skis. There was not much snow, and we clattered noisily across the tundra.

Often on our trap line we encountered the weird effects of weather. For ex-ample, we came upon ice beneath the Wordie Glacier that was like glass. The never-ending, frigid winds that blow down from the glacier had helped to freeze the ice quickly, and to also sweep away all the snow. Trapped in the clear ice, just at the surface, were thousands of lemmings. They must have tried to cross when the surface was slightly slushy, and a sudden drop in temperature, proba-bly caused by the glacial winds, had frozen them in their tracks. They were in strange, contorted poses. It was quite an awesome sight.

Contrary to popular opinion, lemmings do not commit mass suicide by rushing into the sea. Occasionally, when the population gets too large to feed in an area, they begin a migration. Sometimes their path is blocked by open water as they cross the ice, or if on land, by a cliff above the sea. The large horde often unwittingly pushes some lemmings at the head of the group over the edge of the cliff or into the water before the scurrying multitude turns away from danger. Early explorers, having witnessed such a startling sight, began the rumor of mass lemming suicides that persists to this day.

We slid over the entombed lemmings, heading for a patch of clear ground near the base of the mountain next to the glacier. The ground was clear because of the same glacial winds that had swept the ice clean. In this snow-less area we set traps, hoping to catch the rare and thus more valuable blue fox. These animals come from the same family as the white fox. In fact, 10 percent of white fox pups will be blue in color. As they mature, they learn to live in the snow-less areas where their coloration blends in better.

The precipitation in September and the early part of October had been slight, which made for good, thin, hard-packed snow cover for sledding on the fjord, but prevented skiing on land. Near the place where Schjelderup had shot too many musk oxen, and where we had dumped one of the carcasses, we saw signs that the meat had not been "wasted." It had lured many foxes to the area. After all our traps to the east had finally been set, we returned to Krogness for some much-needed rest.

With nothing to do but wait, I was suddenly struck by the rather nerve-wracking fact that a long, black, sunless winter had begun. Even though Norwegians—particularly those in the northern parts of the country—are used to dark winters, at least they have the benefit of towns, cafés, bars, theaters, and, most importantly, people! Our nearest neighbor, Meyer Olsen, the Lapp carpenter who had come on *Quest* to trap, had a cabin a few hours' sled trip away, and even he had gotten so lonely that he made the trip just for a chat.

Meyer was not happy with the long, dark days. I had thought a Lapp would be used to it, but he seemed to enjoy his brooding over the dark. He said, like an orator in a play, "This eternal darkness, I never get used to it. One time with my brother up in Svalbard, looking across Brandy Bay, we watched the last dot of red sun go below the horizon and I wondered, 'Will I ever see it again?' And that is how it is in the Arctic: cold, lonely, and dark." His high cheekbones cast morose shadows on his drawn face and his voice had a mesmerizing effect. If he was so afflicted by the arctic darkness, how would I stand up?

After Meyer had left, I told Kalle how I felt. He laughed and said, "Don't let that old goat get to you. He is a born storyteller, a natural dramatist, and what is a drama without tension? Don't worry. There is a secret to survival during the long arctic nights. I learned it, and I know you'll figure it out yourself. You're made for the Arctic, just like me."

During the eight-day moonless period of the month, we stayed put. Snow fell. At the first sliver of crescent moonlight, Kalle made a crescent with the thumb and fingers of one hand, and said, "It's time. Let's go."

The amount of light given off by even that small sliver of moon was greatly amplified by the snow and ice all around, and since the frigid air was moisture-free, it did not interfere with the dispersal of light. We could in fact see quite well. Labb was excited to be in his harness again, and Kalle and I were glad that we could use our skis over the new snow, even though it was just a few inches deep. The stars sparkled magnificently, and the vault of the sky seemed close enough to touch. There was a curious effect of feeling at once small and insignificant, yet part of the vastness, and tremendously important. As we went along, the moon rose higher, and shadows were more pronounced, but the stars lost their glitter in the moon's growing light. The mountains stood out sharply, and when we looked over to Clavering Island, its glacial top glowed like a jewel. It was a true "moonlit" day.

There was not enough snow to cover all the rocks, and the wind had swept many areas clean. We had to zigzag from one wind-hardened snowdrift to another. Since these drifts were almost always lined up in a northwest direction because of the wind, we learned we could at least use them as a "compass" in an emergency, as most polar travelers soon learn. These drifts are popularly known as *sastrugis*, a Russian term.

Sometimes we had to slide across frozen tundra swept completely free of snow on our way to Villaen, our tiny trap-line hut near the entrance to Loch Fyne. And many times, thanks to the same sweeping effect, we had to dig our way through a snowdrift piled against the door by that "wind-broom." Fortunately, Kalle's experience had led him to tie a shovel by steel wire to the outside wall of the hut. It hung high enough not to be buried, and the wire prevented powerful arctic winds from blowing the heavy implement away.

Everything in the hut was ready for us, just as we had left it. Wood in the stove burst into warm flames with the touch of a match. Loaves of bread with fine, brown crusts were at hand. While dinner cooked, we hung the foxes in the entryway where they would not thaw out. After we had eaten, and I had crawled into my caribou-hide sleeping bag, I thought, *So, this is one of those terrible, black arctic nights? This is heaven!*

Back at Krogness, we would spend the time skinning the foxes. The skins were hung on wooden hangers that looked much like clothes hangers, except that the ends were deeply notched. A slit was made in the skin, near the Achilles tendon, and these holes were slipped over the notches. Thus, the legs were kept splayed. Beginning at the back legs, the skin was carefully disconnected from the flesh. There is a foamy, gelatinous fiber net that attaches the pelt to the flesh. If done carefully, the pelt could be removed with very little flesh attached. Any flesh left had to be removed; gruesome, perhaps, but that was how it was done in those days. We hung our pelts in the small, pelt-storage hut to freeze-dry them. This method, rather than drying them in the cabin, left the fur softer, and the skin more flexible—in other words, more valuable. This was, after all, a commercial venture. The concept of protecting wild species was not yet part of the public consciousness. In 1936, trapping was considered an exotic, daring lifestyle.

We spent most of the time baking bread, repairing our clothes, and seeing that the sled, skis, and rifles were in good shape. When that was done, we'd start all over again, just to keep busy. Luckily, I also had books with me! And my constant desire to explore. Often I went out for walks alone while Kalle stayed at home whistling merrily as if on a holiday in the Caribbean.

While on my walks, I discovered that objects, and even whole landscapes that were miles away, stood out in the moon's light like stunning crystal dreams. And all sounds, even from long distances away, seemed to come from nearby. Though I had often seen the specter-like lights of the aurora borealis in Norway, I was profoundly affected by the first display of the northern lights experienced in my new arctic home. I was alone with Labb at the promontory at Cape Stosch when these cosmic fireworks began. Colorfully streaked curtains began waving like flags at breakneck speed. The curtain seemed to drop all the way to earth, even down to me. Labb was whining. It was like watching cosmic snakes moving gracefully at great speed. The dreamlike quality of the situation got me to laughing at myself and all my previous conceptions of reality.

In the case of a constantly dissolving ego, one has two choices: laugh at yourself, or go mad: I had discovered the secret of arctic survival, just as Kalle had predicted. The secret lay in developing a self-deprecating sense of humor. The Inuit had figured that out long ago. In the Arctic, death was always just a breath away when the nights were twenty-four-hours long and minus-fifty degrees Fahrenheit. One had better think the whole thing rather humorous, or one would certainly go mad. There was no reassuring signpost of humanity, such as a café—or even a signpost, for that matter. You were starkly alone. All the civilized mental contrivances that make most humans feel separate from Nature melt away, and you are left realizing your previous conceptions were mere illusions; even your previous beliefs about the existence of a god or the devil are not spared. The effect can be so traumatic that some men have committed suicide when faced with this rather open-ended perception of reality. And the Arctic certainly tested and teased my mental health more than a few times.

Once, as we headed for Knoph-hytta, we came across a field of deep, newly fallen snow near the base of the "Hindu Temples." It was one of those level, wind-protected areas that Kalle had wisely said we should not set traps in or they would be buried; it was best to set traps where the wind swept the snow away. Here, with no wind to pack it, high drifts of very fluffy flakes had formed. Even with skis to distribute our weight, we sank up to our armpits. The skis were useless, so we put them on the sled. Leaning our bodies into the drift, we did a sort of swimming stroke with our arms to move forward. Poor Labb, heavy as he was, and pulling the sled, had to make desperate lunges from his hind legs, like a jackrabbit, flattening the powder enough to get his footing for the next lunge.

Hoping we would soon get through this snow, we foolishly pressed on, thinking we would save hours this way. Instead, we sweated terribly under the exertion, and often had to stop to air out our coats for fifty seconds at a clip. We continued our grueling breaststrokes for hours before we reached firmer snow. Exhausted, with arms and legs like rubber, we realized that any detour was not worth expending so much energy. We later learned that the German Koldewey Expedition of 1869 had encountered the same rare snow condition north of us and had termed it "swim-snow." It was a damn good description!

At Knoph-hytta, with the stove warming up, the taut, dried fibers of the driftwood walls began to expand and cracking sounds, like gunfire, filled the air. The dense, Siberian driftwood had a fine resonance. It was like a Stradivarius, and we soon grew to like the sound. The room also filled with the heavenly aroma of Kalle's famous Greenland stew of musk ox, seal, potatoes, and whatever else we felt like throwing in. We three basked in the comforting glow of self-satisfaction. Our clothes were hanging up to dry; fox pelts hung in the entryway. After eating, we took to our bunks. Labb, stretched out on his bunk like the Sphinx, yawned leisurely, slowly, over and over again, until Kalle and I began to yawn too. Soon we were fast asleep. In the morning, Labb woke us up with quiet *woofs*; I could tell from his tone it was time to get to work. Kalle, climbing out of his bunk, said, "Labb is worse than a mother; he puts us to sleep at night, and wakes us up in the morning!"

The weather conditions had become a constant source of awe and trepidation. One time we saw two musk oxen in the distance by the weak light of the moon. They were struggling along through deep snow. By that time of year they should have migrated to more windy areas in higher elevations where the ground was kept relatively free of snow and they could get to their food. The deep snow was sticking to their thick coats, and had matted into great, heavy boulders beneath them. The icy boulders interfered with their walking, and obviously drained their energy. Even from a distance, we could tell they were in desperate straits. We did not need the meat, but considered putting them out of their misery. In the end we decided to let nature take its course. It was a grim reminder of arctic realities.

We celebrated Christmas aboard the *Quest*, but first we took our juletide "sleigh ride"—Labb pulling the sled with our gear on it while we skied—down the east coast of Loch Fyne and arrived at Meyer Olsen's little hut. He had moved away from the ship because he and Schjelderup did not get along; Olsen had not visited the ship for a month and a half, even though it was only an hour's sled run away. The hut was barely big enough for the three of us, and Labb had to stay out in the entryway with Olsen's pelts, rifles, and so on. The hut was messy and morose, just like its owner. We spent the night there with me squeezed under Olsen's bunk, and Kalle on the tiny floor. In the morning, Meyer was not willing to go with us. "I am not going to spend one day around that bastard, Schjelderup!" he shouted.

Arriving at the ship, the dogs greeted us with wild yelps; Labb was beside himself, but entered the camp with dignity and a few proper "hellos" to his friends. The ship, now solidly frozen in, had ice up to the railing. It had been winterized by covering the deck with a canvas tent. Blocks of snow were piled high up the sides of the ship for insulation and to break the force of high winds.

A pathway made by sleds, dogs, and men ran from the ship to the shore—a ten-minute walk. A small hole had been cut in the ice, just by the side of the ship, so that bilgewater could be drained away through it. It was covered with boards and canvas to help prevent it from freezing over. On *Quest's* leeward side, small, individual igloos had been built on the ice for the dogs.

Micard still rarely went outside. He said his daily routine was to go out on the ice, walk around the ship, say hello to each dog, walk to shore, then head straight back to his cabin. He said, "Willie, here I have my favorite biscuits, canned pears, and my wonderful mystery novels. What more could I ask for? Besides, it is pitch black. What can one see? I will sit and meditate all winter, and then burst forth like a flower when the sun returns!" We drank a cognac to spring.

Micard had an extensive collection of mystery novels to supplement his good library of arctic and scientific readings. He had a broad knowledge of the Arctic, and loved to learn more. He pumped me for details of what I had seen and felt, and it was a pleasure to oblige. There is little doubt I owed him that much, not to mention it was nice to have someone interested in what Kalle and I were doing.

It was interesting, to say the least, to be among other humans again. The old engineer stuck his head up from the engine room below to say hello. He was drunk as hell, and how he stayed that way was a mystery to everyone for a long time. One day, a crew member was in the boiler room and saw what he thought was a mug of water. He took a sip and discovered that it was pure alcohol! The engineer's quarters were next to the engine room, and there, deep in the hull where it was rather dark, he had come across a fifty-five-gallon drum of pure alcohol left over from the expedition of the year before. It had been meant to preserve scientific specimens, but was pickling the engineer instead.

We had a lively Christmas party, and we all got rousing drunk, the first time for me since Oslo. After the Christmas festivities, Magne Raaum, a Norwegian trapper, came by from the Norwegian weather station twenty-five miles south at Myggbukta. He offered me a dogsled ride to the station, saying he would return to the ship in two days. I jumped at the chance. The day was very dark, but the stars twinkled madly, and gave enough light on the snow to see by. Raaum had the sneakiest method to get his dogs on the run. He would point out into the darkness and shout, "Look! Musk ox! Musk ox!" The dogs believed their boss and would take off running. After awhile, the team would slow down, and look back quizzically as if to ask, "Are you sure you saw a musk ox?" Then Raaum would again shout, "Musk ox! Musk ox!" and point in the direction he wanted to go. The team would renew its dash toward the distant, nonexistent prey. I almost fell out of the sled with laughter every time he pulled that stunt. Sometimes the dogs' faces wore unmistakable frowns of suspicion, and I would have to keep a straight face so as to not give Raaum away.

The trail went through a valley which had a creek that was surprisingly not frozen. Raaum said it came from a lake that obviously was geothermally heated. As we went further along the creek, its water eventually froze up. We sailed along this frozen creek to Raaum's devious cries of "Musk ox! Musk ox!" Never once did he have to use his whip as many dog-team owners did. The dogs were his family, and he would no more have used the whip on them than he would his mother. In this marvelous manner we came to Myggbukta.

The site had a two-storied house, and a storage loft made a small third level. A tall radio mast, guy-wired to the ground, bespoke of civilization. There was a sliver of moon, and its light showed a panorama of great beauty. Mountains across the mouth of Kaiser Franz Joseph Fjord could be seen rising in the distance. Henry Hudson had seen this coast in 1607, but over three hundred years would pass before Europeans had a tiny foothold here. Most of the stations and huts in this area of Northeast Greenland were only about ten years old. Before that, few Europeans had sailed to these shores, and fewer had lived here. And yet there we were, having a party.*

After three days of parties, Raaum and I headed back to the ship. The valley of the unfrozen creek reverberated with shouts of "Musk ox! Musk ox!" Labb greeted me like a long-lost brother. Kalle told me Schjelderup had "conscripted" Labb for some work. The skipper was not necessarily cruel to dogs, but neither did he consider them friends as we did, and often worked them very hard. He used the whip as well. Labb stayed close to us for the rest of the stay.

Micard was in an expansive mood. Sitting in Sir Ernest Shackleton's old cabin, the count told me stories of his childhood and of his life in France. Some of Micard's aristocratic friends at home could not understand why, at his age, he

---

* Author's Note: Magne Raaum and I met in Oslo in 1992 and again in 1995 in Denmark.

kept coming to the Arctic to "suffer so," as they put it. But he loved the Arctic for its great silences and awesome beauty. Micard's father had been both regimented and class-conscious, and his son wanted to be free of that constriction. As a child, Micard had traveled the world in an aristocratic fashion. He did not get to see the real countryside or people. He and his sister, Madame Smet, were raised to be social snobs but rebelled as they grew up. When they were still quite young, they found a medical book with drawings of the human body in their father's library. It contained the first nude pictures they had ever seen. In came their governess, who reported their "perverted reading" to their father; they were promptly locked in a dark closet as punishment. Micard told me he thought this was why he became ill at ease with women, and stayed a bachelor. He told me, "And my friends wonder why I do not care to stay in civilization!"

Micard had a gentle nature that earned him everyone's respect. He was a man of deep thought, and could sit for hours just gazing into the distance, without saying a word. Later, in the spring, he went out with Schjelderup by sled to visit glaciers and mountain passes. The rough trappers never considered the count anything but an explorer, in spite of his colorful umbrella that accompanied him everywhere. When someone suggested Micard should not walk alone—in case of polar bears—when he went off the ship for his daily tour, Schjelderup snorted, "Are you kidding? With that umbrella, he'd scare the hell out of any damn polar bear!"

With the Christmas holiday over, we prepared to head back to our trap line, and Kallehytta was to be our first stop. Norwegian trapper Gerhard Antonsen (also known as the "King of Revet"—Revet being the name of his main trapping hut) had been to the festivities and was now heading back our way. Since he had no sled-load, he offered us a ride. Antonsen had run his trap line at the west end of Clavering Island in an area called Revet for seven years straight. His excuse for not going back home was that no one would be able to look after his dogs the way he did! These dogs actually belonged to the fur company in Norway that bought the skins. The dogs stayed for each new group of trappers that replaced those who had gone home. Antonsen was a kind man who loved his pipe and went about life with regal stature and self-confidence. Even Schjelderup treated Gerhard respectfully, and that's saying something!

We three men were now on Gerhard's sled, with Labb trotting behind and pulling his own. Antonsen's dogs were really something. We were traveling at a good clip, but they always stayed on the edge of the hard-packed ridges of snowdrift, or the *sastrugi*. In between the ridges, the snow was deep, soft powder, and if the sled went off course, the going would have been tough, if not completely halted. But the dogs stayed on hard cover the whole way. With nothing to do but let the intelligent animals take us along, we chatted amiably as if on a cruise. In the distance, by the dim light, we could see Wordie Glacier glowing. We were having a great time, when suddenly the sled slowed markedly. Startled from our cozy chat, we looked around. There behind us sitting on the sled was Labb with a big grin on his face. His sled, of course, was still attached to him, so Antonsen's dogs suddenly had a lot more to pull. Labb looked quite comfortable and wagged his tail to let us know he thought he was pretty clever! Roaring with laughter, we slid over the fjord. Labb rode with us until it was time for "The King of Revet" to go his separate way.

As this was January, the light had started to come back as a dim halo on the horizon. This light actually afforded some visibility. As we approached the coast by Kallehytta, we saw a phenomenal amount of fox tracks leading to our trap line. It looked like a gathering, or like a convention of foxes had passed this way. We hurried to investigate. As we went from trap to trap, which took a few hours, we found more fox than ever in just one run of the line.

Kalle laughed, and said it must be the bait. We had used a pungently aromatic cheese the Norwegians referred to as *gammle ost*, or "old cheese." Kalle had learned this trick in Spitsbergen, following the advice of old trappers who had said it only worked during mating season, and January was the month for that! Kalle said, "It must have the same chemistry as a female fox in heat! We have the sexiest traps in the Arctic."

CHAPTER SIX

Marooned by Storm, Betrayed by Schjelderup, and Saved by Labb

Kalle went out alone one morning to check traps for blue fox at the foot of Wordie Glacier. I stayed at the cabin to get a stew going, and to skin the foxes we had picked up the previous day. When Kalle returned hours later, his eyes were haggard and his face drawn. He could hardly speak. Gulping scalding-hot coffee, he could finally talk.

"Never seen anything like it! Suddenly there was a windstorm at the base of the glacier. So hard, and so cold, I almost didn't make it—couldn't walk. The wind forced me to my damned knees. Ice-cap snow was sandblasting me and turning my back into concrete. I kept thinking about those lemmings we saw that had been flash-frozen in the same damn area. It was a horrible idea to think I'd end up like that! Had to crawl for an hour through drifts before I was far enough away from the windy area to be able to stand up! Christ, Willie! I never want to go through anything like that again!"

He had been caught in an "avalanche" of cold air that had dropped off the ice cap as a single mass. It is like being hit by a solid object. And yet there had hardly been a breeze where I was at the cabin. The Arctic has many such "local weather" phenomena as that which had almost killed Kalle, and that month, in particular, we seemed to experience most of them.

These ice-cap storms produced hard, grainy snow crystals which some-times reached as far as Krogness. On these occasions, the cabin would be hit so hard by winds I was sure we'd all be swept away. It was only because the cabin was frozen solidly into the tundra's permafrost that we did not! The howling, hurricane-force winds drove the fine snow through even the smallest openings between our blocks of sod outside. The specks of ice would find their way among the thick sod pile as if through a maze, and then come through even the tiniest, pin-sized hole in our wooden walls. It was during one of those storms that I really understood why the *National Geographic* pages were so thickly plastered on the inner walls. Even so, the snow still found new, barely perceptible avenues into the cabin. If we did not block up these pinholes, by morning a two-foot drift would be comfortably settled against a wall in the cabin. I would soon learn of a different type of snow, however, that proved to be much more dangerous.

Toward the middle of February a light, fluffy snow began to fall from a cloudy, windless sky. Then suddenly, the snow dumped, as if from a bucket. Without wind to blow it away, the snow piled up quickly around the cabin. We cleared the doorway six times before we gave up. We knew we were going to be snowbound. On the third morning of the snowfall, we opened the door to find a hard-packed white wall blocking the way. Strangely, the window on the opposite wall was not blocked. The draft had been just enough to keep it clear. We knew that if we had to get out in an emergency, such as a fire, we could do it. But we were not going anywhere unless forced to!

As the snow fell, an eerie silence descended. It was unnerving, like the silence of the grave. Shrieking winds would have been preferable, for we knew those kinds of storms would soon end. In this muffled, new world, we instinctively felt we would not soon be free of the cabin. We settled in to keep ourselves occupied, doing anything to keep from thinking. We repaired every hole in every piece of clothing. We cleaned and re-cleaned our rifles. We baked and ate. We did everything slowly, and deliberately. Two Danes who had recently visited before the storm had left a female dog with us who was about to have pups, so we had her to help keep ourselves busy. I read and reread the pages of the old *National Geographic* magazines stuck to our walls. I eventually became tempted to tear them off so I could read their other sides, though of course I did not dare to expose ourselves to interior snowdrifts. Though no winds were blowing to force snow through the cracks, I was taking no chances. I would have to guess what was on the back side of those pages.

After eight days we had run out of fresh meat, but still the snow fell. We tried to make our starchy foods and dehydrated emergency rations more palatable by giving them exotic names, but that did not improve their lack of vitamins and flavor. To help pass the time, Kalle told me stories of his last winter up on Svalbard, the high-arctic island belonging to Norway.

He had spent a year with an Austrian, Herman Ritter, in the most primitive conditions on Svalbard. Herman Ritter had arrived as a typical order-loving Austrian, but you cannot be like that and live long in the Arctic. He quickly adapted and was soon a true arctic man, enthusiastically tolerant of the most primitive—and life-threatening—conditions. He loved the Arctic, and never wanted to return to civilization. A great guy, according to Kalle.

Ritter's wife, Christiane, arrived aboard a tourist cruise ship—yes, believe it or not, there were summer cruise ships to Svalbard in the 1930s!—hoping to get her husband to return home, but she ended up spending the winter with them. They lived off the land as much as possible. Christiane became so much a part of that environment, that when the time came for them to depart for civilization, she did not want to go either. She later wrote an excellent and popular book entitled *A Woman in the Winter Night*. The shack they wintered in, strangely enough, had once sheltered another woman in a previous year. Women were very rare in those parts, to say the least, so it was an incredible coincidence for two women to have lived in the same lonely shack, even if years apart. The previous woman had developed scurvy, and had died on her way back to civilization. Another earlier inhabitant of that fateful shack had left a gangrenous toe there.

When Christiane arrived to spend the winter with them, Kalle had expected her to go mad during the long dark months spent cooped up in the shack. In fact, Kalle told me he had been looking forward to that scene for some midwinter entertainment! Kalle said, "She had only just arrived when Herman and I went off on a two-week hunting trip, leaving her alone! The idea was that she'd never learn to live and love it there if we were around to cater to her. She managed all right. A storm blew up that lasted the entire two weeks. She nearly froze to death, then nearly starved, then nearly went mad. Then, like all of us who make it in the Arctic, she began to laugh at herself, and the task of survival didn't seem so bad after all. One hell of a woman! After that she got used to cleaning the bloody carcasses of seals and polar bears. And then it became nice for us to have a woman around. And though I was already engaged to Ruth, I had not seen her for over a year, so it was me who was going crazy with Christiane around."

Kalle said the best way not to go crazy was to ignore the fact that Christiane was a woman. It must have been tough in a tiny hut, with her husband away much of the time. Kalle was a good boy, though. For all I know, his stories, and our laughter that accompanied them, may have saved us from developing scurvy by generating vitamins from the otherwise vitamin-less food we were eating. As it was, our teeth began to loosen in our gums. After two weeks of being snowbound, even most of the lackluster food ran out. All we had left was flour for bread, and coffee. One morning I asked Kalle, "Are my eyes as milky as yours?" His usually startling blue eyes had lost their inner fire. "They look dead," he told me, but reassured me that it was normal for that time of year.

Kalle soon had a tooth that was killing him. He kept busy, or sane, that is, by thinking of when he would be returning home to Ruth. It was not a matter of *if*; he had to think of his return as definite, predictable as the turning of the earth. He designed the house he would build for Ruth. He even designed a small store he would open so he could eventually stop this "nonsense of spending my life in the lonely Arctic." It was the first time I had seen him morose, and it made me nervous.

Whenever we baked bread, the cabin smelled warm, soft, cozy, and sweet, like a woman. But that's also when the dangerous nostalgia would set in. The flies would also come out of their hibernation in the walls, thinking it was spring, thus adding to our longing for sun and warmth. After two weeks of being snowbound, Kalle watched two flies copulating through a magnifying glass. Suddenly he looked up, laughed, and said, "The devil take me! I've definitely been in the Arctic too long. I'm getting excited!" I swear our laughter kept us from going crazy.

To stay sane, I sketched scenes from the Arctic and from my trip to Africa. I told Kalle the stories that accompanied the sketches, about hot, torrid Equatorial Senegal and the bordellos of Bordeaux (that fortunately I'd had no money for). I went into detail about the diseases in a river in Senegal that made it unhealthy to swim in, even though the heat was killing us. Instead, the captain rigged up a small dunking pool on the deck. I explained how in Bordeaux I had met an American who had come there as a young man with money, but when the money ran out, he'd decided to stay anyway. He was living in the front hallway of a whorehouse, and drank the dregs given away free from the wineries. He had sores all over his body, his teeth were falling out, but he would not leave. When I thought I was through with those stories, Kalle would ask questions about the color of the door in the hallway, and other such minutiae, just to keep us occupied. We were beginning to lose it.

Eventually, Kalle's tooth became so painful that he begged me to pull it out. Using a pair of pliers, I did the job. The blood flowed copiously, and he felt much better, but our lack of health was getting serious. I remembered we had some dehydrated prunes in a small bag out in the entryway. While Kalle slept, I steamed some up for him, and then set them out in the entryway to cool. When I went to get them, I found that the bitch the Danes had left with us was whelping, and she had also gotten to some of the prunes first! I found a few surviving prunes lying in the coal dust of the bags that surrounded her. There was also some of the precious fruit in the afterbirth. Undaunted, I scooped them up and boiled them again, though I never told Kalle about this. He ate them gratefully.

Toward the end of the third week, though we still had bread, we were ravenous. Our thoughts turned to the puppies in the next room. We were just mentally preparing ourselves in case we had to eat them to stay alive. Labb and the new mother shared our rations of bread. If we could have gotten to our hut where the fox pelts hung, we could have had some frozen fox meat, and other rations we had stored there, but it was buried too deeply. Also, the thought of eating fox was repugnant to me. Kalle laughed at that. He said I was just not hungry enough. It is very healthy food. Kalle once saved an old Lapp trapper in Spitsbergen who had scurvy, but was too proud to eat fox meat. He thought it would mean he had become a lower animal! Kalle force-fed him the meat for ten days, and he recuperated from the scurvy.

Lethargy set in, then a feeling of dispiritedness. A sense of the absurdity of our existence crept into our normally positive outlook. Life seemed an overly drawn-out, boring play. Then, in the nick of time, at the end of three weeks, the snow finally stopped. A wind came up and cleared the snow off the roof. We dug a tunnel, starting from our window, crawled out, and stared at an unrecognizable landscape. The deep snow had leveled the land. Wind had sculpted rolling waves on the surface. The sun had technically made its first appearance over the horizon on February 1. Emerging from the cabin, we stood in this strange, new light, weak, but hopeful.

Kalle immediately set out toward Eagle's Nest, where we had musk ox meat stored, but eleven hours later he came back wet, exhausted, and empty-handed. The snow there was so deep that even though the hut had a stovepipe that extended ten feet above the roof, he could find no sign of it! After resting up, Kalle then headed for Kallehytta, hoping the ice-cap winds had swept that area clean, and he could get at the lifesaving provisions in the hut. He was back only a few hours later. The snow was too deep to travel in. He had to turn back before he was completely out of energy. Together we set off to Villaen, by Loch Fyne.

Though we did not have meat cached there, at least we had canned provisions and potatoes. The snow became less deep the closer we got to the hut. Somehow that area had not been as hard hit. It was an example of localized weather phenomena. Trembling from weakness and anticipation, we dug our way into the hut only to find the shelves barren of provisions! I had never known such sadness, and such a sudden drop of energy. Kalle roared, "That bastard Schjelderup has done this!"

I could not believe it. But Kalle roared again, saying, "He can't keep his hands off things 'just sitting around.' The pirate bastard was probably here a month ago. He knew we were finished trapping this line, so he convinced himself we would not need the provisions!"

"It's murder!" I shouted.

Kalle said through clenched teeth, "You're catching on."

I realized just then why it was considered a felonious thing in the wilderness to take another man's cache. If we had seen Schjelderup just then, there is no doubt that we would have killed him, and felt justified in the act. We dragged ourselves back to Krogness even more tired than before. My bones felt hollow, and my legs were weak as feathers. But there was one last hope: to reach Eskimonaes and the Danes. It took us a full day to go the nine miles in the deep snow that covered the frozen fjord, but reaching the Danes, we were saved. We first ate some soup, so our stomachs would not go into convulsions. Kalle knew what to do since he had seen starving men die after being rescued because they stuffed themselves with food. A few hours later we had some bread and meat, and even a beer. Kalle said, "I think I'm strong enough to kill Schjelderup now. Let's go home."

Though February had brought the sun, that month also recorded the coldest temperature of the year at minus fifty-five degrees Fahrenheit. We tried without success to hunt fresh meat to regain our strength. The canned provisions and flour we had received from the Danes were life-sustaining, but left us feeling sluggish and moody. Although we never argued, nor got on each other's nerves, we often traveled in different directions as a relief from each other's constant companionship.

Soon after we returned from Eskimonaes with new provisions, I went down to the mouth of Loch Fyne, and found the swirling waters had opened the ice. The sunlight, such as it was, ricocheted dazzlingly off every point of ice and snow and the wave of churning water. Within this weblike, fantastical display of light, I saw a seal lying on the ice near the open water. I aimed my rifle and fired. The seal rolled over and lay still. The deep red hue of the steaming blood gushed upward in a jet from the bullet hole. I bent down and drank it. I gulped great, desperate mouthfuls, seemingly unable to satisfy my craving. Finally, a warm glow spread over my body. I sat back on my haunches, and heaved a great, happy sigh. I was reborn.

March merged into April. Eventually Schjelderup showed up. We no longer had his murder on our agenda, but at the first sight of him I told him what had happened to us during the three-week snowfall, and what a sono-fabitch, skinflint, penny-scrounging bastard he was. He roared, "This is mutiny!" But he was no longer the great arctic skipper to be held in awe. Kalle looked him right in the eye and told him again what a lousy bastard he was. The captain's face suddenly dropped its snarling mask. He threw his head back and laughed a bit too heartily, as if to show we were sons who had come of age by standing up to him. Even though his laugh sounded a bit nervous, it cleared the air. There was no sense in expecting the tough arctic rat to apologize.

By the beginning of May, even though it was still below freezing, there was such a dramatic change in temperature that the fur of the foxes had already started to shed. We made the rounds of the trap lines and took them down, knowing that soon the pelts would not be worth taking.

Schjelderup came by a few times with a work crew, wanting to use Labb on his teams, but in the freezing air we would hear his dogs' yelps an hour before they came in to sight, and we whisked Labb away on some "emergency mission." One day, when some climatic condition muffled the sound, the dogs got relatively close before we heard them. Kalle got up, put on his coat, called to Labb, and took off across the snow to the east. They disappeared over a ridge just as Schjelderup came into view. The skipper asked me where Kalle and Labb were. I said, "Left yesterday for Knoph-hytta."

"When will they be back?" he demanded.

I shrugged. "Tomorrow, the next day. Don't know."

Schjelderup left, fuming to have come so far out of his way for nothing. It had certainly been a close call for Labb.

Finally, one day as we heard dogs in the distance, Kalle said, "It's time to put a stop to this." When Schjelderup arrived and demanded Labb, Kalle had his turn at venting his anger at the skipper. Kalle told him, "It's our dog, our friend. Not a slave. You don't know how to treat animals."

Schjelderup turned red in the face, shouted that it was his dog, and that he had only loaned Labb to us. He told us, "If I want to work him until he drops, I will do it. And if he does not get up when I beat him, I'll put a bullet in him right there on the spot!"

Kalle calmly told him something like, "There are laws against cruelty to animals, as well as against stealing other trappers' supplies. And we have two witnesses against you." Schjelderup left without Labb, and never asked for him again.

By the middle of May, we had had constant daylight, and not much to do except ready the cabins for whomever was to use them next. This gave me time for some artwork. All winter I had had to thin my oils with white gasoline because in the frigid temperatures, plain turpentine made the oils glob into tiny pearls. Even kerosene did not work. I took a run down to the *Quest* and made some paintings while Halvorsen took photos of me painting in minus-five degrees, and in my Neanderthal outfit. I also made a trip to the little hut where the Danish artist Tutein had lived before the polar bear killed him. I found some brushes just outside the tiny place where snow had melted, and said some words in his memory.

Spring seemed to come overnight. Tiny rivulets began to snake across the crusts of snow. The south-facing slopes were alive with thundering water. We began to see ptarmigan in abundance again, and added them to our menu. The birds had gorged themselves on dwarf pussy-willow buds, and the buds had often sprouted in their gullets, which in turn were eaten for the invigorating vitamins they contained. We two now-seasoned arctic men also grazed on the tundra's reawakening vegetation to supplement our otherwise all-meat diet. Then, suddenly we were eating seal and musk ox regularly again, and some fish as well, and were as alive and revitalized as the land.

The thaw signaled it was time to begin the process of preparing pelts for transport back to Norway. The oily paws were covered in salt, but the fur itself required a more elaborate preparation. We could not leave any oils that would turn rancid, so we tumbled a few furs at a time in a fifty-five-gallon drum partially filled with absorbent sawdust. The drum was suspended between two sawhorses, and a hand-crank was used to turn the drum slowly. Our Primus stove heated the drum, and subsequently the sawdust. Once the furs were tumbled, we would tap out the sawdust containing the oils by gently beating on the skins with bamboo switches we had brought along just for this purpose. The sawdust was then reused, until it was too oil-soaked to serve its purpose. The tumbling and beating also served to soften the skin of the pelt, and fluff up the fur. It was a primitive process but worked just fine. We had 150 pelts. During this work, we discussed the future, and what we would do when we returned to Tromsø. Kalle thought we should team up, go to Svalbard, and get rich trapping polar-bear skins. That was fine by me. I really did not like the idea of returning to city life by this point.

Suddenly there was more time to do painting and sketching. The weather was much warmer, and the oil paints no longer froze so badly. One day I was sketching a view of Cape Stosch from a hill overlooking it, with Labb, of course, by my side, fast asleep. We had climbed to a plateau where we were about a mile away from the cape, and I had walked out onto a small flat area with a cliff below it that dropped abruptly some fifty feet.

It was a perfect scene. A small herd of musk ox grazed on a hill at the foot of the mountains while a lone bull stood watch, motionless on a knoll, as if cut out of granite. As I set up my easel on the solid stone surface, a rabbit watched me warily with eyes like liquid sensors. The terrain below was mostly free of snow, and large hunks of ice in the fjord beyond made a nice contrast to the tundra colors. Even the morning frost on the brown grass had gone, dissolved by the sun into shining, pearl-like droplets. In the distance, the snowcapped mountains of Manley Land and the glacier-capped Jordan Hill framed the frozen flow of Mercanton Glacier. Red-hued clouds roiled above Manley and Jordan. It was a perfect composition.

I had just begun to sketch in the bold lines of those snowcapped peaks with a crayon when suddenly I heard the clatter of hoofs behind me. Whirling around, I saw a musk ox charging me, its head down. According to the textbooks, they are not supposed to charge! Obviously this one couldn't read. With the cliff behind me, there was no place to run or even dodge. The animal's heavy, angry breathing shook its entire woolly frame. It was really quite frightening.

In a single motion, I dropped my crayon and drew up my rifle, but in my haste, the shell jammed in the chamber! Labb suddenly tore past me like a rocket, and snarling like a demon, went straight for the powerful animal's neck. Just a yard from me, the musk ox had slid to a stop with pebbles screeching and flying from beneath its hoofs. It shook its shaggy head to throw off its attacker.

Labb held on, then let go and began to dance wildly around the beast. The musk ox followed Labb in circles with its head down. I cleared the rifle with my knife blade, reloaded, stepped up to the animal and shot it in the ear. It dropped like a rock. Labb yelped triumphantly, and I shouted, "Labb! You saved my life, boy!" He leapt up and placed two paws on my chest. He was big. His face almost reached mine. I hugged him with all the emotion the drama had built up. I told him, "What a dog you are, old boy! And you who were always so afraid of those damn musk ox!" And that really got him yelping, and happily licking my face. What a wonderful dog he was!

The musk ox was a female. We followed her tracks back over the brink of a hill. Partway down the slope, a set of small tracks had branched off from hers. It was clear what had happened. Sniffing us from above, the mother had sent her calf back down to the herd, and had rushed up to the plateau to destroy the enemy she fancied threatened her young. It was sad. Kalle and I only hunted musk ox for meat, and for a long time we'd had all we needed in storage. Kalle, who was out taking photos of our cabin with my camera, heard the shot, and came quickly to see what was up. And that is how I have that picture of Labb and me with the poor beast.

At the end of May, Micard came by whaleboat with Schjelderup and two others from the ship. They were heading for some serious walrus hunting at Cape Mary, twenty-five miles away on the east end of Clavering Island. Another boatload of hunters also carried dogs and a sled. They had used the sled to carry the boats down Loch Fyne, which was still frozen over. At that infamous mouth of Loch Fyne, the water was open to Gael Hampke's Bay, so they had motored to our splendid shores from there. To reach Cape Mary, they boated where water was open, and sledded the boats wherever the ice was still solid. They stayed two months at Cape Mary.

Kalle, Labb, and I headed to Cape Mary for a visit a couple of days later, weaving our way with our small whaler through the loosening pack ice on a calm, sunny day. We first made a visit to Eskimonaes, which turned into a party, and it was two days before we had recovered enough to continue eastward along Clavering's empty coast. After ten miles we came to Deadman's Bay, the site where Clavering, in 1823, had been the last white man to see Eskimo living this far north. I wanted to do some archaeological work, but Kalle was itching to get to Cape Mary to earn some extra money at the walrus hunting grounds.

As we approached the pack ice a mile from the shore of the cape, we saw the unmistakable forms of walrus basking on the pack ice about two hundred yards ahead of us, and we cut our engines. As we glided silently closer through the cold, dark water, the walrus did not even look around for trouble. They were so unused to hunters that they seemed to be sleeping soundly. Suddenly, from behind the cover of a small berg, a whaler appeared with Schjelderup sitting in the bow, rifle in his hands. George, the second machinist, was rowing very slowly. Schjelderup waved us off. We saw Halvorsen suddenly rise up in the center of the boat, camera rolling. The captain motioned frantically at him to sit down so the walrus would not see him. He sat, but never took the camera from his eye, and caught every moment of the dramatic scene as the whaler came ever closer to the herd. They were soon only twenty yards from the herd, camera still going. I couldn't believe my eyes. It was surreal, especially when another boat appeared from the cover of the berg carrying four more men from the ship, plus Count Micard with his silk umbrella raised as if he were heading for a summer picnic.

At the same moment, the bull of the herd suddenly rose up on its flippers, its huge head turning on its thick neck to examine the whirring sound of the camera. Schjelderup's gun roared. The bull just rolled its neck, but a second shot came so quickly after the first that the sound of the two merged and the animal flopped over on its side, flippers flailing. The hunters had not been more than ten yards from the ice's edge when those first two shots filled the arctic stillness with their explosive report. Kalle brought the motor to life and we rushed toward the scene. Because of the shots, the startled herd was panicked into immobility. In a blink, the men were out of the boat and on top of the herd, shooting at nearly point-blank range.

Thirty seconds later, it was all over. Ten massive walrus lay dead or dying. The captain went around and gave those still thrashing the *coup de grâce*, while Halvorsen rushed to film Schjelderup from the side with the best light. After the last shot there was this great stillness. For a moment, all the men were motionless, as if frozen in time. We came to the ice just as Schjelderup stood, rifle in hand, and turned his head slowly seaward. His chin was raised slightly, his eyes half closed. He cocked his head, and his face took on a subtle expression of ecstasy. Kalle and I just looked at each other. The captain shook himself, as if just awakening from a reverie, and said with his famous laugh, "That was all right."

Schjelderup invited the count to climb up on the bull, which weighed nearly two tons. Micard was helped up, and he used his frail, colorful umbrella to balance himself as he stood on the rubbery, rolling flesh while Halvorsen recorded the bizarre scene for posterity.

Had the film been in color, it would have captured the red on the ice from all the butchering that followed. These men had done this so many times that they were like a circus crew taking down the tents for the thousandth time. It was almost instinctual. Sharp iron stakes were pounded with sledgehammers into the ice as if they were tent pegs; then large pulleys were hooked to the stakes. While some men cut around the skin at the neck, then down the fat bellies, others hauled heavy ropes from the pulleys, tied hooks to the ropes, and then jabbed the hooks into the blubbery flesh where it had been cut at the top. The ropes were then tugged on with great effort. As Schjelderup flayed the flesh from the skin, the hide peeled back like a banana—though with much more effort, believe me. Immediately, the hot blood and flesh sent small clouds of fog into the air. This was repeated with each carcass.

Kalle and I helped lay the still-warm and very heavy hides in stacks in the boats, then dragged over the weighty heads still wearing the tusks. The captain shouted to George, who had started on the laborious task of cutting the tusks out, "Can't waste time taking the tusks out, for Christ's sake! Do you know how many trips it's going to take to haul all this to shore?" He then had a thought. "Just load the hides and heads and some meat. There are more walrus than this about. I want the hides and tusks!" We left tons of meat on the ice. We had not motored more than a hundred yards away when hordes of ivory gulls arrived as if out of nowhere. They are very carnivorous, and the only gulls to nest on the ice. The air was filled with their wild cries, and it was all very primal. Schjelderup's mass slaughter of walrus in this region would later be the catalyst for the banning of such hunting for profit! And not a moment too soon.

Back on shore at Cape Mary, Micard invited me up to the little hunter's shack he had settled in. After the usual "how are you?" stuff, he said, clearing his voice diplomatically, that he had heard about the troubles Kalle and I had had with the captain. "And I know how terribly afraid Labb is of him. The captain can be a hard man, but I think I should tell you a bit about his personal life.

"Schjelderup is like the old-time Viking chieftains. He has a large clan he takes care of. It really is like a small, lost kingdom. One can only get to his place by boat. I have stayed there twice now. He has a wonderful large, rustic manor house with a beautiful grass roof, and large barns and storage houses for food. He has the only merchant store for many miles. It sits right on the dock. It is bright red, and stands out wonderfully against the usually gray sky and mountains behind. The store is also the post office, and he is responsible for the mail for perhaps one hundred people who live widely scattered in tiny fjords and bays. You would not believe how backward, but charmingly so, it all is there. Usually, the only source of income for them is through Schjelderup. The money he makes from his ships helps support the whole, private kingdom. That is why he is so tight with his money," the count said. "I know that is no excuse to have taken your supplies, dear friend, but his decisions are colored by his sense of duty to his people back home. I am afraid he just does not care much' for people outside his little world."

"There are a lot of people in Norway like that," I admitted.

"France as well," he said with a smile. He offered me some French pear preserves, and in a much improved mood, I sort of forgave Schjelderup, the old bastard. But Schjelderup's hunting methods had really enraged me. After a week of this walrus butchery, I talked Kalle into returning with me to do some archaeological work at Deadman's Bay before we headed back to Krogness to make ready for the return to Norway.

At Deadman's Bay I saw obvious evidence of archaeological digging done by the Danish archaeologist, Helge Larsen, during the summers of 1932 through 1934, and so I worked on houses not previously unearthed in this well-situated ancient settlement. A broad, shallow bay cut into the land, making it an excellent landing place for kayaks. The just-budding vegetation made the site look luxurious compared to the bleaker hills nearby. A glacial river roared through a canyon in the back by the hills; because of the turbulence in the water there, seal could be taken almost year-round in this area.

I found beautiful, small oil lamps, and tools of all kinds, and in the permafrost I unearthed parts of ropes and dog harnesses made of walrus hide. There were a lot of narwhale remains in the Inuit ruins. Perhaps this meant that these sea mammals had once been in greater abundance. At any rate, this had been a wonderful place for the Inuit to camp for hundreds of years before they disappeared after hearing the thunder of the white man's guns.

CHAPTER SEVEN

Returning to Return

A t the beginning of July, it was time to make ready for the return to Norway, and it was with mixed feelings that we prepared to leave what had truly been a fine home, and a fine life. Kalle and I had returned from Cape Mary weeks earlier, though Micard and the walrus hunters were still there. By the end of July the *Quest* was released from ice, and the old engineer was sober enough to resume his duties. The doctor in Tromsø lost his bet with Captain Schjelderup that the engineer would not live through the winter.

The ship picked up Kalle, Labb, and me, and then sailed to Clavering Island to fetch Micard and company. They were at first nowhere to be seen, though an enormous amount of hides and tusks were stacked on the shore, ready for shipment. It would obviously take hours to load, and whalers were lowered to do the work. On shore, without Schjelderup around to be boss, I begged off from the task of loading, saying this was my last opportunity to paint. Just then, I looked up to the top of the high cliffs at Cape Mary. There I could clearly see Micard's umbrella. Near him stood the unmistakable hulk of the captain. I started the rough climb to the top, lugging my paints and easel. At the top I was greeted by a bizarre sight: Schjelderup and George were collecting goose eggs.

A large number of geese nested on the cliffs. They made their nests high in the precipitous walls where fox and other predators could not get to them, but a man could climb down to the nests if great caution was used. With Halvorsen filming the whole thing, the captain began lowering his underling by rope to gather eggs. George's face was quite white as he disappeared over the cliff's edge, begging the captain not to lose his grip on the rope. With a sudden *whoosh!*, the geese, camouflaged in the cliff face, burst like ghosts into the air. Out of sight, George gave out a loud, frightened curse. Schjelderup laughed and shouted down to him not to be a baby. The captain then had the hapless Halvorsen lowered with his camera to film the whole procedure at close hand. Schjelderup, no wimp himself, took a turn at the gathering, and it is on film today that his was the only hand that stripped the nests of all the eggs, instead of leaving a few as the regulations, to say nothing of good common sense, dictated. With all the seal, walrus, and musk ox meat we had, we did not need food badly enough to risk people's necks for some goose eggs. Knowing the captain, I assumed there had to be an economic reason for all this craziness. And there was.

The Scott Polar Research Institute at Cambridge had asked the captain to bring back some goose eggs from as far north as possible. They planned to serve them at their annual dinner. Not too many weeks later, this meal actually came to pass, and though I never did find out the captain's price for these dangerously gathered eggs, the fete at the Institute was billed as the "world's most expensive omelet"!

Before sailing south, the ship met up with the *Polarbjorn*, newly returned from Norway, near the east end of Clavering Island. Nearby was the *Vesle Kari* (or "Little Kari," named for the owner's daughter), charted by the American explorer, Louise A. Boyd, the only woman polar explorer at the time. She planned to go further north than any American—and for that matter, very few others—and was going to conduct soundings of waters along the way. It was not just an honor to meet this brave explorer whom we had all heard so much about; on this day, Louise and I began a friendship that would last more than thirty years.

Boyd was born to an extremely wealthy family in the San Francisco, California, area. She inherited her family's fortune in 1920 and spent the next few years traveling in Europe. Her interest in polar exploration began in 1924 when she first visited the Arctic regions aboard a Norwegian cruise ship to Spitsbergen. Two years later Boyd chartered a Norwegian arctic sealer ship and took a group of friends on a trip from Norway into the Arctic Ocean. They visited Franz Josef Land, the island chain north of European Russia, where they hunted polar bears and seals. (My great-uncle explored this region in the mid-1800s, remember.)

In 1928 Boyd led an expedition to find the Norwegian Arctic explorer Roald Amundsen, who had disappeared while flying a rescue mission in search of the Italian explorer and engineer, Umberto Nobile. Financing the venture herself, Louise set out on behalf of the Norwegian government on a ten-thousand-mile voyage across the Arctic Ocean, exploring Franz Josef Land in the east, to the Greenland Sea in the west. She was unable to find any trace of Amundsen, but for her efforts the Norwegian government awarded Miss Louise Boyd the Chevalier Cross of the Order of Saint Olav.

Beginning in 1931, Boyd undertook a series of nearly annual expeditions to the Arctic. That year she and an exploring party sailed to Greenland's northeastern coast, where they examined glacial formations and photographed arctic plant and animal life. She earned recognition for her explorations of the little-known De Geer Glacier. An adjoining region was later named Louise Boyd Land. In 1933 Boyd led an expedition sponsored by the American Geographical Society. Her scientific team again studied the fjords and glaciers on Greenland's northeastern coast and, using a sonic device, measured the offshore ocean depths, which is what she was up to when I first met her.

The *Quest* finally sailed south along the coast, heading for Ammassalik (spelled Angmassalik in my time, and now called Tasiilap by the locals). Over eight hundred miles to the south, it was quite a detour from our planned route home, but Schjelderup had a good reason. Before the *Quest* had left Norway, Schjelderup had been asked to pick up a member of Charcot's expedition, who had luckily not sailed with him on his ill-fated voyage. The deal was made before the tragedy, and the passenger we were to fetch was Paul-Emil Victor, who would later become head of French polar exploration at both poles. Of course, Schjelderup would be well paid for picking him up. Micard, who was after all paying for this voyage, naturally considered it a great honor to carry his fellow countryman back to Europe.

When we left Clavering Island, the ice in Gael Hampke's Bay was well broken up, and easy to move through. But as soon as we sailed past Jackson Island, a mere ten miles away, we found ourselves in heavy pack ice. A strong wind was blowing from the east, and it had piled bergs and pack ice up against the shore of the coast curiously named "Hold with Hope." Soon we were pushed against the land-fast ice, while ice from the opposite side was packed tightly against the ship. There was suddenly no sign of open water. The ice squeezed us until our engines were useless. Soon ice was being forced under us, and over us. The railings began to splinter, and then snap in places. For hours the pressure grew. There was little we could do while the ship was squeezed as if held in a vise. The ice beneath us began to "screw" upwards. There was no room for the ship to give, and the deck of the ship began to bow upwards. It was damn frightening to see, I can assure you. Then the wood began to crack. We could hear fibers of beams snapping ominously. Closed cabin doors exploded into splinters!

We had survived so much during the winter, and yet here we were in the summer time making preparations to abandon ship as the creaking and groaning and splintering of wood increased. We knew we could walk across the pack ice to the coast, and it would not be a long journey to the nearest trapper cabin; the crew was more annoyed than anything else. But just then the ship began to lift within the ice, and the pressure was eased. Then the wind suddenly shifted. We could feel and hear the water current moving under the ship. The ice began to flow away from us. The deck settled back to its normal shape. As suddenly as we had been caught, we were released. We then understood why the coast had been named "Hold with Hope"!

We sailed into Mackenzie Bay by Myggbukta to repair the ship, and to give the pack ice time to disperse. We knew that as easily as we had been freed from the ice, we could be trapped again. Even in the bay the ice was thick, and we could not get near Myggbukta, so we anchored on the lee side of Bontekoe Island to make temporary repairs. Although there were large holes in the planking, fortunately they were far above the waterline. The repairs took a day. We then sailed up Franz Josef Fjord, which went west and through a series of connecting sounds became King Oscar Fjord heading southeast. Sailing through this "arch" of waterways, we went in at 73N, and came out at 72N. Though it was a long, roundabout way to head south, we avoided seventy nautical miles of coastal pack ice, while at the same time visiting what have been called the most beautiful fjords in the world. The French call it "The Riviera of the North."

The fjords were indeed incredible. We first came to the multilayered, multicolored spires of the *Teufelsschloss*, or "Devil's Castle," at the head of Andree's Land. Turning southeast, we went around Ymer Island through Antarctic Sound, past Geographical Island, and then past Ella Island. Ella Island was one of the headquarters for Lauge Koch's expeditions on this coast, and it was to here that his plane had accompanied Charles and Anne Lindbergh's plane in 1933 in their search for air routes. It was fantastic to see firsthand that which I had previously seen only in photos, and had dreamed of just three years before. I smiled gratefully the whole way through the incredibly rugged, awe-inspiring scenery—and sketched and painted like mad!

Willie at the Wiiks Hotel in Alta, Norway, dreaming of exploration just before he begins his walk across Lapland in 1932.

At two hundred miles north of the Arctic Circle, Tromsø, Norway, was the starting place of most arctic expeditions in the early 1900s. Willie's ancestors (including his parents) had lived here for decades. This photo is from the 1930s.

Willie at the Canadian border in 1933. Turned away because of lack of funds, Willie missed going on an expedition with Count Micard for the second time.

Count Gaston Micard, with his ever-present Ethiopian umbrella, on board *Quest* in 1936. (Photo by Eigil Halvorsen)

Karl "Kalle" Nicolaisen, who had been sealing since age fifteen, became Willie's trapping partner on his first expedition to Greenland.

Captain Ludolph Schjelderup poses near the stern of *Quest* in Loch Fyne, 1937.

The hut ("Krogness") that served as Willie's and Kalle's home for more than a year. Note the black dog that had to be put down. The mountains of Henry Hudson Land appear in the background.

"The Villa" (or Villaen) by Loch Fyne close to the whirlpool area in 1936. Henry Hudson Land is in the background, Jordan Hill is to the right, and the Wordie Glacier is in the middle right, barely visible.

Labb with his sled under the "Hindu Temples" of Spathe's Plateau where four-hundred-million-year-old fossils were found in 1936.

Kalle feeds Labb a treat while Willie slurps coffee in the warmth of Krogness, while it is minus 30 degrees outside. (Photo by Eigil Halvorsen)

Expedition photographer Eigil Halvorsen at Lock Fyne in 1936.

George transporting musk oxen skins. Labb is the white dog. (Photo by Eigil Halvorsen)

Captain Schjelderup (right) and Gerhard Antonsen, the "King of Revet," in 1936. (Photo by Eigil Halvorsen)

Christmas on board *Quest* at Loch Fyne in 1936. From left is Kalle with Labb; Micard, wearing white scarf; Schjelderup; Ruben Goldman, behind the Norwegian flag; Willie, with his back against the wall; Jacobsen, the cook, dressed in white; and the others, who are not identified.

Willie at Krogness with pelts of arctic fox in 1937, and Labb at his feet.
(Photo by Kalle Nicolaisen)

The sun returns on February 1937 after four months of darkness. This is
Quest, frozen in at Loch Fyne. (Photo by Eigil Halvorsen)

Willie paints the famous *Quest* frozen in at Loch Fyne, in Northwest Greenland in the spring of 1937.

Willie and Labb examine the musk ox he was forced to kill when it charged.
(Photo by Kalle Nicolaisen)

Schjelderup gives a walrus the *coup de grace* at Cape Mary, Clavering Island in 1937. (Photo by Eigil Halvorsen)

Count Micard in a state of contemplation at Cape Mary in 1937. The count could sit like this for hours. (Photo by Eigil Halvorsen)

"Devil's Castle" along the Kaiser Franz Joseph Fjord, northern gateway to the "Arctic Riviera," taken by Willie from on board *Quest* in 1937.

Inuit women and children in umiak in 1937. Photo taken by Willie.

Paul-Emil Victor in an umiak just before boarding *Quest* in 1937 and leaving his Inuit family that he had been with for a year. The young girl looking at Willie's camera was his fifteen-year-old girlfriend, Domedia. Victor went on to become the head of French polar exploration.

Some of the expedition members on board *En Avant* (or *Ringsel*) in Bergen, Norway, just before departing for the Norwegian-French Expedition to Greenland in 1938. Front row, from left: William Jacobsen (cook), Willie Knutsen (leader), Labb, Count Gaston Micard, Kalle Nicolaisen (captain and co-leader). Back row: Jess Tillier (radio operator and first engineer), Ingvald Ingebrigtsen, Sigmund Snarby (second mate), and Edvard Wilhelmsen (first mate).

"Margarine Central," made from margarine crates, was the world's most northerly station when this photo was taken in 1938. The main station, "Micardbu," was built soon after, just north of this site.

Leif Olsen sits near the tent that saved him and Willie during the ice storm in 1939. This photo was taken at Micardbu.

From left: Sigmund Snarby, William Jacobsen, Kristen Hatlevik, Willie and Labb, and Sigbjorn Aamodt sit on the roof of Micardbu in the spring of 1939.

Aamodt at the supply depot near Micardbu in 1938 where the polar bear stole the bolognas. Soon after taking this photo, Aamodt was stalked by the same bear. Note Willie's rifle to the left.

Micard in his library at Micardbu in 1939. Note the lace curtains, the books, and the French pears in glass jars. This photo was sent to newspapers to prove that Micard had not been left alone in a windswept hut as a French paper had claimed.

The Wideroe Airlines rescue plane that transported a deathly ill Micard back from Micardbu to Norway with Willie as his companion in 1939. This was the first air rescue in Greenland.

Willie at an archaelogical dig in Germania Land in 1938. His findings are on display in Norway's National Ethnographic Museum in Oslo.

Ammassalik woman with child in 1940. This photo was
taken by Willie.

Inuit hunters from Ammassalik in kayaks in 1940 that contained floats made
out of the inflated skins. The small white "sail" was for the hunter to hide
behind when his kayak approached prey. The wooden paddles were edged
and tipped with bone to prevent them from being worn away by the ice.

King Oscar's Fjord was seventy nautical miles of wonder. The whole crew ran out of descriptive terms after awhile. Near the mouth of the fjord, we passed a small hut at a place called Antarctic Haven. It had originally been built by Helge Ingstad, who later became world famous when he discovered the Viking ruins of Leif Erickson's settlement at L'Anse aux Meadows in Newfoundland. I think this is a good place to tell a little story about the competition between Norway and Denmark for ownership of Greenland, because Ingstad figured in this argument for the Norwegian side, just as Lauge Koch figured strongly in the Danish position. But first we must look at an earlier controversy. In the early twentieth century there was another land claiming much of the most northerly part of Greenland: It was the United States.

The American, Robert Peary, who despite cries of fraud that still echo today, went down in history as the first man to reach the North Pole. Previous to this accomplishment he had also explored much of the then uncharted top of Greenland. In 1865, the German geographer August Petermann had proposed his theory about a gigantic isthmus spanning from Greenland across the North Pole to the East Siberian Sea. Peary was trying to find out if this was true. And for good reason: America was expanding.

Two years later, the U.S. purchased Alaska from Russia as part of a plan to secure the nation against attacks from hostile powers. In the decades that followed, the U.S. negotiated frequently with Denmark regarding the purchase of Northern Greenland. From 1886 to 1909, Peary sledded back and forth on a large number of expeditions to Northern Greenland. He discovered Independence Fjord and was the first to find evidence that Greenland was an island. In 1892 he claimed he had found a channel that created a large island north of the main body of Greenland, and stated that this island was up for grabs. He added that since he had discovered the island, America had first right to it.

The Danes decided to see for themselves if this channel existed. An expedition was led by Ludvig Mylius-Erichsen. Unfortunately, Mylius-Erichsen, Høegh Hagen, and Jørgen Brønlund never returned from their sledge journey to Peary Land. Survivors of the 1906 expedition included Peter Freuchen, Lauge Koch, and Alfred Wegener, the German who later proposed the theory of continental drift. But these men had not been on the sledge trip to Peary Land, so there was no evidence that Peary was not right in his claim.

Two years later, the Dane, Ejnar Mikkelsen, organized a small, two-man expedition to search for the bodies—and hopefully, the diaries—of his countrymen of the Mylius-Erichsen expedition. While Mikkelsen and his companion, Iver Iversen, were out on sled expeditions, his tiny ship *Alabama* was crushed by ice and sank. The two were forced to spend two winters in harrowing conditions. (Mikkelsen's book, *Two Against the Ice*, became a classic.) Then in 1912 Mikkelsen dramatically returned from the *Alabama* Expedition, bringing with him a cairn report by Mylius-Erichsen containing the statement "The Peary Channel does not exist." In the same year the soon-to-be-famous Danes, Knud Rasmussen—from whom I got my motto—and Peter Freuchen, who became a well-known explorer and writer, reached the interior of Independence Bay on the first Thule Expedition in 1912 and 1913, and discovered a land bridge between Navy Cliff and Heilprin Land. In other words, there was no island as Peary had claimed.

In 1913 the cartographic results of the Danish expeditions were used in an attack that was launched against Peary by the American Congress accusing him of a cartographic swindle. As a result, all official American maps showing the Peary Channel were withdrawn. In 1916 the abovementioned Lauge Koch joined Knud Rasmussen's second Thule Expedition (1916 through 1918). As the expedition's cartographer, he was charged with mapping the northern parts of the so-called Peary Channel. In 1917 Koch and Rasmussen found the channel's northern outlet closed by glaciers. On the basis of this evidence the U.S. relinquished all claims to northern Greenland, and acknowledged Denmark's sovereign rights to all of Greenland (though Norway, of course, had not). When Peary died in 1920, the map showed inland ice where he had originally drawn his channel.

Peary's honesty had been called into question, and this cloud of doubt hung over his name until Lauge Koch embarked on his last expedition to Peary Land on board the hydroplane *Perssuak* in 1938. Upon his return he said to the Danish press, "Peary Land is very close to being an island. . . . Our flight has shown that Peary was practically correct. . . . It pleases me personally that we can restore Peary's name completely. Peary was not right, but he acted in good faith. The Peary Channel is really two fjords and a lake." As Koch pointed out, mapping by dogsled in harsh conditions cannot match the accuracy of aerial photography. Peary's name was cleared, but Koch was not popular with some in Denmark for doing so.

But if we go back to 1924, the year Helge Ingstad "occupied" the Riviera of the North in the name of Norway by building the tiny hut at Antarctic Haven, we find Lauge Koch was not as forgiving of the Norwegian as he would later be with Peary. It seems that Ingstad's solitary presence—plus that of the five Norwegian trappers at Myggbukta, in what Lauge Koch considered *his* territory— had him worried. Added to his concerns was the fact that Norwegian trappers in the area we had just spent the year in had been given police powers by their government. This was a sure sign to Koch that the Norwegians would soon be establishing a permanent colony there.

Koch went to the Danish government and told them they must establish a large, permanent settlement of Inuit as far north as possible. He suggested Scoresby Sound. The new village, he argued, would give them more of a claim to northeastern Greenland in the World Court. This court believed that Inuit settlements under a nation's jurisdiction added great weight to that nation's claims to sovereignty. At first, there was not much interest in Denmark for owning this "empty land," and a skeptical parliament was concerned about the cost, not to mention the ethics, of forcibly resettling the local inhabitants. But Koch persisted until he was given the go-ahead. Part of his argument was that by moving hunters from Ammassalik, the pressure on the hunting grounds there would be greatly relieved.

In charge of this colonization was seasoned arctic explorer, Ejnar Mikkelsen. The Inuit from Ammassalik had reluctantly been sent to colonize the area in 1924. Inuit had not occupied that sound for generations, and even though these new arrivals had been gently prodded into leaving family and friends behind in Ammassalik, they did as they were told. Thus, Scoresby Sound came into being, largely due to Helge Ingstad's small hut at Antarctic Haven.

Ingstad had actually become governor of Erik the Red's Land, from 1932 to 1933, when Norway did as Lauge Koch had worried they would do and annexed that eastern part of Greenland. The International Court of Justice in The Hague decided in 1933 that the territory comprising Erik the Red's Land belonged to Denmark, and so the official Norwegian presence there had to end. This explains why during our stay in Erik the Red's Land, there was no political tension. As we sailed past Antarctic Haven, we drank a toast to Ingstad, the Danes, and particularly, Lauge Koch. The following year, Lauge Koch's aerial photos of Peary Land would clear Peary's good name, but that same year, Lauge and

I—another American—would become embroiled in the Danish-Norwegian argument over the land north of Erik the Red's Land.

The year we sailed by Antarctic Haven, we knew some Norwegian trappers were there, but since we were in a race with the pack ice, we did not pull in. Soon we saw them chasing after us in a small motorboat, so we waited for them. They were fuming. "Bunch of snobs!" they called us. "Didn't you know we have had a terrible time and were almost starving?"

They had been snowed under by the same heavy storm that had holed Kalle and me up for three weeks, except that snow had fallen in their windless area for fifty-five days! Even in May they had had to leave their cabin through a hole in the roof. To top it off, ever since the melt-off, they had had bad luck with hunting. We gave them ample provisions to see them through until their ship arrived. We told them we had seen their ship, the *Polarbjorn*, and then we left, heading southward. I would not see Antarctic Haven again until 1964.

Some hours later, we waited at the mouth of the fjord in Davy Sound for a fog to lift, and when it did, there was a sun-scape so dynamic that I had to paint it. I still have this painting. Everyone, even tough, old Schjelderup, gaped at the scene. No one bothered talking, it was that mesmerizing. And, as the fog lifted tantalizingly, we could see that the ice had slackened and moved out to sea. We had open water southward all the way to Scoresby Sound, eighty miles away.

This coast, called Liverpool, was sliced by bays and inlets too small and too exposed to pack ice to afford any harbor. There simply was no place along the shore for habitation either. But it was beautiful. There was not a dull moment sailing it—or sketching it. There were numerous steep mountain peaks well over three thousand feet. The sun shone here and there through dark clouds brooding over the mountain, creating a sinister, glaring, otherworldly face with its rays. Kalle remarked dryly that it was probably the spirit-god of northern Greenland, angry that we had gotten away alive. Oddly, I had been thinking the same damn thing. I had no canvas or sketchpad on hand, but I found a large square piece of fine sandpaper, and drew the scene using colored chalk. The result was very reminiscent of Edvard Munch's work—not because I was copying his brooding, mysterious style, but because that is simply what it ended up looking like.

After all that we had been through during the last year, reaching the tiny settlement of Scoresby Sound was like coming into a metropolis. The manager of the settlement was named Hoegh. Born of Greenlander-Danish parents, he and his wife were wonderful people, and showed us every courtesy. They urged us to stay and get to know the area. We could not stay long, of course, but I made good use of the visit. I walked up a hill to the radio shack and met the Danish operator and his wife, who invited some of us in for coffee and cakes. His wife's sister was there. A beautiful young girl, she had not seen young men of her race for a long time, just as we hadn't seen women—of any race. (The race issue was a matter of fact in those days, so there is no sense in being phony about it by trying to be politically correct.) It was hard to tell who was more nervous—the young girl as she spilled coffee and dropped pastries, or we men, whose coffee cups shook as she tried to pour.

There were also two French scientists stationed at Scoresby Sound. Members of the *Pourquoi Pas?* Expedition on its last voyage, they had received permission from the Danish government to stay longer, and so, like Paul-Emil Victor, had been spared the fate of their mates. In the village, I met the Inuit wife of Lauge Koch and his young son. The boy was charging around, throwing toy harpoons, and already showing leadership traits.

When we sailed for Ammassalik, the pack ice close to shore looked formidable, so we headed out to sea where we zigzagged our way until we found a break in the ice caused by the famous Irminger Current, a branch of the Gulf Stream. The stream generally sweeps in an arc below Iceland, but obviously had an effect where we were as well. Named for a Danish naval officer, the current afforded fishing to Greenland trawlers when the rest of the coast was locked in ice. During this stretch of the voyage we saw about twenty ships fishing for arctic shark.

The current we rode southward took us quickly to Cape Dan, near Ammassalik, and was so strong there that the icebergs raced alongside the ship. When the current rounded Cape Dan, it literally shoved these bergs into the calmer bay beyond, and there they crowded together as if corralled. I had heard Ammassalik could be a tough place for ships to sail into, and when I saw the village nestled on the shore at the far side of the berg-packed bay, I understood why.

Although whalers had sailed past this coast since the seventeenth century, Ammassalik was only discovered in 1886, just fifty years before we arrived on the *Quest*. One story claimed that the locals had not even known there were other Inuit in the world—let alone white men—and if true, it must have been interesting, to say the least, when the Dane, Gustav Holm, dropped in on them. The more accurate story is that rumors of this settlement had been around for a long time. Probably hunters from southern Greenland occasionally met hunters from Ammassalik along the east coast.

In 1828, W. A. Graah, following up on this rumor, sailed with some Inuit from southern Greenland in an *umiak* up the east coast and came to within sixty miles of Ammassalik before the ice stopped them. An umiak is an open skin boat much larger than a kayak, normally used to carry women, children, dogs, and supplies. Umiaks can be fairly easily hauled over ice or up on land, and using them was really the best way to travel on that rough, ice-choked coastline. Gustav Holm had also used an umiak to reach this northern Shangri-la. His expedition is still called *Konebåd*, or the "women's boat" expedition.

Along the coasts north and south of this district, the land was mostly uninhabitable for a great distance, and because of the constant flow of bergs, ships had always stayed far out to sea. Thus, prior to 1884, none had seen the entranceway. As we approached the entranceway to the fjord, there was a massive berg grounded on the sea floor which directly blocked the view of the entrance. If we had not known the fjord leading to Ammassalik lay behind the berg, we might have just sailed right past it. Every time I returned to Ammassalik over the next thirty years, there was always a berg the size of a New York City block stuck there on the floor of the sea, jealously guarding the threshold to this hidden hunting ground.

The *Quest* was having a bit of a rough time getting through all the bergs packed into the large fjord, but then we saw a small fleet of Inuit kayaks, their owners waving their paddles above their heads in greeting. They signaled that they were to be our ice pilots, and then came aboard for a welcoming party. The Inuit have a marvelous capacity to make every occasion a festive one, and fortunately, their attitude is infectious. We passed out cigars and treats, and we all had a great time before our ice pilots climbed back into their sleek crafts and guided us into the snug cove of the village.

Resting at anchor was a two-masted ship the size of the *Quest*. It was the famous *Sea King*, used to supply villages along Greenland's coasts. It had been the expedition ship used by Knud Rasmussen before he died here in 1933. What led to his death is rather a sad tale.

Rasmussen was half Greenlander, and his people affectionately called him "King of the Inuit." Expecting his arrival, the people of Ammassalik had

prepared a special feast, making a local delicacy just for him. This was ptar-
magin, berries, seal meat, and other tasty bits sewn up in a bladder and left to
"ferment." It was put in cold storage (in the permafrost) to await his arrival. Sea
ice delayed him for many weeks, and by the time he sampled the delicacy it
had turned toxic. He did not survive.

Rasmussen had shown in 1912 that the Peary Channel did not exist. Ejnar
Mikkelsen had done the same, and now here he was, coming out to meet us in
a whaler! Mikkelsen had been the new skipper of *Sea King*, and had been made
temporary head of the village because the director had just died. Ejnar
Mikkelsen, the *Sea King*, and the *Quest* had all gathered at the same time in one
place: what luck! The *Quest* was able to anchor just a few yards from the granite shore where a crowd of smiling and laughing Inuit had gathered to greet us.

Ammassalik! This was another one of the "holy places" I had dreamt of seeing. It was a visual treat and absolutely magnificent. While the ship's crew made
emergency repairs on the planks of the *Quest*'s hull, which had been pierced
by the ice at Hold with Hope, I went exploring. Craggy, flame-like mountains
across the bay constantly drew my eyes. The red houses of the Danish settlement ran neatly up the side of a hill. The ground was green, with patches of blueberries and a type of cranberry. Wooden racks held bright-colored boots called
kamiks, which is an Inuit word that also means "to dry." Hide-covered kayaks
rested upside down on boulders to dry out. Walrus, seal meat, and sides of split
fish hung near every dwelling on wooden racks to dry. Skin-covered tents resembling large door wedges were set up so the long side was like a windshield
toward the west, where strong winds from the ice cap could drop down at any
time. Whole carcasses of narwhale lay on the granite banks of the fjord waiting
to be carved up. They shone white and, with their whorled tusks, looked regal
even in death. Standing on the dock and looking down into the crystal-clear
waters, I saw dead seals tied together at the nostrils, in bunches of threes and
fours. This was nature's refrigerator, but the scene (which can still be seen today)
startles more than a few tourists.

Every few minutes, the air was chillingly filled by the otherworldly howls of
hundreds of dogs tied to their sleds. They were all a fiendishly yellow hue I had
never before seen on dogs, and the animals must surely have been throwbacks
to a very ancient breed indeed. My heart stopped as I saw a toddler waddle toward a pack tied up near a house; surely the dogs would pounce on the child.

But the mother came running out of the house and scooped up the child before it could become their lunch.

That evening the air was often filled with laughter and song. The Inuit went about life as if every day were a celebration. As I went about them, I painted and sketched rapidly, knowing we had only a short time there. As it was summer, drum dances were held under the strangely hued midnight sun, with the shaman swaying eerily in the center of a circle of dancing women and children. They were bathed in a murky red glow as the drummers beat out a hypnotic rhythm. The singers chanted what sounded like secret words created solely to open invisible channels to another world—which is exactly what they were meant to do. It was an absolutely enchanting place.

We had dinner with Dr. Arne Høygaard, the Norwegian biologist and nutritionist, who had come to the village—with his wife and small daughter—to study the health of the people. He was also an adventurer and had crossed the ice cap in 1931 with another Norwegian named Martin Mehren. Dr. Høygaard and his family were to sail on the *Quest* back to Norway. He really knew his stuff, and in a short time we were able to learn a great deal from him about the area's rare population.

Ammassalik was unique in Greenland in that just fifty years after its discovery, its Inuit population was still largely pure-blooded, and it also had pretty much retained its native diet and customs, which is why Høygaard had wanted to study the effects of this diet. Perhaps nearly nine hundred Inuit lived in the village and in camps scattered around the islets, inlets, sounds, and fjords in an area of nearly six thousand square miles—about six times the size of Rhode Island. (Today the area administrated by Ammassalik, including some ice cap, is a whopping one hundred and fifty thousand square miles, which is about half the size of Texas!)

The Irminger Current greatly influenced the Inuit's choice of this area, as it helped to keep the waters open, allowing for almost year-round seal hunting. The fauna of Ammassalik is richer than other parts of the coast, and one assumes this is also due to the warming effect of the Irminger Current. Surrounded by steep mountains and glaciers, there was not much pastureland for large mammals like musk oxen or caribou by the fjord, so these Inuit were experts on water hunting and travel. There had been caribou, but they had been hunted into extinction.

There were actually two distinct tribal groups in Ammassalik: The people of one tribe were shorter than the other, and thought to be related to the Japanese, while the other, taller group was believed to be connected to Tibetans from four thousand years earlier. When we arrived in 1936, there were still blood feuds between the two groups. When one group was trading at the local store, the other kept well away. Though whalers and sealers had stopped in occasionally since 1888, they had left very little of their culture behind, except for a special strain of syphilis. Aside from that social disease, Dr. Høygaard had an excellent "laboratory" to study human nutrition in its pure state.

"My main objective," Høygaard said, "is to study preagricultural, preindustrial nutrition. Like our Norwegian ancestors on the west coast of Norway once did, these Inuit live almost exclusively on meat and fish. The introduction of dairy foods, and refined grains, is probably the cause for many of modern man's health problems. But few agree with me that an all-protein diet would be healthy. I have proven it can be."

This was also the esteemed opinion of the top North American Artic explorer, Vilhjalmur Stefansson, who had spent several years in the Canadian Arctic living off the land and sea, and whom I would first meet in 1940. While Arne Høygaard found virtually no malnutrition among Inuit who ate a native diet exclusively, among the Inuit who ate as white men, he did. One of the men of our crew said, "That is because they have a different metabolism than we do!"

Høygaard differed with him, and asked if any of us had eaten almost exclusively from the land. Of course, Kalle and I had. We told him how we had nibbled on tundra plants, but had otherwise eaten an almost all-meat diet. Høygaard then suggested he take blood tests of the crew, comparing Kalle and me with the others who had eaten more imported foods while living aboard the *Quest* the past winter. Kalle and I were found to be in much better health, and Høygaard said he would include that test in his findings to prove that white men can gradually adapt to a ketogenic diet. He later published his findings, and it caused quite a stir among those who found it hard to accept that "primitives" know something white men have forgotten.

Høygaard had traveled to Inuit camps all over the region to study the natives who lived away from the Danish settlement. Sometimes the Danish priest would go with him to translate and encourage the Inuit to agree to the taking of their blood for samples. Later, the priest told Høygaard the Inuit called his blood-extracting needle the "Big Mosquito," and that many thought he was a shaman who would later use their blood for sorcery. Because they were traditionally very polite, the Inuit never complained during his blood-taking and other tests, but as soon as the tests were done, some of them disappeared into their remote hunting grounds before he could "torture" them again.

Scurvy, the big health problem of the Arctic, was unknown among these Inuit, and Høygaard believed it was partially because they ate seaweed in the winter when no land plants could be used as a source of vitamin C. Only around the trading post did he find any indications of scurvy. The Inuit at Ammassalik also did not suffer from periodic starvation. Their bays teemed with fish, as well as seals. The only health problem they really had were the diseases brought by the ships entering their port. Hearing about the local strain of syphilis kept many of the *Quest's* crew from getting too friendly with the local girls.

Høygaard told us an interesting story about Paul-Emil Victor, the Frenchman who would soon join us for our trip home. Victor and an Inuit named Kristian had traveled by dogsled to Ammassalik from Kangerdlugssuatsiaq, one hundred miles to the north, where they had over-wintered. They had lived for months primarily on Victor's imported foods, grains, sugars, and canned goods. They could have eaten native foods, but Victor preferred food he was familiar with. Both men had developed bad cases of scurvy. On arriving at Ammassalik, Kristian greedily ate seaweed, boiled fresh meat, raw blubber, and raw, dried fish, while Victor could—or would—not. Kristian soon recovered, while Victor spent seven days in the hospital taking large intravenous doses of vitamin C. This, Høygaard said, was conclusive evidence that imported foods were inferior to native foods in terms of maintaining health. It was big news in those days!

Another interesting figure in Ammassalik was the Danish count, Eigil Knuth, who had crossed the ice cap with Paul-Emil Victor, and who was still working in Greenland at the writing of this book! Since he was a sculptor as well as an explorer, Count Knuth had a studio built in the village. As we were both artists and arctic rats, we immediately became friends. He was about ten years older, and through him I learned more tales of the Arctic, and of the Inuit. He, like Micard, had plans to get to Peary Land some day with an expedition, and Micard said he was sorry, but he planned to get there first. The gambling-mad crew started wagers on the spot. My money was on Micard (even though I didn't actually have any to wager).

Of all the interesting characters we met there in that remote happy hunting ground, perhaps Ejnar Mikkelsen's presence was the most important historically. He had done so much, and spent hours telling us in detail the many stories of Peary Land, the Norwegian-Danish—and the American!—claims to Greenland, and his own heroic exploits during his *Alabama* Expedition. I have only given you the briefest outline of Ejnar's amazing exploits in these pages.

At last the ship was declared seaworthy, and we made ready to sail for Iceland, the first leg of our journey home to Norway. When it was time to leave on August 17, we got word that Victor was still up north in Kangerdlugssuatsiaq, so the ship made ready to pick him up there, rather than wait for his arrival. We had missed this inner-coastal wonderland on the way down, having had to go so far out to sea to avoid the pack ice. It was another stretch of awesome glaciers, interesting islands and bays, and fjords with roaring waterfalls. Intensely blue icebergs floated about, the blue color showing the purity of the very old ice.

Suddenly, off in the distance, we saw a small fleet of Inuit kayaks and umiaks heading toward us. It was quite a sight. You do not see the old-style umiaks anymore, not for years. Standing like a conqueror in one of the umiaks was Victor.* Worried that we would leave without him, he had decided to come to us. In the umiak with Victor were his adopted family and his lovely girlfriend, Domidia, who turned out to be just fifteen. According to Inuit custom, there was no moral problem with the arrangement. In fact, when Victor left with us, his good friend Kristian married Domidia. Years later, Victor even dedicated a children's book he'd written to Domidia.

We sailed back to his outpost to pick up Victor's things, which consisted of a huge collection of artifacts, notes, and files, and took up much deck space. He had made unique recordings of the Inuit language, including their songs and fables, and he also had many archaeological and geological samples. Victor would later travel to the Antarctic, and become the head of the French Polar Institute, while continuing to lead *Les Expéditions Polaires Françaises* to both polar areas.

---

* Author's Note: I found the photo Willie took of this scene at the bottom of a carton of notes, mostly junk, in his Norwegian cabin fifty years later. It was a negative, but I knew right away it was Paul-Emil Victor standing in the umiak! I made a copy and sent it to Paul-Emil at his home in Bora Bora, and he sent me a heartfelt letter of thanks.

Indeed, Paul-Emil Victor would become one of the greatest names in modern polar exploration.

The area around Kangerdlugssuatsiaq was even more primitive than that around Ammassalik. Kalle and I were intrigued enough to poke our noses everywhere, much to the amusement of the locals. In one hut we found skin bags full of a fermenting, foaming, liquid, hanging from the ceiling. Kalle looked at me strangely, his face turning white. "What's that?" he asked. "Urine, I think," I said, quickly covering my nose. He ran outside and vomited. Usually Kalle could stand just about anything, and of course, we had kept buckets of urine for tanning purposes ourselves, just as these Inuit did; but that hot foaming brew was too much, even for him.

There in that "Stone Age" world, the ship received the radio message of a new aviation record. The Soviets had flown from Moscow via the Arctic to Vancouver, British Columbia, Canada—a distance of 5,288 miles. They had then flown over the polar route from Russia to San Jacinto, in southern California, making it a total flight of 6,262 miles! Talk about a fast-changing world! We young fellows were talking excitedly about the flight, but Micard warned, "Do not trust the Soviets! They want the world!" We thought he was exaggerating.

The *Quest* sailed at first in sunny weather, but then slowly, the weather changed. The ship left the pack ice only to go into a terrible storm of sleet and hard-driving rain, raging seas, and a black sky that blocked out the light from the midnight sun. The black clouds hung almost to the water and looked like a Stygian fog, which is a very eerie phenomenon. Adding to the aura of otherworldliness, occasionally a shaft of light would pierce the gloom to reveal large and weirdly formed icebergs rolling and bobbing dangerously in the heavy seas around us. We had to stop our motors so that we would not power into one of the bergs in the darkness. It was natural to start thinking about the *Titanic*. I had been born at almost the same time the *Titanic* sunk. I could not help feeling a bit paranoid. Wouldn't it be an ironic twist of fate if my dream of arctic exploration had led me here, only to have me die in a collision with an iceberg? It was not a comforting thought at the time.

After eighteen tense hours, the storm lifted somewhat, and we had light. We saw the icebergs still around us. Wave-sculpted, the bergs looked like the giant heads of gargoyles. This area, infamous for its storms, is where Charcot's ship and expedition members had gone down. Vikings traveling to and from Greenland called it "Troll Bottom" because they believed there were trolls who lived on the ocean floor, who would surface to drag ships down to their underwater lair. Certainly the storm and the mystical-looking bergs we saw rising ominously in the heavy seas explained the Viking name. It was with great relief that we arrived in the calm waters surrounding the port in Reykjavik, Iceland.

A real port! Real houses! And on the quay, hundreds of waving, cheering people! By Odin, we were famous! What a reception. The Icelanders had followed our stormy plight by radio, and reporters from mainland Europe had traveled there just to be on hand when we arrived. We were a sensation . . . and it was all a bit of a shock to us. We had forgotten that ours was the first expedition of its kind in a long, long time. We had been away from civilization for a year, but because of the total immersion into arctic solitude, it seemed more like ten. Suddenly we were being feted in a banquet hall with newspaper cameras popping flashbulbs at us from every angle. I have to admit it was a lot of fun.

Some days later, after we sobered up a bit, we had to say good-bye to Iceland and terra firma. The goose eggs for the world's most expensive omelets were transferred to a ship heading for the British Isles, and we headed off to Norway on the last leg of our long arctic journey. We had just passed Iceland when we were shocked to hear a cry from Halvorsen, who was up in the crow's nest. He called down to us on deck, "Am I seeing an illusion, or is the water getting closer to our deck?"

He was right—we were sinking!

Rushing below, we found the bow storage area totally flooded. It turned out that the bilge pump had quit working. We had left port a little too hungover, and had not been paying attention to the bilges as we should have. The damage caused by our run-in with the pack ice off "Hold with Hope" coast was slowly sinking us. Ernest Shackleton had written that the *Quest* was prone to leakage, but I doubt he ever experienced it to this extreme. We formed a bucket brigade, dipping down into the storage compartment. For hours we bailed until our arms felt like lead, but we were fueled not only by the prospect of our ship sinking, but also by the thought of the ignominy we would suffer if we—the "great arctic explorers"—had to return to Iceland in rowboats!

When the water was too low in the storage area to reach, Ruben Goldman put on a pair of hip boots, waded in, and passed the buckets up to the others.

When the water was low enough to discover the damage, it was found that coal dust from the bunkers in the next compartment had clogged the pump.

Then, as if things were not bad enough, while we were making our repairs in the middle of the Norwegian Sea, a terrific storm hit us. Even under full power, we were being driven off course, steadily northward toward Norway's rugged, granite coast. To top it all off, our boilers quit—we had run out of coal! Schjelderup had not wanted to pay the high price in Iceland, and had thus gambled with our lives. There was nothing we could do but drift with the storm. We did that for hours before the storm lifted.

We could now see the coast, and as we had some wind, we put up our sail to try to tack to a harbor. We came all too close to shore where the wind died, leaving us drifting toward the rocky coast. We began breaking up wooden barrels and crates, and got a fire going in the boilers. Slowly we built up steam to get just enough power to control the ship. In this way we limped into the nearest port, Alesund, which was more than 150 miles north of Bergen, our actual destination. By this time, we were all ready to lynch that cheapskate, Schjelderup.

Nonetheless, we were back in Norway! And on the docks another cheering crowd waited for us. The town had been monitoring the *Quest's* dramatic radio broadcasts through the whole ordeal, and everyone had come out to cheer not only our arrival, but our survival. All of Norway knew of the expedition by then, and Alesund obviously felt honored to receive us. Once again there were international reporters, and even Norway's radio network was there. Because Paul-Emil Victor had been part of Charcot's tragic expedition, he was mobbed by reporters. And what stories he was able to tell them—crossing the ice cap, surviving under the worst conditions, and living among the Inuit in their primitive camps for a year. No wonder he would soon become head of the French Polar Institute!

The only sad note on that triumphant day was that Alesund was the home of Labb's disreputable owner, who was now out of jail. He came out of the crowd like a bad dream, stepped up to Schjelderup, shook his hand, talked with him for awhile, and before we knew it, had Labb on a leash to lead him away. Kalle and I were ready to kill him, but Micard and Schjelderup said that legally, nothing could be done to stop the man from taking Labb; an agreement was an agreement. Labb had only been loaned to Schjelderup. We had forgotten that! By then I thought of Labb as my dog. It was terrible to be forced to accept the horrible reality that we were losing Labb due to a strange twist of fate that took us to Alesund rather than Bergen. Labb left the dock looking sadly over his shoulder at us. It really broke our hearts. I just couldn't believe it. I had come to think of Labb as a partner, and here he had to go off with that man of ill repute!

When we finally made it to Bergen, the *Quest* was again greeted by a large crowd of reporters, politicians, scientists, and cheering citizens. We were not quite Roald Amundsen and his men, but still, these people must have thought we were quite something for them to go through all that trouble on our account.

CHAPTER EIGHT

The Norwegian-French Expedition (1938–1939)

My rather impressive expedition to Germania Land, Northeast Greenland, came about simply because Arne Høygaard asked me about my plans while we traveled together on the train back to Oslo. I told him about my intention to hunt polar bears with Kalle. Høygaard gave a little laugh and told me I underestimated myself. It turned out that on the trip over from Iceland, he and Micard had talked of the need to continue exploration on the northeast coast of Greenland, perhaps all the way to Peary Land. He said, "We both agreed you have the right stuff, and the right spirit for leading a new expedition. You are rather naive in some ways, but I suppose that is refreshing. My feeling is that Micard wants you to approach him with some plan, once you've worked it out."

I was astounded to hear this flattering news, and of course, very excited. Høygaard brought out a bottle of whiskey, and the plans for "The Norwegian-French Expedition" began on the spot.

The plan called for going much further north than Clavering Island, with the goal of exploring Peary Land and setting up the world's most northerly station at Ingolfs Fjord. Only a handful of men had ever been able to go much further than Clavering. Previous attempts to winter further north were hampered by the infamous pack ice. The Koldeway Expedition of 1823 from Germany and the Mylius-Erichsen Expedition of 1906 from Denmark had both met with tragedy. Undaunted, Høygaard and I worked on the plans, and by the time we reached Oslo the bottle was empty.

It soon became clear that doors were opening for me. Høygaard, with instincts for publicity I did not have, got Oslo's top newspaper, *Aftenposten*, to print articles I had written. Next thing I knew, I was a local hero. The only negative note, besides losing Labb, was that my fiancée, Inger, was now engaged to someone else and living in Sweden. I had been gone for more than a year, without even saying good-bye, so what could I expect? Or at least, that was what some of my female friends said when they broke the painful news. Being young, I bounced back— largely due to the fact that I was now planning an expedition of my own.

Visiting my parents in Newcastle, I discovered to my surprise that I was hailed as a local boy who had "made good." The *Evening Chronicle* wrote fine articles about its "local son." There was a good one called MAROONED THREE WEEKS IN BLIZZARD, and another was entitled PACKED IN ICE: UPPER PART OF SHIP CRUSHED, both written by my father after he had received my letters, which contained the pertinent details of these adventures. The university happily let me use the art department to do some sculpting from the numerous sketches I had done of Inuit subjects in Ammassalik. I was reunited with my old mentor in art and archaeology, Dr. Maryon. We spent many hours talking about my archaeological work in Greenland, and of my plans to do more in the future. University geologists were tremendously interested in the four hundred-million-year-old fossils I had found under Dr. Eigil Nielsen's expert tutelage when he had visited Knoph-hytta.

Back in Oslo, I went to work for an architectural firm designing an apartment building. I drew plans all day long in our under-heated office shack on the building site. Since I didn't have much money, I was grateful for work under any conditions, but I did not forget the plans for my expedition. At night I would go over all the details, and every two days or so, I would meet with Arne Høygaard to share my ideas.

Not really sure of Micard's financial support, I devised a necessarily low-budget expedition. Kalle, of course, would be my partner. I planned for a shallow draft boat, just a small one. The idea was to have the boat shipped over on the *Polarbjorn* when it made its yearly supply run to Eskimonaes. From there— or so the plan went—we would weave in and out of the ice. Because of its small size, we could haul it up on shore for the winter. Instead of a mountain of supplies, we would live off the land as Kalle and I had done the last winter. I took my plans to noted arctic experts in many fields, including Thomas Hesselberg, the head of the Meteorological Institute, and also to Odd Arnesen, the lead journalist for arctic stories at *Aftenposten*.

Luckily for me, both men wrote recommendations praising the plans. I was then introduced to none other than Helge Ingstad, the famous man who had started the racket about "Norwegian occupation of Danish lands." Ingstad had by that time spent four years among the Indians of North America. He had lived as a trapper in Canada for four years in the late 1920s, and wrote the best-selling book, *The Land of Feast and Famine*, about his adventures in the Northwest Territories. Ingstad Creek, just to the east of Great Slave Lake, is named for him. His experience in North America spurred his interest in aboriginal peoples, and he set out to learn and write about the Inuit in Alaska, as well as Indians in Texas and Mexico. His book, *Apache Indians*, would be the result of this latter field of study.

We spent some hours together, and I made a sketch of him while he told me his theory that Vikings had been assimilated by the American Indians, citing that he had found hundreds of Indian words that were similar to Viking-age Norse. (In 1939 he gave me a signed copy of his Indian book, and fifty years later, I gave him a copy of the sketch!) Then, through my new association at the Norsk Polar Club, I met my longtime hero, Bernt Balchen, who had piloted Admiral Byrd over the South Pole! Imagine a young man's pride in having the world-famous pilot write a glowing commendation of his plans! And we did not know then that we were cousins, so there was no prejudice involved!

This build-up of support went on for two months, and then one day, Høygaard said, "Willie, you are organized enough. Quit fooling around! It's time to get some help. Why don't you go see Micard? He's not just interested in the Arctic—he needs someone like you to help him pursue his dreams."

I did not have his confidence, but I wrote a long letter to Micard anyway. Reading Micard's reply from Davos-Platz, Switzerland, I was not exactly encouraged:

Dear friend,

I thank you for your interesting letter which I received yesterday. It has caused a great agitation in me and left me a very unhappy man. I have been thinking and thinking all day and part of the night. It [your plan] sounds so inviting, so beautiful. [It would be] the realization of my dream, and my passionate desire to see Independence Fjord. But, as I already wrote to that fellow in Tromsø, it is next to impossible for me to winter in a hut. (It would have to be a real house for me, with a man to look after me, and, regarding the toilet, you know I absolutely can't go out in the cold and the bad weather, and we may be snowed up, etc. . . . .) There are all sorts of difficulties Halvorsen (I am glad to think you will take him, the poor dear boy) will tell you about; I can't help myself. I can do nothing, and would be a dead weight; the others would probably send me to hell. . . .

I am leaving here on February 7 for Paris, and if you would like to make a jump down here (you would be my guest, of course) to discuss things, I should be awfully glad, but I don't think you will be able to persuade me. You can fly from Stockholm to Zurich via Berlin. If you come, please wire the day and hour so that I can reserve a room. Please give my best regards to your sister, and believe me, dear friend, I am

Yours truly,
Gaston Micard

P.S. I heard nothing yet of the arrival of the Xmas presents. In any case, I hope to see you in Norway next spring.

It was rather ambiguous: Would he give me support or not? I hadn't the money to travel to Switzerland, not to mention I was a bit apprehensive about just up and leaving work one more time. I was going to get a bad reputation among architectural firms. My confidence returned when on January 25 I received one of Micard's famous one-word telegrams, saying "COME."

The next day, I received an invitation from the Royal Palace in Oslo! It was from the adjutant to the Crown Prince of Norway, advising me of an audience with the prince in two days, to be held at the palace on January 28, 1938. All my boyhood aspirations were being realized so fast, it felt like a dream.

For the royal audience, I was dressed in my most formal attire. My good friend Per Finn-Hansen had a new car, and he acted as my chauffeur. "And Willie, don't open the door yourself, I'll do it," Per said. "It's not every day that this happens. Let's play it right."

I arrived at the palace in style. I was led to Crown Prince Olav's office, and of course I was very impressed by the regal surroundings, and the fact that I, Willie Knutsen, son of a ship's mechanic, had been summoned there. I waited but a few minutes before the prince came in, greeting me as though we had known each other all our lives. He was an honorary member of the Norsk Polar Club, and was sincerely interested in any updated information on polar exploration.

The Russian Papanin Expedition was in the news just then, and he knew all about it. The members of the expedition had attempted to establish a site on the polar ice near the North Pole, but the ice had drifted so far south that they were in danger of being lost in the open sea off the east coast of Greenland. As the endangered expedition floated on ice within sight of Scoresby Sound, my friend Eigil Nielsen had sent word to them that he had spotted them, and believed he could get to them by crossing ice floes with a dog team.

Prince Olav said, "What do you think of those Russians? They refused Eigil Nielsen's help. Said *they* would be rescued by *their* submarine. A dog team was not good enough for them!" We both had a good laugh. In fact, Papanin denied having been rescued. He said that they had been picked up as planned. In spite of their bravery and great scientific achievements, I really doubted that the Russians had planned to drift on dangerous pack ice for months in the bleakness of winter, and then through the break-up caused by spring warming. Papanin seemed to have forgotten that he had kept the world informed through radio contact of the hellish conditions, the ice break-up, the hurricanes, and their misery.

It seemed that the Crown Prince and I had read the same articles, so we got along fine. I then told him my plans for the new expedition, and discussed its scientific aims. Where I planned to go was called the "womb of North Atlantic weather." To establish a permanent weather and scientific station on the northeast coast of Greenland would immensely ease the dangers to shipping and fishing vessels. The prince told me, "Your work could easily be more important than that of your predecessors, even though they broke the trail." I was greatly honored to have this chance to speak with him, and to find him not only interested but also informed and helpful.

An hour after my meeting I received word that I had won the Roald Amundsen Prize and the Fridtjof Nansen Prize as well. A giddy hour after that, I was having a celebratory beer with Arne Høygaard in the Grand Hotel. He said, "Now you are really ready to go see Micard!" I protested that I hadn't the money to travel. "You *are* naive, aren't you?" he said with a shake of his head. He took me around the corner to Norway's largest publishing house, marched me into the editor-in-chief's office, introduced me, and said I was going to write a book on the previous year's expedition. Without much more conversation, I received an advance of the then handsome sum worth about $3,000 today.

Afterwards, I protested to Arne. "I haven't the time to write a book!"

He snorted, "You idiot! That's your travel money!"

In Switzerland, Micard greeted me like a son, and as we rode from the station I began the speech I had practiced the whole way, but soon got carried away. I heard myself saying things like, "If you will finance the expedition, we will go further north than any expedition has ever wintered before. Go up to Ile de France; explore the land the duc d'Orleans had sighted in 1905. We'll make studies of the aurora borealis from further north than anyone has ever done—perhaps over eighty degrees north! We'll do archaeological digs where man has not trod in centuries!" I was very excited. It was a five-minute ride to the National Sport-Hotel. When we arrived, before the taxi was even fully stopped, Micard said, "I buy it!" The expedition was on!

Micard said we must have a bigger ship—a good, *arctic* ship—and a larger group of scientists. He said the expedition was going to attempt what had never been done before, and it would be best to achieve as much as possible. That night, after Micard had retired to bed, I headed to the hotel bar. A movie about a female skiing champion was being shot in Davos, and the cast was relaxing with drinks in the bar. The star, who had never skiied in her life, took a liking to me, and off I went to her room for the night. I haven't a clue what her name was! But it was a perfect end to a perfect day.

Before I left, Micard gave me a letter of credit for his bank in Oslo, and said, "You must purchase whatever you know we will need. Do not worry about the expense. Buy the best!" Then the aging count hinted that, old as he was, he thought he would like to come on the expedition after all. Of course, I said yes. Imagine his asking my permission to go when he had just given me carte blanche to buy whatever I needed: It would turn out to be a fortune! Not to mention he was good company. Micard's humility always impressed me.

As I traveled home through Austria by train, a frightening incident almost ended the expedition there and then. Hitler had only just taken over Austria, and tourists were not allowed to have deutschmarks, only tourist marks, but a waiter in the dining car had given me some of the forbidden money as change. I hadn't noticed at the time. When the guards came on board and asked for passports, they saw that mine was American, but heard my accent was not, and they grew suspicious. When they found the deutschmarks, they were about to arrest me for being a spy. A German who had eaten at the table with me told them the story, and the waiter was taken off the train. It was a dark sign of things to come for the whole world.

The first thing I did back in Oslo was to wire Kalle about the news, and to tell him to look for a ship. He wired back that the news had already reached him. He eagerly agreed to become my partner, and then began the rather tough job of organizing the expedition. I was just twenty-six, with no experience in purchasing supplies for a large polar expedition; I knew I could rely on Kalle to help me with such practicalities. The next person I hired was the photographer, Eigil Halvorsen. He was in Bergen just setting up a photography shop; hearing my news, he was greatly relieved to be doing something exciting again. He said, "I'm too young to settle down. Next year."

There was a mountain of materials to procure: cameras, clothes, food, fuel, and tools. The list became enormous, from needles to moccasins. I could not just order an electric generator; spare parts of a bewildering variety were also required, as were the special tools needed for repairs. Skis needed extra bindings and spare parts, and so on.

Because of the interest generated by the upcoming expedition, I met many of the old-timers of polar work, men whose names I had grown up with, including the famous explorer, Trygve Gran. Gran had been on Scott's last expedition, and had been the one to find the bodies of Scott and his ill-fated companions, who had succumbed to hunger and cold after they had heroically reached the South Pole.

Gran had also been the first to fly from Great Britain to Norway in 1914. This was an historic feat, the longest overseas flight at the time, but he had landed near Stavanger the day World War I broke out, so his fame was lost to the headlines of the Great War. Gran had also designed the first "tracked" motorcycles—precursors of the snowmobile—to operate in polar areas.

By a wonderful coincidence, when I told him the ship Kalle eventually bought was called the *Ringsel*, he slapped his hand on the bar we were seated at and shouted: "That was my ship! I designed her, and was almost finished building her, when I was called off to explore the Antarctic with Scott. Had to sell her for traveling money. You've got the right ship, all right!" Believe me, the hairs stood up on my neck.

The deck of the small, seventy-foot *Ringsel* would eventually be packed with everything from materials for the sled dogs to coal, but the ship could not carry all the supplies necessary for the expedition. The *Polarbjorn*, which usually traveled every spring to Greenland to bring new trappers and return with others, was charted to carry a prefab house I had designed specifically for Count Micard. (Let us not forget I was a trained architect!)

This house was to be the main station and was preconstructed by students of the trade school I had attended as a bricklayer while preparing for university. The structure was actually a house within a house, allowing the inner house to be well insulated, while the outside shell was used for storage. I also designed a rather chic-looking sled for Micard that looked like an oversized, luxurious baby carriage on sled runners. It had a convertible top and was well insulated with reindeer hides. Because reindeer hairs are hollow, they allow for a lot of buoyancy should the rig break through the ice. One had to consider this possibility. I also designed arctic boots, and sold the design to a manufacturer for a pittance, and the assurance that the crew would receive free footwear.

The planning and purchasing went on for months. I heard from Professor Carl Stromer, a top researcher in theoretical astrophysics at the Massachusetts Institute of Technology, that our expedition had won a grant from the Science Research Foundation of 1919. We were to be loaned rare equipment to undertake aurora photography of the northern lights. Stromer had worked for weeks with the International Association of Terrestrial Magnetism and Electricity, based in Washington, D.C., to get permission to lend us the aurora cameras. We were told that aurora activity intensified every eleven years, during high solar flare-ups, and that 1938 to 1940 were the perfect years to study this phenomenon.

The grant and the special equipment added greatly to the scientific importance of the expedition. The equipment was to be used to make simultaneous, triangulated shots of the effects of the geomagnetic axis of the earth on the aurora borealis. Cameras set miles apart would be coordinated by radio phones to ensure perfect timing. Because of the scientific importance attached to this new project, the team was more determined than ever to reach as far north as possible. Everything was going smoothly—until we discovered that we had some competition.

By receiving permission from Denmark for the expedition, it seems that I had ruffled some fairly important feathers down there—particularly Lauge Koch's. The World Court at The Hague had not yet determined who owned this area north of Erik the Red's Land, and Koch was not about to have a Norwegian presence where no Danish one existed. The fact that we were to start our expedition from a point near where Mylius-Erichsen had died in 1906 seemed to particularly touch Danish nerves. By the loose economic agreement created between Denmark and Norway in 1924, if I succeeded in establishing a scientific station in that disputed territory, my possession and use of it meant ownership. And since my expedition was a privately funded one, ownership would be private, not national. In those days and in that remote part of the world, land claiming was similar to what occurred in the Wild West in America, when first come, first served was the law. That was how the Norwegian and Danish trapping areas around Clavering Island had been divided out—almost a gentleman's agreement—and it had generally worked out just fine. Now, however, I was going where there was no Danish presence. As a result, a Danish team was organizing to go to the same area, with Count Eigil Knuth as leader.

Of course, I had become friends with Knuth in Ammassalik, so I did not think of him as the "enemy," but the newspapers of both countries jumped on the story, and carried headlines that blared RACE TO BE FARTHEST NORTH! and things of that nature. Newspapers in both countries quoted Lauge as saying that my expedition was part of the Norwegian tradition of trying to grab land on the east coast. Norwegians were enraged. Some Danish papers said our expedition was illegal, while others defended us. The exchanges got very heated, and held the public's attention for weeks. One article even tried to make Micard's financing of the expedition sound sinister by referring to it, as we might say today, as "the French connection."

I have to say that I never had the slightest interest in the politics concerning the expedition, and thought the uproar rather funny. But some prominent Oslo people with, shall we say, a more refined political understanding than I worried that the Danes, when stirred to action, would beat me to my objective. Denmark had once ruled Norway for four hundred years, so our national pride was at stake—at least for some people. It was pointed out that Eigil had a seaplane, and that we should have one as well. I was starting to feel the pressure, and thought that maybe the Danes would indeed beat us. My little ship could not carry a seaplane, but if we could afford one, it could be transported to Greenland on the *Polarbjorn*. This was not in the plans I had made with Micard, and I did not dare ask him for more money. I took out a ten-thousand-dollar loan, which was a huge sum for me in those days, considering I didn't have a penny to my name.

Soon a new pile of papers was on my desk from various airplane-sales out-fits answering my inquiries about purchasing a plane. I decided on a Waco bi-plane that was old, but after a new engine and other refitting, was guaranteed to suit the expedition's needs. The seaplane and new propellers, floats, skis, parts, and so forth were to be shipped over from America. The paperwork piled higher. We had letters from the shop which tested our new propeller. We had bills for the shipping and handling of spare parts. We had bills for parts I could not pro-nounce, but were essential to our expedition. Then I received a telegram from Micard: "I have heard about the plane, and your loan. It is all paid for, dear boy. Willie, whatever you need, you let me know!" What a relief. I would probably still be paying off that loan! All in all, Micard's financing of this expedition would have cost around a million dollars today.

Bernt Balchen told me he might be available to pilot the plane. This, of course, would have given tremendous prestige to the expedition. Bernt told me honestly that he needed a job. The Great Depression was still on, you have to understand. But when I told him the small type of plane I had bought, Bernt laughed good-naturedly and told me, "I have a certain reputation to live up to, even if I do need a job!" But he gave me his advice and friendship throughout the preparations for the expedition.

Arne Høygaard found a pilot, Jess Tillier, from Bergen, who had flown for a small company in America. He was also a lawyer, and had the appearance of the good-looking bad guy from a Hollywood movie. Unfortunately, it turned out to be a correct impression. I did not know much about Tillier, and eventually he caused considerable trouble to the expedition. The trouble started before we left. First, after a two-week romance, he married my sister! Then it was found Jess and Eigil Halvorsen, both from Bergen, did not get along. There was some-thing in their history. I knew I could not have such tensions while wintering in close quarters in unexplored and dangerous arctic lands. Unfortunately, I needed a pilot more than I needed a photographer, so I had to tell Eigil the bad news. He took it philosophically, saying, "My wife threatened to leave me if I went off again, so maybe it's time I settled down."

Somewhere during all this preparation I decided to see my parents in England. I did not know when or if I would ever see them again, so I took the time to sail overnight to Newcastle. While there I received an invitation to visit the Scott Polar Institute in Cambridge, and of all things, I met the director,

Professor Wordie. First of all, it was an honor to meet the man whose name was given to the Wordie Glacier, and I told him I had climbed it. Second, he had been a member of the expedition I had vainly tried to join in Aberdeen in 1935. It was quite a good feeling to meet him under such different circumstances. Only three years had passed, and already I had my own expedition. The sun was certainly shining on my path.

Before leaving Newcastle—and I tell this just to show the human side of arctic expeditions—I met a young Norwegian girl, Anita, studying at the university level, and fell in love. We had a favorite song to dance to, a recent hit on the radio, and when I left for Norway, Anita gave me five copies. I felt as if it was the modern equivalent of the damsel giving her scarf to her knight to wear in battle.

By March I was back in Oslo, and preparations for the expedition were almost complete. Count Micard sent a short letter from Belgium announcing his imminent arrival. It also had an ominous ring:

Dear Willie,

Considering the general disturbance, in central Europe as well as in France, I have come over to Belgium the day before yesterday, and I have taken passage on *Bretagne* leaving Antwerp on Saturday, the 19th, and arriving Oslo, Monday, the 21st, noon, and will see you whenever you like. I think it was safer to put myself out of reach of possible complications, and I rejoice to breathe soon the free air of Norway, in anticipation of the yet freer air of Greenland. My heartiest greetings to you and Eigil Halvorsen.

Your friend,
Gaston Micard

Micard's arrival sparked off another round of Danish versus Norwegian newspaper salvos. Lauge Koch was preparing his now-famous aerial mapping expedition over Peary Land, and his expedition ship, the *Gustov Holm* (named after the man who discovered Ammassalik), would carry his plane first to Norway, then to Svalbard, and then as close to Greenland as possible. Koch made it clear to

Norwegian reporters that he thought the Norwegian-French Expedition did not have the "legal permission to go as far north as they plan to." When asked if he did not think a weather station in that land would be a good thing, he simply replied, "That will not be an easy thing to do." He added, "I don't know much about meteorological things," which was his way of avoiding the acknowledgment that our expedition was a scientific one that would do everyone good. Even the Danish paper, *The Danish Way*, attacked Koch for planning this aerial expedition while there was an ongoing court case against him. Eleven Danish geologists had accused him of "scientific theft." When asked about that by Norwegian reporters, Koch snapped, "A stupidly written article with old-fashioned ideas!" He might have had a point at that.

In May, the Danish-Norwegian "war" heated up again when Lauge Koch returned from his historic aerial mapping flight over Peary Land. As I reported earlier, Koch said he had shown that Peary had not cheated, but had made an understandable mistake in thinking he had found Peary Channel. Many of the survivors of sled expeditions who felt they had proven Peary a liar were furious. They were worried that, armed with Koch's observation, the U.S. might take back its claim to the area. And there I was, an American citizen, backed by a Frenchman whose grandfather had helped France "take over Egypt," about to commence a Norwegian expedition to the contested area. No wonder some Danes were nervous! The fact that Koch, whom some of these "nervous" men now disliked, was against my expedition did not seem to matter to them; they still smelled an international conspiracy. The whole thing boggled my simple brain.

In June, Micard planned a big farewell dinner at the Bristol Hotel's Moorish Hall. It was to be a large gathering that included supporters such as Bernt Balchen, Thomas Hesselberg, K. S. Klingenberg, Olaf Holtedahl, Odd Arnesen, Arne Høygaard, the Norsk Polar Club, the expedition's bankers, two English arctic explorers who were in town, the press, my sister Signy, with her new husband, Jess, who was also my pilot, and the friends, wives, and girlfriends of the expedition's scientific members. Kalle and the crew were too far away in Tromsø at the time to make the party.

The day before the dinner party, I received a phone call from an old boyhood friend of mine named Thomas Kristofersen. He was a furrier who lived in the countryside outside of Oslo. He told me he had been reading about the expedition, and that he had also read newspaper accounts of my adventures on the last one. He told me, "I was sorry to read about your dog, Labb, being taken from you." I agreed it was a hell of a blow. Then he said, "You won't believe this, but I think I have him!"

Labb's owner, the scoundrel trapper and tanner up in Alesund, owed Kristofersen some money, so he had given Labb in payment. It seemed to be his favorite method of paying his debts. By a fantastic stroke of fate, Labb and I were to be reunited. Kristofersen then cautiously told me that Labb had gone on a "hunting" spree in his neighborhood, killing chickens and other farm animals. I was happy to pay for the damages, of course, but I had to wonder about the once-docile, pampered pet that had been afraid of his own shadow—and of lemmings! But then I remembered his sudden conversion when he had attacked the musk ox.

In the middle of the formal dinner party, with everyone in their best attire and exhibiting proper decorum, Kristofersen arrived with Labb. The whole place burst into cheers and applause as Labb rushed over, leapt up on me with his big body, and showered my face with joyful greetings! When the excitement of the reunion had died down, my wild killer sat politely at the table like everyone else, listening to the speeches and verbal accolades as he daintily ate his dinner of sausages from a plate. The management, although glad that the famous canine affair had concluded so happily in their posh hotel, said it was the first—and probably the last—time that a dog would be allowed at a dinner party.

CHAPTER NINE

Victory!

A t the beginning of July, the *Ringsel* arrived in Bergen, and we took the train over the mountains to join it. In honor of Gaston Micard, the ship was renamed *En Avant!*, which means "forward" in French. As final preparations were made, we received bad news. Jess Tillier, flying the seaplane from Oslo to Alesund, where the *Polarbjorn* was to take it on board for transport across the Norwegian Sea, had crashed! He had tried to set it down on a glassy lake in the middle of Norway, had thought he was closer to the surface than he actually was, and had cut the engines. The plane hit hard, sank, and then resurfaced as a wreck. Tillier had floated unharmed to the surface, still gripping his pipe between his teeth. I know that last little detail because a coworker of my sister Signy's just happened to be waiting on a train at a station by the lake, and that is how I have a photo of the plane today. It also seems Tillier swam to shore and snapped at the flabbergasted local policeman who came to see if he was all right. Tillier said that he didn't need any police assistance, that all was as it should be, and that it was no big deal!

Hearing this news, I tried to stay calm about the plane, but I could not help thinking Tillier was not as good a pilot as he had claimed. Even I knew that on a glassy surface, a pilot should find his position above the water by looking at the shoreline. He had cost me my photographer, and now my plane! Expensive barrels of aviation fuel had to be unloaded from the ship as we would no longer be using them. And, to top it off, I had not taken out insurance on the plane since the premiums on arctic expeditions were out of this world. I phoned Tillier's mother in Bergen, told her of the crash, but quickly added that Jess had gotten out of the water alive. What this well-educated, socially polite woman then said should have warned me of the troubles to come. "Drown? Jess?" she asked. "Young man, you listen to me now: 'He who is born to hang will never drown'!" And with that she hung up the phone. I hung up the receiver, quite startled. In spite of the warning by his own mother, I told Jess by wire to come to meet us in Bergen as quickly as possible. He would stay with the expedition as a radio man.

I did not want to fire my sister's husband, but not doing so would turn out to be a mistake. This would not be the only personality problem to arise before we left.

Arne Høygaard had asked me to take along his assistant, Kaare Rodahl, who was to monitor our nutritional intake and health for Høygaard's continuing study. While the loading of the ship was going on, and all hands, including scientists, were expected to pitch in and help, Rodahl apparently thought it beneath his station. I was not around, but I heard from the crew that when they were taking a break, and had grabbed a few beers from the supplies, Kaare had told them it was theft, and that he would report them to me. "He's a damn snob!" they said. "If he comes with us, we guarantee we'll throw him overboard before we get halfway to Greenland!" He would have been a valuable scientific member, but I could not afford to have personal antagonisms on our dangerous expedition. I told him he would have to stay behind. (He went on to do important work over the next two decades in Greenland and Alaska.)

The Norwegian-French Expedition—the French newspapers naturally called it the French-Norwegian Expedition—was set to leave. The key members of the expedition were Count Gaston Micard, the financier and philosophic advisor; myself as expedition leader; and Kalle Nicholaisen as ship's captain and second in command. Kalle had hired Edvard Wilhelmsen as first mate, and Ingvart Ingebrigtsen as chief engineer, while his second was Sigmund Snarby. William Jacobsen was our cook. We were fortunate to have the famous trapper Nils Nois as our main hunter. For the scientific team we had Kristian Hatlevik, geophysicist; Sigbjorn Aamodt, meteorologist; and Jess Tillier as radio operator. At the last minute I took on a strong young man named Leif Olsen, who had begged to come as "all-around handyman, and without pay!" Remembering my own history of begging to come on expeditions, I said he could come along. There were plenty of provisions for an extra man. To our chagrin, he brought an accordion with him he was just learning to play, and almost drove us crazy with his practicing when we later crossed the Norwegian Sea.

The press and radio people assembled on the dock, along with half the town. The dog teams, including pups, were also on the dock, quietly awaiting boarding procedures. One of the radio announcers, who had interviewed me in Oslo, whispered, "Willie, this is boring! Can't you get these dogs to give the listeners the real feel of the expedition?" So, while the whole nation listened, Kalle and I got the pack to start howling and barking by playfully roughhousing with them—all in the name of showbiz!

We finally left on our great endeavor, with our little ship, on July 7 at nine in the evening. Bergen had been the starting point for expeditions to both poles since Amundsen's in 1893, and the *Bergens Tidende* newspaper wrote, "None of these—not even Hubert Wilkins with his World War I submarine, the *Nautilus*, had a ship so unimpressive in size, just a little over seventy feet. Still, they had on board twelve men, fourteen dogs, supplies for seven men to over-winter on land for two and a half years, and the great plan to build a weather and scientific station as far north as possible. . . . and we hope that this station will be the basis for important studies and weather reports in the years to come . . . under the most northerly Norwegian flag in Greenland." It wasn't necessary for them to add that last taunt to the Danes.

We steamed off to make history—we hoped—with our unimpressive, over-loaded ship, and fortunately were able to unload much of the cargo in Alesund onto *Polarbjorn*, which now, thanks to my brother-in-law, had ample space on deck where my plane should have been. The *Polarbjorn*, which of course carried our prefab station house, would also pick up twenty-one more sled dogs, making thirty-five in all. So in truth, we really were not that small of an expedition; we just had a small ship, per my plan. This was the biggest Norwegian expedition since Amundsen, and yet it was the only one ever financed by just one man!

Arriving in Tromsø, we discovered that Helmer Hansen, the great veteran of Amundsen's Antarctic dash to the Pole, was still the harbormaster. As he had done when Micard's *Quest* Expedition had left Tromsø in 1936, Helmer drank toasts with us and studiously ignored the fact that the water was almost licking the deck because we were a "few" tons over our weight limit. A reporter later wrote: "Anyone watching the boat leave would have shaken his head. Loaded as *En Avant!* was, it looked like a submarine just surfacing!"

Finally, on July 17, in beautiful weather, the "submarine" eased its way from port. We were on our way to making history, with the water nearly on the deck. The dogs, who had to stay on deck, looked uneasy, but Kalle gave me the thumbs-up sign. Micard probably wondered what he was doing on a ship with two madmen. We crossed the awesome Norwegian Sea, then the ice-spattered Greenland Sea, and arrived four days later at Clavering Island, without a hitch!

Micard put up his beautiful silk umbrella, and the expedition members went ashore to see old friends at Eskimonaes.

What a greeting! Niels-Ove Jensen was still in charge, and we had a grand reunion for two days before we had to make way again, and sail to meet the *Polarbjorn* on the other side of Clavering Island. We sailed in a light fog, and had to go slowly. I went below to get some sleep after all the celebrating at Eskimonaes. I awoke when I felt the ship hit something. There was a commotion on deck. Hurrying topside, the fog was so thick I could not see to the end of the ship.

"We've run aground on a damned sandbar!" Kalle told me. "The men had been sounding, but sandbars slope steeply here. You are on top of them before you notice the shoaling waters. We're on soft sand, thank God, but the damn tide is going out!"

Helplessly we watched the ship list as the waters receded with the tide. Slowly *En Avant!* started to lean. When it reached a 45-degree angle, we began to get some of the dogs off the deck and to shore by using the whaler. The dogs that were left on board were perched at the high side of the deck, their legs splayed out to keep themselves from sliding into the water. Water was coming into the hold a little, and supplies that shouldn't get wet were laboriously moved. The anchor was run out, and drawn tight to help keep the ship from listing any further. We anxiously awaited the return of high tide. We prepared for that event by tying our two outboard launches to the ship, hoping that even their little horsepower might help pull the overladen ship off the sandbar at high water.

At high tide, the ship righted itself. The motors on the two boats were started up, and then slowly the tow ropes were pulled taut. Kalle yelled to the engine room, "Start the engines!" When they roared to life, we could see sand churning in the water, but by god, we began moving! Kalle looked at me with a let's-not-have-to-go-through-that-again expression. The expedition had almost been wrecked before it began, but Micard said, "I told you that you boys were the right ones for the job." He had a nice way of making near disasters seem like triumphs.

The fog cleared, and we had a fine sail around the back of Clavering. There we found the *Polarbjorn* waiting for us, along with the *Vesle Kari*, carrying the redoubtable Miss Louise Boyd! When we drew within shouting distance she suggested—rather, commanded—we all meet on shore for a shindig. She shouted that she would supply "the goddamn booze!"

There we were on shore, three crews of toughened sailors and arctic expedition men, and it was she who was barking orders that we all assemble for a historic photo. It was difficult to ignore her. We assembled. Then the party began. When she spoke—occasionally taking a swig from a bottle of brandy she carried around with her under her arm—I was reminded of a brothel owner in a Hollywood Western. This in no way detracted from her professionalism, nor from the years of important research she did in the Arctic; quite the contrary. She was a great scientist and a wonderful person.

Louise Boyd's plan when we met at Clavering was also to go as far north as possible, and make a photographic record of the coast and bays and fjords. She had with her a huge aerial surveillance camera capable of making detailed, sharp photos. She had hired three husky Danes to lug the heavy apparatus up and down the mountains. They told me, "Easy work, and she pays well!" When the *En Avant!* and *Vesle Kari* finally sailed away together, she shouted good-natured bets as to which ship would get north to Denmark's Haven first. We should have bet on whether we would make it at all. Very few ships had in the past.

We soon stopped at Sandodden, the Danish trapping station. A neat little setup, there were three frame huts, built like the one I had designed, so that there were two cabins built one inside the other for insulation, with all the comforts of home. I mention this brief stop because the remote site would become the stage for a tragic drama during World War II, involving Kalle's old Spitsbergen trapping partner, Herman Ritter. Both Bernt Balchen and I would also play prominent roles in this nearly forgotten saga of the war.

There was a formidable blockage of ice piled up between Pendulum Island and Shannon Island, and also at Bass Rock. We were encountering the infamous coastal pack ice that had always limited ship exploration of the coast. The 1823 expedition under Koldewey had completed the first scientific studies of this coast on the Pendulums. The expedition had set up a concrete platform for a pendulum to study the magnetic movement of the earth. In 1906, Alfred Wegener, as the only German on the ill-fated Mylius-Erichsen Expedition, came to Greenland to study arctic air currents. He arrived at Pendulum, took readings, and would later note that the island had moved from its first reported position of 1823. This gave him the data for his theory of continental drift, a theory we now know is a reality, though he was scoffed at by the experts of his day.

Over the course of his life, Alfred Wegener took part in four expeditions to Greenland, "the happiest times of my life," he later wrote. His last two Greenland expeditions in 1929 and 1930 led to the construction of three ice-cap stations and plans for creating an all-year meteorological and glaciological profile of Greenland's inland ice sheet. In November 1930, on the way back to West Station, Wegener and his companion, an Inuit by the name of Rasmus Villumsen, died trying to provide the central Eismitte station with supplies for the winter. The expedition was completed by his brother. (The idea of continental drift did not become widely accepted in Europe until the 1950s. By the 1960s, geological research conducted by Robert Dietz and Harry Hess led to its acceptance among North American geologists.)*

The ice was too thick for us to penetrate, so we weighed anchor to wait to see if it would slacken. We went ashore on Pendulum to hunt for musk ox, and found a herd on the top of a ridge, about an hour's walk from the shore. We got five, and began to lug the meat back. Labb carried a whole head, horns and all, by gripping the hair with his teeth. Labb was big, but that was one oversized load, even for him. His neck arched from the weight and looked like it would snap. But he made it back to the beach before he would give in to what had to have been terribly painful cramps. My canine "Ferdinand" certainly had undergone a remarkable metamorphosis. I had come to love that dog.

After two days, a strong wind came up and moved the ice around enough to create a lead of open water. Following that, the *En Avant!* crawled north to Shannon Island. The island was where Ejnar Mikkelsen had left his doomed ship, the *Alabama*, in 1910 and 1911 while he went off looking for Mylius-Erichsen, or his remains. We had somber thoughts as we edged northward.

Finally, the ice between Shannon and the mainland was so thick, *En Avant!* went out to sea to work its way through ice that was not so stubborn. In that way the expedition inched another thirty-six miles north to Big Koldewey Island.

---

* Author's Note: for more information on the subject, visit
  http://www.awi-bremerhaven.de/
  http://www.brainyencyclopedia.com/encyclopedia/t/th/theory.html
  http://www.enchantedlearning.com/subjects/dinosaurs/glossary/Contdrift.shtml]
  http://www.pbs.org/wgbh/aso/tryit/tectonics/
  http://www.engr.usask.ca/~mjr347/prog/geoe118/geoe118.057.html

There we found solid ice landward again, making our return to the ocean ice pack necessary. With the current and ice against us, we bumped, and ground, and gained another fifty nautical miles. At last, the northern tip of Big Koldewey Island was reached. We squeezed our way through ice to go past Little Koldewey Island and into Dove's Bay, near Denmark's Haven, on August 8. We had reached 76 degrees, 45 minutes north.

Denmark's Haven was the old station built by the Mylius-Erichsen Expedition in 1906. His plan had been to chart the coast from there to Peary Land, where Peary's exploration work had ended. We all were thinking of Mylius-Erichsen's tragic end north of here while on an exploratory sled trip. Where we had arrived was devoid of humans for hundreds of miles in all directions. No one but a long-vanished Inuit culture had ever settled north of this point, and to go beyond was the Norwegian-French Expedition's goal. We were alone—for the moment, anyway—and that made our thoughts of the history of this place all the more poignant.

We did some land exploration, and I climbed a high ridge to see how far north of us the ice went. I could see solid ice all the way to the horizon. We knew it would be a while before that jam would break up. The old station was in usable condition, but the expedition had no intention of staying there. It was, however, a very picturesque bay, and a natural settlement place. There were two small rivers nearby, and two small lakes. I found the remains of Inuit ruins, many of them dug up by Thomas Thompson and Bendix Thorstrup of the Mylius-Erichsen expedition.

While we were gazing out on the huge bay, in came the *Vesle Kari*. We hurried to our boat and motored out to meet Miss Boyd. Her ship had penetrated as far north as Ile de France. This was the second most northern landing ever made by a ship that anyone among us knew of, and certainly the furthest north by an American. Boyd had come within thirty miles of the most northerly point reached by the Duc d'Orleans in the *Belgica* in 1905. In 1930, the famous Canadian from Newfoundland, Captain Bob Bartlett, on his ship *Morrissey*, had reached about twenty miles south of where Miss Boyd had landed; hers was an historic voyage.

Miss Boyd's ship had found it impossible to sail along the coast we wanted to go up, and had had to reach south, where we were, by going further out to sea, and then cutting in to shore. It showed what a difficult task lay ahead of us if we were to establish a land-based station. While we were joking about beating her here with our little ship, in came another ship! It was the *Gamma*, Count Eigil Knuth's ship from Denmark. It was getting crowded on this unknown coast; there hadn't been this much activity here since 1905. And certainly they did not have three ships.

When Knuth came aboard the *Vesle Kari*, he told us with a sardonic smile, "We made our way here inch by inch through the pack ice out to sea, always in danger of being trapped and crushed. But everything we had heard from the old-timers said it was the best way to get in at this unpopulated latitude. Then, as we finally approached land, we saw smoke—and now, we find you here! We have come miles through dangerous ice to be where few men have ever been, and we find not just other men, but a woman with red lipstick walking around with a bottle of brandy under her arm, and a French count walking about with a silk umbrella!"

Knuth and his men were proud of the polar boots they had bought from the outfitter, Kolbjorn Knutsen, in Oslo (no relation to me). Lined with lambskin, the boots had a flexible russet exterior, with only the heel and sides made of leather. "Best European footwear known to me," said Knuth. "The shoes give way softly when you walk, and are easy to thaw out over a Primus stove. Roomy, lots of space for layers of socks and some insulating bladder sedge. And the soles have thick double layers of felt sewn between two layers of leather!" We let him go on for a while before Kalle finally revealed that I had designed the boots, and then sold the idea to Kolbjorn Knutsen. I had not made much money, but the look on Knuth's face made up for it. Young men always want to upstage their more experienced elders.

Knuth's expedition included Eigil Nielsen, the paleontologist who had found the four hundred-million-year-old fossils near Krogness the year before. There was also the famous zoologist, Alvin Pedersen, a veteran of other trips to Greenland. Knuth's ship had brought the De Haviland Gypsy Moth seaplane we had heard about. Their pilot, Michael Hansen, had had to learn the techniques of landing on water only a few days before the expedition left Denmark. I almost said I wished my pilot had admitted he had never landed on water, but kept my mouth shut. No sense being churlish.

During the voyage to Denmark's Haven, the plane had enabled them to see that ice conditions inside Koldewey prevented sailing that way, and so the

Gamma had headed out to sea. Further conversation proved that the plane could be a hindrance as well as a help. At one point, the radio had failed to operate properly, and the pilot had experienced some dangerous hours not knowing where the ship was. The ship, meanwhile, had to wait for the plane's return, rather than continuing on, making progress. That, at least, provided some consolation for the loss of our craft.

Knuth's plane was unloaded, and the open water around us allowed it to take off to scout the ice to the north. But the flight only confirmed what we had already told Knuth, based on our view from the high ridge. We kidded him about the unnecessary expense of a plane, while at the same time wishing we still had one.

Every day was crucial in the Arctic. After two weeks of waiting, the ice had still not broken up. It was the end of August, and all hope of further break-up was almost abandoned. The *Gamma* dropped off supplies for Knuth's wintering site twenty miles to the west of our ship, then headed south, with the plane on deck, to return to Denmark. The *Vesle Kari* also weighed anchor and headed south. Miss Boyd had never intended to winter over, and was happy with the results of her three months' expedition. We found ourselves alone again, wondering if we, like Knuth's wintering party, would have to be content to stay at Dove's Bay. Repeated climbs to our observation ridge showed no improvement in the ice along the coast to the north. Micard told me not to worry; there was always next year. I had forgotten that we might be there for two years.

We then had a ten-day spell of warm weather, followed by days of high winds. When the winds abated, I climbed the ridge and saw a lead. It was not a long lead, but it was encouraging. I hurriedly returned to the ship and we set out of Denmark's Haven. Our patience had been rewarded. We traveled ten miles along the coast of Germania Land before the ice was too packed to penetrate further. The small promontory, or point on shore, where we anchored is called "17 Kilometer Ness" (or "17 Kilometer Point") on the Danish maps. There we found a snug harbor, just big enough for the ship. We sat there, wondering if the ice would come back in and pin us there. While we waited for the weather to determine our fate and the direction of our movement, on the deck we assembled what has to be one of the most improbable huts ever devised.

We had crates and crates of margarine which had been sold to us at a huge discount as a gift from the manufacturer. We were not fond of the margarine, but the dogs liked it, and of course, the oils were essential to the health of all of us, humans and animals alike. But we did not need the crates, so the walls of the prefab hut were lined with slats from crates that boldly advertised the product's manufacturer: MARGARINE CENTRAL.

I took further advantage of the waiting period by going ashore and digging in some Eskimo ruins. Typically, if we found a sheltered cove, long before us the Inuit had too, and had built settlements there. I could tell that the Mylius-Erichsen group had dug here as well. I unearthed a deep, permanent, winter-type dwelling. It had a rock and earth-covered entryway leading into a circular room. The arched, stone ceiling of the room was only partially collapsed. When I was finished clearing out rubble from the interior, the dwelling was almost usable again. While we were digging, we also bagged some nearby musk oxen. The ancient Inuit had not hunted musk ox, as the herds did not arrive before the demise of the Inuit in that region. But in my diggings, I found a drinking cup made from the horn of a musk ox. As I had never found one before, and as it appeared rather new, I surmised it had been fashioned by the archaeologists in 1906.

After three days another storm blew up, lasting for twenty-four hours. When it calmed, we saw some open water but did not have a high enough observation point on land to see how far north the lead stayed open. I decided to take the whaleboat, a radio transmitter, and Leif Olsen—with the damned accordion—and see how far the open water went. We took enough food for several days, plus the pre-fab pieces of the homemade hut we had just made out of margarine crates, and we were off. It was not long before we came up against some flat ice floes that *En Avant!* would have had no trouble going through; unfortunately, Leif and I had to haul the launch up on the floes in order to reach water on the other side. We did this portaging often, and while it slowed us down, we gradually gained another ten miles up the Germania coast until the ice finally stopped us.

The whole coast had been absent of any sort of harbors. Steep gravel cliffs and windswept beaches covered with boulders was all we found. The ice conditions were not favorable for *En Avant!*, so it was decided that we would wait to see if conditions improved. We had hugged the coast where no one had been ashore since 1870, when the Koldewey Expedition had sledded inland from just about where Leif and I stood. Koldewey had written: "We are the first and last people who will ever see this dreadful place, where no humans could live!" We got busy setting up the hut at that very place.

Our "Margarine Central" hut went up quickly. We set up bunks inside made from leftover margarine crates, and piled sod and rocks on the outside walls. There was barely room inside for two men. Outside, we still managed to set up bamboo poles, stretching radio antenna wire between them to create a "scientific station." It was not much, but at that moment, we had the most northern station on the planet!

We scouted around for two days until another storm blew up, again with favorable results to the ice. I radioed Kalle, and in four hours saw the smoke of our ship—the first ship on this coast that we knew of—plowing toward us. What a sight! I took a great photograph of this historic occasion. While waiting down by the water's edge for the ship, I found an empty vodka bottle. I could only assume that it had drifted here on the currents, like Siberian timber. It was possible that the Papanin Expedition had tossed the bottle into the sea as their ill-fated expedition floated south on ice floes, the sole record of their perilous journey.

Our ship progressed northward, mile by mile. We came to shore-fast ice, and were forced to follow its border, which gradually forced us farther out to sea. On August 24, at 77°-04'2 north, the open water stopped dead. The shore was about a mile and a half away. I decided this was probably our last chance to take the time to unload the ship; this shore would host our main station. Feverishly, we unloaded the prefab materials for the house, plus sleds, dogs, food, and fuel. While we piled everything on the ice, one group began sledding supplies toward shore to set up tents for camp.

The ice was rough and full of impediments, including huge outcroppings of piled-up ice near the shore, so the sledding was not easy. A wind began to drive from the northeast, bringing with it more ice. Before we were able to unload all the supplies, Kalle had to quickly set sail so the ship wouldn't get pinned in. He headed south for the relative safety of the small bay the ship had come from earlier. The wind suddenly grew much stronger. Snow began to fall—or rather, whip along—at a great speed, and the men at the unloading site left for the cover of the tents already set up on land. We left a mountain of material still to move, along with one chained-up dog with her five pups, snug in a little doghouse. There simply had not been enough time to move them. The storm had increased in velocity so quickly that the last men barely made it back before a whiteout blizzard was in full swing.

The tents had been set in the lee of a huge cliff, but the weather still got a chance to test their durability. Kalle and I had designed them to be double layered, with dead space between the layers for added insulation. The outside material was the strongest ever made. A man could barely stand up in the center, but all in all, they were comfortable little tents. Micard was really happy. He was experiencing the real rigors of an Arctic storm without his usual snug shipboard quarters. As the storm raged, he and I were actually able to discuss, while eating warm food, the historical significance of our being the first people to be this far north at this general longitude since his fellow Frenchman, the duc d'Orleans, stopped briefly. The duke had been far out to sea, however; we were the first to actually land this far north. Micard was very, very happy, even though we were not able to leave the tents for ten hours.

By radio, we heard that Kalle and the others on board the ship were having a hell of a time. He had had to run anchors to shore, as well as to sea. He had run all the hawsers he could to shore, and wrapped them around boulders. Still, he had been forced to keep the engines going at full power in order to avoid being driven ashore. It was a tremendous relief when the storm broke and the sun came out. Stepping out of the tents into a snow-covered landscape, we saw to our dismay that the coast to the south was almost free of ice. The whole shelf seemed to have broken up, and the swift current had cleared the coast!

We could not see where we had left our pile of materials because the old masses of piled ice near the shore blocked the view. We rushed down to the edge so we could see around the ice masses, and we were greeted by five little pups with their tiny tails wagging happily. The ice to the north had been cleared, almost to the shore, except for one wedge jutting out to sea which was still attached to land. At the tip of the wedge was the life-saving pile of supplies! We tried not to think about the mother of the pups. She had been left chained up, so she might not have survived.

We rushed our dogsleds out to the edge of the ice. Our aluminum radio masts, and some of the prefab walls for our station, were hanging partway over the ice's edge, dangling above the fast-moving, open water—but nothing had been lost! We could not believe our eyes, or our luck, when at the newly carved edge we saw the little doghouse with the mother, still chained, and happy as hell to see us!

We put all our energy into getting the supplies off the ice. The dogs worked like demons, pulling overloaded sleds. To give them some initiative, I got our hunter Nils Nois to run in front of the team with Miss Hansen on a leash. Miss Hansen was useless as a sled dog, but the cute coquette with a tail like an ostrich feather was in heat. The dogs pulled triple loads across rough ice to try to be the first to her.

The men had to maneuver around a few small water holes churned open from the currents below. Kristian Hatlevik, enthusiastic to be in the Arctic for the first time, was not paying attention to where he was going, and slipped into one of these open holes and disappeared. When he bobbed up, he was laughing. I grabbed him by his parka, and hauled him out, still laughing. He was having a ball!

Kalle arrived with the ship, but with the ice shelf so dangerously unpredictable, the rest of the cargo had to be unloaded at a point about forty-five minutes away from the station, which was already being built by several of the men. The storm had cleared so much ice that the ship could be maneuvered quite close to shore to unload the remaining supplies. At this relatively short distance from the station site, they could be stored in a supply depot.

After the ship was unloaded, and while the station was being assembled, Kalle and I and the crew took advantage of the open water created by the storm to take the ship further north. We wanted to try and set up a substation, inching our way north, bit by bit, establishing supply depots along the way. The key to successful polar exploration had proven to be logistics. Instead of making a rash dash, which had been the death of Mylius-Erichsen and his team in 1907, we would ease our way north, leaving reserves of supplies that would sustain us in case of emergency.

We sailed up to a spot near Ile de France, but the ice was too thick to get close to shore. We returned to about fifteen miles north of our main site. Huge icebergs were stranded on the bottom of the shallow water. We anchored in the lee of their natural breakwater, and there unloaded more material. The following summer, we hoped, we would inch our way north again, hopefully to reach the "impossible" goal of Ingolfs Fjord at last.

We next anchored off a point called Thomas Thompson's Ness—named after the archaeologist who had sledded to this point in 1906—to do some digging in the ruins that were apparent everywhere on the rocky shore. There was a tiny shack there, and Leif Olsen and I went ashore to fill it with emergency provisions and do some repairs to a door that a bear had obviously taken objection to. Kalle left us there and set sail far southward to find a harbor on the inside of Little Koldewey Island for the winter, where the pack ice could not crush the ship.

When two days later Leif and I made the long walk back to the main site, we were greeted by an amazing sight: The station was nearly completed. Prefabrication had made this possible. The three tall aerial masts were up, weather gauge boxes were erected, and final touches were being added to the large and roomy house. The kitchen had a large stove designed to easily melt snow for water, and a storage tank in the next room could hold many gallons. Micard's room was next to the kitchen, graced with fine French lace curtains on the windows and a good library. I had my own room—rank has its privileges. The rest of the men paired up in rooms for sleeping quarters. Aamodt had a radio room where he could keep his meteorology and aurora borealis work organized; he often slept there too. In the specially designed room at the back of the station, the diesel electric generator *putt-putted* cozily. With electric lights and a hand-cranked record player, all in all, it was a truly civilized weather station, and, by a few miles, the northernmost in the world!

We dubbed this new site *Micardbu*, or Micard's Place, and celebrated with French champagne, of course. A tremendous feeling of camaraderie and accomplishment bonded us together. I wondered if my grin was as wide as everyone else's. We had done what no one before us had done, but we could not afford much time for fooling around. We were the most northerly station, and certainly, it was the most remote; but most importantly, Micardbu was the most ideally situated for making the most helpful weather reports for North Atlantic shipping. We began sending three radio messages daily with weather reports. Besides the satisfaction of our being there, science was our real objective. The world would now have better forecasts than ever before, and a window to an unknown world was opening up to mankind.

CHAPTER TEN

Micardbu

The landscape around Micardbu consisted of rolling hills leading to steppes, which in turn led to a glacially capped mesa about six miles from the station. The view around us was similar to what the mesa areas of Utah, Arizona, or New Mexico might have looked like during the Ice Age. Behind the main house was the cliff we had tented near during the storm, and a great pack of permanent snow swept down its face and almost to the sea's edge, about fifty feet away. After the main house was built, an emergency shelter was dug into the hard-packed snow cliff. In it was stored extra sleeping bags, clothes, food, and fuel; the entrance was sealed with blocks of icy snow, and then marked with tall bamboo poles. This shelter was created in case a fire burned the main house down. Everything had to be thought of in advance; nothing could be left to chance. This was to be serious exploration, not an adventure. Roald Amundsen had once said that people who have "adventures" obviously did not plan well enough.

Before too much snow fell, driving musk oxen to remote, protected valleys, we hunted them while they were plentiful and relatively nearby. We killed a large number and cached the meat in the snowbank behind the main house. It would prove to be our key to survival later. And survival had many facets in Germania Land. Once, while Leif Olsen and I were hunting, we saw one of our dogs come running across the tundra at full speed, with its tail tucked between its legs and a big bull musk ox right behind it. The damn dog ran to hide behind us! Here was further proof that musk oxen had never read the books that said they did not charge. The bull charged us as if in a Spanish bullring, making three fast passes, as we did clumsy pirouettes with the frightened dog underfoot. The shaggy, rough coat of the angry bull gave off a powerful, wild smell. And its heavy, hot snorting sounded ominous. Musk oxen are not tall, but ask a man who has been hit by one whether or not it's a laughing matter! And they have a nasty habit of jumping up and down on enemies they have laid low. At last Nois put a fatal shot into it.

We soon discovered we had set up Micardbu in the middle of an ancestral migration track of the local polar bears. From our depot to the south, to Thomas Thompson's Ness to the north, we had invaded their ancient homeland. While moving materials from the depot, we often saw their tracks. It gave one an eerie feeling, because polar bear are clever enough to wait in ambush for a seal. They are not to be regarded as anything but a death threat. Soon after the station was in operation, I went with Sigbjorn Aamodt to the supply depot. Sigbjorn was not carrying a rifle, because in spite of his name (*bjorn* means bear in Scandinavia), or maybe because of it, he did not like the idea of shooting a bear. He was a scientist, and Sigbjorn figured hunting was for Nois. But all around the depot that day, we saw bear tracks in the snow; a single trail with only the rear paws imprinted in the snow led out to the sea ice, where we saw a dark spot. We went out to investigate.

Along the trail we discovered seven huge, half-eaten bologna sausages. Arriving at the dark spot, we found it was a crate with ten bolognas still inside. The bear had carried the crate in its arms, walking upright. It obviously had seen us, though we hadn't seen it, and had run off on all fours to dive into the open water. Apparently, the bolognas were a fee exacted for our use of the bears' ancient trail.

The snow was packed hard around the boxes in the supply depot, and Sigbjorn was digging to find a crate of his containing radio tubes and other materials for a set he had designed. He told me, "Go on back, Willie. I'll catch up when I find the damn crate." Later on, back at headquarters, someone spotted two forms coming toward us. Through binoculars the men saw Sigbjorn striding at full speed on his skis, and parallel to him about fifty feet away, a huge polar bear was casually keeping pace. It most certainly had never seen a human, and was probably wondering if this thing was edible. We quickly harnessed the dogs, and took off. The bear, hearing the dogs, turned and lumbered out of sight over a hill. Out of breath, and terribly frightened, all Sigbjorn could do was stutter: "B-B-bear. F-F-Followed all th-th-th-the way . . . d-d-d-depot. Never left m-m-my s-s-s-side. Never so happy . . . hear dogs!" He never went anywhere again without a rifle. Schjelderup had been right.

With the other men set to go about their experiments and studies, I prepared to go south overland by sled to explore, and to visit Kalle and the ship's crew at Koldewey Island. To give the station a break from Leif Olsen's accordion practicing, I took him along. We headed first for Margarine Central. We cut cross-country to Denmark's Harbor. It was a good decision, because first we came across a strange little beetle that lived in miniature igloos, something I had never seen, nor heard of, and a few hours later on the trail, we came to an area that held the icy, exotic remnants of a "dead" glacier. No longer moving, nor attached to an ice cap, it had been weathered by wind and rain, possibly over many centuries, into magnificent carvings. There were large, arched bridges, and we crossed one, feeling tiny and awestruck. Colossal hummocks, separated from the main, decaying body, lay scattered in the old curving path of the once-live glacier. Huge, beautifully sculpted walls showed the stratified layers marking each year's snowfall. It was the catalogue of the centuries, with rocks, gravel, and other debris included.

Karl Koldewey had quoted some of Dante's descriptions of Hell to capture his horrified impressions of the land that Leif and I were now dazzled by. Of course, Koldewey had had no dogs, no radio, and no other humans within hundreds of miles. Suffering from malnutrition, Koldewey had been in snow four feet deep when attacked by a polar bear. He had escaped only by tearing off bits of his clothing, which the bear had stopped and puzzled over. No wonder Koldewey had considered this place to be Hades! And he hadn't had the benefit of learning about this area from previous explorers, as we had. Our knowledge had been greatly enhanced by reading about the experiences of Koldewey and the Danish expeditions.

By the time we had crossed that wonderland, a storm started to blow up. We were then well south of Margarine Central, and though we had not brought tents, we did not want to go back there. I decided to head to the coast where our ship had waited, in the snug harbor near 17 Kilometer Point, since the big storm when we first landed. I had dug up Eskimo ruins there, and now planned to put them to good use. The tarp I had with me would cover the small opening in the roof of one of the best-preserved homes. When we arrived, the storm had moved northward, so we just rested up. It was, however, comforting to know we could use ancient Inuit homes for our survival if need be. It was a tremendously empty land, empty of all civilization, yet ironically, a long-vanished culture could still furnish us with life-saving shelter.

From there, it was just six miles overland to Denmark's Harbor, and we sledded in fine spirits. I had read a bleak description of the marvelous land we were traversing. It may have been by a member of the Mylius-Erichsen Danish Expedition of 1906, but in any case it went like this:

[. . . a] wasteland, and barren country, deserted by God and man. Vast gray stony surfaces, relieved here and there by a hill. Here and there, decomposed rock, emerging up from the sand. Or near the shore, some Eskimo ruins, which makes the depressing feeling of death and destruction even more unendurable—thus appears the coast . . .

This was not our impression of it at all. We were having fun, but that was because we had comrades, and well-stocked stations, unlike our famous predecessor, Mylius-Erichsen, who had died somewhere in the area.

Reaching Denmark's Harbor, we expected a deserted station, but a tiny wisp of smoke drifted up from the main hut, and we noticed another change in the hut's appearance since we had last been there: The door was filled with the protruding sharp ends of spikes, and a square of shiny aluminum glinted at us from the center of the door. As we came up to the hut, a voice from the roof greeted us. It was Alvin Pedersen, the famous Danish zoologist who had come with Count Knuth's ship.

Alvin explained that he was there on a specific mission: to take photos of the polar bears eating. Apparently, no one had ever done that before. He had left a rotting seal carcass to lure the bears, and then he would photograph them through an aperture cut in the door. The patch of aluminum on the door was designed to reflect the camera's flash outward. He had been afraid the flash might anger the bears, so he had spiked the door shut, and had then driven more spikes through the door so if bears tried to smash it in, the pain in their paws would discourage them. It was an old trick used by Scandinavian mountain folk.

We had to enter the hut by the trapdoor in the roof, usually reserved for when deep snow nearly covered it. Inside, despite the fact that the hut was filled with smoke, it was still cold and damp. I don't know how anyone could have lived in there. The stovepipe was clogged with soot, probably from 1906! The pipe could barely draw, so the stove could only generate smoke, and very little heat. Pedersen was a good thirteen years older than I was and a veteran of half a dozen Greenland expeditions. He was a good zoologist, but knew nothing of stovepipes. We got the pipes cleared, and soon had a warm, smoke-free hut.

Pedersen had been told he would be picked up after a week. He had been there two weeks, was almost out of food, and was understandably worried and annoyed. Because he was a scientist, he had always been looked after on previous expeditions, and he did not know how to live off the land very well. I asked Pedersen why he had not hunted the herd of musk oxen that Leif and I had just passed on the hill. He told me rather sternly, "That is against the conservation regulations of Denmark, and I am an appointed game warden!"

The Danish regulation was only a guideline, but since Denmark had given me permission to do the expedition here, to ensure future expeditions, I said hastily, "Well, I only meant you could shoot one rather than starve to death." He told me, rather pompously, "Well, I'm not starving yet!" And this was true—he was quite overweight! I began telling him about the musk ox that had attacked me the year before. "You must have dreamed it!" he snorted. "Musk oxen never charge. They always go into their instinctive protective circle when threatened." I argued that the instinct to circle was for wolves, and works fine when dogs come at them, but Pedersen just smiled tolerantly, as if I, the young explorer, could not be blamed for such a mistake. I gave up.

We decided to take Pedersen on our sled to Eigil Knuth's station at Morkefjord. We mostly sledded cross-land, staying close to shore. It was obviously the route used by the Inuit for centuries, traveling through passes and generally following the path of least resistance. I was leading the way on skis as we took a short cut across a small bay that looked well frozen over and smooth. But soon we came to ripple-topped ice, which indicated that the surface was thin. Ripples caused by wind on water that has flash-frozen disappear as the ice thickens. I shouted frantically to Leif, who was inexperienced on such ice, to keep moving! Stopping would have placed too much weight on one spot, causing it to give way. He grinned back at me in his smart-aleck way and told me not to be nervous; I had to cuss at him to get him to understand the gravity of the situation. When he saw fine cracks appearing beneath his sled, he lost that youthful, know-it-all grin, and snapped his whip furiously above the dogs. It was bloody tense going. Even the dogs seemed to be holding their breath until we reached shore. I didn't have to bawl Leif out. He was white as a sheet.

Not long after, we came up to the top of a narrow pass, and encountered a small herd of musk oxen blocking our path. They showed no intention of moving, dogs or no dogs. There were seven of them, including one very large bull. Hoping to use this as an excuse to get some much-needed fresh meat for the dogs and ourselves, without getting Pedersen upset, I suggested I shoot one to disperse the herd.

"Nonsense!" he said. "I will merely drive them away with a clap of my hands."

He walked ahead of us about fifteen yards, stopped, and loudly clapped his hands. Like a well-rehearsed comedy, the big bull charged him, with the whole herd behind their leader! Pedersen came running toward us, his overweight, heavily clothed form moving with unaccustomed speed as he shouted desperately, "Shoot! Shoot! For Christ's sake, shoot!"

The bull was catching up to him quickly, but there was too much chance of hitting Pedersen with our guns. The herd would soon be upon us. I grabbed my knife and cut the dog team loose. The dogs dashed forward, and the musk oxen slid to a thunderous halt. Quickly, they formed their instinctive, protective circle. The bull stood just outside the circle, head lowered, ready to do damage. I dropped him from just a few feet away. Leif shot another, and I one more. Still the other four did not disperse. I looked at Pedersen. His face was white from fear-caused anger. He shouted, "Shoot them! Shoot them all!" So we did. Pedersen thanked me for saving his life, adding with a laugh that he would rewrite his data on the habits of musk oxen. But believe me, I would learn much more from him than vice versa.

It would have been impossible to carry all that meat. The sled was already overloaded with Pedersen's cameras and other equipment. We cached what could not be carried under a pile of large stones, and marked it with a bamboo stick topped by a red flag. This is what arctic travel is all about. It is not dehydrated packs bought in a fancy sports shop. Oh, we had those, too—but we would not get many calories out of them!

Late in the night, we reached an empty trapper's hut at Snenæs. We set some more hunks of meat under heavy stones there as well. It took another long day of sledding across cold and barren land to reach the camp of three Danish trappers who had arrived with Count Knuth's expedition. The leader was Kristian Jensen, who would later be a leader of the famous "Sled Patrol" during World War II. They had been on their way to fetch Alvin, but had first needed to stop and hunt, as they had run out of meat. Of course, when they had not needed the meat, there had been plenty of musk oxen around. Obeying the Danish regulations, they had waited until they were out of provisions to look for herds, but then none could be found. We told them about our cache, and though it was late at night, two of them took off immediately in sleds in the direction of where we had come.

Reaching Morkefjord ("murky fjord"), I realized it was so named because of the silting caused by a nearby glacial river. One could see that the station looked much like Micardbu—radio aerial antenna and all—although the geography was markedly different, with mountains towering nearby. Knuth congratulated me on the establishment of the northernmost station. Knuth and I were always very cooperative with each other. We talked long hours about archaeological diggings we had each done separately. I drew him maps of the coast of Germania Land, and the interior Leif and I had recently crossed, and Knuth did the same for me of territory he had just explored. Knuth, Eigil Nielsen, and cartographer Svend Solver would over the next year cover hundreds of miles by sled up and down this unknown coast, vastly increasing man's knowledge of one of the last "dark" areas of Greenland.

Knuth had originally hoped to use the floatplane—now returned to Denmark with the *Gamma*—to determine if the fabled "Fata Morgana" (Phantom Islands) existed. Several early expeditions on ships had mentioned seeing what looked like islands somewhere between Spitsbergen and Greenland. But later expeditions, whose members looked in the same area where the islands had been reported, found none. Lauge Koch's aerial photographs had shown nothing. It was an intriguing mystery. Naturally, I wanted to be the one to finally solve the puzzle of these "Fata Morgana." Twenty years later, I would find myself on one of these islands.

The cooperation Knuth and I enjoyed was not shared by all the members of the two expeditions. The station's dogs got in a heated fight over one of my dogs, the flirt, Miss Hansen. Labb, who usually was above such uncouth behavior, got into a scrap with some of Knuth's dogs over the pretty hussy. Being so large, he just waded into the pack, but this proved his undoing. A much smaller mutt reached up with his mouth and firmly secured Labb's scrotum. The mutt did not bite, but Labb froze, as if a statue, with one leg in the air. There was nothing any of the men could do but watch. Finally, its point being made, the dog released Labb from his undignified position. Labb slunk back to the sled to reassess his dignity.

Kristian Jensen arrived, announcing that he and another trapper were heading north through a pass to Flade Bay, a distance of about thirty miles; he wanted to know if Leif and I wanted to go along. As this would take us to the other side of the ice-capped, flat-topped mountain behind Micardbu, through territory we had not yet seen, we readily said yes. Our route went north through a pass over the highest range we had seen on the fist-shaped peninsula that makes up Germania Land. An interesting rock formation that looked just like the profile of a man was located in this pass. Knuth called this "Michelangelo's Statue," and it was quite impressive to see in such an unpopulated land. Labb barked at it as the sled passed beneath this "face." From there on, it was relatively easy going, and very pretty country. We arrived late in the evening at Flade Bay, which was frozen over. Judging from the records of the past few explorers who had come in the summer months and had seen Flade Bay, it may have been frozen solid for centuries.

In the morning, a light, gentle snow had begun to fall. Leif and I headed across the ice to go around the northern tip of Germania Land. While the glacier only capped the mesa behind Micardbu, here it was present all the way down the slope of the mesa to the sea. Its slope looked inviting, and the top was not much more than a thousand-foot elevation. A cloud hung at the top, but I decided we should go up and over it, thereby taking a shortcut down into our home range. We made good time until we suddenly came upon a gaping ice crater, almost a funnel. We peered into it with awed respect, and decided to go a bit slower. The snow fell thicker and heavier, until visibility was nil. Heavy snowflakes muffled all sound. The thought of another ice crater slowed us to a crawl. What should have been a quick climb to the top was taking a long time, and since we didn't have our tents, I decided to build a snow hut until the storm stopped. I did not want to make the downhill ride in zero visibility.

I knew we had to be near the plateau of the glacier, and not wanting to sleep on a slope, we pushed forward. We could barely see the tails of our nearest dog, but we had at last reached level ice. Suddenly, as if we had stepped through a stage curtain, we were in blazing sunlight! Behind us, a sky-high white curtain of gently falling snow ran north and south for miles in a perfect line. Turning around, we could not see through the snow, even though it was just a few feet away. But ahead of us we could see for miles, up and down the coast, and far out to sea. Though we could not see the house at Micardbu, we could see the spot on the coast where the station lay. Looking northeast, we could make out the promontory of Thomas Thompson's Ness, the only promontory in the area, and far north of that, we could make out the ice-covered Ile de France. Pleasantly stunned, we sat on the packs on our sled admiring the view and the phenomenon of the vast snow curtain behind us.

We found a gentle slope for our descent. Though there was not much snow covering the usually windswept, sea-facing slopes, we had enough to sled on, and descended the steppes in great spirits. Near the base of the great mesa, we came across another crater, about a hundred feet in diameter, this time gouged in the ground by the powerful water-melting action of a now-vanished glacial flow. The edge all the way around and down its slopes was sharp with rocks, and we were glad we had not come this way in the dark or in a blinding snowstorm. When we got back to the station and told the others about the snowstorm, they said they had had no snow all week, but had seen the curtain hanging there in the distance for days.

CHAPTER ELEVEN

The Forbidding Land

A round the middle of October, the temperature warmed, and rain fell for nearly three weeks—extremely unusual that far north. Kalle radioed that the surface of the bay ice by Koldewey was flooded in many areas, making travel difficult there, and sometimes impossible. I knew how he felt. Sledding was impeded on land near Micardbu as well. Then the temperature plummeted, freezing the land over with a thick, slick glaze. In the Arctic, rain and its inevitable after-freeze was feared more than snow. These periods were the most dangerous climatic conditions for travelers. Clothes got soaked, and then froze; sledding was often dangerous; and there was no snow to make igloos. The freeze-up also made the musk oxen move away from the coast. The frozen surface prevented them from getting to their food, forcing them to retreat to higher elevations where snow, not rain, had fallen; here, they would be able to dig through the surface snow to find their meals. Consequently, our meat supplies ran low.

About this time, I heard via radio from Knuth's station that they needed meat, and musk oxen were nowhere to be found. Because they had conscientiously followed their conservation regulations, the Danes now found themselves in a tough spot. Even the ptarmigan had migrated south early. Anyone with any sense was heading south! The ice stuck to our radio antennae wires, and then winds caused them to snap on more than one occasion. Repairing the lines in such conditions was hard and dangerous work because of the ice on the poles, but we had to keep sending weather reports, and we needed to stay in touch with Kalle, so the lines were always quickly put back up.

As mentioned earlier, this freeze-over phenomenon was probably the reason why the caribou had left this area in 1899, the year a large migration of herds was seen coming in on the northwest coast. Unable to paw down to their food through the concrete-like ice cover, they had had to move to land not subject to the rain-freeze cycle, which seemed to be accelerating around that time on the east coast. Count Micard and I had been reading some of the old books of that era, and we marveled at how the herds could have instinctively known they would find better pastures across the mammoth ice cap. We discussed the possibility of the herds using celestial navigation, and whether they had any memory of past migrations. All we could come up with was the obvious: Instincts are very mysterious and interesting.

The fact is that human instincts are sharpened when one is in the Arctic, particularly if one lives off the land. One's senses become more attuned to the surroundings. Often I knew the location of musk oxen before I saw them. It was not just that the senses of smell and hearing were heightened, but also that a connection was made between the nervous system and the environment. It was possible, then, that the caribou had possessed an even more finely attuned connection to the environment, and sensed a migration west was their best bet for survival.

There has also been discussion on the effects of polar magnetism on psychic awareness. Many arctic travelers have mentioned the same heightened perceptions as the ones I had developed. The famous arctic pilot, Sir Hubert Wilkins, is one example. He crashed his plane in the Canadian Arctic, and when the search was at last given up, his wife told the searchers she had seen her husband in a dream. She told them where to look, and there they found him! Out of all those millions of square miles, she had pinpointed his exact location. What does one say to that? Mental telepathy, however, is not a field I know much about, so I mention these phenomena simply as examples of how the Arctic induced a special sense of awareness in many of us.

Finally, Kalle radioed that the bay was frozen over, and he hoped canned goods and radio supplies could be brought down. The ship's crew had set trap lines along Koldewey Island, and established small supply depots, so they did not need meat. I loaded a good supply of musk oxen meat anyway. Then Leif Olsen, his accordion, and I made another sled trip south. We knew the way by then, and had an easy time of it. Reaching the ship, we found the ice was piled so high around it we could walk from the surface onto the deck.

Kalle and I had a private party, just two old partners shooting the breeze. We each had a beer, and as Kalle told me of establishing the trap line along Koldewey, the conversation turned to the Koldewey Expedition of 1869. We recalled one of the tragicomedies of that unlucky group. The Germans had believed that alcohol would prevent scurvy, and drank the pure stuff daily. Vitamin C was not yet widely known as the main cure and preventative of the debilitating disease. The expedition had had a terrible time just east of the island named later for Karl Koldewey. There they had encountered deep snow, the "swim-snow" Kalle and I had such a rough time with the year before, and the effort to walk through it exhausted them.

They finally reached the area we would later call Denmark's Haven, and then looked across the land my expedition now occupied. It was there that the leader had written nothing but those depressing remarks about what a "dreadful place" it was. Kalle said, "No wonder—they were tired and depressed, and they must have woken up each day with a hangover!" That expedition, of course, did not have any of the benefits we had, such as radios, or even maps. They had no real idea where they were or what lay ahead of them. When Kalle and I considered what they had gone through, we drank a toast to their unbelievable courage and accomplishments. Thanks to them, we were better prepared, not to mention—once again—that we had the psychologically liberating factor of radios.

I headed back to Micardbu, leaving Leif and his accordion there to help out. I brought back Snarby, the engineer, so he could have a change of scenery from the ship. We had a fine trip over the land Koldewey had said was a "dreadful place, where no humans could live," and which the Danish Expedition—I think—called "waste and barren, deserted by God and man."

Micardbu was prepared for winter. Nils Nois had set his trap lines. The station was running smoothly. Everyone had worked long hours every day, and it had paid off.

Hatlevik stayed busy with his cosmic ray apparatus, counting the arrival of particles from outer space. Daily, for long hours, he stayed glued to his desk, recording each *ping* that announced another arrival. In the 1950s, the American scientist, Dr. Van Allen, realized that these *pings* were coming from a layer far above the earth now called the Van Allen Belt. He called them the "birth pangs of the Universe." His work was very impressive, but I think my team may have been the first to hear them.

Sometimes Hatlevik had only a few hours of sleep each night. He was so involved in his work, he never changed his Icelandic sweater, and after a while its arms and body were so stretched out that he looked like a creature from another planet. His tireless efforts and constant good humor made him a valuable member of the team. Hatlevik, by the way, would go on to become a top politician in Bergen.

Toward the end of November, Count Knuth, Svend Solver, and the two Inuit—Eli and Zachaeus—came by for a visit on their way back from establishing a depot north of Skaerfjord. Solver was a meteorologist, geologist, and cartographer. Arrangements were made with him and Knuth to be part of the historic trimetric photography planned for the aurora borealis. Through radio contact between Knuth and Solver at Morkefjord, Kalle and Tillier on *En Avant!*, and Hatlevik at Micardbu, we would make several simultaneous, historic photographic shots. A triangle of the size suitable for the computation of the height of the mysterious northern lights would thereby be created.

Before he returned to his base, Knuth expressed concern over his expedition's lack of fresh meat, even as he said the problem could be remedied by fishing for Greenland shark beneath the ice of Dove's Bay. The men of Micardbu promised to help him out if his group really got in a jam. This type of cooperation was natural in the Arctic. The competitive spirit of civilization waned under the rigors of arctic reality. The true law of nature that Darwin revealed was the fact that the species which cooperates most effectively survives the best—not the one that is the most cruel or ruthless. Cooperation is what makes you strong, especially in the Arctic; that, and a good sense of humor.

The winter nights grew longer. Heavy snowstorms lasted for days, and then strong winds would blow the snow into huge drifts. When weather and light permitted, Nils Nois would venture out to check his trap lines. During one of the many times when Nils and I went out together, we arrived at the hut at Thomas Thompson's Ness and found the door had been smashed in by a polar bear. Once again, a bear had levied a tax for our use of its land. A big broken crate lay outside, and large blocks of goat cheese had been sampled, with huge bites taken from them. It was a reminder of the hazards of living in that true wilderness. We repaired the door, but took the remaining, tempting cheese with us. I cannot overemphasize the need for secure, undisturbed huts in times of emergencies. Imagine coming to a hut hoping for life-saving shelter only to find the door smashed because a bear could smell some stinky cheese inside.

In the deep darkness, especially during storms, we usually stayed put at Micardbu, snug and secure. Sigbjorn Aamodt had to go out daily, even in blinding snowstorms, and walk the fifty yards to the small weather box to take readings and precipitation samples. He had a guide rope so that he would not get lost.

Even though polar bears were not expected at that time of the year, after his scary encounter some months before, Aamodt always carried his rifle.

One may well wonder how we were able to be in such cramped quarters for so long without getting on each other's nerves, or even going a bit mad. The fact is that such conditions were quite normal for Norwegians. All of us had, at one time or another, spent days, or even weeks in tiny huts in Norway's mountains during ski trips. In other words, we were raised to put up with such conditions. But, perhaps more importantly, Norwegians traditionally have a philosophical attitude more akin to paganism, or naturalism, than Christianity. We are fatalists. We love life, but believe in fate. Adversity is to us just another interesting challenge to overcome. Complaints only give the complainer a bad reputation, and a reputation, as the old Viking saying goes, is the only thing left of you when you die. Having a good sense of self-deprecation helps as well; you cannot take yourself or your position in life too seriously under arctic conditions and expect to maintain good mental health. During one of these dark periods, Kalle radioed that the ship was again in dire need of some radio tubes since some of them were failing. I did not enjoy going out in such conditions, and if it were not for science, I would not have. I grumpily harnessed my team in the pitch-black, frigid day, and wondered why I was in such a very un-Nordic-like mood.

The journey seemed ten times longer in the dark. The lack of sunlight drained all of my energy and motivation. I felt old and downcast, and I was beginning to understand a little bit of how the early explorers must have felt here. The old hut at Denmark's Haven looked like an icy mausoleum, deserted and depressing. Heading for the frozen bay, I saw my salvation. During low tide, the ice attached to the shore also moved lower, breaking away from the shore and exposing a temporary sliver of open water. At this gap I found clumps of fast-frozen seaweed. These were mostly the type with bulbs of air on their fringes, called bladder wrack. The next incoming tide would shove more seaweed up between the land and ice, until the ice at high tide froze solidly again to shore. Knowing that part of my depression was from lack of vitamins, I ate the seaweed like candy, and it was amazing how quickly my mood improved. Early explorers, not knowing this trick, had died of scurvy while surrounded by masses of frozen seaweed.

Crossing the ice at Denmark's Haven, I had to be alert during every long, agonizing moment of the six miles in case the eddying currents there had scoured open a water hole. It was a great relief to reach the ship. This time, the ice was so high around *En Avant!*, I had to step down to the deck. The crew was in good spirits, but I did not see young Olsen around. Kalle explained to me, "We put him down in the hold where he can practice that damn accordion without driving us crazy!" I took the hint: Olsen was to return to Micardbu with me.

On the trip home, we sledded on the sea ice along the coast north of Margarine Central. It was dark, and the going was rough. I was on skis in front of the dogs, while Olsen drove the sled. Suddenly the ice gave way beneath me and the team. A large slab of ice, made thin by some current beneath it, broke away from the thicker ice, and the dogs and I were descending slowly as if on a sidewalk freight elevator. The dogs immediately began to fight, as if they blamed their leader for not seeing the thin ice. Snarling, biting, and thrashing about in the frigid water, the team began to get tangled around me. Olsen was holding the sled back with all his great strength so it too would not plunge in, taking me and the dogs down with it.

In the mass confusion, I had to reach beneath the water, which by then was up to my waist, to undo my skis. The bindings were tight, and the dogs bounced against me. I finally got the skis off, and was able to haul myself up on the hard ice. With Olsen still holding the sled with all his might, I cut the dogs free of it, and helped them get back on firm footing. The name-calling and placing of blame continued there, and it was only with some well-aimed kicks to their ribs that I got their attention. Olsen tied the harness back to the sled with a crude knot. I dumped the load of provisions off the sled because we needed speed. I was beginning to freeze up! We took off at a good clip, the dogs' fur frozen, and my legs and waist wearing a hard crust of ice. The ice had actually created an insulating layer from the freezing air, but I was fortunate that we did not have far to go to reach Micardbu.

Fortunately, all the days and nights were not quite so dramatic. There was time for relaxing, reading, and, for me, painting. The men stayed occupied with their scientific work, or repaired clothes, traps, and rifles. There was no end of things to maintain. We tried repeatedly to get the trimetric photographs of the aurora lights that we had so carefully planned for, but the conditions were never quite right. We were in constant contact with Solver at Knuth's station, and with Tillier, who had gone down to the ship, so that we would all be ready when the conditions were right.

In the meantime, single, and sometimes, double-position shots were taken, depending on which of the other stations was clear when we were. During this period, Bæck, the radio operator at Morkefjord, called us to report with great excitement that he had reached Copenhagen, Denmark, directly by radio phone. This was a scientific first in those days, and wholly unexpected. He was actually bouncing the signals off the stratosphere, something we had never heard of before. To us, it was nothing short of miraculous. On Christmas Eve, Bæck was able to make an historic phone connection to Denmark, sending greetings to family, loved ones, and an astonished nation. In those days, when a loved one went on an arctic expedition, those at home did not expect even a letter but once a year, and that, of course, happened only in the summertime when ships could come into the coast there. Try to imagine the surprise and joy of hearing news in the middle of the winter. Of course, we take such calls for granted now, but believe me, it was astonishing in those days. Meanwhile, at Micardbu we contented ourselves with messages relayed home via ships in mid-sea.

That night, after we had just eaten dinner and the kitchen was being cleaned up, William Jacobsen, the cook, said, "I hope you all don't mind canned pemmican for Christmas dinner. We just ran out of fresh meat!" The mountain of fresh meat had dwindled to nothing. We knew sooner or later it had to run out, but to hear this news at Christmastime! There was an unusually somber silence in the house. Arctic-toughened men tried not to sulk, but even so, Aamodt went sullenly out in the darkness to his weather station, forgetting even his now-beloved rifle. What a time to run out of fresh meat!

Suddenly Aamodt burst back in the door, shouting, "Musk ox! Grab your rifles!" He was greeted with hoots of derision. Nils Nois told him, "We don't fool that easily! I haven't seen musk oxen in weeks. They're gone for the winter." Aamodt assured us he was serious, and ran out again. We followed suit, carrying rifles. Through the thick snow we could see four musk oxen. We were believers! Christmas dinner so providently provided! And so the first, well-supplied Christmas dinner was had at the northernmost scientific winter station in the world. Jubilation reigned for days. Then came the New Year's festivities, followed by yet another celebration nine days later.

On January 9, a moonless, stormless, and fogless night, Micardbu, Morkefjord, and *En Avant!* were able to make the first triangulated photos of the aurora borealis as it blazed across the sky to the north of Micardbu. At two A.M., the aurora was so bright we could read the thermometer gauge easily by its light. Never had a herald of scientific achievement waved so beautifully and brilliantly across the sky. Hatlevik, who had so patiently stayed by his instruments for so many weeks, was silently delighted. Over the radio the men shouted congratulations to each other. At Morkefjord, Bæck said he would try to reach Copenhagen with the historic report, which he did.

Micard, forgetting his all-important financial support as usual, thanked me profusely, in a manner that only a true Frenchman can, for helping him to be present for this historic moment. Quickly, I got out his French tricolor flag and stuck its pole into a high snowdrift. We all sang the French national anthem. We then set up the Norse flag and solemnly sang Norway's national song. I said I thought we should also sing America's national anthem, on account of my nationality, but it turned out I was the only one who knew the words, and I was not going to sing alone with those merciless jokesters around—historic occasion or no historic occasion!

CHAPTER TWELVE

Where No One Could Possibly Live

S oon after that triumphant day, temperatures plummeted, reaching minus-fifty degrees Fahrenheit. A strong wind was blowing, forcing a two-week period of hibernation. In those conditions, exposed flesh freezes in just fifty seconds. The only thing I really remember of those two weeks was that the recording I had received in England from Anita was "accidentally" dropped by Aamodt and broken. He pretended to be sorry, but I knew the rest of them were sick of me playing it during those two weeks of confinement. I told them cheerfully: "Oh, no problem, I have another copy. And when you break that one, I have two more where you'll never find them!" They groaned. We had fun—most of us, anyway.

As soon as the monthly deep period of darkness ended and the moon showed itself, I went south with Leif Olsen to the *En Avant!*. There I exchanged Olsen for my brother-in-law of doubtful character. He was, despite his shiftiness, pretty good with the radio. My plan was to sled over to Morkefjord to see if Bæck could reach Norway by his radio phone. His intermittent success reaching Copenhagen intrigued me. I brought Tillier along hoping Bæck could show him how we could adapt our radio sets the same way.

We reached Knuth's station just before a strong storm blew up. Bæck was still excited over the success of the aurora photography, and was also anxious to see if his radio phone would reach the Oslo newspaper, *Aftenposten*. Incredibly, via a connection through Alesund, Norway, he made it. I asked the paper's switchboard operator for my friend, the reporter, Odd Arnesen. When he was put on the line he had no idea the call came from Greenland—the equivalent, at the time, of being told he had a call from the moon.

"This is Willie Knutsen, calling you from the northeast coast of Greenland!" I shouted over the radio. Of course, he was astounded. He said, "My God! Is it possible? Wait . . . wait a minute!" I heard him calling to others. Then he returned. "Willie, this is historic—the first phone call from Greenland to Norway. The world will never be the same!" I was sitting in a chair talking with Odd in Oslo, while an arctic storm swirled outside. It was absolutely astonishing. (Years later, in 1969, when man reached the moon, I was less astonished. In fact, a mere fifteen years after that phone call, technology had made such great leaps in the Arctic that I and other arctic men who had had a front-row seat to watch the new technology being tested in the Arctic were predicting the moon walk.)

Arnesen promised he would reach all the families of the expedition with the good news that all was well. It was a very emotional moment. None of us had dared think such contact with family and loved ones could be possible. In those days, we really were, relatively speaking, on the moon. Later, when the expedition returned to Norway, we found the story had made the headlines of *Aftenposten*, Norway's largest newspaper.

The celebration at Morkefjord went on for hours. The station gave me a bottle of aquavit, a strong, vodka-like drink, and Eigil Nielsen gave me a book on art. A day or so later, the storm broke, and when we stepped outside, we could see a low, thin bit of light to the south, a warm-looking, happy glow to eyes accustomed to weeks of darkness. The sun had returned! To the north, a bluish-black light, with hints of orangey red, hung close to the earth and appeared cold and gloomy. It was as if the dark arctic winter was signaling its displeasure at the sun's return from the south.

While Jess and I were on the return trip to the ship, heading across the bay through Far Sound, the sliver of southern light had disappeared. We traveled in a light fog through the dark. About halfway to the ship we passed North Orient Island, and then reached a tiny islet. I thought I saw the form of a musk ox there. We kept the sled and dogs back, and I went a few feet ahead to investigate. There on a small beach stood a bull, just three yards away. Aiming through the murky fog, I shot. Behind me at the same instant, I heard my lead dog yelp. The bull was still standing. I took another shot, and the bull dropped.

My first shot had ricocheted off the horns and winged my dog; fortunately, the bullet lodged just below the dog's skin, and I was able to remove it without too much trouble. The bull had been stranded on the island when the fall storms had opened up too much water in the ice; it was unable to reach land and migrate to winter grounds. When the ice was finally solid, it was too late to move. Puzzling over how the bull had been able to find food on the island, we discovered that it had been eating seaweed that was frozen in long, great clumps on the shore. The musk ox had made a deep walkway up and down the narrow beach, munching contentedly while awaiting the chance to reach the mainland in the spring. Bladder wrack seaweed is truly a fantastic food.

A happy ship's crew helped unload the meat. Though they had plenty of seal meat, musk ox was favored. We all had a celebration to commemorate the success of the aurora photography, the phone connection to Norway, and the return of the sun. In the morning, a break in the fog allowed another glance at the still-climbing sun. Each day, as the sun climbed up a new "Hen's Step," as the old-timers called it, it gave us renewed enthusiasm. I took advantage of the weather to head back to Micardbu with Leif Olsen.

After all the darkness, it was great to be able to actually make out geographic positions, even if dimly, such as mountains and bays in the distance. Reaching land at Denmark's Harbor, we found the weather was still good. I could see the tops of small mountains three miles to the north. At the peaks, strong winds blew puffs of powdered snow, making the mountains look like steaming volcanoes. I knew that could signal a storm coming, so we increased our pace. We pushed northeast to 17 Kilometer Point where I had dug up Eskimo ruins before.

There, Olsen and I set up an emergency depot consisting of food supplies and a tent set up in the wind-protected hollow of one of the ruins. The sudden storms on that coast had taught me we needed more shelters. We had not gone more than a few miles when snow indeed started to fall. With the wind velocity increasing as we headed north, we hoped to reach Margarine Central before we were caught in the storm. I had never before seen such a quick, ferocious change in the weather. The snow came at us in blinding blasts, and we had to lean far forward to keep from being blown over. Progress was measured in inches. We could not see our hands unless we held them directly in front of our faces. We did not know if we had yet reached Margarine Central, or if we had passed it. The wind then actually came at us so powerfully that forward motion was impossible. We had no choice but to erect our small emergency tent and wait out the storm.

The wind was now pressing down on us like a freezing, pneumatic crusher. Fighting to put up the tent, we had to kneel and crawl our way around. As we struggled, we had to yell to each other to be sure the other was still there, even though we were only a foot or so apart. The dogs tried to snuggle together around us, bumping us around. Using one hand, I would push one away as I held the tent with the other hand. With a shove, one dog would disappear into the thick blizzard, and then another would pop out of the white like an apparition. When at last the tent was up, we anchored the sides with hefty blocks of snow. Inside, we slid into our reindeer-hide sleeping bags and hoped the storm would not last all day. Labb stayed in the tent with us. The wind hit against the tent like massive, well-rounded fists, over and over with resounding, staccato *cracks* that sounded like a flag in a squall. The super-strong tent material stretched like a lung, first in, then powerfully out, but at a rapid speed. Snow was compacting into ice against the walls of the tent, building bricks. As these "bricks" built up, we soon realized we were being buried alive!

We hit our elbows against the walls to knock down the blocks, in an attempt to keep from being crushed in an icy mausoleum, but the storm never relented, and we wondered how long we could keep the ice walls outside from building up. Hours passed, and then the day was over, with no sign of the storm slackening. Body condensation began to dampen the insides of the bags, causing a loss in their insulation capability. If the storm kept up much longer, and the bags could not be aired, we were in trouble.

The tent's powerful slapping was unrelenting, and the ice kept building over it. I had a flashlight that of course had to be kept inside my bag to keep the batteries from freezing, and occasionally I'd shine the light to see where the building ice against the tent needed a kick or an elbow thrust. The day had passed, and soon, the night as well. The typhoon-strength winds rarely slackened for more than a few minutes, and then to just slightly lower velocity. A second day came and went. For food we had only a bag of dehydrated eggs, which we took small spoonfuls of now and then. Conversation was useless in the cacophony of the screeching winds and the slapping tent. Each of us lay in his own dark universe.

Finally, the fabric of the tent could take no more, and ripped across the top. The snow came in quickly through this ten-inch tear, but nothing could be done about it. The material would have to be held together to be sewn, and I always carried needles and strong thread on these travels, but we did not dare go outside in the subzero temperatures, and, I suppose, one hundred-plus-mile-an-hour winds. Damp as our clothes were from perspiration, the wind would have quickly frozen us clear to the skin. I made an interior roof by holding a blanket over us, and letting it freeze in the shape of a dome. We used Labb as a hot-water bottle, and he draped himself over us as best he could. He held still for hours so that we would never be without his protective warmth. We did not even dare think how the dogs outside were doing.

Every few hours Leif would shout loudly over the storm, "Willie, are you alive?" I would answer through the darkness with a laconic "Yes," not wanting to waste strength on speech. Then no words would be heard for hours. Sleep was fitful, somewhere between heaven and torture, as the mind tried to deny its terrifying encounter with the deepest forces of nature. In my dreams I saw tables well laid out with steaming platters of food, and a warm, sunny forest provided a backdrop for the feast.

On the third day, I lay in cold, damp misery. My veins and arteries felt like windblown glacial valley passes. My mind and body became more and more disconnected from each other. Well-dressed butlers, with kind eyes, now served the steaming platters of food, and pleasant conversation murmured reassuringly around me in a warmly lit, elegant, but cozy dining room. Then, at the edge of my reverie, I thought I heard the wind abate. I had had many clever illusions by then, and did not want to return to a torture of icy hunger and loneliness to test if what I had heard was real or imagined. It took all of my willpower to slowly, agonizingly extricate myself from the beautiful peace I had found in another world. But bit by bit, I realized the wind actually had slackened.

Over the infinite, painful hours, I had listened to the patterns of the wind against a nearby cliff. If there were many short pauses in the wind, but shorter than the length of the previous blasts, a return of horrendous power was signaled. I had learned this trick of arctic survival the year before from Kalle. This time, the wind's pauses gradually became longer than the periods of blasts, slowing to what would normally still be considered severe, but sounded like mere breezes in comparison to the past three days' hurricane-force winds. It was the break we needed.

Gathering all my strength, I yelled to Leif, "This is it! Outside! Quick!" Half dead, and dazzled by his own reveries, Leif still managed to scramble outside. He held the powerfully flapping edges of the ripped tent fabric together while I sewed from inside with numb, blue hands that just barely functioned, but functioned out of desperation. We finished, and Leif dashed in, just as the fists of wind returned in spiraling fury. The tent resumed its endless beating, but the seam held. We curled up in our bags in the dark, and let the dreams return.

Sometime hours later, I heard Leif calling me urgently. He had had a dream. His mother had appeared to him dressed in a white dress and shawl. She told him he could not give up, that he must not die, because his brother was at that very moment drowning. I told him it was only a dream, and to leave me to mine. I just barely heard him say sorrowfully, "I wish I had some aquavit." And then a little later, in a very weak voice, he shouted the best he could, "If I had some aquavit, I might want to stay alive."

It was then that I realized he really was losing his will to live. Alcohol was the last thing a man should drink in those horrible freezing conditions, but since it might well be the last thing he ever did anyway, I brought out from my sleeping bag the bottle the Danes had given me. He had not known I had the bottle, so he was pleasantly stunned when I handed it to him. I told him to just take a sip. We settled back into our private sufferings. After a few hours, Leif repeated his need for aquavit, and I handed him the bottle again; there was no sense letting him die unhappy, and the word *aquavit* derives from *aqua vitae*, or, the water of life—so who knew?

As the hours dragged on, excruciatingly complex thoughts tortured our every moment. At one point I was psychologically overwhelmed by the fact that I had once sledded over this area, happy, and laughing at the horror stories told by the last explorers to this region. A terrible thought flashed through me: I had the paranoid sense that I had been tricked into a false sense of security by some unknown, malevolent power. I shook off the horrendous implication. But my predecessors' words made chilling sense now: ". . . a waste and barren land . . . Eskimo ruins, which makes the depressing feeling of death and destruction even more unendurable . . . ," and "We are the first and last people who will ever see this dreadful place, where no human being could possibly live."

On the fifth day, the storm broke. The silence was numbing. We lay there for a long time, suspicious of the quiet. We finally crawled out of the tent, numb, stiff, and haggard, into a comparatively windless and dimly lit day. Still too shocked to feel jubilant about our survival, we stared at the landscape in disbelief. We did not know where we were. The ice storm had changed the topography, making rocky cliffs disappear into long, sloping ice hills, filling ravines and creating geographic confusion everywhere.

Next to the tent, the dogs slowly emerged from ice caves tailored to each individual animal by the force of storm and their own body heat. As the snow had piled and compacted around them, they had wriggled upward just enough to keep from being smothered, while maintaining enough snow insulation to protect themselves from the deadly, freezing wind. Two dogs did not emerge, however. What we had feared would happen to us had happened to them: They had been crushed flat. Beneath opaque slabs of ice we could see the grotesque forms of the poor creatures. One was old, and had been unable to struggle for its life; the other was young and inexperienced, and had died for the same reason. As our eyes grew accustomed to the light, and our wobbly legs developed some composure, Leif and I realized with grim irony that we were barely a hundred meters from Margarine Central! We staggered to it, and slowly dug our way to the door. Soon we had a fire going, food in our bellies, and finally, enough energy to feel jubilant about still being alive.

We finally reached Micardbu, to the great relief of our friends who had been in radio contact with the ship, and so knew we had not weathered the storm there. Micard was so relieved he held me by the shoulders at arm's length for a long time, muttering, "My dear boy . . . my dear boy . . . my dear boy." It was quite moving, to say the least.

Our disappearance had coincided with that of two Danes south of Koldewey Island, yet all stations had been frustratingly stormbound, and helpless to search for any of us. Svend Jespersen and Anders Johannesen were never seen again. In the summer, their sleeping bags were found floating in Roseneath Bay. The message was simple: Never, ever, ever get complacent in the Arctic.

Kristian Hatlevik took me aside to tell me another result of the storm he had learned of by radio. I waited a few days for the sun to gain more "Hen's Steps," bringing more psychological encouragement before I shared that radio message with Leif. For one thing, his mother had died, and for another, a fleet of Norwegian sealers had gone down at sea near Iceland in the storm. Eerily, his brother was among the many that drowned. Leif said nothing for days, then finally told me in private, "If it had not been for that dream, and the aquavit, I would not have had the will to make it that last, horrible day. I mean that." He walked away, and never mentioned the mysterious incident again.

CHAPTER THIRTEEN

A Hard Spring

I n March, the days were light enough so that we could easily see an open lead in the sea ice, two kilometers offshore. We knew it had been more or less open all winter, just the opposite of what one would expect this far north and on this coast infamous for its impenetrable ice. Since we were really the first to winter on the coast, we took pictures to verify the presence of the six- to ten-mile-long lead. It always astounded us to see it. We had had such a hard time penetrating these ice-locked waters even in late summer, and here was open water in the winter.

One morning as I stepped out of the station house, a strange light hung in the air. There was an orange tinge, with green blotches hovering here and there. There were also dapples of pale pink, and indeed all the colors looked a bit washed out, as if they were aquarelles. Stranded bergs on the shore looked like giant, colored plastic toys that had melted in a great fire. I had seen many of the wonderful arctic light phenomena, including the famous geometrically perfect sun dogs and moon dogs (bright spots caused by ice crystals commonly equidistant to each side of the sun or moon, low on the horizon), but this was sheer chaos, a riot of colors. Even the dogs whined. They may not have seen all the colors we did, but they were certainly noticing that something was unusual! Labb stood beneath one oddly sculpted berg and just stared up at it while the colors kept moving and changing. Then the colors began to fade. In a few minutes all was back to normal. I never saw such a sight again in all my years in the Arctic.

Nois resumed his hunting and trapping, as the storms seemed to have ended—at least for a while. With the longer days came preparations for exploration further north, planned for April. Though we no longer held hopes of establishing a station at our original goal of Ingolfs Fjord—almost two hundred miles further north in Peary Land—we wanted to familiarize ourselves with as much new coastline as we could for the next expedition, which we were already planning. These lands were so little known that we did not hope on our first year there to make but the most basic observations for mapping and geology, and with luck, to complete some preliminary archaeological work. But now that Micardbu was established, and also Eigil Knuth's Morkefjord, the pathway was made easier—so to speak—for others. Scientists could now come and concentrate on their specialty, rather than just struggling for survival. If all went well over the winter, in the spring some of us could sled for Ingolfs Fjord. We were feeling pretty self-satisfied, and figured that with the new reputation we had established for ourselves, support for further expeditions would be forthcoming.

But fate intervened.

One night, Micard was telling me again how fortunate he felt to be with us. Others had financed expeditions, but few actually went on them, and certainly not wintering ones. Micard, however, did not think of himself as courageous, but rather, fortunate for having come. While we were making plans for spring travel, Micard told me, "Willie, I would like you to promise me that if I should die on this trip to Peary Land, for whatever reason—" he paused, and said with a laugh, "perhaps old age—I want you to bury me up here. I am quite serious. You know my family would object, but I will put it in writing for you." Micard asked me to look at a sketch he had made. It was of a crude cross, with the lettering of his name and date of birth. He had indicated the date of death with question marks. He said, "Just fashion a cross from driftwood, Willie, and make a stone cairn over me. That would be the best monument I could ever have!" There was no sense telling Micard that this talk of dying and monuments was unnecessary, that there was no danger inherent in our travel plans for April. He was too deep a thinker to be psychologically coddled. I told him I would carry out his wishes if it became necessary.

This was followed by another period of heavy snowstorms that kept us housebound. One day, I was in the storage space in the loft, searching for something or other. Of course the warm air from below rose to this area, and it was very hot as I rummaged around. I could hear the reassuring *putt-putt-putt* of our gas-powered generator in its own room below. After about fifteen minutes, however, I could not remember what I was doing there, and felt light-headed. Going back down the ladder, I almost fainted upon reaching the floor. Nois, who had been standing by the door getting some air, grabbed me and threw me out into the fresh air. Soon another person lay next to me. It was Hatlevik, looking white as death. I staggered to my feet. I had figured out the problem. Our house was filled with deadly exhaust fumes from the generator! I went in to turn off the generator, and to help Nois who was carrying out our half-dead friends. Rushing to Count Micard's room, I threw open the door. He looked up from playing solitaire by his window, and said, "Why, hello, Willie! *Mon Dieu!* You look awful!" His room had been the only one spared the noxious fumes.

It turned out that snowdrifts had slowly built up over the end of the exhaust pipe that stuck outside the wall. The heat had formed a tunnel downward, the fumes had found an opening between the walls, and had entered the house that way, slowly poisoning the house. For days, those who had been poisoned suffered heart palpitations and pounding headaches. In my pain, I tried not to imagine Micard the only one left alive, fashioning crude crosses for the graves of the rest of us, instead of us fashioning one for him.

Knuth showed up again, with the Greenlanders Eli and Zachaeus, from a sledding expedition to the North. His whole group at Morkefjord had had a rough winter. Without fresh meat, some of his dogs had grown so hungry they had broken into a cache of salted fish. Five had died from intestinal distress as a result. Other dogs had simply disappeared in storms, and some in open water holes in the sea. Without sled dogs, his goals might be sharply curtailed, so Micardbu made him a present of four of our dogs. He said he would never forget it. I reminded him of what his team had done for us. He said, "That was just a radio, and some photography. These are dogs!" True arctic men know what is really important in life.

On the first day of April, Nois returned from a trip to Thomas Thompson's Ness. He told me to follow him with my sled. He had shot two polar bears, and when we arrived at his kill, we found four live young cubs beside the dead mothers. We put the cubs in a wooden crate we got from the hut, and carted them and the fresh meat back to the station. This was our first fresh kill in weeks, and the station was elated when we returned with the meat. Count Micard had Jacobsen fix him some steak tartare—ground, raw meat, with a raw egg cracked on top. This was a Parisian favorite, though polar bear was an exotic adaptation to the recipe. That polar bear meat could contain a variety of the trichinosis larvae was not known to us at the time.

Sure enough, Micard soon fell ill. He was suffering from abdominal cramps, and he could not urinate. But it was not trichinosis—Micard was fast getting uric poisoning! His belly became swollen, and he could not help occasional screams of agony. Radioing to Norway for emergency medical instructions, we were told to catheterize him. We had a catheter, but none of us was trained in its use. Micard convulsed with unbearable pain when we tried to insert it. Helpless, we gave up trying.

We took turns sitting with him, talking to him when he was able to listen. Usually the cook, Jacobsen, stood guard during the day, looking in on the count from time to time from the kitchen. By night the others took turns staying with him. His yells of agony penetrated every corner of the house, and all the men's hearts went out to him. He and I tried to make jokes to keep our spirits up, but he had lost a lot of weight, his eyes were yellowed, and his skin had a deathly looking tinge. His suffering was nerve-wracking to watch, and his pain, so apparent, almost entered my own body. Micard, even in his agony, was sensitive to this and was touchingly sorry for the "problems I am causing the expedition." He told me I must go on with the expedition northward, since there was nothing we could do for him. He felt he was just a burden. But how could I concentrate on exploration knowing he was suffering? I told him I was not going anywhere until he improved. I meant it. What was the use of exploration and science if the suffering of a friend could be dismissed as unimportant?

A few nights later, his eyes dark from the suffering, he took my hand. "Willie, I beg of you, kill me! Put a bullet in me. I cannot stand the pain."

"Gaston!" I protested.

"I have written a letter absolving you of all blame. Please call in Jacobsen as a witness."

My protest only brought on more courageous assurances that he knew what he wanted. I brought in Jacobsen just to calm Gaston, but his letter was not signed by us as he wished. Instead, I told Aamodt about the situation and asked if we could get a rescue team together via the radio to Norway. After all, this was Count Micard! All of France and Norway and the world knew we were there, and there had to be some way to mobilize help for him.

A few days passed, with Micard sinking closer to death each day. Finally, a message arrived that a rescue plane might be brought by ship as far as the pack-ice belt. The message said that if a landing strip could be prepared, the first plane rescue to Greenland might be attempted. Over the radio I told them about the open lead offshore from us, but they thought I was crazy, and said so. Not one of them had ever been there, but they were all "experts." Suppressing my anger, I told them we would prepare a landing strip. Then I was told there was a catch. "Who was going to pay for this?" they asked.

Not able to believe my ears, I told them, "Micard, of course."

"Could you guarantee that?" they asked coolly. Steaming, I went to Micard.

I told Gaston the good news first, then hesitantly, told him about the money angle. I had never seen Micard curse, or even truly angry, but sick as he was, he sat up in a fury. Pounding his chest with one fist, he shouted, "I have always paid my way! We left Norway with headlines! Every banker in Norway knows me, and my credit! Who are these bastards? Money is discussed after the life is saved, not before!" He swore like a sailor, "Have these cretins never heard of making arrangements with one's bankers? Tell the bloody vultures to phone my bankers. It is nothing! The payment will be guaranteed!" Then he slumped, exhausted, back on his pillow.

Aamodt, who had heard all this, angrily repeated Micard's instructions to the radio operators.

Micard told me, "Willie, I know it is a lot to ask of you, especially since you are ready to head north to Peary Land, but I must tell you the truth: I would like for you to accompany me back to Norway. You give me strength. I am a bit superstitiously afraid that if we part, the cord of life will be broken, and I will not survive long enough to reach a hospital." It killed me to think of curtailing my plans, but without hesitation, I said, "Of course!" He was not fooling about his health. His eyes had just a tiny spark of life left, and were frightening to look into. If Micard's "superstition" was keeping him alive, then naturally, I would accompany him home.

A floatplane from Wideroe Airlines, which still operates in Norway today, was put aboard the *Vesle Kari*, and the ship headed for Clavering Island. Though the men at Micardbu were sure the plane would be able to land on the lead that had been open for months, just in case, the whole station went to work leveling a makeshift landing strip. We dragged a wooden beam across a level field of ice to smooth it out a bit, filled in ruts with snow, and then tightly tamped down the fill snow. It was long, laborious work, but we had plenty of time. The ship had to cross the sea, and then penetrate the pack ice.

Micard had become a mere skeleton with a grotesquely swollen abdomen. Every night I sat with him, told him of the day's progress with the ship, and the landing strip. I told him he must not die, as it would make me look bad, and this brought a smile to his face. "I will try not to ruin your reputation, though otherwise I would happily die. This is truly awful."

By the middle of May, with the whole station ready to collapse from tension, the rescue ship had succeeded in reaching an open spot of water near Shannon Island. Kalle arrived by sled with the Dane, Gelting, who had come to *En Avant!* from Knuth's station. Gelting had letters and scientific dispatches he wished the ship to carry back to Norway, and then sent on to Denmark.

Kalle and I went over plans for him to take over the expedition's leadership role when I was gone. Aamodt would be in charge of Micardbu, but under Kalle's command. Kalle told me that my returning to Norway was a golden opportunity to get working on new support programs for next year's expedition. He was trying to cheer me up for having to leave, but he also had a point about the value of my early return.

If Micard's deathly sickness and my having to leave the expedition for an uncertain amount of time were not enough, Aamodt called me into the radio room. "Willie, I think you'd better hear this." He took off his earphones and turned on the speaker. I was shocked to hear Tillier talking to a Dane, Elmer Drastrup, at Morkefjord. I heard Tillier plainly say, "This is my chance to take over the expedition. None of these bumpkins have what it takes to run this show. Uneducated, every one of them! And Willie is weak. He treats these classes like equals. He'll not have their respect that way. And he is only going back with Micard so he can be with his fiancée! He can't take the strain of isolation away from girls!"

We heard them laughing, then Tillier continued in a spiteful tone. "Willie goes back to civilization, and we're left here to do all the work, and he'll get all the credit."

I turned to Kalle. "How long has this been going on?"

"Oh, he mouths off all the time about how he's a lawyer, and trained in leadership, while you and I are just naive adventurers. The crew and I did not want to say anything. After all, he is your brother-in-law."

I took a dog team and lit out for the ship. When I arrived, I went right up to Tillier. I do not remember ever experiencing this level of anger before, and certainly never as much as I felt at that moment. I blasted out, "You are fired, you back-stabbing son-of-a-bitch! You are a phony! First, you crash my plane — now you plan mutiny. You are fired! We will feed you until the expedition returns, but you are only to sit on your ass until then! Do not touch anything. Do not touch the radio! Do not leave the ship. You are under arrest! This is my land, and I am the law!"

I looked around at the crew, all trying to suppress grins. "Everyone understand?" They mumbled yes through teeth shaking with repressed laughter. I would have laughed too—I have to admit, telling Tillier off was a good feeling—but I had to play at being stern. I jumped back on my sled and headed for Micardbu feeling light as a feather. And it *was* my land that I then sledded over, at least as far as Norway was concerned I legally owned it, from Cape Stensby, south of Margarine Central, to Thomas Thompson's Ness—in other words, almost the whole coast of Germania Land, a fiefdom of 350 square miles! And, by the agreement of 1924, even Denmark had to allow that. Until the matter of national ownership was settled in the World Court, I was the rightful owner of the coast of Germania Land. Now the problem was, how long could I hold my rights? I would have to possess or make use of the station. An absence of five continuous years was grounds for loss of ownership. And here I was, headed back to Norway with the financial backer of my private fiefdom. Though I planned to return as soon as possible to Micardbu and my team, I was worried about the war spreading in Europe. Anything could happen. It would be a terrible blow for me to have to give up my so recently and dearly won fiefdom. Of course, the exploration and scientific research was what was really important and interesting to me, rather than the ownership. I had only used my status to impress Jess, and from the shocked look on his face, it was obvious he had not realized my exalted—though perhaps fragile—legal tenure as lord of the manor.

The plane coming for Micard took off from an open lead 150 miles off Shannon Island on May 19, and headed for Micardbu. It was almost a two hundred-mile flight, and we watched the sky nervously for signs of bad weather, and kept a watchful eye on the open lead to see if it stayed that way. Finally, we saw the plane, a tiny speck in the vast sky, and soon after, it made an open-water landing on the long lead, much to the astonishment of the pilot, Erik Engnaes. The "experts" had told him this lead could not possibly exist. Upon emerging from the plane, he said, "This is the only open spot on the coast for hundreds of kilometers, and such a damn long lead, too!"

It was a historic flight—the first plane to land here, the first plane rescue in Greenland, and the first airmail to and from Greenland. Erik Engnaes and the navigator, Helge Bjornby, flew the count and I southward to the *Vesle Kari*, where a doctor awaited. From the plane I saw the glacial-topped mesa where Leif and I had stepped through the "snow curtain." Along the coast I saw where Leif and I had suffered so terribly in the storm, and where sledding trips had taken me to archaeological discoveries, to wonderlands, and to horror stories. That inhospitable strip of the coast of Germania Land belonged to me as long as I could maintain Micardbu. I saw an awesome panoramic view of the immense arctic land we had occupied in the name of science, and realized it was astounding we had ever considered we could do it.

PART TWO

CHAPTER FOURTEEN

War!

The "ambulance plane" had a tailwind and good weather. We reached *Vesle Kari*, harbored on the back side of Shannon Island, in one and a half hours. When we touched down in an open lead next to the ship, we saw the crew wildly waving their hats. When Count Micard was carried out of the plane they sent up a rousing cheer. Gaston looked bewildered. Pilot Erik Engnaes said, "All of Europe has been following this drama for days. This is history! I want to thank you for getting my name splashed in newspapers from Norway to France." Gaston looked pleased.

Dr. Blom Hartvigsen, seeing the count's yellow skin, immediately had him catheterized, which did drain the count's bladder, but the doctor said we'd better get back to Norway, and fast. Nature had other plans: As soon as the ship left the coast it was pinned in by ice. It took the captain, Johan Olsen, probably one of the most experienced in arctic sea ice, twenty-two nerve-wracking hours to get us loose and sailing again. Because of that delay, it took five days to cross the Norwegian Sea. Micard lay near death the whole way. And, as he had requested, I stayed at his side.

We at last anchored near Trondheim on May 26, and the floatplane was set immediately into the water. Two and a half hours later we landed in Oslo's inner harbor, where an ambulance waited dockside to whisk him to the hospital. Also on the quay was the count's sister, Madame Smet, newly arrived from France; there were dignitaries, the pilot's wife, crowds of cheering well wishers, and of course, a small army of reporters. The rescue had been more than dramatic: it was historic. The whole operation, from flying the plane from Oslo to Alesund where the *Vesle Kari* took it onboard, to the return flight to Oslo with Micard on board had taken just twelve days, and had covered three thousand miles. It was a record. The world was stunned that such a thing was possible. The rescue created a sensation, and beyond that, it created a clamor for air-rescue services in Europe; if it could be done in the farthest reaches of the arctic wastelands, and using a ship to boot, why not in Norway or other places with remote towns? It was the beginning of air-rescue services in Europe.

In Oslo I went to see Micard in the hospital. He had had surgery for kidney stones and his prostrate gland. He had nearly a cup of stones removed, and cheerfully rattled them for me when I went to visit him. The official word was that he would have died in two days had he not been catheterized on the ship when he was. He and Madame Smet were reading articles from some French newspapers. They were laughing when I came in.

A French newspaper known for stretching the facts had written a fantasy story of how the count had been dying alone in an old, windblown shack in the Arctic, abandoned by the Norwegian members of the expedition before he was rescued. We decided to counter the dramatic embellishment of the facts. A Norwegian paper published a photo we furnished of the count reading in his library at Micardbu. His French lace curtains on the window next to him gave a rather different impression of "the old, windblown shack." Micard was pleased and said, "Too bad the photo does not show my French cookies, French tinned pears, and Bordeaux wines!" I added, "Or most of us walking around in a house too warm to wear shirts!" All in all it was good fun, and it was great to see Micard smiling again. The downside was that some days later Micard told me with heavy heart that he could not go on funding the expedition. Of course I understood. He had first spent a fortune on my plans and ambitions, and now had used up another to save his own life put at risk by following my dreams. Few people had ever used their personal fortunes to such good use as he had. Arctic exploration was greatly advanced by this one man's generosity; he had done enough. I began to look for support elsewhere. I had to radio Kalle and the others with the bad news, though they took it pretty well. I think after a rather exciting year, we were all ready for a break from the breakneck adventure.

Kalle and the other expedition members came back to Norway at the beginning of August. I went up to Tromsø to greet *En Avant!*, and there we had a moving reunion. Labb leapt off the ship and charged to greet me. Their triumphant return made the front page of all the newspapers, and radio stations were there to greet the ship, but the expedition's arrival was overshadowed by the gathering clouds of war in Europe. Kalle and I, young and optimistic, kept reassuring each other we would soon be back at Micardbu. We even made inquiries in Tromsø about supplies for our trip back to Greenland.

Kalle had some bad news. He had learned that Gerhard Antonsen, "The King of Revet," had been marooned in a small trapping hut by a fierce storm up at Tyroler Fjord, far from his main cabin at Revet, when the wind had blown open the door, breaking the catch. Antonsen used his knife, jabbed into the door frame, to hold the door shut until he could fashion a new catch. One of those powerhouse punches of wind we knew all too well had blown open the door, and the knife had flown with eerie accuracy into "The King's" left eye! Antonsen had survived, returned home on the *Polarbjorn*, and was in Oslo recuperating.

After a week in Tromsø, at last I said to Kalle, "See you later, partner," and something like, "Keep the engines warm," and Labb and I returned to Oslo. I went to see Antonsen in the hospital.

He told me the whole story. When during the storm he had pulled the knife from his eye, not only did he become covered in blood, but because of some sympathetic reaction of his nerves, he also could not see out of his good eye. In the morning, when he had recovered from the shock, though he still could not see, he had hitched up his dogs, put himself in his dogsled, and covered himself up in furs and blankets. Because his dogs knew the terrain perfectly, and where each hut was between them and his main cabin, "The King" had simply told them to take him "home," and this they unerringly did. There, he was able to dress the wound, though he could still not see.

Because he had not made a visit to the Danish regional headquarters at Es-kimonaes in such a long time, two Inuit working with the Danes had set out to look for him at Revet. They never would have thought to look for him at Tyroler. When I saw him, the sight in his good eye had returned, and eventually he re-gained limited use of his injured one. In the hospital, Antonsen said to me, "The doctor told me that if I had received that wound in a city, with all of its bacteria and irritants in the air, I would have lost the eye. I roared at him, 'Hell! If it wasn't for my dogs, I would have lost my life!'" Antonsen had stayed eight years at Revet, simply because he could not bear leaving "his" dogs behind. They certainly had paid him back for his love.

After an emotional farewell dinner, Count Micard sailed back to France. I was soon busy looking around for sources of support for a new year in Green-land. I had a plan. Micard had given me legal ownership of all films and pho-tographs taken during the two expeditions we had gone on together. With the movie film from the first expedition, slides from the second, and a presentable collection of archaeological findings, I started out on the lecture circuit, determined to drum up support for the next expedition—not to mention the fact that I was broke and needed an income. Despite all the money Micard had given me for the expedition, I had forgotten to pay myself a salary! Fortunately the lecture fees soon provided me with a modest income.

Under normal circumstances, I would have been able to garner enough funds from various sources to re-supply Micardbu. I was now well known; my ship was paid for; Kalle, of course, was willing to go again; and I had received The Roald Amundsen Award for the second time. Then, in October, *Aftenposten* devoted an entire front page to me—something that had only happened twice since the paper had started in 1860. The other two recipients were Nansen and Amundsen, so I was definitely in good company, not to mention famous. I could not believe I was given the same high regard. This was like having the whole front page of *The New York Times* or the *Los Angeles Times* devoted to my adventures. Though I was obviously overwhelmed by the honor, I hardly saw myself in the same ranks as Nansen and Amundsen; nonetheless, with this level of publicity, further support seemed assured. I was confident I would be sailing back to my polar work in short order. The fickle forces of history soon intervened.

Back in September, the Germans had invaded Poland, England and France declared war on Germany, so arctic expeditions were no longer a priority. The *Aftenposten* front page in October still provided me with a few weeks of hope. By November, the Russians had invaded Finland, and all arctic expeditions were cancelled. The world was at war. Instead of preparing for more arctic exploration, I felt lucky to get on the lecture circuit. Naturally, my plan to visit my parents and Anita in England had to be cancelled due to the new danger to shipping lines. Plane travel was out of the question as well, even if I could have afforded it, which I could not at that point. I had a chance to see my folks in 1945, but I would not see Anita again for thirty years.

The lecture circuit kept me busy. At one particularly important event at Oslo University's lecture hall, which is the same auditorium used during the presentation of the Nobel prize, I was met outside by a small but irate crowd with signs saying NO CRUELTY TO ANIMALS! The famous *Aftenposten* article had included some of my sketches, plus the photo I had taken of the two polar bears that Nils Nois had shot at Thomas Thompson's Ness. In the photo, the four orphaned cubs lay curled beside their slain mothers. The photo had been included simply because it was a dramatic one, but was now being used by animal rights groups who were against further polar bear hunting, particularly up on Svalbard where decades of hunting had seriously affected the bear population. I lamely told the group it wasn't me who had shot the bear, and that the hunter had not known the bear had cubs. I then went inside to a packed house.

Luckily, in January, the Norwegian government asked me if I would sell my rights to my fiefdom on Germania Land. The government wanted to claim a weather station in that territory where national ownership had still not been established. With my land, Norway could have further claim to the region. I readily said yes, and I was given the token sum of twelve thousand kroner—about forty thousand dollars in those days. It was not much for a kingdom of that size, and with a modern weather station to boot, but I almost fainted with relief when I heard the news. I really had been quite without funds.

By the beginning of April 1940, Labb and I were in rainy Bergen, staying at the Hotel Norge, where I was to show the film and give a lecture to a sold-out audience. When I say rainy, I should point out that the unofficial symbol of Bergen is an umbrella. No one went anywhere without one. Even on a sunny day, businessmen, truck drivers, shoppers—you name it—all carried the famous symbol. Showers could fall in the blink of an eye due to the high mountain located between the city and the North Sea. I went to the lectern dressed in tails, top hat, gloves, cravat, and . . . umbrella, and received hearty applause for that final touch of proper dress. It was a long presentation, and the party afterwards lasted long into the early hours of the next day.

The photographer Eigil Halvorsen was there, as well as my good friend, Joachim Grieg. Joachim was a descendent of Edvard Grieg, the famous composer. Joachim had with him a guest, a friend he had attended school with in Switzerland and who had escaped Germany when the Nazis began to round up Jews for the gas chambers. His friend, Arnold, was part of a family of international investors, and was hoping to get to America. Meeting him really brought home the reality of the horror that was enveloping Europe. I learned from my uncle Johnsen, then the brewery master of the famous Hansa brewery, that while we enjoyed ourselves with food and drink, just outside the fjord in the North Sea, German and British warships waged bizarre sea battles: Each side politely took turns refueling at Bergen, or at any of Norway's other neutral ports, and then returned to the North Sea to do savage battle. It was getting light, and we had hardly gone to our rooms when the sound of bombs exploding in the distance rapidly grew nearer. I thought it was the Germans and the British. I looked out the window and saw people running through the streets, screaming in terror. German warships were steaming into the harbor, with guns blazing. Nazi planes flew overhead, dropping bombs. In a matter of minutes, German troops were unloading at quayside, and running through the streets!

No one knew if the Germans would soon be followed by British ships in hot pursuit, or if Norway had been invaded. With every hour it became more obvious that the Germans had no intention of leaving anytime soon. Because no channels of communication were open with the capitol, or the rest of the nation, rumors flew. No one knew if the king was captured or safe, if the English had come to our aid, or if we had been left alone to fight the might of Germany. Arnold was naturally terrified.

Labb and I went with Joachim Grieg and Arnold to Joachim's aunt's lavish villa where we hid out in the basement. It was stocked with hams, sausages, and hundreds of bottles of good wines and champagne. We stayed drunk and well fed for three days, then left with more provisions to go up into the mountains where we knew we could find summer huts to stay in. Cabins dotted the landscape there, and we found ourselves joined by several other men our age with the same idea. After three days of that, I decided to put my American citizenship to the test and return back down to town to see the American consulate. At that time, I believed Germany did not want to have any trouble with America. The others thought they would go back down as well, but Arnold decided to take his chances and walk to Sweden! Joachim gave him maps, addresses of friends and relatives, and hints on the best way to cross Norway. He eventually made it to Sweden, and eventually to America, where he would become a big name on Wall Street.

The American consulate, Mr. Dunlop, could not help much, though he was friendly and did his best. My papers were in Oslo, and all communications had been cut off, so he could not get hold of the embassy in Oslo. Mr. Dunlap, told me, "You have been in Norway all your life, and everyone knows you. The Norwegians will give you papers to cover you until you reach Oslo." He did not want to offend the Nazi invaders, as he thought they would soon leave. He was, after all, a diplomat. I went to the Nazi headquarters myself.

The Nazis easily believed my story of being an American, and amazingly, even knew of my arctic work. How else could they have known unless they had spies in Bergen for a long time before the invasion? But I did not think like that in those days. I was just glad they said I could go on to Oslo. They told me I should just show my American papers at the newly established Nazi headquarters there. It was a shocking thing to hear that the Nazis were already running Oslo. They said I was free to move about as I wished. They magnanimously said I was free to stay in Norway or to return to America. Germany had no quarrel with America, they told me, with seemingly honest smiles. I should have been suspicious.

I volunteered with the International Red Cross to help reunite families separated during the confusing terror of the invasion. More German ships arrived. A particularly ominous-looking one, painted black and gray for camouflage, was tied to the dock next to the old warehouses of the Hanseatic League. This league had been founded by Germanic merchants, and in 1370, they had extended their organization to Scandinavia. The Nazis used that fact as a propaganda tool, saying Bergen was really a Germanic city, and they were "liberating" it!

Early the next morning I was walking by the docks with Labb when I first heard, then saw a small plane diving from the sky toward the harbor. It did not look like any of the German planes we had seen. Then other similar planes followed behind the first. Then I saw the British markings. Germans on the dock were shouting and pointing as the first plane went straight for the dangerous-looking ship. It dropped one small bomb, which miraculously went right down the smokestack. The whole waterfront detonated in a blinding blast. The concussion knocked me flat, taking the breath right out of me. I thought I was dead. It felt as if my stomach had exploded through my skull. So quickly did it happen, and so hard had I been hit, that there was no sense of fear. When the air returned to my brain, Labb was whining and licking my face. He was low enough not to have been in the shock wave of the blast. To the sound of anti-aircraft fire, I got unsteadily to my feet only to be nearly run over by the fire chief's car, which came roaring along, followed by fire trucks with their sirens screaming madly. More bombs from the other dive bombers went off by the ship, but they were like firecrackers in comparison to the first explosion. Then the planes disappeared. The anti-aircraft fire went silent only to begin again as a single dive bomber suddenly screeched through the sky and dropped more bombs at the ship, which was already settled on its side. The plane shot away. Then came one more! It dropped its bombs, but to no avail, and then left.

The whole area along the quay seemed to have gone up in flames due to that first massive blast. Obviously, the ship, the *Konigsberg*, as it turned out, had been filled with ammunition! Fires raged through the mostly wooden buildings and homes. Screams of pain and death mingled with the roar of flames. German trucks passed by carrying bodies of dead and wounded German soldiers. Running back to the Red Cross headquarters, I found it packed with injured and terrified people.

An old woman told us she had lived just behind the warehouses where the ship blew up. She said, "I knew there was something sinister about that ship. I was looking out my window when I saw that plane come flying in. I thought it was another German plane, but then I saw it carried the British emblem. It dropped a little bomb that went right down the smokestack! I remembered that in case of bombing, one should get under a doorway, so I did; then the ship blew up. I watched one wall of my house collapse, then another, and then the third. The only wall left was where I stood. My family has lived in that house for generations. Everything is gone!" She paused, then with a twinkle in her eye said, "But thank God I saved my umbrella!" and she waved the symbol of Bergen proudly over her head like a sword. For the first time in what seemed an eternity, we all laughed. We laughed until tears ran down our faces. The old woman's courage and unflagging sense of humor renewed our faith in ourselves.

Germans began arresting city officials, thinking they had tipped off the British about the ship.

Getting to Oslo was not so easy. The railway to Oslo was too damaged to be used. Refugees had fled to mountain summer homes, or to tiny fishing communities up and down the fjords and coast. By incredible coincidence, I ran into George, the assistant engineer and hunter from my first year in Greenland with Micard. He was the poor guy Schjelderup had lowered over the cliff to collect goose eggs for "the most expensive omelet in the world." Happy to see each other, we teamed up because each knew the other could handle emergencies. George, who lived all the way up in Alta, had wanted to head north to Trondheim, but fighting was reported all along the coast, so he planned to go to Oslo and then take the train north. The first thing we agreed on was that it was time to get out of town before the invaders' shock from the ship's bombing wore off, and further reprisals started. A friend lent me a backpack. All I could carry was food and some clothes, and had to leave my precious film and slides behind. (I never saw them again.) George and I, and my constant companion Labb, hopped on the back of a truck heading east out of town.

The dirt road ended at a small fjord called Bjornefjord. There we begged a ride on a small ferryboat across to the other side; once reached, we took off at a fast walk to put as much space between us and the Germans. We were in fine shape for such easy walking. The next day we arrived at Hadanger Fjord, where we hitched a ride in a small skiff that was delivering eggs to remote homes. It would have taken a hundred times as long to walk around the fjord. We then crossed the land until we reached the next fjord. Not a single person was there, so we helped ourselves to a rowboat and crossed the fjord. On the other side we followed roads or foot trails until we came to another fjord where we either flagged down a small boat, or requisitioned one on our own authority. Most of the few people we ran into did not know we had been invaded, and when they heard, they gave us food for our journey. We hopscotched through the country-side in this manner for ten days, traveling a hundred miles down the coast. We went from fjord tip to fjord tip, from island to island, until we reached Sta-vanger, where I had relatives on my father's side.

An uncle owned a butcher shop and a grocery store. George and I were able to rest up there and hear the news. The king and his family had escaped, and were probably on their way to England. If we wanted to get to Oslo, buses would take passengers to where the rail still operated, sixty miles south, at Flekkefjord. My aunt gave George and I a good supply of food for the journey, and off we went. A group of about eighty travelers gathered by the buses to get passes; soon, the Nazis arrived to question us. A bull-necked German glared into my eyes when I told him I was an American. He was looking for signs of nervousness. I told his interpreter to call Bergen Gestapo Headquarters for confirmation that I was allowed to travel. In a few minutes the interpreter returned, whispered to the still glaring soldier, who then said in a more congenial tone that I could board the bus. I still did not wonder why I was able to move about so freely without papers.

All about us lay the evidence of war. Bridges were down, making the journey slow. Passengers would have to leave the bus, cross over the tangled wreckage in order to get on buses waiting on the other side. It had all been organized very quickly considering the circumstances. While crossing the last bombed-out bridge, Labb had a particularly rough time balancing as he made his way over the twisted steel to where a train awaited us. At last we arrived in Oslo, which was now an occupied city. German troops were everywhere. George and I said our goodbyes. I went immediately to the American embassy. Then, with newly issued passport in hand, I reported to the Gestapo headquarters, where strangely enough, they had been expecting me. They were extremely polite, and gave me "permission" to travel, even if I wished to go to Tromsø to reach my ship. They seemed damned well informed on the details of my life for having known me such a short time.

After I had been in Oslo for a few weeks, I was contacted by Adolph Hoel, the director of the Polar Institute. The Institute wanted to charter *Ringsel* to bring relief supplies to a Norwegian family at a weather station on the southeast coast of Greenland. The war had stopped supply ships from reaching them. Also, I was to bring two relief weather reporters—we called them "weather beaters"—who would replace the couple that would be going back to Norway. The war might be raging, Hoel said, but business had to go on. Hoel was also of the opinion that the Germans would soon have to leave. "The British will promptly drive them out," he said, adding casually, "War is just an annoying distraction in the long scheme of things." Micard had said something along the same lines. At any rate, I was now able to return to Greenland, courtesy of the Norwegian government. I was cautiously elated. There were those troublesome thoughts about leaving friends and family behind, but the truly harsh hand of the Nazis had not yet been felt in Norway, so I innocently prepared to go with a clear conscience.

On the streetcar en route to the Polar Institute, where I would sign the contract to go to Greenland, I was shocked to see posted in the advertising spaces over the seats several reproductions of my photo of the two dead polar bears with their cubs. These posters warned CRUELTY TO ANIMALS WILL NOT BE TOLERATED! and they were signed by the occupying forces of the vegetarian, Adolf Hitler. Mine was now a well-known face in Oslo, and an elderly woman sitting by me winked, but dared not say anything about the grotesque irony of the notices because two German soldiers rode at the end of the car.

Outside the doors of the Polar Institute, I was stopped by two young Norwegians. "We heard from friends inside that you are going to Greenland," they said. "We'd like to go with you. We want to get to England to join the Free Norway resistance!" These two men, Sundt Jacobsen and Hans Engebritsen, had been fighting the Russians in Finland, and when Norway was invaded, they had returned. Fresh from their fighting in the snows of Finland, they wore heavy sheepskin coats, and hatred for the Nazis shone in their eyes.

Since my ship was now chartered by the Polar Institute, I took them to Hoel to get his okay. He asked them why they wanted to leave, noting that the Germans would give them good jobs repairing the damage caused by the war. "We would kill ourselves first!" was their answer. Hoel tsked, and said the war would not last long, so why should they put their young lives at risk? He added that he could not risk the important mission by giving the young men official sanction to leave Norway. I suggested they come as guests of mine, which would leave Hoel off the hook with the Nazi authorities. Hoel agreed to this, but he still did not want the men traveling with me to Tromsø, as I was officially his responsibility until the mission was completed.

Back outside, I made plans for the two men to get to Alesund, from where *Polarbjorn* was to carry much of my equipment to Tromsø. I sent a telegram about the sailing plans to Kalle, who wired back that he had already prepared the *Ringsel* for departure because he had been ready to leave on a sealing trip to the Barents Sea as far back as March, when the fighting between the Russians and Finns in the area had stopped all hunting there. Therefore, everything we needed for Greenland was already on board our ship. A few days later, after an emotional farewell with my sister—Jess wisely did not bother to show up to wish me *bon voyage*—and friends, Labb and I were on the train to Trondheim.

A few hours outside of Oslo, the train suddenly halted. The bridge at Minnesund was down. Once more Labb and I crossed over twisted steel wreckage with the other passengers to the train waiting on the far side of the river. Hours later, at Trondheim, we found that the passenger ship, the *Hurtigruten*, no longer plied the coastal war-zone waters. Instead, we had to take an extremely slow train that wound through 250 miles of mountainous terrain to the end of the line, at the port of Mo i Rana. From there, Labb and I hitched a ride on a small fishing boat that was heading for Harstad, just sixty miles south of Tromsø. The boat would actually carry us over two hundred miles.

Our trip was lengthened because the boat had to hug the coast and sneak behind small islands that ran along the entire coastline. Though it was summer, the midnight sun was obscured by black, low-hanging clouds. The cold North Sea wind and rain cast a damp chill over everything. The high coastal mountains, craggy and magnificent in sunlight, were now half buried in fog. After a hundred miles, we came around a bend and saw through the gloom the smoldering ruin of the town of Bodø.

There did not seem to be a single inhabitant left in the town. Anyone who wasn't dead had apparently fled inland. Of all the buildings, only the old, granite customshouse by the docks still stood, and, further back, one wing of the small hospital. Not another building or house by the docks was spared! We were stunned. Why destroy a fishing village? The orangey glow from several fires along the docks made an eerie scene. As the ship drew closer, the lonely outline of a single person could be seen sitting on the quay with his head down. Behind him, the bleak, granite shore bathed in the hellish glow provided a heartbreaking backdrop. When we tied up to the quay next to him, the man looked up, then said with a tired, but still slightly sarcastic voice: "Well, well, if it isn't the great arctic explorer, and his heroic mutt, too." It was Captain Schjelderup!

I had not seen him since returning from my first expedition to Greenland. I had forgotten that Schjelderup's home was near Bodø. He looked ten—not the actual three—years older. He knew the ship's crew, and asked to join us. The *Quest* and another one of his ships were on sealing expeditions off the coast of Newfoundland, but he had another ship in Tromsø, and he was going to take advantage of the war to do some hunting in the normally off-limits areas.

"Greenland walrus don't know there's a war on, and I'll be the only one out there hunting them!" Schjelderup said. "And those damn Danish rangers with their rules and regulations are a bit tied up in Denmark with the Krauts just now." He laughed in his loud and fearless way. He hadn't changed a bit. Somehow, I couldn't help but admire his sheer self-confidence and bravado.

As we helped load his considerable gear already stacked on the dock, just waiting for the first handy ship, the sun peeked through the clouds, revealing more of the devastation of Bodø. A few Germans marched prisoners around the dock area.

"Polish slave laborers," grunted Schjelderup, then added, "The British had been using the port when the Germans came in. Don't know which side did the most destruction." The Germans ignored us. They looked almost as unhappy to be there as the prisoners did. Just before we shoved off, a young Norwegian girl ran to the dock and asked for a ride to Tromsø. She carried her new baby, which had been born in the undamaged wing of the hospital just as the other wing was hit by a bomb. She of course was taken on board. The ship's crew refueled by helping themselves to what had been spared in the fighting, and we sailed away from the sad scene. I had been to Bodø as a youngster to visit relatives; I was glad they had long since passed away.

The ship once again hugged the coast as much as possible, threading the islands to stay well away from open waters. We had been told that a tremendous battle had raged here between the British and the Germans. The voyage across any open water to the islands had everyone on edge. Submarines prowled unseen, and we could be mistaken for an enemy by either side. We diverted our attention from the danger by trying to think of a suitable name for the new baby. Someone suggested "Bombardina," and though we all laughed, the young mother thought it not such a bad name. Even along these sparsely populated islands, many tiny port towns lay in ruins, especially ones that had fuel storage tanks ashore. Columns of oily, black smoke rose up to the dark sky, marking where once quiet fishing villages had nestled along the rocky coasts. Reaching Harstad, the largest of the island towns, and where I had first met Kalle in more innocent times, we went ashore. Our fishing boat was finally at its home port.

The dock area was empty except for a few Germans who wandered about aimlessly, looking as if they were wondering what they were doing there. There was no food in town, and the townspeople were in a panic. They had forgotten how to feed themselves without a store to provide food. Schjelderup and I said good-bye to the others, and then went down to the edge of the water to do some fishing. The townspeople were going hungry even as the water teemed with fish! We caught enough to eat, simply by jigging. We found old tin cans, scoured them out with sand, gathered some driftwood, and made a cook fire on the shore. We returned to the dock to eat our improvised meal. While we were chowing down, scraping the fish out of the cans, Schjelderup laughed and said, "Look at us! The two ship-owning arctic explorers, living like a couple of bums."

It wasn't long before a small fishing boat arrived at the dock, and its single, glassy-eyed fisherman told us about seeing dead, bloated bodies floating in the waters outside Harstad. I found out much later that prior to the Allies' quitting of Norway, the German High Command had learned the British were readying to pull out of the town. While we had sailed in shallow waters to avoid just such craziness, a German naval task force comprised of the *Gneisenau*, the *Scharnhorst* and the *Admiral Hipper*, accompanied by four destroyers, attacked the shipping at Harstad.

On the morning of June 8, the German task force met and sank three ships, one of them a transport. The German ships also met and sank the British aircraft carrier *Glorious* and her two escort destroyers, *Ardent* and *Acasta*. Before *Acasta* went down, however, she made a torpedo hit against *Scharnhorst* and caused heavy damage; this caused the German fleet commander to cancel further operations, even though the Brits were now out of Norway. Except for some submarine action, this was the last naval battle of the Norwegian campaign. The battle for Norway was over. For awhile.

The fisherman talked of bloody seas, and floating, human carrion covered with flocks of frantically pecking gulls. He told his grisly stories with a strange, stuttering laugh. He had half gone mad! But we were able to get enough information out of him to secure a ride aboard another tiny fishing boat going to Tromsø. The boat was so small that just the three of us—including Labb—filled the deck. It was a slow ride, and a wet one, but a ride nonetheless. Reaching Tromsø, Schjelderup shook my hand farewell, and told me that for a city boy and an architect, I hadn't turned out so badly after all. This was high praise indeed from a tough old bird like him. He even patted Labb on the head! I never saw him again, but I would certainly hear of him and his arctic shenanigans many years later.

I went quickly to say my hellos to my relatives, and to commiserate with them over Norway's agony. The British had just left, and a few Germans had arrived. Kalle showed up and a bit nervously informed me that he now planned to take his wife and father with him to the United States via Greenland. "Well, skipper," I said, clapping him happily on the shoulder, "I didn't know how to break it to you that I had no intention of bringing the ship and crew back to Norway after our run to Greenland. Not as long as this damn war goes on! I am heading for the States, too, so this sure is good news!" Although we were happy about it, we had to keep this plan to ourselves. We did not want any of the crew blabbing in a pub!

The *Polarbjorn* arrived a few days later carrying Jacobsen and Engebritsen, the two men I had planned to smuggle out. Then it turned out that a Captain Von Krogh would also be aboard as a representative of the Arctic Bureau. I knew Von Krogh slightly. He had been aboard the *Vesle Kari* when it rescued Count Micard. I was told Von Krogh would technically be leader of the expedition that would bring the two replacements, Fidjeland and Hjort, to the Greenland weather station. I wondered why he had been assigned to this simple task of bringing two radio operators to Greenland. Did Hoel think we needed babysitting?

Von Krogh's father had been a famous admiral, and I worried that his sense of duty to family and country would make him look unkindly on my plans not to return to Norway with the ship after our trip to Greenland. At this time, I was convinced the war would be over in a few months. Von Krogh indeed seemed suspicious that Kalle's family members were making the trip, and Kalle's explanation that he and Ruth were newlyweds was not much of an excuse for a Tromsø boy. Tromsø women knew that to marry a seaman meant not seeing him for months, or even years. And if this was a sort of honeymoon, why was the father tagging along? Fortunately, Von Krogh was distracted when an Icelander suddenly showed up at the ship and asked if he could come as well. He was a shipowner who had been in the process of buying a ship when the war started. I speedily told him yes, and told the crew to go aboard. Von Krogh now had met someone more of his station—Norwegians could be very class-conscious in those days—and got into a conversation with the Icelander. That was the diversion I needed. I walked quickly to where Jacobsen and Engebritsen were hiding behind some crates of cargo, and told them of the problem with Von Krogh. There was no way I was going to let them down, so I told them to make their way out of town to a point nearby where a water tank used for supplying ships was located. I would meet them there. It was best to assume my ship might be under Nazi surveillance at the docks, but I doubted very much there would be anyone by the water tank. And even if Von Krogh protested, it would be too late for him to take his complaint to harbor authorities.

A storm broke out, which helped clear the dock of snooping eyes, and we slipped our ropes and headed out of Tromsø. Because of the thick cloud cover, it was fairly dark. When we stopped to take on the water, most of our crew went ashore to help get the water hose to the ship. Von Krogh was in his tiny cabin. The two resistance fighters slipped on board unnoticed, except by Kalle and me. I took them to the crew's quarters where a small door led to a storage bin filled with coal sacks and other supplies. In they went, and I closed the door behind them.

Once the water and crew were on board, Kalle headed the ship out through the treacherous currents that snaked among the islands. He knew these rather tricky waters well, and did not expect anyone would care to try to follow him. At last we headed north for Spitsbergen. It was four hundred miles away, and twice that far out of our way, but the direct route to Greenland was a battle zone, not to mention that because of the fighting, the only place to get enough coal for a possible wintering-over in Greenland was at Spitsbergen. The *Polarbjorn* was headed there for the same reason.

The heavy cloud cover protected us until we were far out to sea. A startled crew member came to tell me that two dirty, dangerous-looking stowaways had just emerged from the hold next to his bunk. I introduced him and the others to the resistance fighters who had finally come out for some air. When they came on deck, Von Krogh was still asleep, but suddenly, like a scene from a movie, a small German plane came through an opening in the clouds. I told all unauthorized passengers to go below so the pilot would not report I had a large group on board. The plane buzzed us, but was not amphibious, so it could not land to search us. It circled us a few times and then headed back in the direction of Norway. I worried that it would radio for a seaplane. The heavy clouds returned, however, and kept us hidden until we arrived at Longyear Bay on Spitsbergen, the main island of the Svalbard group.

Svalbard is an old Viking word meaning "The Land of the Cold Coasts." Russian monks trying to escape civilization had settled here as far back as the 1600s. I mentioned earlier that my mother's uncle was the first to circumnavigate this group of islands. The town of Longyear was named for the American, John Longyear, who had established the coal mining company there, though it was now a Norwegian concern. The mines would soon draw the attention of the Nazis, and then the Allies, but when we arrived, *Ringsel* sailed past the impressive glacier-topped mountains, and up to the quay, where a small group of men awaited. They were the crew of the coaling station, and had not had many visitors since the fighting had begun raging to the south. They were very glad to see any sign of life from the outside world. Behind them loomed the dismal-looking buildings of the mine.

Among the men, astonishingly enough, was William Jacobsen, my cook from Micardbu! Also on hand to greet us was Ruben Goldman, the radioman from the *Quest* Expedition with Micard in 1936 and 1937. Spitsbergen was turning into an arctic travelers' reunion. Ruben was now first mate working on board a small icebreaker used to keep the local waters open for ships seeking coal. Soon the *Polarbjorn* arrived, captained by John Gjaever. Gjaever had been skipper for Louise Boyd's expeditions, and I had twice met him that way. He had hunted near Clavering Island before my time, and also had done some archaeological digs there. He had been part of the first wave of Norwegians to set up trap huts by Loch Fyne during the early 1930s when that method was being used to establish Norwegian sovereignty there. Gjaever was a good writer, and had had some books published and even translated into English.

His mission when I met him this time at Longyear was to bring Norwegian trappers home from Myggbukta, and he was also bringing Danish personnel to Clavering and Sandodden. On board his ship was the Dane, Ib Paulsen, who had been at Eskimonaes on Clavering Island when I had been at Micardbu. Paulsen carried a letter for me from Count Eigil Knuth, who was stranded back in Nazi-occupied Denmark. Knuth had heard via the "Mukluk telegraph" that I was headed to Ammassalik, and wrote to say I could use his studio hut there in his absence. Imagine a man being that thoughtful in wartime! But this was typical of the "polar brotherhood." John Gjaever also told me to watch myself as I crossed over to Greenland, as there were submarines and other warships prowling about. Every time I had met John, it felt as if we were brothers with me being the younger one. What we both experienced on the way to Greenland made us even closer.

Kalle and I were told the by the skeleton crew at Longyear that they were no longer equipped to carry on business, and, fortunately for us with our limited resources, we could help ourselves to all the coal we wanted. We also hunted seals to stock up on fresh meat. Things were going fairly well under the circumstances.

Heading at last for Greenland, my ship stuck to the pack ice. This was familiar to us, so we had no fear of it. What is more, there was no chance of being torpedoed there by either side of the warring parties. It was an uneventful, relaxed passage, except that our radio set soon gave out. In blissful ignorance of the goings-on in a troubled world, we worked our way through to Greenland, arriving at Brestrup Glacier just a bit north of Ammassalik where we anchored. Two Danes I knew from my first visit and two Inuit came aboard, drank some beer with us, and then wanted to know if we carried any weapons on board.

"Sure," I said, "our hunting weapons." But they wanted to know if we had machine guns and so forth. They were acting rather peculiarly, so I told them to search for themselves. They returned to have more beers with us, satisfied that we were not Norwegian Nazis arriving as an invading force! We were flabbergasted they had ever thought such a thing. But with communications more or less cut off from the rest of the world, the village was full of rumors. Just before we had arrived, some Greenlanders had come paddling furiously in to the settlement to report that a German war machine had landed near a remote hunting camp. It had turned out to be a runaway British barrage balloon, but this was the kind of panic-stricken atmosphere we had entered into. After all, the Germans had Denmark, so the locals expected the Nazis to arrive soon to claim Greenland as well. The Americans would soon put a stop to that fear.

When Denmark had been invaded by the Germans, Henrik Kaufmann, the Danish ambassador to the United States, had, of his own volition, given provisional governing status over Greenland to the U.S., although this had to be kept unofficial at the time. The Americans had then established a consulate at Gothaab, the capital of Greenland (which is today called Nuuk), and an American Coast Guard cutter was also stationed there. The Coast Guard cutter patrolled the east coast, so the Germans could now only arrive covertly, and at great risk of bringing the United States into the war.

Now twice glad for my American citizenship, I sent a radio message from Ammassalik to the Americans that I had arrived. A message came quickly back that the *Northland* would soon be calling at the village. We arrived the next day with our rudder damaged by ice. While waiting for the *Northland*, the crew of the *Ringsel* hunted for seal and repaired the ship's rudder. I showed my letter from Count Knuth to the Danes, and a key to his studio was found for me. I was happy to paint and work on my sculpting, as I was not much good at ship repairs. Also, it was very diplomatic of me, the boss, to butt out and leave the crew alone, since I had noticed many of the local girls were hanging around the ship. I was right. A wild party went on far into the night, and I, out of hearing range in my cabin, did not have to pretend that I didn't hear or see a thing.

The people of Ammassalik impressed me once again with their daily celebration of life. In the midsummer's light they still held their drum dances, twirling around to hypnotic chants and drumbeats. Sometimes I would look out my window and see a group of Inuit slowly going up a hillside, picking at this bush, and that herb, grazing on the vegetation as they went. Kalle and I used to do the same thing when we set up our trap lines, and that was one of the reasons we had stayed so healthy.

One night, while a group of Danes joined us in conversation over beers at a Danish trader's house, the trader turned to me, bleary-eyed. He was drunk. He pulled out a revolver and pointed it unsteadily at me. "I am going to shoot you,

you Nazi sympathizer. I know all about you, and your crew!" I jumped to my feet, ready to knock him down for that remark. The Dane's wife was in hysterics in the kitchen. The rest of my crew grabbed me and escorted me out of the trader's house.

In the morning when he had sobered up, he told me he had received a message from Clavering Island saying that the Norwegian ship, the *Fridtjof Nansen*, sailing under the British flag, had steamed into the bay there and taken the *Polarbjorn* captive as a German spy ship! My friend, Captain John Gjaever, had been arrested! The message had come from my Danish friend, Niels-Ove Jensen, who said that the British were after me and the *Ringsel* as well. I asked the now-sober Dane, "If I were an agent for the Germans, why would I call the Americans to let them know my whereabouts? You were with me when I made the damn call!" He told me that the war had made everybody crazy. There were collaborators in Denmark, people he never would have thought would do such things. Months would pass before the mystery involving my ship and the *Polarbjorn* was solved.

The American Coast Guard cutter *Northland* arrived, commanded by Rear Admiral Edward H. Smith. "Iceberg" Smith had earned his nickname the hard way. He had been the first American to attend the Mikkelsen Institute for Arctic Navigation established in Bergen, Norway, after the sinking of the *Titanic* by an iceberg in 1912. (There was that *Titanic* connection again!) Smith had experienced sailing in arctic ice in Alaska as well as here, though he was rather new to east Greenland. He and I had a meeting during which he came right to the point.

"Look, Willie," Smith said earnestly, "you are an American. I am going to tell you unofficially that America is not going to stay out of the war forever. President Roosevelt himself has activated plans to protect Greenland from being used by the Nazis. We need you, Willie! We don't have anyone who knows this coast. We don't even have decent maps of Greenland, for crying out loud," he said. I showed him some maps I had made during my expeditions. "That's what I mean. We need you! I strongly urge you to return to the States with the *Northland*. We are going back for a refitting. What do you say?" Fate had stuck out a hand, and I grabbed it. But now I had to tell Kalle.

The *Ringsel* was under contract with the Norwegian government, but that was just a technicality now that the Germans were running it. Kalle was ready to stay in Greenland with his family, or to go to Canada to join the Norwegians at Little Norway. But we worried about Von Krogh. As an official representative of Norway, he might raise a ruckus if my ship did not return him home. We decided to wait on a decision until we had reached Torgilsbu Station with the relief crew. We still had to contend with the Norwegian couple there that was expecting to be returned home. It was a terrible burden to be responsible for so many lives during wartime.

Labb and I sailed the three hundred-mile-trip to Torgilsbu on board the *Northland*, as the *Ringsel* was very crowded and could use the extra space. It was a rough journey, with storms that pushed huge bergs about like corks. The effect of the midnight sun was hardly seen that far south. In the stormy night, the Coast Guard ship's searchlights shone dramatically against towers of ice that bobbed violently all around us. We lost contact with *Ringsel*, and we entered the narrow fjord to Torgilsbu with still no sign of my little ship.

A lonelier spot for a couple with a small child could not be imagined. High mountains plunged into the fjord, giving it a hemmed-in feeling. This area was named for the Viking, Torgil, who one assumes found this fjord—probably by accident, as there is no indication Vikings ever lived there that I had heard of.

The ship anchored near the tiny station, and we were greeted gaily by the Norwegian woman who could scarcely conceal her utter relief at seeing us. A few hours later the *Ringsel* arrived, much to my own relief. But the situation concerning evacuation plans became confused for all concerned. The Norwegian couple was split on wanting to return to Norway. The man did not want to, but the woman was hysterically homesick.

Previously, Herculean efforts had been made by many parties to bring her supplies and to make her life at the wild, remote station as comfortable as possible. Greenlanders, for instance, hearing that she had no milk for her child, had at great personal danger brought a goat by a kayak-escorted umiak from more than a hundred miles away. But by now her daughter was two years old, and the woman had reached her limit. Her long separation from home and her growing fears for the rest of her family living in Norway were too great. None of our arguments for her not returning made sense to her. She was from a tiny fishing hamlet on the north coast, and the thought of big America, where she knew no one, frightened her.

I did not know what to do. Since Von Krogh was technically in charge of the mission, I assumed he knew what he was doing, and he thought his duty was to return to Norway. He roared, "The war will be over in a few months!" This was 1940. Between the heart-rending pleas of the Norwegian woman to be returned home, and Von Krogh also clamoring to get back, I left the decision up to Kalle, since I already knew I was heading for America, and was therefore out of the decision-making process. Also, as the ship's captain, he could legally make any decision he wanted.

Reluctantly, Kalle agreed to take the *Ringsel* back to Tromsø. While all this was going on, a Norwegian sealer arrived at Torgilsbu. It had come from Halifax, Nova Scotia, and had been sent by the exiled Norwegian government's headquarters in Canada to bring supplies to the station. Norwegian ships stranded on that side of the Atlantic by the war were now under control of the Free-Norwegian authorities. The sealer was returning to Halifax, and Jacobsen and Engebritsen asked if they could sail with them. It was a perfect opportunity, and arrangements were soon made. But just as the two men began rowing a skiff out to the ship, it steamed away without them! No one could understand it; it was outrageous. Jacobsen and Engebritsen suspected that Von Krogh, not wanting any trouble back home with the Nazis when he returned to Norway, had officially ordered the ship to take off without them. Why a ship under Free-Norwegian command would ever listen to Von Krogh, who acted under a Nazi-occupied government's command, was beyond me. At that point, I was having a hard time understanding my fellow men, and having been the recent victim of rumors myself, I reserved judgment on Von Krogh. He was otherwise a fine man, but perhaps officialdom was his weak spot.

I gave Engebritsen and Jacobsen a lot of provisions and coal to ensure their comfort at the station until they could get a ship to Little Norway, the resistance center in Canada. These two brave men later served in the Free Norwegian Air Force in Great Britain. Their plane was accidentally shot down off the coast of Scotland by friendly fire. Floating in the chilly waters, Jacobsen died in Engebritsen's arms.*

With the diplomatic row now over, the *Ringsel* was preparing to go back to Norway. As I moved my things onto the *Northland*, Smith asked me, "You are not

---

* Author's Note: In 1992, Hans Engebritsen told me Willie was an unsung hero, and should have earned a medal for getting them out of Norway.

going to bring Labb with you, are you?" Smith, Labb, and I had become friends. We had done some archaeological digging together in the area while waiting for the confusing local "political situation" to sort itself out. I told him, "Sure. He's family!" Smith already knew that, so he wanted to know why I wanted Labb to have to endure a six-month quarantine when we reached New York. I was afraid that in six months Labb would go crazy being cooped up alone, not knowing where I was. And then Smith mentioned that in just a few weeks I might be assigned somewhere three thousand miles from New York.

Labb had become a close friend. The big white dog, such a pampered pet when I had first met him, had become strong and courageous through his experiences in Greenland. He had saved my life from a musk ox's charge. A lonely quarantine in a kennel was no place for him, so I decided that Labb should return with Kalle to Norway. Kalle and I vowed that when the war was over we would have a great party where we would make plans for our next expedition. Labb put his great paws on my shoulders to say good-bye, and then leapt on board his ship to join Kalle and the others sailing back to Norway. I never saw either of them again.

CHAPTER FIFTEEN

Sailing to Vinland

The *Northland* sailed along the south coast of Greenland, and I felt fortunate that we were able to stop briefly at the ruins of one of the settlements begun by Erik the Red a thousand years earlier. At the end of the fjord, a small patch of stunted trees were growing in a sheltered valley. Trees on Greenland—what an unusual sight! We visited the still-standing stone walls of the old church at Hvalsey. According to an Icelandic record, in 1408 a wedding was performed in the Hvalsey Church. This is not only the last known service at Hvalsey, but perhaps also the last written record of the Viking presence in the region. There is evidence that some settlers remained for another eighty or ninety years, but then were forced to leave by the deteriorating climate. That they struggled for this long, still clinging to the remnants of their Christian culture, is conjectured in a letter in the Vatican library dating from the 1480s. This would mean that records of Christian weddings and burials were kept in Rome, and so the existence of Greenland could well have been known to Europeans like Christopher Columbus. The earliest mention of land beyond Greenland is found in Adam of Bremen's *History of the Archbishops of Hamburg-Bremen* from 1075.

"He also spoke of another island," Adam wrote, referring to his interview with King Svend Estridsen of Denmark, "which many have found in this great ocean, and which is named Vinland because grapes grow wild there, and yield the best wine. There is also an abundance of self-sown grain, as we know not from hearsay only, but from the sure report of the Danes." I bring up this Viking connection with America because during the next few years of my arctic journeys, their reported travels were often interwoven with my own.

When we reached the town of Julianehaab, it turned out the *Northland* would not be sailing for New York City right away. Ice had damaged the rudder, so Smith arranged passage for me on the USS *Campbell*, which was heading for New York. Smith kept the skeletons and artifacts we had found, and said he would get them to the Smithsonian, and that we would meet later in Washington. "You'll be famous!" he promised me.

The USS *Campbell* headed for the United States, skirting along the coast of Labrador, where Leif Eriksson was said to have landed and made a settlement. This had not yet been proven in 1940. Some have suggested that the Vikings came as far as the Hudson River, and the *Campbell* followed that route all the way to New York City. When I landed again in America in 1940, it was not to the acclaim and fame and instant appointment to arctic work for the American military that "Iceberg" Smith had predicted.

In New York City harbor, the ship dropped me off by the customshouse, and then went on to the naval yard. The customs officials treated me with great disrespect and suspicion. Why did I have these rifles and radio equipment, they wanted to know. And, they said, no one had told them about "no USS *Campbell*"! There was no one around to back up my story. It took hours to get things straightened out, but they were going to charge me a customs fee of a hundred and fifty dollars because I might profit from selling all my arctic gear! I had on me a total of twenty-five cents, which I had earned making a sketch of the *Campbell* for one of the officers. My thousands of Norwegian kroner were worthless because of the German occupation. With no money, the customs officials kept all of my things, including my books and some of my archaeological findings that I had carried with me. Thank god Iceberg Smith had kept those skeletons! That really would have put me under even greater suspicion. The final injury came when an obviously Italian-immigrant customs officer told me—I, who had refined my English at university in England—to "drop-a dat-a phony English accent, Knutsen. You're-a back in the-a U.S. of A. now." Thus, I arrived in the land of my birth, not to fame and acclaim, but broke, alone, and a bit flabbergasted at my reception.

I had just enough change for some bananas and that all-important shoeshine; I may have been broke, but I wanted to arrive in style. Then I spent my last five cents on a subway to Brooklyn where I hoped to stay with family friends, as I had done on my last visit in 1933. Unfortunately, they were away. I had to walk through the asphalt jungle near Prospect Park, where I had been born, to reach the Norwegian Seamen's Home, hoping to find food, shelter, and some good news. Trudging along, with police sirens screaming some blocks away and the din of the traffic making my head spin, I could not help wondering about the fickleness of fate. Only a year after receiving a full front page in Oslo's *Aftenposten*, here I was, a forgotten bum in Brooklyn.

Reaching the sailors' home, it seemed fate had decided to give me a break. Not only was I fed, but everyone knew me, or had heard of me, or at least knew my father. We drank beers and swapped stories. I was told the Norwegian consulate was giving two hundred dollars to each refugee!

The consulate general knew my father, and of my arctic journeys, and was all set to hand me the handsome sum, when suddenly he asked, "Willie, aren't you an American citizen?" Sure, I said. "Well, I can only give financial help to Norwegian citizens!" It was unbelievable, but regulations were regulations. I told him my circumstances, and that I had smuggled two resistance fighters out, and had even given them expensive coal and food.

"There's our solution!" he said. "You get this money as reimbursement for aiding Norwegian combatants!" He also exchanged my kroner, at nothing close to their true value, but he made up for this, I think, when he gave me the address of a Norwegian artist who had lived in New York for decades. "A real Bohemian!" he said. "Born in Bodø, for crying out loud, but studied art in Paris. Knows Picasso and that lot. Hemingway apparently asked her several times to marry him. I was at a party when she said, 'I am an artist! Artists don't get married!' "

Gunvor Bull-Teilman greeted me like her long-lost brother. I was not to live anywhere but at her studio on Washington Square in Greenwich Village, she said. Her large apartment was everyone's idea of an artist's studio in 1920s Paris. She was a popular and moderately successful artist. She had even been selected to illustrate the American edition of *Kristin Lavransdatter*, the popular historical novel written by Sigrid Undset, which eventually earned Undset the first Nobel Prize for Literature ever awarded to a woman. Sigrid had just arrived in New York after escaping Norway, and I would later briefly meet her through Gunvor.

Gunvor told me, "I'll introduce you to everybody!"—and she did. Edward Hopper, the realist painter, lived in the building next to her; above her lived Frederick Stokes, the aging artist who had been on arctic expeditions to Greenland with Robert Peary. When I met Stokes in his high-ceiling studio and said that I had almost made it to Ingolfs Fjord in Peary Land, his Vandyke beard quivered with rage.

"Don't mention that man's name around me!" he fumed, sputtering expletives, as he walked over to ceiling-high rack of artwork. He dug around a bit, and then said, "Since you are a real explorer, and an artist, and have actually been in the area, take this." He tossed me a small oil sketch of Inglefield Gulf, on the northwest coast, done on board the ship during the 1893 Peary Expedition. He had casually tossed the canvas to me, but I caught it like it was a great treasure. I never did ask him what caused his falling out with Peary. I couldn't risk giving him a heart attack.

I went to the The Explorers Club to meet the great arctic explorer, Vilhjalmur Stefansson, who was also the president of the club. We had corresponded during the planning of the Norwegian-French Expedition, and he told me when we at last met face-to-face that he was really glad to have another, as he put it, "real arctic rat" around. He immediately nominated me for membership in The Explorers Club.

The Explorers Club! Just off Central Park East, it was architecturally reminiscent of an English baron's estate. The interior featured the same high ceilings, leaded windows, and ornate woodwork on both the ceilings and floors. Paintings of exploration from the Arctic to Africa hung on the walls, and artifacts from around the world hung everywhere, drawing the eye in for closer inspection. Though there were women members, with the hardy Miss Louise Boyd among them, it was in many ways similar to an exclusive men's club. I hasten to add that race and religion were also not considerations for membership, just an interest in exploration and discovery.

However, I soon discovered that dinners at the club could be very formal affairs, where one was expected to wear a tuxedo, not just a suit and tie. While most of the long-standing members had their own custom-tailored tuxedoes, I had to make do with renting mine. At one event, the featured speaker was Amos Burg, who had just finished a long canoe trip through Alaska. He arrived late by train, and showed up in a sports coat. Some eyes were raised at this breech of etiquette. Amos strode to the podium, and began his talk by apologizing for not wearing a tuxedo. "I came in late, and rushed around town to rent a tux before all the stores closed. None was to be had. In the last shop, the owner told me he was sorry, but the last tux had just been rented by the president of The Explorers Club!" The members burst out laughing, and all was forgiven. President Stefansson, in his hand-tailored tux laughed the loudest.

Stefansson was my second savior in America after Gunvor. Not only did he nominate me for membership in the prestigious Explorers Club, he also gave me a job. He had just been commissioned by the government to write a textbook on Greenland. He had never been to Greenland, and he told me my arrival had been just what he needed. The book had a tight deadline, and there was no time to waste. He even gave me office space in his apartment on Morten Street, in the Village. I was paid twenty-five dollars a week. This was a livable sum during the Great Depression. I would not be able to save anything, but my fortunes were quickly improving. "Stef" even bailed out my things that had been confiscated by the customshouse. I paid him back by giving him a top-notch batch of rare arctic books from my collection.

During my first few weeks in New York City, it would be an obvious understatement to say I was experiencing culture shock. I walked daily from my newly rented hotel room at the Earle near Washington Square along the overcrowded sidewalks to Stef's apartment on Morten Street. Car horns beeped continuously, and police and ambulance sirens blared all too often. Flower vendors sold their fragrant wares; sidewalk artists drew rough portraits of tourists; and taxi drivers shouted insinuations to offending drivers about their mother's morals. Crossing busy Tenth Avenue, I was particularly mindful of the fact that the quiet and beautiful east coast of Greenland was a world away. It was always a relief to turn off onto the tree-lined sanctuary of Morten Street, where the noise level mysteriously dropped several decibels. It was like entering a time warp. Stefansson's home was filled with history and art, and it was easy to work there. New York City, I must say, apart from the constant noise, was a very exciting place to be. As huge a city as it was, each area was like a self-contained village, where many of the locals had known each other from birth. New Yorkers were friendly and generous, and everyone from street cleaners to shop owners to stockbrokers seemed to be fairly well-educated. There was a sense of destiny in the air, as if the future belonged to New York City, and exciting things could happen at any moment.

One day, while visiting Gunvor at her studio around the corner from my hotel, she told me there was a good art exhibit up at the Russian Tea Room. Having nothing else to do that day, I went uptown. I was admiring the rather good artwork on the walls when I bumped into someone; I said, "Excuse me," and he did the same. Suddenly, we both stared in disbelief. It was Anton Berger, the Oslo photography shop owner whom Micard had commissioned to develop all the photos and movie film from the 1936–37 expedition! We were exclaiming over the coincidence of our meeting when he suddenly said, "Willie! Your photos from the Micard expedition! I have them. Here! In New York!"

Anton was a Jew, and had wisely fled Norway to go to Sweden, and then on to Russia. He had taken the Trans-Siberian Railroad to Vladivostok, and then sailed by ship to America. He had come to New York by train, and during the entire journey from Norway, he had carried with him five shoeboxes full of photos and negatives from my first expedition! Micard had given me ownership of all these historical photographic records, but I thought I'd never see them again. It was unbelievable that they would end up in New York via the Trans-Siberian railway, for crying out loud. And then, to meet in the Russian Tea Room! We were both quite overcome by the miraculous meeting, and had to get some drinks. We spent the rest of the day sharing our stories of escape from Norway and arrival in America.

It was not long after meeting Anton that I was contacted by the then Brooklyn-based Norwegian-American newspaper, *Nordisk Tidende* (now the *Norwegian Times*). I wrote an article for them about my journey from Norway to America, which the paper declared "followed the route taken by Leif Eriksson." It was a slight exaggeration, but was more or less true, and it had a nice ring to it—not to mention that I got fifteen dollars for the article. The article announced my arrival to a wide audience, and *The New York Times* later picked up the story. I soon had all the lecture invitations I could handle, and my financial situation started to improve.

While giving a lecture to the Norwegian Literary Society, one woman asked, "Do you think explorers should marry?"

"No," I said. "It would not be fair to be away so much of the time, as explorers must be." I was speaking from my experience with first Inger, and then Anita.

Later that night, I went into Shakespeare's Bar in the Village, just a couple minutes' walk from Gunvor's studio and my hotel. Gunvor had painted the murals that covered every wall. It was late, and a few elderly patrons were there, all hanging around a very good-looking young woman. She was talking about the theory of relativity. The radio was blasting a commercial about a furrier shop that had just received silver fox skins from Greenland. The announcer was saying that a Norwegian refugee had arrived with the skins. I thought I heard him say the trapper's name was Solver, and who else could that have been but Solver from Morkefjord! I was smiling into my beer when the charming girl said, "Advertisements! That's what's wrong with America!" She turned to me, her contemporary in age, and asked, "What do you think?"

I said, "Yes, it is rather annoying, especially since I think I know the trapper mentioned on the radio. If it's who I think it is, I trapped foxes with him in Greenland!"

And that was how I met Alice Coen. Alice had an expensive artist's studio around the corner from the bar, in MacDougal Alley. She took me home to show me her sketches, and we were married two weeks later. So much for my advice on explorers not getting married. But we were not to get married without first jumping over a cultural hurdle. Alice was an Irish Catholic from Rhode Island. Her family's house in Edgewood, near Providence, was not far from a Catholic bay-side chapel—overlooking the yachts—whose tower had been paid for by her father, Sylvester Coen. Sylvester, who had recently died, had been a drinking buddy of Honey Fitzgerald's—John Kennedy's maternal grandfather. In other words, these were serious Catholics, while I was a so-so Protestant Lutheran. Her priest said that in no way would he marry a girl he had baptized to a Protestant infidel! I was stunned. Organized religion had never been an important part of my personal philosophy. Some days later, I remembered Count Micard's uncle had been Pope Pius IX. I sent Micard a telegram, explaining the problem. He cabled back that he would take care of it, and not two days later, the priest told me that he had had "a change of heart, me son."

Stefansson, who also got married not long afterwards, had a celebration dinner for us. He told Alice, "You know, you will have to get used to being second place. With us explorers, exploration comes first. And all explorers are prima donnas!" Well, in my case, a fairly broke prima donna.

Alice laughingly apologized for not being able to provide a dowry suitable for "an arctic explorer." Her father's death was due to a heart attack sustained during a period of financial losses to the tune of a quarter of a million per week—anyway, a large sum—due to the Depression. He had been a director and major stock holder in the oldest brick company in America, the Barrington Brick Company in Barrington, Massachusetts. The way it was told to me, Sylvester, after reading each day's terrible stock results, had pretended to hit himself, saying, "Another quarter of a million, right on the jaw!" Although Alice and I were thrown a lavish wedding and reception, we were not lavished with wedding cash. Not that I expected anything—I just knew that my twenty-five dollars a week writing for Stef was not going to support a family in the manner my wife was used to! But Alice had an idea to get us going.

———

Alice had an uncle named Tony Dimond, who was U.S. senatorial representative from Alaska. This was, of course, before it became a state. He had long fought for statehood for Alaska, and was trying to get Congress to see the wisdom of building a highway from Alaska to the rest of the nation. We went to see him at his office in Washington, D.C. Alice thought he might be able to hurry things along regarding my long-promised position in the military as an arctic advisor. While Alice and I waited for things to happen, we stayed in a lodging house in the capitol. A letter from "Ice berg" Smith was forwarded to me there. He had finally got the Inuit skeletons to the Smithsonian, and said that the famous physical anthropologist Ale Hrdlicka had been excited to receive them, and I should go see him. Hrdlicka, a Cech, was an early pioneer in the development of American physical anthropology and had been at the Smithsonian since 1903. Though he was indeed happy and impressed with the skeletons I had donated to the museum, it was soon obvious his main concern right then was the Nazi occupation of his beloved homeland. He said excitedly to me, "You are young and strong. Go, run to the nearest recruiting office and sign up to liberate Europe!" He went on and on and had me so wound up at the end of a long harangue that I was halfway down the hall toward the exit and heading to sign up when I caught myself and went instead for a much needed beer. A lot of good a pacifist dogsled driver like myself was going to do the army!

Soon after that close encounter, I met the staff at the National Geographic magazine through Tony Dimond, as well as Gilbert H. Grosvenor, who had been president of the National Geographic Society since 1920. I was startled when they commissioned me to write an article. It was an amazing moment: I was going to be in *National Geographic* magazine! Nice things were happening rather fast. I told them how the pages of an old copy of one of their magazines used to plaster the walls of my old hut in Greenland. The editor, Andy Brown, who would help me write the article, as well as become a good friend, said, "We *do* cover the globe!" I was very impressed with the friendly way in which I was treated. I guess I expected a more aristocratic, detached demeanor from such a world-famous and influential geographical society. But I was in America, after all.

Then someone mentioned that Bernt Balchen was in town! I got his phone number and we had a reunion at a restaurant. When Alice and I got there, John

Gjaever was also there! Over dinner, he cleared up the mystery surrounding the not-so-funny rumor of our being Nazi operatives.

It turns out we had been set up. The Germans had allowed a message about me and John to be intercepted by the British. The message said that we were setting up Nazi weather stations on the east coast of Greenland! While the Norwegian ship *Nansen*, under the British flag, had chased after us, the real spy ship slipped into northeast Greenland and set up a weather station. This had obviously been planned for a long time, and explained why the Germans, particularly the dreaded Gestapo, had been so congenial with me. The British finally believed John was not a Nazi spy, but he had spent a long time in a "dungeon" at the Old Bailey during the horror of the Blitz before he was released.

When John had finished the bizarre story of his arrest due to diabolical Nazi cunning, Bernt announced that there was one more serious matter I should know about. He took out a Chicago-based Danish newspaper that he had with him, and showed me the relevant article. I couldn't believe it: It said that I was a Nazi spy! It even said I had broken into Eigil Knuth's hut at Ammassalik, and had come to the United States as a prisoner on board the *Campbell*! I immediately got up and rang the Danish Embassy, and they said they had read the piece and knew it was false. The next day Alice and I visited the embassy because, fortunately, I still had the damn note Eigil had sent me with permission to use his hut. The Danish Embassy sent a copy to the newspaper, telling them to "print no more of this about Willie Knutsen!"

The newspaper did stop publishing such nonsense, but they never apologized. I had a sneaking suspicion that this sabotage of my name and character had been the work of someone—whose name will not be mentioned—in the higher ranks of Danish Arctic affairs who still fumed over my selling Germania Land to the Norwegians! It really shook me up to think someone would stoop so low as to put another man's freedom and reputation in jeopardy simply because of some nonsense about who owned a frozen strip of lunar landscape on the Greenland northeast coast. And rumors get started easier than they are to stop. Even years later I would occasionally come across some article containing reference to *Ringsel* and *Polarbjorn* having been German spy ships. Luckily John and I were not mentioned, but this serious error about our old ships kept popping up like crabgrass.

Bernt had told me he would try to get me a job with the military, but that it would take time. When I finally did get a job, at the beginning of 1941, my assignment was to design small buildings for an Indian reservation near Juneau, Alaska. I had to go alone, nearly three thousand miles from Alice and the child we were expecting. My daughter was born while I was away, and it took the day that will "live in infamy" — December 7, 1941 — to bring me back from the beautiful isolation of the northwest Pacific coast to my family in New England.

At the news of the sneak attack on Hawaii, Juneau was panic-stricken. Japanese fishing boats in great numbers had been seen by Juneau-based fishing boats for a long time, and some now believed these were actually warships in disguise. Many in Juneau wanted to get back to the lower states, but Juneau had no road out over land. The only way out was by boat, and rumors of Japanese submarines off the coast did not help the emotional state of the capital city. Tony Dimond had for years urged Congress to build a highway connecting Alaska with the rest of the U.S., but no one had listened until the attack. At the time, I personally did not see why Japan would try to extend its reach all the way to Juneau, but many of the people in this small city were really nervous. When I boarded the coastal steamer *Denali*, the native name for Mount McKinley, it was packed with these people. It was with mixed feelings that I left the quiet beauty of Juneau.

I left the ship at Vancouver, Canada, and took the first train available heading cross-country. We made a stop in Winnipeg; watching from my window, I saw a small train waiting on the spur that went north to the arctic port of Churchill. Churchill sat on the south shore of Hudson Bay, so was actually in the Arctic. Trains carrying grain bound for Europe would use this line during the summer months to unload onto ships that could sail in unfrozen waters to the Atlantic. It saved the huge expense of land transportation from the "bread basket" of the Midwest to the Saint Lawrence Seaway. Since it was not summer, I was watching a passenger train bound for Churchill. I was suddenly seized by an impulse to leap from my train to catch the train to Churchill! My marriage, a life in civilization — it had all happened so quickly. I felt like I was caught in a trap. My brain raced with adrenaline. It was the call of the wild, and it was only by doing some rather strenuous mental gymnastics that I managed to restrain myself. I realized my relatively carefree past was over. The world was at war, and it was time for me to grow up.

The attack on Pearl Harbor by the Japanese made war preparations first priority, and so even though I had thought I was being brought back from Alaska to do arctic-related work, I found myself working as an architectural draftsman for government buildings.

Finally, on August 16, 1942, I received a telegram from the head of the Army Air Corps, General Henry "Hap" Arnold. I was to meet him at his headquarters in Washington, D.C. At a meeting in his office, he said, "Willie, our air crews are not trained to survive arctic conditions if they crash. Have you heard of the 'Crimson Route'?" I shook my head.

"It's the route used by planes loaded with men and cargo, bound for the European theater of war," he continued. "That is, up to Labrador, across to Greenland, Iceland, and then Scotland. The 'crimson' part was apparently dreamed up by Churchill—because of the dead and wounded being brought back, you see. We are losing planes and crews, particularly over Labrador. Your knowledge of arctic survival would help Allied flight crews. We've got an Arctic Survival School started in Maine. I'm going to send you there, if that's all right with you."

I said, "Of course!"

"I thought it might be" he said. "The sooner you can start the better." He then introduced me to Colonel Charles Hubbard, who was to be my commanding officer. Charlie Hubbard had flown mapping surveys of Labrador, and so was one of the few members of the "top brass" familiar with the perilous flight path of the Crimson Route. Hubbard welcomed me to what he called "one of the most important jobs in this war!" He then told me the people in the front office would arrange my orders and travel plans. I was almost to the door when Arnold added, "Oh, by the way, Knutsen—you are now a lieutenant in the United States Army Air Corps. Congratulations!"

It was rather dizzying, but in a good way.

The Crimson Route! This was the same route that early arctic pilots and explorers had predicted would someday be important in modern warfare. From Stefansson in the early 1900s, to Bernt Balchen and General Simon Bolivar Buchner in the 1930s, their predictions were unfortunately correct. This flight path, pioneered in tiny, single-engine planes by the Lindberghs and a few other hearty souls just a little more than a decade before, would become the most heavily trafficked sky in the world. Huge planes, undreamed of by most a decade before, roared off to war, and other planes roared back, carrying the carnage of the conflict raging across Europe.

Near the tiny port town of Goose Bay in Labrador, a huge refueling airstrip had been constructed in cooperation with the Canadians at great speed. Once our planes left the United States and crossed the Saint Lawrence River, there would be very little human contact. The staggeringly vast wilderness beneath the three hundred-mile flight path to Goose Bay probably contained no more than a few hundred humans. If your plane went down there, you would be met with 110,000 square miles of rugged, empty wilderness. The only survival equipment issued for planes in those days was geared for jungle survival. It was no wonder that downed crews were dying.

The site of the Survival School—at Presque Isle, in the northeast corner of Maine—had been intelligently chosen. Heavily forested and mountainous, it had a long, cold winter with a lot of snow. Nearby was Mount Katahdin, with its 5,268-foot-high steep and wild terrain. Until the turn of the century there had been native caribou on the mountain. Its higher elevations provided a perfect reproduction of Arctic tundra. It was an astonishing place, and I felt right at home there.

The first thing anyone was told upon arrival at the Survival School was that when the morning sun hit the top of Mount Katahdin, its setting rays were on Attu, in the Aleutians. Therefore, the sun never set on the USA! The second thing we learned was that our rescue operations in the Arctic were dismal. No one had thought about providing flight crews with the thick eiderdown sleeping bags needed for deep-cold survival; and the crews had no detailed maps for the region.

There is one particularly sad story concerning that lack. Coming back from Greenland to Goose Bay, a B-26 had crash-landed in Northern Labrador, and though the crew had managed to survive for months, they had not been found until it was too late. The cruel irony was the fact that unknown to them, Hebron—an Inuit settlement—was located just a short distance away. One of the men had kept a diary, posthumously entitled *Diary of One Now Dead*. The diary revealed that the men had not known how to live off the land very well; reading of their heroic attempts to do so moved us all. We were determined to tip the scales in our men's favor.

General Arnold and Colonel Hubbard had gathered all the available men who had any experience in the Arctic, or the Antarctic, to teach at the school.

Some of this experience in polar weather consisted of traveling on a navy ship into polar waters; nonetheless, there were so few Americans who had even that much experience that they were instantly regarded as experts. The majority I worked with at the school had at least some dog-driving experience, and that was something. One of the first men I met was Eddie Goodale, who had driven dogs for Admiral Byrd in the Antarctic. He and I became fast friends, and eventually he became the godfather to two of my children.

Eddie Goodale was a New Englander of old stock. In his youth he had belonged to a dogsled club in Ipswich, Massachusetts. He had started by hitching his German shepherd to a small sled, and it was this experience that launched him into polar life. While still young, he had worked a few months at Northwest River, Labrador, at the Grenfell Mission, and because of this additional experience, he was chosen to go with Byrd to the South Pole—without pay, of course. Eddie had friends from the same dogsled club in Massachusetts who had also graduated into polar work, including Norman Vaughan and Alan Innes-Taylor. The three men had been dubbed "the Three Musketeers" by Byrd. Vaughan had also spent some time at the Grenfell Mission, and so was well qualified to be our commanding officer in Labrador. Another of that Ipswich group was Bill Robertson. We all gathered at Presque Isle.

The commander of Presque Isle was Major Jack Crowell, a man with great physical strength, and strength of character. He had had experience in Baffin Island setting up one of the outposts there in 1942. He had sailed there with the great explorer, Donald MacMillan, and had a small island there named after him.

Crowell's first visit to Frobisher Bay, Baffin Island, was in the mid-1920s on the Rawson-MacMillan Expedition, sponsored by the New York Museum of Natural History. This expedition included Sharat Roy, the University of Chicago geologist originally from Kashmir. These men had been the first scientific team sent to Frobisher Bay since Francis Hall arrived with just his Inuit guide, Kojesse, in the 1870s. The only other non-Inuit to visit there had been the crew of an occasional whaling ship. Although a few missionaries and Hudson's Bay Company fur buyers had paid infrequent visits to that remote land, almost nothing was known about it when Crowell arrived to set up the base.

We were lucky that our commanding officer was so qualified for his position. I say this because too often we ran into phonies who had little or no experience, and had only achieved their position of command through their personal connections. These types particularly grated on those of us who had honest experience, and were forced to listen to their foolishness because of their senior rank. Fortunately, "Hap" Arnold had foreseen that the Arctic would have no place for such characters, and so we were generally in the hands of competent senior officers.

Along this same line, I found that among the men I trained, those who learned the fastest, and had the most enthusiasm to get to the Arctic, were some boys from the deep South. These guys had no pretensions about their knowledge of anything north of the Mason-Dixon Line, but somehow they became the ablest arctic men, and later, the ablest arctic instructors. This also held true for some Cherokee Indians who found their way into my hands. Conversely, there were men who had some experience, and thus, thought they knew it all; they did not take to learning new things as well as those with no experience whatsoever. Fortunately, the majority of the men at the school were a good bunch.

We had only three complete dog teams at the Survival School. Most of the animals were veterans of the Byrd expedition the year before. In charge of these dogs was a New Yorker, Sergeant Louis "Tony" Colombo, who had been with them in the Antarctic. What a good man, and what a sense of humor he had! Another top dog handler was Norman Bright, the first man to climb Mount McKinley in Alaska with Brad Washburn. Washburn was executive director of the New England Museum of Natural History, and also had an impressive record in mountain climbing in Alaska. Bright, a brilliant photographer, also had "climbing fever," and all too often put himself in dangerous situations on Mount Katahdin.

Two other interesting men named Bob Slobodin and Dick Fuller also came from New York. They had gone by canoe from the Hudson River to the Yukon. Portaging, fighting rapids, and so on, they had taken two years to accomplish that remarkable feat. When Slobodin and Fuller mentioned to me that they had been in Juneau, I told them I had, too. As we talked about the large gold mine there, Fuller asked, "Did you see the monument and plaque to the mine's discoverers, Juneau and Harris?" I told them I had; as a sculptor myself, I always looked at such things. Then I remembered the artist's signature; it was "Fuller." The pair had been out of money in Juneau, so Fuller had taken on that little sculpting job in order to earn enough money to get home! They were men right after my own heart.

My first job at the school was to train the men who would then train flight crews in how to survive the harsh winter conditions of Labrador. The new recruits kept pouring in. Then came the pilots, navigators, and flight crews; the weathermen, chefs, and maintenance men, and so on, who were all to be sent north. They poured in for intensive training—and it *was* intensive. The war was raging, and no one could afford to take it easy.

In three months, thousands of men came through, took a few days' "crash course" on surviving arctic crashes, then left again. We taught them how to quickly erect an igloo, or, if in a forest, how to dig a cave under the branches of an evergreen. The trees provided some metabolic heat. "Stay out of your metal planes!" we told them. "They are colder than being outdoors! Dig yourselves a cave; get out of the wind. Use your parachutes to line your shelters, to make boots, and even for use as buckets." Basics like these were necessary for boys who had, until just recently, been occupied with playing baseball, or tinkering with their cars. The Crimson Route, although never easy or completely safe, was slowly becoming more controllable.

It's also possible that our training site may have helped to popularize skiing in America. Men who had never skied before watched in awe as I flew down snowy slopes, something I had been doing since I was six. They all wanted to learn how to do it, and learned damned quickly, if you ask me. I couldn't have asked for more enthusiastic pupils.

After three months of training, I received orders to fly to Goose Bay. From there I would fly seven hundred miles further north to take over the rescue station at Frobisher Bay, on Baffin Island. The year before America joined the war, and with the permission and cooperation of Canada, small outposts like Goose Bay already had been built, in reasonable anticipation of our entering the war. So, before the attack on Pearl Harbor, the U.S. already had manned outposts near the Crimson Route. This scattered line of rescue sites included locations in Ungava Bay, Baffin Island, Northern Labrador, and Greenland. But these sites were often manned by men inexperienced in the Arctic. The arctic survival teams being taught at Presque Isle were to replace those early crews. What excited me was the fact that Frobisher Bay—although technically beneath the Arctic Circle—was, because of geographical conditions, actually arctic terrain. I was going home!

Alice and I had bought an old farmhouse near the base at Presque Isle, and we had friends living nearby—some Alice had known since childhood—so I knew I was not leaving her and our daughter totally alone. I was able to head off for the arctic wilds with a somewhat relieved mind. Flying first over Maine, and then New Brunswick in Canada, all one could see was forest. There were occasional glimpses of humanity, but the forest canopy camouflaged most towns, and by the time we came over Labrador, it was obvious we had left civilization a long time before.

Below us, in Labrador, was a sub-Arctic land of 110,000 square miles of rugged forests, mountains, lakes, and streams. Most of these water bodies and waterways flowed downward to the east, dropping rapidly in elevation until they came out in the Hamilton River (renamed the Churchill in 1965). This river eventually emptied into Goose Bay, which was actually a fjord 150 miles in length that came out at Hamilton Inlet on the North Atlantic. From the inland lakes to the sea was a good seven hundred miles, as the water coursed. This region of *terra incognita* was then home to just a few Indian tribes of the Algonquin, some Inuit in the furthest north along the coast, some French Canadian trappers, and a few Christian missionaries. The vast majority of the rest of Labrador's burgeoning population of 7,800 humans lived along the coast, most of them fishing for a living.

Arriving over Goose Bay after flying over a thousand miles of wilderness, it was astonishing to suddenly see an air base, already quite large and modern for the time period. It eventually would be the largest airfield in the world for a time, and when we touched down, one could almost feel the electricity that marked the importance of this remote airfield to the war enflaming Europe.

After a two-day layover in Goose Bay, we were soon winging our way over the rugged north end of Labrador. Below us, the heavy evergreen forests thinned, then disappeared, replaced by a raw, rocky landscape that stretched as far as the eye could see. This was the beginning of the Arctic terrain as we approached Ungava Bay.

Rumors at the time claimed that Vikings had harvested trees at Ungava. Excavations on the west side of Ungava Bay, carried out in the 1950s and 1960s by Canadian archaeologist Thomas Lee, did indeed suggest a Norse presence in the region. The C-54 we flew in was far larger than anything I had been in previously; the only other time I had flown over the Arctic was when Count Micard had been rescued from Germania Land. Below us was an astounding view of seemingly endless, utter bleakness, but it was beautiful to me. The other men

played cards and tried not to think about what was beneath them, even as I experienced these powerful emotions. This all might have been happening under
better circumstances, but at least—*at last*—I was back in the Arctic!

As we passed over Resolution Island off the southern tip of Baffin Island,
we were flying over the route probably once followed by Leif Eriksson and the
other Vikings, whom legend had it had plied their ships along this frigid coast
around A.D. 1000. From their settlements on the west coast of Greenland, the
Vikings could have followed the currents northward along the Greenland
coast, all the way to Disko Island, where Norse artifacts have been found.
There, the currents swung to the west, across Davis Strait, and so it made sense
that the Vikings would have made landfall on Baffin Island anywhere from
near Cape Dyer to Resolution Island. This area of natural flagstone beaches is
thought to be the *Helleland,* or "Flagstone Land," mentioned in later Viking
sagas. I had seen photographs taken of the coast from the sea, and also some of
the glacial-covered, rugged mountains near Cape Dyer, to Resolution Island
below me. Picturing it from the air, I had the most interesting sensation of carrying on the Viking legacy of exploration. This is only natural, I suppose, for a
Norwegian-American, and an arctic man.

There was another interesting aspect of this flight. I learned that the commander of Frobisher Bay was Colonel Bert "Fish" Hassell, a legendary pilot. I
had read about him for years. He was the twentieth person to qualify for a U.S.
pilot's license, so he had been around! A friend of Charles Lindbergh's, in 1928
he had been the first to attempt to fly to Sweden in a small plane called *The Spirit
of Rockford,* after his hometown in Illinois. He hoped to fly from New York to
Greenland, to Iceland, to England, and so on. On the leg to Greenland, he had
crash-landed on the ice cap, north of Sondrestrom Fjord. I remember reading
about it when I was thirteen in Oslo. There had been no hope of his being found
alive. Three weeks later, nearly starved, he and his copilot, Parker Cramer, had
staggered to safety. Cramer had attempted the flight again in 1930, and this time,
he disappeared. (Years later, I read that a trawler from Hull, England, had
dragged up a watertight flight pouch in its nets, three years after Cramer had disappeared; it was Cramer's navigator's flight log.) I had heard of "Fish" Hassell for
years; I could hardly believe that this legend would now be my CO.

It had been just fifteen years since man had started to try flying over the Atlantic with small, primitive aircraft. Pilots like "Fish" Hassell were regarded as

fearless gods. A mere fifteen years later, we twenty-six men, complete with equipment and crew, were now flying the same route in one plane at a speed and altitude that would have previously been considered impossible. It may not seem so astounding today with our jet planes and international travel, but we could not help being amazed at the rapid change in arctic affairs.

The C-54 approached Baffin Island, a land as large as California, flew over Meta Incognito Peninsula, over Frobisher Bay, and approached the primitive, sandy landing strip at this outpost at the end of the world. Everyone held their breath; no one had ever landed here before. Our pilot, whose name I forget, knew his stuff. He had learned to fly in the old days before paved runways, and had been chosen for this flight for that very reason. When we touched down, we came to an abrupt, uncomfortable halt in the deep sand—but we had made it. An Arctic first: On this wild, unexplored Arctic island, the first aircraft had landed!

CHAPTER SIXTEEN

The Crimson Route

The first view we had of Frobisher was of a broad, yellowish sand strip. On some low hills were the huts, shacks, and bedraggled-looking hangar of the "base." No vegetation greeted us but the barest hint of minute, dwarf willows at the edge of a small brook that percolated along by the low hills. There were also a few fugitive tufts of grass that crouched miserably between some rocks. Northward there were no mountains visible, just the broad valley, and low hillocks. A river to the west ran southward toward the bay. Far across the bay to the south rose the high mountains of the Meta Incognito Peninsula.

It was low tide, and the bay was empty of water for as far as the eye could see. The bay normally had a thirty-five-foot tide that went up to forty feet in the spring. Huge boulders covered what in high tide would be the bottom of the bay, but when we arrived, looked like land. A jumble of grotesquely shaped icebergs lay stranded everywhere, while some even balanced precariously on top of the boulders where the tide had deposited them. This was our first impression of this new arctic base, code-named, "Crystal Two."

The headquarters at Frobisher Bay, or Crystal Two, was a typical field-base shack. I marched rather smartly inside, I thought, and presented myself to Colonel "Fish" Hassell, a childhood hero, with a formal salute.

"Well," he said in a gruff voice, "with that accent, Knutsen, are you Norwegian, Danish, or Swedish?" He then began talking to me in a mixture of all three Scandinavian languages—"Scandihuvian," as he called it. He told me that although he had been born and raised in Rockford, Illinois, he had spent some childhood years in Sweden with his grandmother. Our first meeting was the beginning of a long and close friendship that would continue up to his death in 1969. Hassell had a reputation as a gruff, cussing man with a heart of gold. "My grandmother in Sweden taught me how to cuss," he told me. He also eventually told me how he got his nickname.

In the early days of flying by the seat of your pants, pilots often followed roads, rivers, or railroads to guide them from town to town. The landing fields were just that—flat farm fields—and the weather-reporting service was far from perfect. Like many early pilots, including Charles Lindbergh, Hassell had had a mail route in the Midwest. He was in the air one day when a horrendous rainstorm hit. He was able to reach an airfield in the almost pitch-black downpour. The startled men on the ground heard a splash on the water-covered field, and saw a plane roll to a stop. When he sauntered into the terminal shack, his perennial pipe sticking carelessly out of the corner of his mouth, the men said, "No one can fly in weather like this—you must be a flying fish!" The name stuck.

After Hassell, one of the first men I met at Crystal Two was Herman Andresen, a trapper I had known in Greenland. And then I met another Norwegian from Tromsø, Sverre Strom, who had been with the Byrd expedition in 1929 and 1930, and was a friend of Bernt Balchen's. As Strom and I shook hands, he said he had known me as a child. "I used to bounce you on my knee!" he said with a chuckle. And also in that tiny, remote outpost I met another man from my past, Knut Olsen. I had met Knut briefly at Torgilsbu when I was bringing in the relief crew on the *Ringsel*, to take over for the Norwegian couple who had been running the weather station there. As I continue saying, these wonderful reunions, or coincidences, were really quite frequent in the Arctic.

Andresen was the harbormaster, working for the Johnson Construction Company that was busy building the base. He told me stories about the incredible tides of the bay. Apparently, just before I had arrived, Colonel Charles Hubbard had landed on the bay with a PBY, a large amphibious aircraft. Sverre had been directing him with hand signals, indicating that he should not come any closer to land, but Hubbard had misunderstood, and the plane's floats had struck a hidden reef. When the tide went out, the craft balanced precariously on the rocks, high above the now empty seabed. Another time, the same thing had happened to a ship. Both the ship and the plane were lucky enough to stay balanced, rocking dangerously, until the tide returned and they could be floated off. It was really a rough place to navigate into, to say the least. The transport ships that brought in building supplies and materials had to anchor far offshore and unload onto tracked, amphibious landing craft, which then brought the cargo to shore.

Through Hassell, I learned some of the history of the base. This was such a bizarre and out-of-the way place to the first American arrivals that many of the men, most of them civilian construction workers, thought they had been dropped off the end of the earth. To them, civilization had disappeared, and therefore, for many of them, so did discipline. Many of the men had gone "native"—that is, they let their beards grow, and lowered their standards of personal cleanliness (for example, urinating wherever and whenever they pleased).

There was one character, an officer, whom Fish had just sent to another site because he had gone more native than even the civilians. His name was Dave Irwin, and I had heard about him from Vilhjalmur Stefansson, and subsequently had read the old newspaper accounts of him, so it was quite a coincidence to hear Hassell talk about him. The story, as I knew it up to that point, was that Irwin, a Pennsylvanian, had somehow gotten a job as a reindeer herder while he was in Alaska. That herd of five hundred deer had been brought by ship to Nome from Lapland, and was being driven across the vast land to be introduced to the Arctic areas, so that the Inuit would have better hunting. The native caribou had been steadily dwindling in number, and the government thought it would be cheaper to introduce a new herd than to pay welfare to the Inuit. (You will remember my meeting Issak Hetta, the Sámi in Kautokeino, who had been traveling with this herd.)

Dave Irwin had gotten fed up with the drive, and had struck off on his own. He went from trapper station, to native village, and in that way covered quite a piece of territory for someone with little knowledge of the land, or of arctic survival. Eventually, he had gotten lost, and was on the edge of death when an old Inuit woman found him, and nursed him back to health. He had written a book about his adventures called *Alone in the Arctic*. Vilhjalmur Stefansson had told me Irwin had come to visit him, as a fellow "explorer." Stef had told me, "I sensed the man was something of a 'Walter Mitty,' though not a complete fraud. I didn't even invite him in. He was really nothing more than a bumbling, carefree soul, who was lucky enough to have been fed and saved by real Arctic people." But through his book, Irwin had gained a reputation as an arctic man, and so had been sent to Baffin Island to work for the military.

Hassell told me, "Irwin arrived with a sack full of steel traps; he was planning to set up a trap line! He had used the Army Air Corps as a free ride back to the Arctic. He would be clothed and fed, and paid by the taxpayers, while he ran his illegal trap line. Naturally, he completely ignored his military duties. One time I sent him with some prefab material to set up an inland rescue depot. He just dumped the material at the proposed site, and went off on his goddamned dogsled to hunt and trap—didn't see him for two damn weeks!" We both had a good laugh, but Hassell's second in command, Captain Bunting, was in the room when Hassell told this story, and he did not share our sense of humor. He said rather righteously that the "Dave Irwins" of this world were no laughing matter during this grave time of war.

Bunting obviously wished he were anywhere but Baffin Island. He was far too prim and proper for such an assignment. He prided himself on being a good shot with a pistol, and kept our nerves on edge with his constant practice, "just in case of an invasion." No one else there expected an invasion. After my unit had been on the base for a few days, we were standing guard near the airfield, where work was progressing. Bunting came up excitedly. Hidden in a rock cairn he had found a note written in what he said must be a secret code; he was convinced the note had been left by enemy saboteurs. Fish looked over the note, scratched his head, and then handed it to me. I tried not to laugh. It was written in Inuit! (An Inuit dictionary was slowly being pieced together starting with missionaries in the 1880s, though regional language differences made it difficult to produce a dictionary suitable for all Inuit peoples.) Probably the note was left by a passing missionary. Bunting looked rather annoyed at this news. This was the state of affairs in the "new" Arctic, the changing Arctic—but damn, was I glad to be back!

Frobisher Bay had once been home to many different Inuit groups. The Pre-Dorset people arrived first about four thousand years ago. Then they had left around a thousand years ago when geological and meteorological changes drastically eradicated their ice-hunting culture. The arctic ice pack, for example, substantially retreated, and with it the walrus and seal herds that had depended on pack ice for their survival. The Dorset Inuit population of Baffin Bay seemed to have moved to better walrus and seal hunting grounds to the west, around the shores of Baffin Basin. They were replaced in Frobisher Bay by people of the Thule Culture, who hunted the bowhead whale that swam in the newly opened water of the bay. It may have been that some Vikings paid a visit around the same time.

It has been estimated that annual mean temperatures in the region around that time must have been about two degrees higher than at present, with extreme January minimum temperatures six degrees warmer than they are today.

During the same time, the warming period had allowed the Vikings to settle in Iceland. And from there, the now famous Erik the Red sailed and settled Greenland. A wooden figurine of a Viking carved by an Inuit was found in a fifteenth-century house near Lake Harbor. This would indicate an early encounter between Viking and Inuit cultures somewhere in Hudson Strait. When Frobisher and his expedition arrived in 1578, he sailed up this 120-mile-long bay hoping he had found the "Route to Cathay," to China, and a place in history. But instead of the Northwest Passage, he found shoaling waters, dangerous tides among treacherous islands, a dead end, and unfriendly Inuit. It may have been that Frobisher was greeted by belligerent natives with a long oral tradition — natives who warned generation after generation about white men in long wooden ships. That's how I like to imagine it, even if it's not historical fact.

Frobisher's expedition at Frobisher Bay also found some heavy, black rock that was believed to contain gold. Returning to London without achieving his goal of finding the Northwest Passage, he found it difficult to get funding for a second attempt, until he convinced Queen Elizabeth I that gold might be a second-best goal. Eager to strike it rich, London merchants, courtiers, and even Queen Elizabeth I herself generated enough capital to send a third expedition to Baffin Island in 1578, without ever having tested any of the sample ore they had just received.

Over four hundred people aboard fifteen ships left Portsmouth, England, in May 1578, en route to the Countess of Warwick Island (or Kodlunarn Island), where the vein of supposedly rich minerals had been located. Confident that the area was rich in minerals, the expedition planned to establish a colony of a hundred people on the island. Miners, soldiers, carpenters, and mariners were to be left with provisions for eighteen months. After a perilous crossing of the North Atlantic, during which the expedition lost goods, ships, and manpower to ice and spring storms at sea, twelve ships reached their destination by mid-July. Among the missing ships was the *Dennis*, which was transporting prefabricated barracks essential to the founding of a colony.

Meanwhile, the "gold" turned out to be mica flecks! Frobisher was accused of fraud, disgraced, and his dreams of discovery ended. Temporary though the colony therefore was, the first English settlement in North America was actually on Kodlunarn Island, not Roanoke, Virginia, as most believe. Canadian archaeologists have worked at the site of the "gold strike," as have members of the

Smithsonian, including William Fitzhugh, who contacted me during the process of writing this book. He said he had done some of his thesis work on my Inuit ethnographic collection at the Smithsonian Museum in Washington, D.C. Until he wrote, I had forgotten I had a collection there! From his work, and that of his colleagues, I learned that although the site was abandoned more than four hundred years ago, a number of features were still visible on the surface.

The most obvious apparently were the abandoned mines, the foundation of a small cottage erected on the highest point of the island, and the foundations of two laboratories where ores were assayed before being loaded on board the ships. Less distinct were the bulwark, what seems to have been a blacksmith's shop, a ditch dug on the west side of the island to gather water during the summer of 1578 that was spent on the island, a possible burial ground, and what may have been a turf-walled hut.

Now here is where the debate about a Viking presence on Kodlunarn Island comes in. The first discovery of Frobisher's settlement was made by Francis Hall in 1861. There were Inuit tales of early white men living on this island and hauling their ships up for repairs. The Inuit told Hall that white men had lived there long ago, but it is believed they were referring to Frobisher's visit in the 1500s. Hall found a clump of smelted metal which he gave to the Smithsonian, and which was assumed to be from Frobisher's time there. However, tests by the Smithsonian Institute were not made until 1981 when the metal was dated to around A.D. 1200. Some assumed it as of Viking origin. But others debated the testing technique. The most recent evidence favors the Frobisher origin of the iron, especially since lading lists have been discovered that indicate Frobisher purchased iron blooms from a shipyard on the Thames, and the smelting material has been dated to the sixteenth century. My prejudice would have naturally hoped for a Viking date instead.

Five centuries after any Vikings might have been at Frobisher Bay, European whalers arrived. We know the Basques and other fearless seamen hunted whales there, and they may have brought diseases that further reduced the native population. In 1914 the Hudson's Bay Company opened a trading post at Ward Inlet, forty miles from Iqaluit's current location, and by the 1920s the company had established trading posts throughout Baffin Island. By the 1930s fur prices crashed, and many southern traders withdrew, leading to hard times for the Inuit as game had been over-hunted and southern commodities became scarce. Whaling was no longer commercially viable, and so for a decade Baffin Bay was quiet and tranquil—until we arrived with our planes and bulldozers in 1942.

While preparing the runway for flights to follow ours, a grader unearthed the entire skeleton of a whale. No study was done to determine its age, but as it lay about thirty-five feet above sea level, it was clearly from a geological age with substantially higher sea levels than we have today—an age earlier than even that of the Dorset Culture.

Have I mentioned that this was a damn lonely land? Weeks went by without a plane landing. Frobisher Bay was way off the heavily trafficked main section of the Crimson Route. The men felt forgotten, even nicknamed themselves "The Forgotten Bastards of Baffin Island," or the "FBI" (GIs are not always logical or literate in their acronyms). I, who was supposed to be setting up a rescue station, did not even have a dog team. There was, of course, no sign of the war where we were, but the base had received an order to set up anti-aircraft posts. My unit went about the rather useless mission of filling sandbags with the ample supply of sand we had available, and used them to set up anti-aircraft posts around this desolate and not-likely-to-be-attacked outpost. At last, Hassell, who was tired of waiting for headquarters to send material for my survival team, told me to use whatever was available and set up the rescue team myself.

There were already sled dogs at Crystal Two, but they, like some of the early military human arrivals at the base, had "gone native." Uncared for, they had lived wherever and however they could. There were a few that lived beneath the mess hall, gulping down whatever scraps of food were indecorously tossed out the window by the cook. These animals had grown unhealthily fat on lard drippings and other discarded food. Their coats were dull and crud-encrusted. They were half wild, and attempts to round them up had them cowering in the inaccessible confines beneath the kitchen or other shacks. One group of dogs had taken to the wilds, and was now living in a cave and raising a litter of pups there. The male of this family had once been the expensive pride and joy of Bill Shearer, from Massachusetts, whom I had met at Presque Isle, and whom had been stationed at Crystal Two with the original founders of the camp the year before. When Bill had to leave, he was not able to catch his dog.

One of my men was Harley Anderson, a fisherman from Coos Bay, Oregon. He and I made nets to catch the dogs, and we chased them around for days until we had them all. Once we had them contained, we used the nets to catch fish to feed them, since salmon, arctic char, and other fish abounded at the mouth of the Sylvia Grinnell River. Nets were set at high tide, and harvested at low. It was "easy pickin's"! Naturally, we ate the fish as well, particularly since the rations sent to us from the States were so deplorable, and vitamin-less. We also set up drying racks, and a smokehouse, though there was scarcely any wood suitable for the smoking except the minute dwarf willows. I had seen dwarf wood used for smoking fish at Ammassalik, so knew it could be done.

Later, we found that our nets were regularly being raided. A fish trawler that had been converted to a coastal-watch ship by the Canadian government was anchored nearby. It was manned by the fishing crew, not navy men, so we got highly suspicious. Hassell ordered guards set out to watch from hidden positions. Sure enough, late at night a small launch from the trawler came sneaking out toward the nets. A shot high over their heads—and in fun—put an end to the "fish war." The ship's crew had taken the fish in fun too, just to relieve the boredom. There was plenty of fish about for everyone. This comedic episode was the closest Crystal Two ever came to a fighting war.

As I was the only one with sled-driving experience, and with winter coming up, Hassell told me I could hire an Inuit for my outfit. As I have said, this land was no longer fit for Inuit to easily live off of by hunting, so it was not as easy to get a driver as one might think. An Inuit named Palouchi, who had been a driver for Jack Crowell the year before, had been hired by Hassell. One of Palouchi's jobs was to protect the base against polar bears ever since the enlisted men had reported seeing one. It was hanging around the camp, searching for garbage to eat, and the men did not want to stand guard, which was reasonable.

Palouchi was needed because regulations prevented non-natives from shooting the bear unless attacked. The Inuit could hunt polar bear, but only if they needed meat. Waiting for an attack was getting on the men's nerves, so Hassell told Palouchi to shoot the creature, since natives were not bound by the regulations that tied our hands. But Palouchi merely sat in his plywood shack instead of walking about, watching for polar bears.

"I have no proper mukluks," he explained (even though he did indeed have the appropriate footwear). He used every excuse he could think of. He had enough meat, was Palouchi's next bit of reasoning, so why kill the bear? Finally, the Mounties told him it was all right to dispatch the bear. Palouchi still felt put out, but did the job anyway. I watched all this with dismay. I understood his line of reasoning about the bear, but I needed a sled driver who might bring a bit of enthusiasm to the job of dog driver, and, obviously Palouchi was not going to be the man!

I finally found a desperately poor family down by Ward Inlet. This was the family of a man named Etuachia, who became my driver and friend. With Etuachia's expert help, we eventually had the dogs retrained and healthy. Soon, the first rescue squad on Baffin Island was ready for any emergency.

At that time, Crystal Two was being constructed, and the sound of the machinery was the most obvious change in the Arctic. Gone was the endless and healthy silence. An observer might stand with his eyes on primitive, unpopulated lands, which unflaggingly represented the astounding history of past eons, while his ears were locked into the snarling, combustion engine noise of the modern era. When the bulldozer that was excavating the runway pushed up the bones of that ancient whale, the moment was both exciting and sad. History was momentously unearthed, but at the same time history was carelessly being trampled under heavy metal treads.

Some of the men who now came to the Arctic were also part of a new breed. War and its commanders' directives had brought these men here rather than the pure scientific inquiry and natural curiosity that had motivated those of the "old school." That difference totally changed the Arctic. I never saw such indifference to the magnificent arctic world which had so transfigured me and most of the other arctic men I had known. Even the rough, tough, unsentimental trappers of the northeast coast of Greenland would suddenly stop their work and stand awestruck by the silent magnificence of their surroundings. But many of the new men rarely went off the post, and never contemplated the vast, unpopulated Arctic territory of their planet. They never had the slightest interest in the land, the plants, the animals, or the ancient culture of the Inuit.

Was it the machines that made the new men so lackadaisical? I'd read that somewhere. Was it the mounds of supplies, foods of all kinds, the ear-numbing sound of gas-powered electric generators, the blasts of dynamite, the smells of diesel fuel and paint, or the easy availability of building materials that made the majority so benumbed to the wonders of the unexplored land around them, that brimmed with such history and natural wonder? Whatever the reason, I never did understand this shocking indifference. Thankfully, my crew was a totally different matter. They wanted to learn everything, and they stuck to me like glue.

My crew and I were out one day scouting the terrain near the base. On a ridge overlooking the river delta, I looked down and could just barely make out the traces of ruins etched through the ground which covered them. I had seen similar sights in Greenland. When we descended the ridge, I loosened a bit of the tundra turf, and, sure enough, there were ruins. In 1887 Francis Hall had reported seeing many Thule Culture ruins just where I had found them, though I had not known of his report at the time. Though the Rawson-MacMillan Expedition of the 1920s had sought the ruins Hall mentioned, they had not found them. When Sharat Roy came to Frobisher in 1944, he and I talked about his 1920s visit. He told me that he and Duncan Strong had been standing right on top of where I eventually discovered the ruins, and had not seen anything. It was only my fortuitous view from the ridge, plus a bit of experience, which had allowed me to become their re-discoverer, and the first to work on them. The Canadian government even issued me an official permit to search the ruins.

Part of my findings—later to be called the Knutsen Collection—were donated to the national Canadian museum at Ottawa, and of course the Smithsonian. The late Henry Collins, the Smithsonian's ethnographic curator and a friend of mine, learned of this site from me, and later came to work on the same site. He dug deeper than I had, and discovered an earlier Dorset culture, four thousand years old! I have to admit I am damn proud to have played a part in their discovery. I believe it must have been my findings from this site that William Fitzhugh, who took over for Henry Collins at the Smithsonian, kindly wrote to tell me about.

During that first summer, the famous Newfoundlander and explorer, Captain Bob Bartlett, came into the bay aboard his ship the *Morrissey*. Amazingly, and typical of Arctic coincidences, Vilhjalmur Stefansson arrived soon after by plane. That this isolated outpost should be visited by these two arctic legends at the same time was only just short of miraculous. It certainly was not planned. They had not seen or spoken to each other for decades—and that is just the way they had wanted it.

Bartlett and Stefansson had once explored the Arctic together in the early 1900s. The source of their tension was the Canadian Arctic Expedition of 1913 to

1918. Stefansson had been the leader, and Bartlett was skipper of the lead ship, *Karluk*, in an expedition that ended in tragedy. Briefly, the situation was this: The *Karluk* had become ice-locked off the northeast coast of Alaska. Food provisions became scarce. Stefansson, who had already learned to survive in the Arctic, went hunting with a few of the men, leaving mostly young scientists with little arctic training on board with Bob Bartlett. A horrendous storm came up, *Karluk* was pushed away from its position, and Stefansson, after futile attempts to find the ship, had to live off the land for five years! Under Bartlett's command, the twenty-five others on the ship, including an Inuit, his wife, and two young children, drifted helplessly for months before the ship sank, and they had to take to the ice. They suffered tremendously for another six months. Bartlett went for help and covered seven hundred miles of frightful conditions to bring back a rescue party, but not before eleven men had of died of cold, starvation, and suicide.

Bartlett blamed Stefansson for not providing leadership for the inexperienced men. Stefansson wrote that he had assumed the crew had made it to land, and that local Alaskan Inuit would have found them and led them to safety. Therefore, he added, he turned his mind to exploration. He covered hundreds of miles, going deep into the Canadian Arctic Archipelago, discovering three new islands along the way. He returned, not knowing World War I had come and gone, to a hero's welcome, complete with awards and public acclaim. But in any event, the case of both great men had been aired in the newspapers of the day, books had been written, and I would guess the whole literate world at the time was held spellbound by the details of all the accounts. Not since 1917 had these explorers talked to each other, let alone set eyes on each other, and yet here they were, fatefully brought together at Frobisher Bay on the edge of nowhere!

Stef had heard that I was there, and the first thing he said was, "Let's take a look at those dogs of yours; I've heard about them all the way back in New York." Stefansson heartily approved of the whole operation. Later, in his autobiography, he referred to me as "a man who knew dogs." In his mind, this was a very great compliment, and I took it that way.

Stefansson had not been to the Arctic in a very long time, and he was not at all happy with the modernization the camp represented. He and I talked about living off the land, the beauty of the stillness and solitude—in short, "the good old days." He thought the choice of the site of our base was a poor one. President Roosevelt's son, Elliot, who had come there in 1940, had recommended this spot for the base. Stefansson's disapproval of the choice was based on the fact that he'd heard the hunting was poor in this area. An explorer who lived off the land, Stefansson's main criteria for a military base was that it have good seal and walrus hunting. Never mind that this site was the only one possible for a runway! But I knew what he meant. If we were ever truly cut off from the airlifts of food and supplies in the winter, most of the men at Frobisher would not live long.

Though I knew of the feud between Stef and Bob Bartlett, I thought I would try to arrange a meeting between them. Fish Hassell had flown down to Presque Isle for a briefing, and the protocol was left to me, not unpleasant duty in this case. I had met Bartlett briefly in Washington, D.C., and I rowed out to his ship for a reunion. During our lunch aboard his ship in Frobisher Bay, he astounded me with how much he knew of my career, and of course, we discovered we had many mutual arctic friends. When we had met in Washington, he had been on his way to Baffin Island with my old friend, the indomitable Louise A. Boyd, who had chartered his ship. She had quite a reputation as a domineering type to her skippers. Even tough Norwegians had buckled under her will. Bartlett, who disapproved of women leading expeditions, told me about the trip.

"She was the biggest dictator I ever met!" Bartlett said. "But I put a stop to her nonsense first thing. The rest of the voyage had no love in it, I can tell you!" I, who loved the old girl, could not help smiling at the thought of two strong wills sailing on one small ship. Louise, by the way, won a medal for her work on that expedition, which greatly helped the military to make accurate maps of the coast, and of the sea bottom.

Also on board the *Morrissey* was Dr. Alexander Forbes, the famous cartographer, and writer of *The Quest for the Northern Air Route*. Forbes had chartered the vessel for the government to make soundings of the bay. And it was about time, too! After we had eaten, I asked Bartlett if I could sketch him, which he consented to. As I sketched, I casually mentioned that the explorer, Stefansson, was ashore. Bartlett, whom I had been told in his later years had become religious and had foresworn cussing, sputtered, "Explorer, my ass! The only thing he has explored since 1918 has been Greenwich Village!"

When I had finished the sketch, Bob's brother privately told me he had never seen the old sea dog sit still that long. Back on shore, I politely asked Stef if I should arrange a dinner and invite Bartlett. Stef, who was not young anymore, was younger than Bartlett, and he said with a kindly, though obviously coy voice,

"No, no. He's getting on in years, and you ought not to tire him out." That nicely let me off the hook, protocol-wise, and prevented a possibly explosive meeting—but it certainly would have been interesting to have instigated that reunion.

Few white men came this far north because they wanted to. The war had brought most of them. A remarkable exception was an Englishman named Tom Manning, who came by the base for a visit one day. I did not recognize him at first because of his long beard, and it had been ten years, but after we got to talking, we realized with astonishment that we had met in Alta, Lapland, in 1932! Tom had come to the Canadian Arctic a few years later. He lived, usually alone, on the east coast of Baffin Island, and had become a legend. He had met a Canadian nurse at some remote outpost, and they had been married aboard the Coast Guard ship, *Nascopie*, the captain being the only one in hundreds of miles authorized to conduct a marriage ceremony. Several marriages were held on board that ship, in fact.

Tom and his wife spent two years living like the Inuit on the west coast of Baffin Island, but when the war broke out, he had joined the Canadian armed forces. Manning's ship lay at anchor in the harbor. While Tom was out roaming about our camp, Herman Andresen told me that Tom had killed a large polar bear with a knife while on Southampton Island in 1942. In the evening, I asked Tom if the story was true. "Well, it was not such a large polar bear," he said casually.

Winter began its radical transformation of the land. The bay froze over. When the tide went out, the ice stayed behind; when the tide returned, it piled the ice in enormous jumbled walls that could tumble at any moment. Travel on that end of the bay was almost impossible. The land was wracked by frigid winds; men staggered about their duties, miserable and gloomy. Our landing field was in perpetual darkness. During the long, dark days we constructed small igloos along the sides of the runway. When small oil lamps were lit inside, the whole dome glowed from the outside like a dim lightbulb. We also made larger ones that served as aerial navigation markers, the "Baffin Beacons" so eagerly sought by pilots of the Crimson Route who had errantly drifted this far north off the main flight path.

Our first rescue mission involved bringing food to a group of starving Inuit on Peugh Island, seventy miles down the bay on the shore opposite us. An emaciated Inuit had staggered into our base with the distressing news of his people's near-death situation. Etuachia and I took a sled down the coast, and then went on foot to the island. We crossed the treacherous jumble of ice, slowly and ago-nizingly, literally inching our way along. Reaching the island, we found the peo-ple in the most miserable condition imaginable. Many lay near death, but luckily, our rescue came in time. When we noticed that a nearby government supply cache (left by Jack Crowell the year before as a storage depot) still had plenty of provisions, I asked the Inuit why they had not broken into it. They replied that the missionaries, long since returned to civilization, had told them they would go to Hell if they stole, and especially if they stole from whites!

Before the arrival of white missionaries, the Inuit regularly took whatever they needed from one another without asking, since all was more or less com-mon property. Early white arrivals had been treated in the same manner. The job of teaching the Inuit the subtleties of theft had been given over to the mis-sionaries. The missionaries left these trusting people with such mortal fear for their souls that they would not help themselves to food that would have saved their lives! There has been a lot written about the harmful effects the mission-aries often had on the Inuit, and unfortunately, it was often true. A few mission-aries were the much-needed exception, most of whom lived among the Inuit. There is a story circulating in the Arctic about an overzealous missionary who became enraged when, warning his flock about the fires of Hell, he had been told by the natives that that sounded like a good, warm place to go!

CHAPTER SEVENTEEN

Mercy Mission to Lake Harbour

I n the first week of January 1944, I was harnessing my sled dogs on a cold, dark, quiet morning. I prepared myself mentally for a grueling, hundred-mile trip from Frobisher Bay, across a rugged, barren mountain range, and then down to a small military outpost at Lake Harbour. The temperature was minus-thirty-five degrees Fahrenheit. The dogs were grouchy as I wrestled with their straps. By that day in 1944, I had spent four out of the last seven years in the Arctic. There had been some pretty close calls, some dramatic adventures, and some historic and scientific firsts. There had also been some pretty dumb moves, but the mission I was about to undertake on Baffin Island seemed to me to be the most absurd.

Though our tiny station was free from the "spit and polish" of many military units, and though we had comfortable quarters, plenty of good food, phonograph players, and very importantly, work to do, some of my men were not very happy to be there, unlike me who had made the Arctic my life's work. Most of the young men (I was an "old-timer" at age thirty-two) had not known the privations we earlier arctic explorers had gone through. Complaints were therefore natural. And it did not help to tell the guys, accustomed to American life, baseball, and so on, about how rough it was in the "good old days." But I had to put my face in my hands and shake my head in wonder when I was told, "Lieutenant, the cook at Lake Harbour has gonorrhea!"

The cook had carried his infection from the States. Although Hassell had consulted a medical book, which said the disease could only be transmitted sexually, naturally, no one wanted the cook in the kitchen, and I had had to radio for a replacement. So, there I was, harnessing the sled dogs for the trip to Lake Harbour.

With me as I readied the dogs was the Inuit driver, Etuachia, and two Canadians, Pepin and LeBlanc. Etuachia would carry the new cook on his long, narrow Baffin Island-style sled. The other two were on a clumsy, "rocker-type" sled invented by some inept explorer of earlier years. I had a "Nansen" sled, a superior type I had used in my earlier work in Greenland. Before we set out, I asked the cook if he had received any arctic survival training. "Sure—in Denver, Colorado," he said. I had heard there was a survival school there, and as I pictured the snow-clad mountains of Colorado I had seen in photos, I felt better about him. I knew we were in for some rough arctic traveling.

As we set out, the dogs looked at me as though I were stupid to be going out in such weather; I couldn't blame them, but we headed out anyway, with them howling and yelping bravely to get geared up for the journey. Above us the sky seemed a frozen deep black. In only a few minutes we were alone. A patch of open water on the bay, caused by currents, shot up fog like a volcano. It enveloped us for the first part of the trip, crystallizing everything it touched. The dogs quit their enthusiastic racket to save their lungs from the frigid fog, and settled in for the long pull across the mountain pass.

The mountainous area of Baffin Island we had to cross is called Meta Incognito Peninsula, which was an accurate analysis of the geographic and historic situation there. So few humans, including the Inuit, had ever been into these mountains that it was laughable. New arrivals to our outpost were always astounded when they learned that unexplored wilderness existed all around the base. After all, there were maps, weren't there? However, the maps we used had often been based on maps from Martin Frobisher's brief visit in 1578, when he had so gloomily named the land I was sledding over.

Since that time, the American explorer Charles Francis Hall had come into Frobisher Bay in 1861 and made an outstanding map, and recent aerial photography had added further details, but still, no one had actually walked through the damn place. The pass itself had been used by the Inuit for centuries. And in modern times a few Royal Canadian Mounties, a few trappers, or an occasional missionary would make the hard sled trip through as well. Sharat Roy was the only person I knew who had done any scientific work there; that is, traveled off the "beaten path" of the pass. There is a peak there named for him. Among our little group, the only one who had made this journey before was Etuachia, and that was many years before.

As I drove my dog team through the frigid wilderness of Meta Incognito to deliver a replacement cook for the one with gonorrhea, I did so with my mouth set in a tight, sardonic grin. A situation like this was surely not what General "Hap" Arnold had in mind when he said the U.S. needed me in the Arctic!

Free of the freezing fog at last, we were presented with the somber view of the dark, craggy peaks far above the foothills we now struggled over. The snow was deep, and a stiff wind blew, ripping at clothing and stinging and numbing our exposed skin with hard, sand-like grains of snow. I was in the lead, breaking the trail. The dogs were exerting themselves heroically. Against my advice, Etuachia's dog team included a pregnant one he insisted was needed for the trip, but she was pulling as hard as the rest. After a few hours, we were going so slowly I let my team pull without me, and walked back to see how the cook was doing. He was huddled under blankets, but I could tell he was in trouble. He had lost his mittens to the wind! Too proud to tell us, he was suffering terribly. Also, his nose and chin bore the warning signs of frostbite.

I said to him, "For Christ's sake! Why didn't you tell us you were freezing to death?" The rest of us quickly built a snow shelter, covered it with a tarp, and got him inside. A Primus stove soon had the cramped quarters warm. When his color returned, I said, "I thought you told me you'd had Arctic training in Colorado?"

"Well," he said rather sheepishly, "we had classes for a few hours in a hangar on the base. And I guess I wasn't paying much attention, anyway."

I was speechless. Fortunately, exhaustion prevented any further attempts at conversation.

In the morning we started out again. The wind was still strong, and the trail got steeper and steeper. The rocker sled was almost useless, and was slowing us down. I told the men to divide the sled's load between the other sleds, and we left the damn thing there. For all I know, it is still there. Before we got moving, Etuachia said excitedly, "Tuk-Tuk! Caribou!" and did a waddling attempt at running in the deep snow toward a solitary caribou silhouetted in the distance. Except for the rifle he carried, it was a dramatically timeless scene. But it was hopeless; the animal was too far away. Reluctantly he came back to the sleds, and we struggled upwards again.

The dogs were leaning into their harnesses, sometimes needing to make lunges in the snow. Pepin and LeBlanc walked alongside, pushing when necessary. At times we had to push with all our strength. Still, the trail got steeper. For hours this went on. The ridge loomed far above us, and more hours passed as we continued our ascent. Finally, the crest was just above us. The last few yards were extremely steep. I was first over the edge and on level ground. A little ways behind me Etuachia's sled came creeping along. On the last, steepest part, his pregnant dog began to whelp! The pups were dropping out into the snow. Some of the dogs behind her were trying to snap up the pups for food, and others were trying to mount her.

"Can't stop!" Etuachia shouted to me. "We'll never get going again on this slope!"

He ran forward, and was beating the dogs that had been driven lustfully insane by the smell of the birthing. Pepin and LeBlanc were frantically pushing the sled from behind. I shouted to Etuachia to kill the poor, damn little things. He was busy beating the dogs, and shouted back that he couldn't do it, couldn't face it. He was willing to leave the newborn pups to freeze, but the usually tough hunter couldn't bring himself to kill them.

I lumbered, stumbled, and slid back down to where his sled was just barely still moving. A snarling male was trying to gulp down one of the pups, and I banged him in the head with the butt of my whip. As the pups emerged and dropped, I put the tiny creatures out of their misery, and deep into the snow, with the heel of my boot. The male dogs, now less diverted, pulled forward again as one. The suffering mother was merely hanging in the harness and being dragged along, but the sled just made it over the top. The dogs, knowing the worst was over, dropped exhausted to the snow. So did we. Steam poured off all our bodies, creating a small cloud of bio-fog, and there we lay for a long time.

While we rested, we fed the dogs hunks of frozen walrus meat Etuachia had bought from the local Inuit at Frobisher back in the fall. I didn't want to think what the meat would smell like if we allowed it to thaw. We cached a small supply of pemmican as we rested, and marked the spot with a bamboo pole with a flag attached. I had learned in Greenland to make supply depots wherever and whenever possible. When we took off, it was downhill, but gently so. The bitch that had just whelped rode on my sled. The temperature was now minus-forty-five degrees. We drove all day with only short rest periods for the dogs. When the snow became so deep that the sleds got bogged down, I went ahead on skis again to break a trail. Whenever we stopped to build a cache, or rest the dogs, the cook just sat there like a lump. Now he was getting frightened. He moaned that he didn't want any part of this Arctic. He suddenly went berserk, screaming, "Get me outta here! I'd rather die. I want out of here! Get me outta here!" He was getting hysterical because the dark, cold immensity and forbidding nature of the land had become the smirking mask of death to him. This happened to many an unprepared mind in these conditions. We took a break.

"Look," I said to him, "if I was just sitting there, I'd be scared and freezing too. Get off your dead ass and get some exercise!"

He just looked at me with no expression, so I told him, "That's a goddamn order!" and yanked him off the sled. Soon the sleds were moving right along. The cook ran in a wobbly-legged fashion, but I knew he would soon feel better. He had no business being in the Arctic without proper training.

Toward the end of the day, while we sledded over the upper region of the frozen Soper River, the dogs began to have the runs. It was caused by that semi-rotten walrus meat, and it stunk unbelievably. To make things worse, some of the dogs were scooping it up and eating the stuff as they ran! The cook, back on the sled, looked as if he was about to go mad. I couldn't blame him that time.

When it was dark, one of the dogs started running drunkenly; I knew that was a sign of a frozen lung. I wrapped the dog up in blankets and put it on the sled. The mother had to take its place. Such was life. We kept going over the frozen river, making occasional rest stops, far into the moonlit night. After three hours, I began to search the land ahead for a landmark that a Royal Canadian Mounted Police officer friend of mine, Doug Webster, had warned me about.

Doug had said, "When you see that, Willie, make a stop. There is a drop-off at a frozen waterfall. You'll have to lower the dogs and sleds by ropes. I learned the hard way. I saw the drop-off, but by then, it was too late, and since we were going downhill, the dogs just kept going. I rolled off just before the whole mess went over!" Doug continued, "Thinking I was now out in the middle of nowhere without a team, I figured I was in a hell of a fix, not to mention I'd lost the government a valuable bunch of dogs. I peered over the edge, and there they all were, staring up and wondering what had happened to me! The lucky bastards had just rolled, slid, and bounced their way down, ass-over-teakettle. But it's a lot better to lower them, I'm sure."

We slept like the dead in a camp just above the falls, and in the morning we began the slow process of lowering dogs, sleds, and all. The cook was learning fast, helping out and keeping busy, and admitted he was getting to like the Arctic. Soon the sleds were *shushing* along smartly downhill through the gloomy darkness. Sledding just a few miles, we heard another dog team coming our way, making quite a cacophony. As I've said before, sound travels far and loud in the frigid air, and it was a long time before we saw a large team of about eighteen dogs coming up the slope. On the sled was the Inuit, Shutiapik, with Bill Carter, the Hudson Bay Company's area manager, and my RCMP buddy, Doug Webster. They had come from Lake Harbour, a two-day sled trip, and were on their way to Frobisher Bay.

We had a grand meeting out there in the middle of nowhere. The dogs howled greetings while we men sat down to chat and share some food. Doug cracked open one of the boxes of supplies on the sled bound for Frobisher Bay. It was a case of VO scotch! He pulled out a bottle, then sealed up the case. It was 80 percent alcohol, but in that weather it was slush. We drank an entire bottle anyway, and made a dumb joke about the Mounties always getting their man, and that it was "The Case of the VO: Case opened; case closed!" Corny, but obviously the stuff was having the desired effect.

Though drinking alcohol in such weather is not too bright, we soon felt pretty good. As we jawed about this and that, mostly about the Arctic, the cook said to me, "Say, Lieutenant—things sure must be changing fast up here from when you started out in the Arctic." The wind was blowing snow among the boulders near us. I looked at him, thought of the ridiculous reason why we were sledding him across this dangerous wilderness in the first place, looked at the case of scotch, then said, "You're goddamned right!"

CHAPTER EIGHTEEN

Pirates, Spies, and Rescues

T he absurdities in the new Arctic did not end in that frozen pass. When I arrived back from Lake Harbour after two hard weeks on the trail, Hassell told me that I was taking command of a small outpost even further north, at Padloping Island on the east coast of Baffin Island. He added, almost as an afterthought, that I was now a captain! This remote base was code-named Crystal Three. I should have been suspicious from reading my orders: There was a long, detailed section about how men in remote sites often tended to neglect their duties, and that there was a need for discipline, especially in "these kind of places."

I flew from Crystal Two to my first command with Eddie Goodale and the famous meteorologist, Colonel Merriwether. We zoomed over the arctic in a then very modern military transport version of the DC-3, the C-47. The C-47 was also called the Sky Train, and was capable of carrying twenty-eight troops or six thousand pounds of cargo. Such capability was undreamt of only five years before, and yet there we were, flying in relative luxury 275 miles northeast over Hall Peninsula, then Cumberland Sound, and then Cumberland Peninsula—which means some of the most magnificent scenery in the world.

Along Cumberland Peninsula were mountains that looked like Empire State Buildings lining a large fjord. Glaciers flowed down ice-capped mountains for as far as we could see. Our flight maps said the highest elevations were four thousand feet, and we were somewhat above that. Obviously, whoever had made the maps had never been as close to them as we were, because the pilot, who had been relying on the maps, had to veer sharply and head for a pass. As close as we were, and at that speed, we would have smacked into the mountainside, thousands of feet below the top! The mountains were twice what the maps said. It turned out the pilot was using maps that borrowed findings made by Franz Boas in the 1880s, and by Hall in the 1870s. This shows how little was known of this land during the period the U.S. military was struggling to set up bases and outposts.

There was no landing strip on the island of Crystal Three. The coast was a wall of high, glacier-capped mountains, and we had to make a bumpy, hard landing on the frozen bay, the surface of which had been dragged smooth of some of the worst bumps and ruts. We emerged shaken but undamaged into a beautiful arctic scene. It was sheer wilderness. If Frobisher Bay had seemed past the edge of the known world to the new military arrivals, Padloping must have seemed a new planet to them! And to back this up, we arrived at a station that was halfway between a comedy and a nightmare.

Padloping had been intended as an emergency hospital zone for the Crimson Route, and a large hospital building was nearly finished. Other buildings in various stages of completion made the site look like a large base peopled by many men. I knew there should be only fifteen men, but there were at least that many buildings—one per man. And yet not a soul stirred. No one greeted the plane. We had the feeling that we were entering a ghost town. When we finally found the CO in his quarters, it was obvious he had gone a little goofy. With a heavy southern accent, he babbled as he packed, telling me that all he could see were "cotton fields," referring to the snow, and all he could smell was "nigger-sweat," referring to the Inuit who did domestic chores on the base.

The men on my team from the South told me they could handle him, and I gladly let them do it rather than have to suffer his company. His seedy-looking second-in-command was also his bodyguard, complete with a .45 on his belt, because of the enlisted men's deadly dislike of their CO. Strangely, neither knew where their men were. "I don't give a good goddamn where them nigger lovers have got to!" was all we got out of the man I was replacing.

After the plane had left with these two strange characters, I searched for the enlisted men, since the sleeping quarters seemed unused. It turned out some of the men were living with Inuit women in rough shelters off-base. Others had set up individual, spacious quarters in unused buildings. A nightclub worthy of any town had been set up, complete with a fake fireplace that had a small fan blowing strips of colored cellophane to imitate a fire.

Generally speaking, the men had gone even more native than the men at Crystal Two. All basic ideas of cleanliness, shaving and such, had been abandoned; they had forgotten there was a war on. The mess hall was a pigsty, and passageways were dangerously cluttered. Vehicles were in disrepair, furnaces were not working, and some buildings were filling with snow because doors had been left open. I then discovered that one of the warehouses was locked with a padlock. When I asked for the key, one of the men curtly said it was a private lock, and looked at me as if daring me to do something about it.

I ordered the lock cut, and found that the warehouse contained a fortune in furs and pelts. Two of the men had started a pirate "Hudson's Bay Company." They were buying cheaply from the Inuit, and turning a nice profit by selling to pilots and crews just passing through. The warehoused furs were waiting for buyers who would ship the goods south on government planes, at taxpayers' expense! And these two birds seemed genuinely put out that I had put an end to their operation. It was as if I was the criminal.

Though the pirates knew that only the Hudson's Bay Company had a license from the Canadian government to deal with the Inuit, these two thought that since they were in the wilderness, no one would catch on. It had not occurred to them that the Hudson's Bay Company buyers were going to know something was wrong when they arrived at Inuit camps to buy furs and pelts, and there weren't any! I had only been at the base a few days when, sure enough, an angry agent arrived by dogsled. When I turned over the furs and pelts to these agents, the pirates felt sorely aggrieved and demanded that they be compensated for what they had paid the hunters. Eddie Goodale said he thought ten years in Leavenworth might do the trick, and that shut them up.

I did not make myself immediately popular when I put a stop to the pirate operations and ordered the men back to the barracks to relearn basic cleanliness and military behavior, but when I began painting murals on their barroom walls, they seemed to forgive me. They even stopped griping when I had them do daily marching and drills. Soon the station became what it was supposed to be: a weather reporting station and rescue site.

The history of that little-known coast was interesting, though somewhat bizarre. Of course, the signs of the vanished Inuit peoples were everywhere. Also, it seems the coast had once been the landing spot for Vikings who followed the currents from Greenland. A missionary, Reverend Turner, one of the decent men in his occupation, came by sled for a visit. Reverend Turner told me about finding what he believed to be Viking runes while on a dogsled run in the mountain pass that linked our coast with that of Cumberland Sound. The runes had been inscribed on a rock, but he had not been able to dig it up, and later, on subsequent runs, he could not find the spot again. That was understandable, as flagstones by the tens of thousands littered the entire sixty-mile-long pass. Turner's brother, also a missionary, had been killed with his own rifle while helping an Inuit. Crawling through the entrance of the Inuit's shelter, the gun had accidentally gone off.

Centuries after the Vikings' arrival, when whalers plied the coast, a nearby cove had been used for anchorage, but another bit of local history was enough to make one sigh for the folly of mankind. About sixty miles south, at Exeter Sound, a group of Englishmen had tried to set up an agricultural colony a hundred years before. Where they had got the notion they could farm that arctic coast is beyond me, but their endeavor was short-lived. Large heaps of rusting equipment still lay scattered about as a monument to their imprudence.

Crystal Three had just begun running smoothly when I received a telegram directing me to Goose Bay, Labrador. Since there was no explanation, one of the thoughts I had was that I might have unwittingly trod on the toes of some big shot when I shut down the pirate Hudson's Bay Company. Arriving first at Baffin Island, Hassell told me over a welcome-back toast with whiskey that I was going to Greenland for a few days. Seems I was to advise a commando outfit there about the best way to dislodge some Germans who had set up a weather station on the northeast coast!

The station was on Sable Island, south of my old stomping grounds in Germania Land. Of course, no one in the attack team knew anything about the lay of the land, the best way to get in, the weather conditions, or the pack ice, so that is why I was called in. This is the best part: These characters at the Nazi station were the ones who had been involved in the plot to paint me out as a spy. While the British had been busy arresting John Gjaever and trying to find my ship, these were the spies who had slipped in to the coast unnoticed. This assignment to help flush the bastards out was going to be a particularly pleasurable one.

Arriving at Narssarssuaq, I was first met by a securities officer. A real cloak-and-dagger type, he showed me the book on Greenland that I had had a hand in helping Stefansson write. He asked, "Are you the Willie Knutsen who helped with this book?" I admitted I was, and then he relaxed and led me to the briefing room, where I was told about the situation.

My old friends—the Danish trappers at Clavering Island, Hold with Hope, Ella Island, and so on—had, on their own steam, created a coastal watch called "The Sled Patrol." Going singly, or in twos or threes, these men drove the dogsleds up and down the harsh, lonely northeast coast. The patrol's leader was

Ib Paulsen, the man who at Spitsbergen had given me the letter from Eigil Knuth, granting me permission to use Knuth's studio at Ammassalik.

Marius Jensen, Kurt Olsen, Peter Nielsen, and Eli Knudsen were among the members of the patrol. Eli Knudsen had stumbled upon the Nazi meteorological station. The Germans had ordered him to halt, but his dogs kept pulling toward them. Eli was shot and killed. Marius and Peter had later been captured, but escaped when the leader of the Germans had, astonishingly, given himself up to Jensen. They then had made it safely to Ella Island where the alarm was sent up. Here is the amazing part: The German leader was none other than Herman Ritter, the Austrian who, along with his wife, Christiane, had wintered on Spitsbergen with Kalle! Ritter, chosen for this role because of his arctic expertise, had been a reluctant leader of the Nazi weather station, and at Eli's death, had sickened of the whole affair. I was so astounded at hearing this coincidence that it took me a few minutes before I could share the story of Kalle and Ritter with the men I was briefing. It was agreed that if it were put into a movie script, people would have thought it far-fetched!

Eli Knudsen had been killed in March 1943. The Americans, hearing of the enemy weather station, had bombed the site some months later from the air. Bernt Balchen had been in charge of that bombing run. Kalle, Ritter, and I had been involved in this affair, and now, so was Bernt. It was truly amazing. Later it was found that the Germans had been warned of the attack through the interception of radio messages, and had built shelters in snowdrifts. After the attack, they came out and reestablished another station. A ground attack was attempted next, but the commando group had run into weather trouble and had to be rescued from the fury of the Arctic. None of the men had had survival training, but that was being remedied. Balchen had remembered that this was my old stomping ground, and that's why I had been sent for. "Iceberg" Smith's prediction of my usefulness on that coast had at last come true.

At Narssarssuaq I met many of the men I had known at Presque Isle, including Norman Vaughan, who was now the commander of the whole Crimson Route. Norman is one of the most decent men I have ever met. A nondrinker, nonetheless, whenever the rest of us got a bit wild and funny from drinking, he could get right into the mood with the rest of us.

But most of the time, just to make it clear, these guys were busy training the commandos in the basics of arctic survival. I briefed the commandos on the area they were to raid. I drew maps, and described the best routes, the dangers they might encounter, where they might still find supply depots, and so on. After a week I was flown back to Goose Bay. Ultimately, the dangerous mission to unseat the Nazis in Northeast Greenland was successful. Three weather stations were destroyed in 1943. One was on Little Koldewey, where my ship had wintered in 1938 and 1939.

This story was not released until early in 1944, when Bernt Balchen told a stunned American audience: "You did not know the Nazis had actually established a foothold on this side of the Atlantic. You did not know, all last year, that their planes were flying within bombing distance of the shores of North America. Their well-equipped weather station on the undefended east coast of Greenland was sending communications to Berlin daily. Nazi submarines were refueling there, and then going after our ships heading for England and Murmansk."

What Bernt did not reveal to the audience was that he had received medals for rescuing downed bomber crews on the Greenland ice cap. The planes had been lured there by a radio beacon placed by the Nazis. But not all his rescues on the ice cap—and there were several—were due to German tricks. Greenland's notorious weather was the cause of most crashes. In one incident, a plane was in whiteout conditions when the navigator yelled to the pilot that the instruments showed no flight speed. They had landed softly on the high, gently sloping ice cap without knowing it.

One of the officers who had been with the naval attack on the Nazi weather stations was Norman Von Rosenvinge, from Rockport, Massachusetts, who later became a friend of mine when I moved there after the war. He had been on the *Northland* with Iceberg Smith when they captured a German ship attempting to evacuate their comrades after Bernt had bombed them. When Von Rosenvinge returned to Goose Bay, he told me a side story about the raid.

After the raid, the ship had sailed to the tiny, mid-Norwegian Sea island of Jan Mayen where a Norwegian weather station operated. There, Norman had overheard some trappers drinking a toast to my memory and sad death! Norman cut in to tell them that I was alive and well. They had thought that I, not Eli Knudsen, had been killed in 1943. It turned out they had heard the news over a badly crackling radio, so it sounded like Willie Knutsen. (In 1964, I would visit Eli's grave at Sandodden, near Clavering Island.)

Arriving back in Goose Bay, I found that Hassell had taken over command there, and he had made me head of Goose Bay Rescue Operations, the main rescue site on the Crimson Route. We unfortunately stayed very busy there. During May, June, July, and August of 1944, 2,373 tactical planes passed through on the way to Europe, and many arrived back to refuel on their return trip to American hospitals. Not all arrived. The long flight across the Atlantic strained engines and wore out crews. The weather around Goose Bay was often horrendous. And I cannot emphasize enough that this central part of Labrador, and the adjoining province of Quebec, are heavily forested and extremely rugged. The four thousand-square-mile area to the north was not even surveyed.

A glance at a map will also show thousands and thousands of lakes and rivers. Lakes were at differing elevations, so even if they appeared to be sitting cozily next to each other on a map, they might actually be at quite different elevations, so sharp and rough were the cliffs. The cliffs might run for miles like folds in an accordion. This terrain is a craggy forest wilderness of ravines, thunderous cataracts, and awesome falls. When planes seeking Goose Bay had navigational or mechanical problems, there was one large, nearly unpopulated territory to get lost in if there was a crash. There were certainly precious few places to land safely. Planes went down, and we went looking for them.

In the summer, hordes of mosquitoes made the wearing of face-nets on rescue missions imperative. They were so numerous and vicious, animals such as caribou were often driven mad by the stings, and it was also dangerous for men without protection, as one can literally be stung to death. A much earlier attempt to start a timber industry in the region failed simply because the mules and other draft animals were rendered useless, or even killed by the innumerable bites they suffered. Even on the water, we were plagued by the notorious Labrador flies that were only the size of a pinhead. You don't see them until they've bitten you, leaving a burning pain. Back in Maine, these bastards had been called "no-see-ums." They got into our ears, up our nostrils, and bit our eyes, faces, and hands so much that we scratched until we bled. My shirtsleeves at the wrists were caked hard with blood by the end of many a day out in the lovely wilds of Labrador. Even going over cataracts, with white water showering us, the flies persisted with their attacks.

The only solution was to sew headgear out of parachute nylon, and then sew mosquito netting for a face mask. This contraption had to be worn over a hat with a wide brim so that the headgear would not touch our faces—otherwise the bugs would just sting us through the net. There was another kind of fly the size of a dime that seemed to take chunks of flesh when it bit. The local French Canadian trappers called these flies "bulldogs," and swore they could be shot out of the trees! Conversely, in the winter, heavy snowfalls and minus-forty-degree temperatures created another kind of torment for downed flight crews.

On top of all the other problems in the area for flight crews, Goose Bay is subject to a lot of electromagnetic disturbances that hamper navigational equipment. And there was another hazard that went hand in hand with the magnetic one. In the summer, particularly around August, the inland temperatures could be in the eighties and even the nineties, and the heat creates fog due to the cold waters of the bay and the huge fjord beyond. Flights coming back from Europe should theoretically follow the flight path that took them north of the fjord where there were no mountains, and usually less fog. But a plane could have navigational problems, end up approaching the base from south of the fjord, and then run into thick fog just before the wicked peaks of the Mealy Mountains. These peaks were from two to four thousand feet high, and covered four hundred square miles. Unfortunately, I spent far too much time in those treacherous mountains.

Terror, suffering, and heroism are good terms to describe what was required of my men during daily life on the Crimson Route. For example, a plane had gone missing over the Atlantic off the coast of Labrador. Later, in the spring, rumors reached us of a plane wreck discovered by an Indian in the Mealy Mountains. A flight over the area confirmed the report. The wreckage was in an area inaccessible by plane. The crew had been missing for a long time, so we did not expect to find survivors; we were there to recover the bodies.

My pilot landed our amphibious plane on a lake miles from the site. Exiting the plane, we were met by a dark cloud of mosquitoes. Without our facenets, we would have been eaten alive. We took to our canoes. After going upstream for miles, and portaging dangerous cataracts, we finally had to give up that means of travel and take to our feet. We began to go cross-country over the most rugged terrain imaginable. The land was a jumble of ravines and ridges, sort of a tortured stone maze for giants. Tiny lakes glinted everywhere in the sun. Bogs often made passage impossible, forcing us to make long detours. We clambered up one steep, rocky, tree-covered ridge and down the other side, then up the next, over and over again. Of course, there was no trail. We crashed through brush and limbs of evergreens on the steep sides of the ravines. We crawled over and under boulders. To make just half a mile as the crow flies, we sometimes covered five. Reaching the coordinates of the crash site, at a fairly high elevation, we found the wreckage and the bodies of the crew. One man lay partially submerged at the edge of a small, icy lake. His hair and nails had continued to grow long after his death, and some mineral in the water had tinged his hair a strange yellow hue.

It was impossible to carry the bodies out. We could barely carry ourselves over that tortuous terrain, and we did not yet have helicopters. We could only mark the graves with pieces from the wreckage. Strangely, we found no identification, no wallets or ID tags. Perhaps the Indian had brought them with him for identification. I did find a .45 pistol and took that with us on our return trip. I was so exhausted that the .45 began to feel like fifty pounds, and I soon discarded it, setting it in the crook of a tree. I have often wondered if it were ever found, and if so, what the finder must have thought.

The crashes, though not numerous when one considers the amount of planes and the conditions they flew in, still kept the rescue teams busy. I spent my thirty-third birthday in a tent, waiting out a late snowstorm before trekking further to find and rescue a downed crew far west of Goose Bay. In the first thaw of spring, amphibious rescue planes often landed in water with dangerous ice floes floating about. Taking to the air again might mean paddling the craft among hunks of ice, looking for a spot clear enough to effect flight. Later in the summer, sometimes we landed amphibious planes in shallow streams, hoping there was enough water so that the pontoons would not hit bottom. One time we luckily found two survivors, one who was disappointed that we had shown up with the rescue plane so soon, as he was enjoying the fishing! But when we tried to taxi for takeoff, the pontoons kept hitting sandbars. After two hours we finally lifted off. Flying over Goose Bay's water landing site at Hamilton River, we had the ground crew take a look at our pontoons from the ground to make sure they were still in one piece after the many scrapes they had undergone on the takeoff. We were signaled to land on the river; once safely down, we found the pontoons had been sanded bright and shiny.

On one rescue operation, involving five men who had parachuted from a B-17, our floatplane landed in little more than an oversized pond to search for the men. The pond was deep, but not wide. A dangerous angle had to be taken in order to land and stop in time before running out of water. We found three men alive, and they were flown out while my men and I searched for the others. But on the next attempt to land, the plane came in at too steep an angle, and flipped over! We were stunned, and stood on the beach, unable to move for a moment. Fortunately, we soon saw two of the crew crawl up onto the overturned craft, dragging an injured man with them. Seeing the craft settling in the water, we hurriedly inflated a raft and paddled out toward them, only to find ourselves sinking—the raft was leaking! We barely made it to the plane. As the plane we sat on slowly sank, we speedily patched the holes in the raft, and got everyone safely to shore. Unfortunately, we found the other two parachutists by dragging the lake.

Operations such as these could last for days, and often the rescue crews had to live off the land, which was not very difficult in summer. Labrador is well stocked with all types of wildlife. Ten- and twenty-pound fish in the Hamilton River were not unusual. The thousands of small lakes of Labrador were full of trout, as were the rivers, and so one would have to be really working hard at it to go hungry. Geese and ducks were numerous in season, and blueberries were nearly as plentiful as the mosquitoes, while moss berries and the so-called appleberries were also readily available. Porcupine is a delicious meal, and we occasionally got lucky and bagged a caribou. If it wasn't for the mosquitoes, and those damned flies, it would have been a fine place to live!

One rescue took place right on the base. A "Mosquito" fighter plane exploded above the airfield. I was in the operations building talking with Eddie Goodale when we heard the noise and then saw pieces of the craft raining down. Then, horribly, we saw a body hit, leaving a long, deep furrow in the dirt. Amazingly, we also saw someone descending in a parachute, but as it got closer, we could see the man was tangled in the shroud lines, and was coming down headfirst!

With Eddie driving a jeep, we raced across the tarmac, then across sandy dividers on the runway. Eddie wheeled us around, changing directions as the wind blew the man about. Finally, we were able to position ourselves just at the spot where the man was about to crash into the runway—and infinity. As the unconscious man neared the ground, I jumped from the jeep and stood directly under him. I was able to flip him over at the last second by pulling him up at the shoulders, thereby landing him on his rump! RAF pilot Captain Roberts suffered—as the doctor's report put it—"a dislocation of the left humerus, fracture of the left tuberosity humerus, and lacerations about the head, face, legs, and chest." But he lived. Hassell, writing a report on the incident, called it "perfection in search and rescue . . . arriving at the scene before the accident!" During the citation ceremony held for us, I was asked what ran through my head at the last moment. "Frankly," I replied, "all I could think about was how damned red his face was!"

There were so many rescue operations that it would take a whole book to give sufficient credit to all the men and dogs involved. I do want to mention that we made the second mass rescue by helicopter in history. The first was in the Orient—just a few days before ours—when three men were rescued. Hardly a "mass"! We saved eleven! In the middle of April 1944, eleven downed Canadian men had been stranded for twelve days in horrendous conditions. Their Canso (a Canadian version of the Catalina floatplane, also called a PBY) had crashed three hundred miles southwest of Goose Bay. When the weather cleared, a pilot flying over the heavily wooded crash site had read a message stomped in the snow: MAN DYING. There was no way I could sled that distance in time to save the dying man, nor even the rest of the crew.

Our only hope was to get a hold of a new flying machine called a helicopter. The first reliable helicopters, manufactured by Igor Sikorsky, had only been purchased by the U.S. military the year before. Sikorsky had pointed out, "If a man is in need of rescue, an airplane can come in and throw flowers on him, and that's just about all. But a direct-lift aircraft could come in and save his life." Hassell frantically called stateside hoping for one of the few "direct-lift" aircraft then in existence. The Coast Guard had six of the rare birds at Floyd Bennett Field, New Jersey, just outside of New York City.

While the whole base at Goose Bay waited nervously, on May 2 the tiny and then strange-looking R-4 chopper was disassembled and flown to us via a Douglas R5D. The "eggbeater," as my men called it, was quickly reassembled by experts from Sikorsky, and flown in at the last moment to save the dying man's life, and to then evacuate the other ten men. The chopper, piloted by Lieutenant August Kleisch of Cincinnati, had room and lift power for only one man besides the pilot, so it had to make eleven flights back and forth in the cold winter weather. Both pilot and craft performed beautifully. At the time we were told it was the first mass evacuation by helicopter in history, but much later we learned that a week earlier, an R-4 helicopter in Burma had rescued three British soldiers from behind Japanese lines.

We also believed we had pioneered the parachuting of rescue dogs into re-mote areas. Many of my men had suggested this tactic for getting teams and sleds close to downed crews, but sled dogs were expensive, not to mention rare, and no one dared risk experimenting with the animals. There was however one dog at camp that had become a habitual biter and constantly attacked the other dogs. Hassell had put him on death row, but when he heard about our plans to test the parachuting of dogs, he said we could use this condemned canine as a guinea pig, and added: "If the mutt survives the jump, he'll be given clemency." It was a bit like the movie, *The Dirty Dozen*. We had to have a special harness sewn, but the normally aggressive animal let us strap him into it. When he later came floating down to earth, he had the most dumbfounded look on his face, and thereafter was as gentle as a lamb, and a wonderful team player!

There was a very human side to Goose Bay, as well as the dramatic, larger-than-life rescue operations. A general who knew my wife came to Goose Bay for an inspection tour. He took me aside and said, "Willie, I'm leaving for Presque Isle tomorrow, but I'll be back in a week. Why don't you hop on the plane? Make a quick visit home to Alice." I told him I'd never get permission to fly. "Willie, just tell Hassell you are going some damn place with your sled dogs for a week. No one will ever know. I'll tell the operations fellow not to put your name on the flight manifest." That is how I got to visit our home in Maine not just once, but twice, in two years.

To continue with the "human interest" stories about the Crimson Route, Goose Bay also had a visit by Marlene Dietrich, and another time Vice President Harry S. Truman came up for an inspection tour. I was up in northeast Quebec setting up a rescue and weather-reporting station at Indian House Lake when Truman arrived at Goose. I was frantically trying to finish my job before winter set in. Indian House Lake was 250 miles from Goose, and needless to say, it was remote.

It was estimated that over a hundred flights with our two large Catalina floatplanes would be necessary in order to transport all the needed equipment. Once winter began, the men would be on their own, so everything had to be fin-ished by then. One of the Catalinas that was ferrying materials was suddenly taken away from us. We were abruptly told by a visiting officer that it was needed to take "Harry" on a fishing trip! I was fuming. That was the kind of officialdom nonsense that put lives in jeopardy. We had been working sixteen hours a day while being driven crazy by insects, just to be sure we could operate effective rescues. I am sure Harry "The Buck Stops Here" Truman would not have approved had he known that his fishing trip might have jeopardized a rescue mission. Fortunately, between Hassell and me, we were able to convince our Canadian counterparts to lend us one of their Catalinas, thereby saving the mission. It was one of many examples of such Canadian-American cooperation. One Canadian who deserves mention is Scotty Alexander, a Royal Mounted Police officer of the highest caliber, whom I met in Goose Bay. Scotty and I worked together off and on over the next decade. In the 1950s, when mutual cooperation between Canada and the U.S. was of world consequence, Scotty and I became specialists in smoothing the ruffled feathers of high-ranking, touchy patriots of both countries. We should have gotten the Noble Peace Prize.

We also experienced the lighter moments of life on the Crimson Route. One porcine incident in particular at Goose Bay deserves mention. The canned food we were usually served on base tasted bad and quickly became boring, so Hassell came up with a solution. In a gruff voice, as if daring me to laugh, he told me, "We need some fresh meat, and we have a lot of wasted garbage from the mess hall. What I am planning, Willie, is to raise pigs!" He had already sent for a planeload of five sows and twenty-five piglets, and he put me in charge of "Operation Porkchop." I didn't laugh. Pens were built, and when the plane arrived with the pigs, we were set. The flight crew was not amused by the smell their passengers had left in the hold, but the operation was a success, even the envy of many another site without fresh meat. Naturally, I was dubbed "Porkchop" Knutsen.

I enjoyed the operation, although I had dreams of pigs lined up in military review while I pinned medals on them. To help keep the pigs healthy, I grew vegetables, including corn on the cob for the pigs, but we ate the fresh produce as well. In the long, hot summer days, the produce grew at an astonishing rate. Eventually, Hassell found a suitable replacement for me, a sergeant from the Midwest with a farming background. He became the new "pork master," and went happily about the life he was used to, while I went happily back to mine.

The work continued. I hopped by plane to such exotic-sounding spots as Mecatina, a tiny outpost, and Magpie Lake. There was also Mistassini, and Mistasin. From Chimo, or Crystal One, far up on Ungava Bay, Quebec, to Mingan, a large base at the mouth of the Saint Lawrence River, my crew and I flew hundreds and hundreds of miles, canoed, portaged falls, hiked, climbed, dog-sledded, and skied to rescue downed flight crews. Sometimes these heroic efforts were just to give downed air crews a proper burial.

It is difficult to give credit to the men and women for all the work involved: the training of pups to be sled dogs; the maintenance of equipment under harsh conditions; not to mention the maintenance of good humor during this danger-ous and rugged work in so primitive a place. All this work took the dedication and expertise of many men and women, too many to be given proper space in this book. My hat is off to them and to their memory.

CHAPTER NINETEEN

Dogsleds over Paris

I n late 1944 Germany was clearly losing the war. The Russian Red Army was steadily closing in on the Eastern front while German cities were being re- duced to ruins by intense American bombing. The Italian peninsula had been captured and liberated by the British and Americans and their allies, and our armies were advancing rapidly through France and the Low Countries.

By December 1944 the Allied forces were nearing Germany. The men and women at Goose Bay read about the advances in the daily bulletins as ardently as turf men follow the horse races. They followed the advances of generals Patton, Bradley, and Field Marshall Montgomery. They read about the liberation of Toulon, Marseilles, and the push up the Rhone Valley by Sir Henry Maitland Wilson's troops. We knew our troops were pushing through Belgium toward Germany. The men and women of the Crimson Route, and other support groups far from the front lines, could see the results of their work. There were cheers with each victory, and groans of dismay at setbacks. The planes returning with the wounded increased in number the closer the Allies came to Germany. We saw the terrible results of the front lines, a long, long distance away. This distance would soon change for some of us.

On December 6, 1944, eight German armored divisions and thirteen German infantry divisions launched an all-out counteroffensive on five divisions of the United States 1st Army in the heavily wooded Belgium-Luxembourg-France area known as the Ardennes. Because the American front line as drawn on a map looked like a bulge in the line, this fierce German counteroffensive became known as the Battle of the Bulge. This would become the largest land battle in which the United States was involved. Something like a million men were engaged in this desperate struggle. The 5th and 6th Panzer armies, which equaled eleven divisions, broke into the Ardennes through the Losheim Gap against the American divisions protecting the region. At the same time the 5th Panzer Army was attacking the U.S. VIII Corps some hundred miles to the south. This corps had not seen much action in Europe and their lack of experience was taken advantage of by the Germans. The Americans were quickly surrounded and there were mass surrenders. A lot of American prisoners were shot. When the Americans in the city of Bastogne were then surrounded, the German commander offered them the chance to surrender. This was the moment Brigadier General McAuliffe uttered his now famous reply: "Aw, nuts!" The siege continued. The only way the Americans could get supplies was by air drop, but the winter weather was so bad, nothing could fly. Wounded GIs in the forests of the Ardennes were freezing to death in the large snowdrifts.

In January 1945, a time when the Battle of the Bulge was in full, fiery agony in the midst of a frigid, snowy winter, I received a telegram from Norman Vaughan: ASSEMBLE FROM ALL SITES ALL BEST DOG TEAMS AND MEN NOT ABSOLUTELY NEEDED FOR CRIMSON ROUTE RESCUE OPERATIONS.

There was no further explanation. I gathered my men and dog teams from Chimo to Indian House Lake. Other teams from Mingan, Frobisher Bay, and all around, arrived at Goose Bay to await further orders. We waited and waited for days. Then we received another telegram: BE PREPARED TO FLY OUT AT ANY MOMENT. We waited and waited for the order. Finally, on a dark winter day, with a temperature of minus-forty degrees Fahrenheit, we were ordered to fly to Greenland. There was still no explanation, of course, as this was security procedure. We had three planeloads of dogs, totaling 209 of the most well-trained creatures, plus seventeen drivers, also pretty experienced in their jobs. The plane I had charge of contained forty-six dogs—and their sleds—plus five of my men. The uninsulated metal planes were so cold that even those of us with years of arctic experience were shaking and miserable, though the dogs seemed happy enough.

In Narssarssuaq, Greenland, we landed to take on dog food. Amazingly, the man in charge of loading the cases of food was a Norwegian, Hans Sievers, who had trapped at Myggbukta, and so we had a lot to talk about. Taking to the air again, we found ourselves headed for Prestwick, Scotland. There was still no word about where we were headed, or what this secret mission would entail. Halfway to Scotland we found out that we were heading first to France, then to Belgium to rescue the snowbound wounded at the Battle of the Bulge.

Norman Vaughan, our commander, had been in charge of this operation. In fact, it had been partially his idea. Someone had come up with the idea of using sled dogs to rescue the wounded in the snow-covered, forested battlefields of the Ardennes. Norman Vaughan had said it could be done, though it took him some time to convince the higher-ups. And so there we were, headed for the shooting war at the front lines.

We landed in Prestwick after an uncomfortable flight, made worse by the odor of the natural activities of forty-six dogs. We splashed down at Prestwick on a rainy day early in the morning, dark and wretched weather. After we unloaded the dogs, we noticed that quite a group of distinguished-looking people had gathered, as if to greet us. There were British military brass, American brass, the local mayor, and other officials, all dressed up in their best clothes or uniforms. There was even a brass band! They did not seem all that happy to see us, and so their presence was even a greater mystery on that early, miserable morning. The greeting committee disbanded gloomily, and only later did we discover what had happened.

As we approached Prestwick Airfield, which of course had no prior word of our arrival or mission, Vaughan had sent them this message: ARRIVING WITH FORTY-SIX DOGS. VAUGHAN. The airfield staff, thinking this was a coded message, sent it to London for decoding. London radioed back that "dog" was the code name for Delano, or President Roosevelt; the "forty-six" was taken to mean forty-six dignitaries; and "Vaughan" was interpreted as General Vaughan, Roosevelt's military liaison officer! Since even London knew nothing of such a visit, everyone assumed something historic was about to take place. Hence, our official greeters—and hence, their dismay when our crud-encrusted dogs and frozen, bedraggled crews spilled out of the planes!

To make matters worse, we staked out our dogs on the American commanding officer's lawn, the only available turf on the base that was handy to our planes. Not only was he made to feel the embarrassment of his mistake over Vaughan's telegram, but he also had to listen to our dogs howl all night. In the morning, his lawn littered with dog crap, he rashly ordered us to take off for France, even though there was zero visibility. This bit of personal irresponsibility—to put it nicely—nearly caused the end of the whole mission, and the lives of the crews and dogs.

The planes were soon separated. Reaching France with no contact from the other two planes, we were still experiencing zero visibility. Homing in on Orly Field, things were no better. Paris had just been bombed by the Germans, and the airport could not or would not turn on their runway lights. On one approach attempt we luckily saw a tree we were about to hit and powered a pull-up, which caused the dogs to get sick all at once. The plane banked, and then lost an engine under the strain. We radioed for the airfield staff to send up flares to light the field, which they did, but heading for the light, we saw they had fired it right from the tower! We could see men running down the steps and diving for their lives as we came hurtling at them! Another power pull-up caused the dogs more sickness. The whole crew donned gas masks to escape the smell.

We were all past fear, and made plans to bail out. We would head to the coast and ditch ourselves into the water. Just then, we were radioed that the only clear spot in France was Marseilles. It was a hell of a long flight for the fuel we had left, but we headed for Marseilles anyway.

Our navigator had no maps for that area. I was the only one on board who knew European geography, but then again, I had grown up in Norway. I told the pilot to head southeast, as I believed we would eventually see the Rhone River, which led to Marseilles. After a nail-biting flight, we saw a few rays of moonlight glinting on a large river, piercing the otherwise cloudy sky. I told the pilot it could only be the Rhone. He turned south. With only these occasional glimpses of moonlight to guide us, we finally emerged from the cloud cover close to our destination, only to have a second engine go out! And our fuel was almost spent. Approaching Istres LeTube Field, we radioed our approach, and we saw the lights go on. But soon a Buhl fighter plane shot toward us. Its pilot demanded over the radio, "What is the code of the day?"

"How would we know?" our pilot shot back. "We were supposed to land at Orly, but they sent us here because of the fog."

"No one at Orly told us anything about you!" we heard the suspicious pilot say. The lights of the field went off.

"Take a look at our insignias!" our pilot shouted back in anger and desperation, for we were almost out of fuel.

"The Germans have used that trick against us before," said the still suspicious voice.

Our pilot screamed, "Goddammit! We're out of fuel, you bastards!"

That must have convinced them we were real Yankees, because the lights went on. We landed, and rolled to a stop. We could not even taxi off the strip; we were completely out of fuel.

A jeep came hurtling across the tarmac. A nervous-looking major, obviously a little drunk, came aboard with his hand on his concealed .45. I spoke a few words with my Norwegian accent, which sounded like German to him, and the major's pistol went off in his pocket, blew a hole in his pants, and missed my foot by inches as it plowed through the floor of the plane!

The pilot came screaming out of the cockpit, "Goddammit! We're Americans! We're Americans!" Embarrassed, the major let us disembark. It turned out that the field had just been under attack, that scattered groups of Germans still combed the countryside, and everyone was understandably jittery.

It was five in the morning. A truck took us to an inn for billeting. We asked the proprietor for some drinks, but he said it was too late. We were in no mood for formalities. One of the crew pulled a pistol.

"We've been betrayed and double-crossed. We've nearly crashed a dozen times. We've been threatened and shot at by our own people, and we've smelled dog shit and puke for hundreds of miles. By Christ, we're going to have a drink!"

Our baleful glares must have convinced the good man. After a few bottles, we realized our navigator was missing. One of the crew said he had last seen the man mumbling about never going into the air again. We set out to find him. We went from brothel to brothel. At each establishment we had to go through a veil of suspicion. We had to assure each madam that we were not going to report the place to the police. At last we found our navigator, asleep in a back room, cuddling a bottle of brandy.

As we walked through the still-dark morning, trying to find our way back to our quarters, we passed a POW camp with tall guard towers. "Who goes there?" a guard demanded, shining a light on us. One of my men whispered, "Willie, don't say a word, or we're dead!" One of the other boys spoke up and told the guy to "F—— off!" This was apparently the password, because the guard took the spotlight off us. We staggered off to get some sleep. It had been the worst experience of my life, worse even than the three-day, frozen nightmare in the tent with young Olsen in Germania Land. I'd rather be killed by nature than man any day!

Our plane's wiring had been too damaged by the gunshot to be quickly repaired. Our dogs, who could not take the sudden, one-and-a-half-day change from minus-forty degrees in the Arctic to plus-seventy-five degrees on the Mediterranean Coast, had to be constantly hosed down while we waited for a new plane. Two Gooney Birds were sent for the dogs, sleds, and material, and a third for us. In this way we finally came to our destination near Luxembourg. By the time we reached the front lines, the snow was gone! The worst snowstorm in recent history had created a demand for the dogsled teams, but a sudden warming had melted the great drifts. The snowy nightmare of the Battle of the Bulge had become a hell of mud and clay.

We never did use the dogs or the sleds. Holed up near Verdun, we did see the horrors of the war when the wounded and mangled bodies, military and civilian, were brought into the field hospital. That terrible job was one we were not sorry to have missed. All about us was the cacophony of radio men shouting into their phones while noisy army trucks roared by, horns beeping. We felt useless and out of place, but the dogs were a hit, even if they had not been used on the battlefield. General Patton, under whose command our operation had been attached, issued orders that the best available meat be delivered for the dogs, and he even came by personally to see and pat them. During our few days' stay, my crew, trained to be resourceful under all difficult conditions, took some of the canned meat we no longer needed for the dogs and traded with the meat-starved locals for wine and cognac. I was so proud of them.

Norman Vaughan's team, however, which we had last seen shortly after taking off from Scotland, had arrived to the battle area with his dog teams while snow was still on the ground, and had made some rescues before the snow turned to mud and mire. They braved enemy fire, subzero weather, and deep snow to rescue the wounded and get them to hospitals. His group was dubbed "Vaughan's Voyageurs." His story of the sled dogs in France made the American radio and newspapers, although I believe this is the first time the whole, harrowing—and sometimes, hilarious—experience that my team went through has been told.

Later, it was learned that a general who had been at Orly Field when the planes had attempted to land in the fog and rain was heard to mutter, "Who sent these poor bastards out in weather like this?!" and an investigation was launched. From the commander at Prestwick, to the men in the control tower at Orly who did not inform Istre of our rescue team's imminent arrival, to the major with the .45 who plugged our plane, repercussions were felt. The commander at Prestwick was relieved of duty and sent back to the States. The others were reprimanded.

Once I had arrived in Paris, two wonderful events occurred. I ran into my old arctic explorer friend, Paul-Emil Victor, who was in the U.S. Army as a lieutenant. We talked about the first time we had met, north of Ammassalik. He had come to greet the *Quest* in an old walrus-hide umiak, one of the last of its kind, escorted by a flotilla of graceful kayaks. That had been a scene out of antiquity. Sitting in Paris, we said a bit ruefully, "Look at us now!"

I also was able to see my old friend and benefactor, Count Gaston Micard. He had just returned to a liberated Paris from Switzerland. Micard! I had thought I'd never see him again. He was his usual self, and apologized for the theft of the arctic artwork I had given him by saying, "Probably taken by the house staff during the war, Willie. Cannot blame them much. One had to survive anyway one could during those dark days. They might well have sold them to the Germans!" It was some of my best work, too. We spent a fantastic weekend at his home reminiscing, and talking of expeditions we would certainly do together after the war.

Then I got word that I could have two weeks off before heading back to Labrador. I caught a military plane to Newcastle to visit my mother and father. Meanwhile, the dogs and crews were returning to Goose Bay by ship, and later we officers would fly back. By the time I returned to Goose Bay in April, the men, dogs, and sleds were just arriving. Soon the crews were heading north again to Chimo, Frobisher Bay, Padloping Island, Mingan, and Indian House Lake. The war was still on, planes were still crashing, and rescue missions were still needed. I arrived back in Goose Bay just as the ex-commanding officer of Prestwick, Scotland, arrived on his way back to the States after being removed for sending us into the air in zero visibility.

"Fish" Hassell, who had heard the whole story, shook the man's hand and said with a straight face, "I'd like to tell you how grateful I am that you met my men and dogs with the brass band and dignitaries!" The disgraced officer did not laugh. Though we did not use the dogs in battle, still, all the members of the operation received battle stars for the Battle of the Bulge. The dogs received nothing, but seemed relieved to be back in the north.

It was May 1945 and Europe was being liberated, country by country. There was a special elation I felt when I heard Norway was free again. After a week's trip up to Frobisher Bay on an inspection tour, I returned to Goose Bay. I had only enough time to take a few breaths when Hassell said to me, "Willie, I have a job for you. I think you'll like this one. Members of the Royal Norwegian family—the children—are passing through on their way home, and you're to be their official escort while they are here."

By a stroke of luck, the famous violinist, Isaac Stern, was in Goose Bay with his accompanist, Alexander Zakin, and the singer, Polyna Stoska. They had just been entertaining in Frobisher, of all the "forgotten places," the week I had been there on inspection tour. (Stern was then just twenty-five, but had already played at Carnegie Hall. From Carnegie Hall to Frobisher Bay: what a contrast!) They had been made honorary members of the Forgotten Bastards of Baffin Island Society, and readily agreed to perform in Goose Bay for the members of the Royal family and their entourage.

It was a tense wait. No one was used to greeting royalty. The plane was four hours late. The security officer had gotten so nervous wondering what had happened to the royal family that he had started to take shots of liquor to calm down. But at last the plane arrived. Accompanying the royal children on their long trip back to newly liberated Norway was Count Wedel-Jarlsberg, Nils Jorgersen, and Captain Østgaard. I had met Østgaard, the famous skier and friend of the then Crown Prince Olav, at the Royal Palace during my visit with Prince Olav, before going on my Norwegian-French Expedition.

Young Crown Prince Harold, now the new king of Norway, was about eight years old then, and the first thing he did when emerging from the plane after the long flight was to slip on the tarmac and fall headfirst onto the pavement. His older sisters, Astrid and Ragnild, said, "Poor Harold. He is so tired!" I introduced myself using the local Oslo slang, and added that I had once met their father at the Royal Palace. They attached themselves to me like I was their link to home. We were soon sharing local jokes only Oslo people of the "younger generation" knew. When I accompanied them into the terminal building, the girls burst out giggling. There, in a chair, passed out and snoring, was the security officer. The girls, happy to have met someone from home, went around to the U.S. and Canadian military men of the greeting committee, and speaking very good English said, "Just imagine—Captain Knutsen over there knows our dad!"

The Isaac Stern concert was a great success, especially since he played "The Song of Norway" from the hit musical of the same name then playing on Broadway. I should think, however, the children were more impressed the next day when I took them and their protectors to the kennels in the forest outside of the base to see all of my huskies. There were about one hundred large, half-wild, magnificent creatures, including two that were 100 percent wolf! I am certain Count Wedel-Jarlsberg, Nils Jorgersen, and Østgaard also enjoyed the dogs' howling concert-in-the-wild. When I met Nils Jorgersen thirty years later in Oslo, he at first tried to place me, and then exclaimed, "Oh, yes! The man with the dogs!"

After the royal contingent had flown off to Europe, I let out a sigh of relief and went to the officers' club. There I was greeted with what can only be described as the American Way. "Yes, yes — he hobnobs with royalty!" the American officers jeered. "Okay, we're impressed. But Willie, you were not raised in America, so you probably didn't learn the unwritten law — any American hobnobbing with royalty has to buy the drinks!" They stood there, tongues firmly planted in their cheeks, and there was nothing I could do but buy a round.

By June the war in Europe was over. The planes were now streaming back, loaded with the victorious soldiers. And, sadly, some planes still crashed into the cruel wilderness due either to being lost or to mechanical problems. And so, the rescues continued.

We traveled by foot, canoe, and plane to the remotest places. We used snowshoes, skis, and dogsleds. Along the way we saw small bands of Indians living primitively. Many of these showed French ancestry, and wore berets as if to prove it, particularly among the Montagnais I met living along the Nascaupee River. Sometimes their shelters were tents with evergreen boughs for an insulated floor, even in winter. Though there were such modern amenities as tin cups, rifles, or even factory-made canoes, their old life of trapping, hunting, and fishing went on as it had for centuries. It was interesting that few had ever ventured far from the main rivers. They knew little of the interior, except to talk about "ghost trails." Local tales abounded of hunting groups that had been lured into the interior by following herds of caribou that disappeared, leaving the hunters far from camp and without food. Journeys over the tortuous overland trails required a tremendous expenditure of calories. Water fowl are obviously not too prevalent in the thickets, and caribou are a tough target in the forests. The remote inland trails were littered with evidence of hunting parties that had not survived the ordeal. "Stick to the big rivers," was the advice of the locals, and it was damn good advice, too.

The Indians hunted for caribou at Indian House Lake, and at the Barren Grounds River, where it widened into a large lake to make an easy crossing for the herds. One year could yield a bonanza of a thousand caribou killed, and the next, nothing. If you came a day too late, you'd never catch sight of the herd again that year unless you foolhardily went on the "ghost trails" after them. And what would be the point? Far from the rivers, carcasses could not be transported back to villages before they rotted. As it was, I never saw Indians at Indian House Lake. The caribou herd populations had dramatically dropped since 1900 (although I understand they have made a remarkable comeback as of the 1980s). We did find two canoe forms for making birch-bark canoes, and racks for drying meat and fish. It was a beautiful area in the summer that unfortunately attracted hordes of mosquitoes. I had learned more than one invaluable lesson from the Indians along the Nascaupee, but perhaps the best was to remove the "galls" growing on birch trees and light them, thereby keeping the mosquitoes away!

In spite of the advice to stay on the rivers, planes had an inconvenient way of crashing far from the beaten trail, or from a traversable river system. Though we could, in good weather, have supplies dropped to us on long searches, we hunted, and gathered berries, and nibbled other wild foods as we tramped through rugged ravines and mountains searching for downed flight crews. At the beginning of summer, I had just returned from a search operation in the Mealy Mountains. There, we had had a hard time in the wilderness getting to a wreck, only to find all the crew dead. On our return to base we heard the news of Hiroshima and Nagasaki.

The war was over.

We thought that would be the end of warplanes crashing into the wilderness. Most of the men were leaving to go home, including me. A quiet settled over the wilderness. But the nuclear age, and its resulting nightmare for mankind, had begun. And soon I would be assigned to the Far North to set up defenses for the new enemy, the USSR, when they, too, acquired The Bomb.

During the war I had heard that my old friend, Gerhard Antonsen, the indomitable "King of Revet," had made his way from Clavering Island to England, then to Little Norway, in Canada. There, of all the damn things, he had been killed while felling a tree. My sister Signy wrote to say that that blackguard husband of hers, Jess Tillier, had collaborated with the Nazis, and had fled Norway to escape jail. He left Signy alone with their one-year-old daughter to fend the best she could. Jess, that amoral creature, had also sold many of my sketches and paintings to the Germans. More bad news was yet to come.

Kalle wrote to say that when he and the ship had arrived back in Norway from Greenland in 1940, the *Ringsel* had been confiscated by the Germans as soon as it docked. Kalle and the crew had been taken into custody, though they were soon released. Labb was taken to be used as a sled dog for the Germans in their fight against the Norwegian Resistance. While pulling a sled loaded with ammunition through the high mountains of Lapland, the sled had been ambushed by Norwegian resistance fighters. Labb had been killed. I kept seeing him that last time we were together, happily saying our good-byes at Torgilsbu. It took a long, long time to get over it, but I never forgot him. Good old Labb.

CHAPTER TWENTY

The Secret of Prince Patrick Island

I had been asked to stay in the military to take over at Presque Isle, and though Alice and I had bought that farmhouse near the base, I felt I was ready for the civilian life. What convinced me was a warning delivered by one of the enlisted men, a fellow Brooklyn boy, who advised me not to take the job as base commander. It seems that jeeps and other government material had been stolen and shipped south. Whoever was in command when this was finally discovered might be held responsible, even if he had not been there during the period of the actual theft. He told me: "Willie, dees guys, knowing you're sort of a foreigner and don't know the ropes, are plannin' on tying youse up in dem!" Being offered that post had not been the honor I thought it was; I was being set up! At the beginning of the war I had been set up by the enemy; now, at the end of the war, I was being used as a patsy by some amoral men on my own side. Dishonesty really seemed to be a virtue to these types, and those who played by the rules were considered saps. I would fight against this trend for the rest of my life. I left the military just as the whole world was plunging into the collective insanity called the Cold War.

After a short tenure in my old job as an architect for the Army Corps of Engineers, I took advantage of the GI Bill and attended the Rhode Island School of Design. At the same time, I taught art at Tabor Academy, a private school. My wife and I had had another daughter in 1944, and a son just at the end of the war (the one who helped to tell this story). I did what most men with young families did at the time: I bought a house that was affordable because it needed fixing! We had bought a small pre-Revolutionary saltbox in Swansea, Massachusetts, that had no plumbing (water was fetched from a well), but it was home. We remodeled the house and life began to resemble something normal after the hell of the war. It would soon become apparent that "normal" was a fleeting concept.

In 1948 we moved to Rockport, Massachusetts, where we bought a large, desanctified church of the Swedenborgian order on Pigeon Cove, overlooking the Atlantic. We began to convert it into more of a home, but we fancied ourselves as Bohemian artists and so were in no hurry. Rockport was also home to Norman Von Rosenvinge, the man who had brought me news of Eli Knudsen's death by the Germans on Greenland. Norman's family and mine became good friends. He was a lawyer, and the Danish Consul with an office in Boston, but he also painted and hung out with artists, so we knocked around the idea of starting an artist colony. After all, Rockport had long been a magnet for artists, and the Rockport Art Association was world famous. I bought the old, water-filled granite quarry on Pigeon Hill. We envisioned an art studio, and perhaps artists would build studios around the rim of the pit. I became a member of the Rockport Art Association, and was invited to be the judge during some sculpture exhibits. One of Alice's favorite cousins was the well-known artist Russell Cowles, and he and his wife became great friends of ours. Russell's family owned LOOK magazine and a raft of newspapers. He laughingly called himself the "black sheep" of the family, even though it turned out his family did not think that way of him at all and was extremely proud of his artistic success. With people like Russell around, life was like an artist's dream: intelligent, interesting people coming around once in awhile to bounce ideas off each other before each went back to the quiet isolation of his own art. Then things began to unravel. Alice had begun to have wild mood swings. She was happy as hell one moment, and snarling, sneering mad the next. This was followed by bouts of depression. It turned out she had had these swings since she was a teenager, but now they were getting worse. As we had never really lived together for very long before this period, I had never noticed her problem, and no one had seen fit to mention it to me. I hoped the problem would just go away. That's a Norwegian trait. You don't talk about things.

That same year I got a letter from Kalle that the *Ringsel* was found abandoned and in bad shape after the Nazis had finished with it. Someone had claimed salvage and was running into great expense trying to fix it. Interestingly, I got a letter from Helge Ingstad, asking my permission to use that damn photo of the two dead polar bears and their living cubs in his new book. I gave him permission, and mentioned that I had heard from a few farmers and fishermen from a remote spot on Newfoundland that they had seen metal objects that might be Viking in a place near L'Anse aux Meadows. I did not know at the time that as early as 1914, this had been written about by W. A. Munn, of Harbour Grace, Newfoundland. Ingstad, who had of course lived in Labrador a few times during the 1920s and 1930s, turned out to be familiar with Munn's work, but was glad to hear I had some "grassroots" confirmation about a possible Viking site in Newfoundland. (In 1961, Ingstad uncovered the site and proved the Vikings had beaten Columbus to America by five hundred years. As if we hadn't known—but here at last was proof!)

I had no sooner settled down to life in Rockport than I received a wire from Charles Hubbard, now head of Arctic Meteorological Studies in Washington, D.C. Charlie and I had been friends since the first time I had met him in General "Hap" Arnold's office when I was commissioned and received orders to set up the search-and-rescue stations. The message was mysterious: DEAR WILLIE— PERHAPS YOU HAVE HEARD THROUGH THE "MUKLUK TELEGRAPH" THAT THERE IS A BIG PROJECT ABOUT TO START IN THE ARCTIC. I CANNOT TELL YOU WHAT IT IS, BUT I THINK YOU CAN GUESS. CAN YOU MAKE YOURSELF AVAILABLE IN THE NEAR FUTURE?

The "big project" was to last two decades! But at first I begged off; I had had three children, and had not been home for any of their births. Alice was losing her long battle with manic depression, and I thought my previous long absences certainly hadn't helped. However, the messages from Washington continued until at last I said yes. So, Alice's mother moved in with Alice to help with the kids while I went to the Capitol.

Many of us in arctic work had known of the Russian threat via the Arctic for a long time. Stefansson had told the U.S. government, "The Russians are the best-informed people on the Arctic!" And Bernt Balchen, who had fought the Russians when they invaded Finland in 1939, detested the Soviets. He had repeatedly issued warnings about the threat they posed, even when the Russians were our Allies, and it was not a popular thing to say. The fact was that the quality of long-distance bombers had exponentially increased, and America was no longer invulnerable to attack. Although this situation was not general public knowledge in the late 1940s, Washington knew all about it.

When it was clear to America who the new enemy was, Bernt Balchen told Congress: "The Arctic is to us what the Mediterranean was to the Greeks and Romans—the center of the world. We have to push out there for our defense!" General Hap Arnold had told the West Point Military Academy in 1946, "The first line of the nation's defense lies now to the North, between America and that attack, which if it comes will surely come from over the Pole. From that transpolar air attack, no land army or naval force can defend the nation. It will be an air defense system."

Most of us who knew our arctic history often talked of how the Russians had flown nonstop to the U.S. over the Pole—the shortest route between the two lands—in bomber-size planes as far back as 1927. At the end of that flight in 1927, five thousand people had gathered in Seattle, Washington, when the Soviet plane landed, and the aviators had been showered with flowers. A decade later another Russian plane flew nonstop from Moscow across the North Pole, landing first in Vancouver, Washington. This pilot had completed a daring 63-hour, 5,288-mile flight. They continued from there on to southern California, totaling a record-making 6,262 miles. There, they also received a tumultuous welcome. During the war, Soviet pilots ferried planes from the U.S. to Russia via the arctic routes, just as planes were ferried to Europe over the Crimson Route. But by 1948, the honeymoon with Soviet Russia was over. Though the rest of the nation, and even most of the military high command did not know it, America was at war, albeit a secret one. And the threat of this conflict had been around for a long time.

Tony Dimond, still Alaskan delegate to Washington, had warned via the media back in 1940 that tens of thousands of Russians, supposedly colonists, had settled on Big Diomede Island in the Bering Strait, only five miles from the American island of Little Diomede. All the Russian Inuit had been removed, army bases were being built, along with coastal gun installations, submarine bases, and airfields—all, one assumes, for the "colonists."

Judge Dimond wryly pointed out to the press, "The U.S. does not threaten Russia's position in the northeast part of Asia, and Big Diomede is far from Japan's plans for Asiatic mainland expansion; therefore, it could only mean a Soviet plan against a sparsely populated and poorly defended Alaska, which was Russian territory before the United States bought it." He also pointed out that Soviet newspapers were devoting a lot of attention to the riches of Alaska that, as they said, "had once been ours, but had been ineptly lost or corruptly sold later when the dynasty became decadent." The young soldiers on Big Diomede had been told that the glorious revolution included getting Alaska back. A Vladivostok newspaper said that their mission was "to get their hands on Alaska, which was so idiotically sold to capitalist America by the Czarist Government." The Soviet intention could not be any clearer, though Pravda reputed Judge Dimond's allegations. Dimond said that the Inuit on Little Diomede were getting nervous, and that the rest of America had better be, too! World War II had diverted attention from the Soviet threat in the North. Eight years later, we still had not done enough about an Alaskan defense against a Soviet attack.

It was a strange new kind of war, a war of nerves and psychology. Someone would soon designate it as the Cold War—meaning a war without the "fire" of bullets and bombs—but it was also an apt name because the line of defense and attack was to be the frigid Arctic. A mammoth construction job was planned for the defense line to be set up in the Far North, stretching over three thousand miles, from Alaska to Iceland. When Charlie Hubbard finally gave me my mission, I knew my brief flirtation with civilian life, the arts, relaxation, and remodeling was over. I put down my brushes and chisels and hardly picked them up again for the next twenty years.

My mission in 1948 was to scout out sites for arctic runways. These would be emergency landing fields should an aerial war with the USSR become a reality. America already had planes patrolling the Arctic frontier. These flew from bases in Greenland, Baffin Island, and Alaska, but there was a two-thousand-mile gap between Baffin and Alaska with no far-north, arctic bases. This area included the most northern Canadian arctic islands of Ellesmere, Axel Heiberg, Devon, the Sverdrups, the Ringnes, Mackenzie, Bathurst, Melville, and the most remote of all, Prince Patrick. In all there are more than fifty islands, covering about a thousand square miles.

Beyond Prince Patrick to the west there were well over eight hundred miles of the Beaufort Sea to travel before reaching the coast at Point Barrow, the northernmost tip of Alaska. This was a huge, undefended area. Victoria Island, to the south of Prince Patrick, is about the size of Wyoming. It turned out my destination was Prince Patrick Island, the only unexplored island in the Canadian archipelago. The political situation concerning the Soviets was so serious and my mission so secret that only a handful of the top military strategists knew what we were about to undertake. All I was told officially was that my job was to make a scientific station for arctic research, and I believed it at the time.

The nearest thing to exploration of the island was done by Lieutenant Mecham of McClintock's expedition in 1853. He had explored Prince Patrick with a spyglass. Mecham later wrote that no country could possibly be more barren and desolate. Vilhjalmur Stefansson thought he might have stumbled across it when he had been forced to spend two harrowing years (1915 to 1917) in the area on foot, from there to Banks Island, but he couldn't swear to it. Certainly no one had been there since then, though Sir Hubert Wilkins had landed a plane briefly "nearby"—some hundred miles—while searching for a lost Russian aviator.

Before I left New England for Prince Patrick, I called Stef to tell him I was headed North, though I could not tell him where, of course. He asked me to look out for herds of musk oxen. He had seen some when he was on Melville Island, and wondered where others might be, and if so, in what condition they were in. At the time, he had just heard of a disease that had affected herds in the Arctic, and was eager to know how the herds had fared.

I flew to Goose Bay. The base was still growing at an amazing rate. New bombers lined up smartly by new, huge hangars. Next, we flew to Frobisher Bay. Landing at my old base at Frobisher was poignant for me. I remembered the first landing we had ever made on the sand. Now, of course, the base we had started was a bustling site. Entering the mess hall, I saw my old dog driver, Etuachia, scrubbing floors with a mop. A memory swept over me of him in the wilds as we dogsledded, his eyes alert for caribou, and for hidden dangers. When he saw me, Etuachia's eyes widened, and a great smile spread across his face.

"Hey, Willie! Gone are the days of the noble dog drivers, eh?"

"For Christ's sake, Etuachia! How are you?" I asked, trying to ignore the slight embarrassment I saw in his eyes.

"Eatin' regularly." He was smiling broadly.

"That's something in the Arctic," I agreed with a laugh. His wife, nicknamed Susie, was also engaged in maintenance work on the base. He told me, "If you white men leave, it's back to blubber."

"Looks like we are going to be here for a while," I said, thinking of the scientific stations being planned for the high Arctic.

"That's good. My rifle is not much good anymore."

I told him I'd get him a newer one, and I did. The Hudson Bay boys owed me for saving all those furs from the pirates at Padloping.

At Frobisher Bay, Charles Hubbard and Alan Innes-Taylor joined the flight, but in a separate craft. Innes-Taylor was a dog driver on the Byrd Antarctic Expedition #1 and chief of field operations for Expedition #2. During World

War II, he had helped to establish weather stations on the Greenland ice cap, and commanded the Arctic Training Group at Echo Lake, Colorado. Stefansson and Innes-Taylor corresponded often about pemmican, musk ox, and various arctic subjects, so we had with us another authentic arctic man.

We flew northwest, heading for Cornwallis Island. As this was only the end of March, the temperature outside the plane was minus-forty degrees Fahrenheit. Naturally, the seas were still frozen solid. At first, the going was clear, but as we reached the northern part of Foxe Basin, a bay 340 miles long by 225 miles wide, vast clouds of frigid fog rose like smoke from the sea, obscuring our view of the unexplored land. The fog was caused by vast areas of open water (created by currents) which, when rushing through the narrow Fury and Hecla Strait, helped to stir up wheeling eddies that kept the waters from freezing over. For eight hundred miles, the sea, the islands, and the northern end of Baffin Island were obscured.

We were just gloomily reconciling ourselves to this bad luck of not being able to view the fabled land—and had started a game of poker—when the cover broke. Off in the distance we could see Devon Island bathed in the golden light of the spring sun. Vast ice caps spread magnificently. We stared in silence. Once again, the awesome size and majesty of the Arctic was overwhelming. All the rest of the way to Resolute, on Cornwallis Island, we had crystal-clear viewing. We landed on a frozen lake, all of us enthusiastic and happy to be back at work in the Far North. (About two months later, during a rare clear day over Foxe Basin, a plane spotted an island not previously shown on any maps. The island was as big as Connecticut! No one had ever seen it because of the infernal fog. That same day, Prince Charles of Great Britain was born, so the island was named after him.)

Resolute was a tiny weather station, and it was commanded by Bill Robinson, one of the "Ipswich Dogsled Club" boys I had first met at Presque Isle, along with Eddie Goodale. Bill immediately gave me bunk space in his small quarters, and privately told one of his men to set Innes-Taylor up in "The Cooler." This was a small warehouse that was unheated and had its inner walls covered with thick hoarfrost, a very uncomfortable situation. I asked Robinson, why the rough treatment for Alan?

It seems Innes-Taylor had been in charge of recruiting for Byrd's Antarctic expedition, and had turned down the then youthful Robinson's heartfelt pleas to be on the exploration team; instead, Robinson was assigned to ship duty. Robinson was finally getting Alan back—years later. Arctic men have long memories!

Bill recounted a recent tragedy that had hit the station. There had been a polar bear marauding about the garbage dump, but Canadian regulations strictly forbade the shooting of polar bears. (For that matter, even shooting foxes was against the rules.) A Canadian radio operator had gone out in the dark morning to relieve himself, turned the corner of a hut, and had run right into the animal, which savagely knocked him down and began to bite into his head. The cook, hearing his screams, got the Canadian colonel, Claigborne, who, still groggy from sleep, ran to get the only rifle on the site. By the time the bear lay dead, the poor man was so badly bitten that although he would live, he would never regain consciousness. He was flown out by a rescue plane from Thule, Greenland; although 450 miles away, Thule was the nearest large base, which in those days consisted of twelve Canadians and twelve Americans.

Because of that awful event with the polar bear, dogs were later sent up to remote sites to warn of other such intruders. This belated improvement showed the natural problems that arose when inexperienced people in Ottawa and Washington, D.C., made decisions concerning supplies and equipment to be sent hundreds of miles into the unknown arctic. The bureaucrats had assumed dogs were no longer necessary, since these sites usually had motorized snowmobiles. The "early warning" value of dogs had been forgotten. Because polar bears were endangered, rules were instituted to protect them, and though laudable, and necessary in most instances, these rules did not take into account the reality that men had to face living there! I never went anywhere outside unarmed—damn the regulations.

From Resolute, the two planes flew northward up the Wellington Channel, then over Queen's Channel past Devon Island to the east and Bathurst Island to the west. These were truly uninhabitable lands that were bleak to the point of disbelief—the veritable "End of the World." I longed for the beauty, and livability, of northeast Greenland.

Our first destination was Ellef Ringnes Island, named for the Norwegian brewery owner who financially supported Otto Sverdrup's expedition of 1899 to 1902. As we flew over the islands and straits of the Sverdrup Islands, we could see why early explorers had had such a hard time trying to navigate the waters, and why sledding was nearly impossible on the frozen sea. Endless jumbled masses of ice rose in tortured ridges caused by the great pressure of swift currents. If we had experienced engine trouble, we certainly could not have landed on the frozen sea in that area.

On Ellef Ringnes Island, a site called Isachsen was to be used as one of the outposts, and was to be commanded by Innes-Taylor. This site had been chosen by cartographers who had never been there, and it was up to the pioneers aboard the planes to see if it would indeed serve this purpose. We landed hard on a frozen lake near the site—but at least we landed—and unloaded cargo for the new post. After a week's reconnaissance of the area, we determined that the site was going to do the trick. We left Alan and his crew and took off for Prince Patrick Island. In my plane we had only the four-member crew, and two Canadians who were to remain on the island with me after the plane left us—alone in the middle of a frozen nowhere.

My teammates were Patrick McKay, who was to be our station's radio operator, and Paul Chorney, who was our "weather buster." We were to make the landing, and if we did so without mishap, the second plane with Charlie Hubbard aboard would return to Resolute for the bulldozer and other equipment necessary to make a crude runway.

As we flew toward the low profile of Prince Patrick, I was carefully searching for herds of musk oxen and caribou as Vilhjalmur Stefansson had asked of me. It was a strange experience to finally be seeing this immense emptiness, this remote frozen world which Stef had struggled across in 1916. I had read his accounts of the harrowing five years he spent marooned in the Arctic. He had walked, or rather struggled, more than three hundred miles. It was a land unpopulated even by Inuit. With only the food he hunted, he had survived five long, freezing dark winters, and the dangerous melting of sea ice during the summers. Now, thirty-two years later, the second visit would be by plane. A longtime ambition of mine would be realized: I would be the first to go where no human foot had trod—well, as far as we knew—and that was close enough. The truth is, I actually did not take those kinds of "firsts" very seriously. But it was fun.

On April 12, 1948, we flew over Mould Bay, found a frozen lake that looked land-able, and made our historic approach. Our stomachs were in knots as we wondered if the snow would be hiding boulders. The ground was coming up fast. We hit the lake with a hard bump, and then a series of more rapid, jarring bumps seemed to squash my insides, and I was afraid my teeth would lose their fillings. The pounding seemed to go on forever. We made the landing, of course, but it was a lousy place to land! And so we five Americans and two Canadians were the first men to land on Prince Patrick Island. I took unapologetic advantage of my position as mission leader, and was the first to step onto the island.

The first order of business was to check the plane for damage. The motors were kept running so the oil lines would not freeze up. I then set off to survey the "landing strip." The cold, dry, virtually moisture-free air had formed rock-hard hunks of ice on the lake's surface. Deep snow had camouflaged this hazard. The air was so dry that a strip of sand by the edge of the lake was unfrozen, as dry as the sands of the Sahara. I went off immediately on skis to a higher spot to survey the terrain, to see if a landing field could be made in the area. At the highest spot I could tell from the rugged views that greeted me that we needed to find a more suitable site; nothing close by would work. I made a rock cairn were I stood on the ridge, wrote a note, and placed it under the rocks. The note read: WILLIE KNUTSEN WAS HERE, APRIL 1948—JUST FOR THE FUN OF IT.

Just as I finished my "scientific" work, I heard Charlie Hubbard's plane flying in low, as if to land. I could see my men were waving them off with the signals we had previously agreed on. But the plane kept coming in. My heart was in my throat as I saw the plane touch down hard, and then momentarily disappear in a cloud of churned-up snow crystals. Then the tail popped up out of the top of the cloud as the craft came to a sudden halt. The tail dropped slowly back into the cloud. I shot down the slope on my skis, and I could see the men from my plane rushing to see if our friends were all right. By the time I arrived, the cloud had settled, and Charlie and his crew were staggering out of the plane. No one was hurt, just badly shaken up, but the nose wheel had been damaged. Fortunately, the motors were still running, but we did not know if the craft could get airborne again. McKay asked why they had landed when they had been waved off.

"We thought you signaled us to land!" was Charlie's reply. I immediately thought of how his floatplane had gone aground at Frobisher in 1943 when he had mistakenly interpreted Sverre Strom's signals to stay out of a boulder-strewn area of the bay. Secretly, I think Charlie wanted to be able to say he had landed on Prince Patrick, too! I couldn't blame him.

While we surveyed the damage and pondered whether it would ever fly out of there, the pilot shut down the engines, and the fuel lines were quickly removed before they could freeze up and crack. Watching this procedure, my pilot suddenly remembered he had turned off his engines before he had come running over to Hubbard's craft. He went running back, but it was too late. The oil lines had cracked! Now we appeared to be stranded on the most remote spot in the Arctic.

Night was fast approaching, and we had to get tent shelters up quickly. We had not planned for such a large group, of course, but at least the planes were supplied for such an emergency. In the morning, I remembered it was my birthday—April 13. It was the fourth birthday in ten years that I had spent in a tent in the Arctic. Unfortunately, there was no time for a party. It was decided that Hubbard's group would attempt a takeoff in his plane by putting all the weight in the tail so as not to put pressure on the damaged nose wheel. While I and my tiny team watched with more than a little apprehension, the plane's fuel lines were re-installed, the motors then came to life, and the plane soon roared its way across the bumpy lake surface, became airborne, and just barely cleared the low hill at the end of the lake by two feet. I never wanted to have to go through that again!

A plane carrying the spare oil lines from Resolute arrived the next day, and made a bumpy but safe landing. While one crew fixed our plane, the other crew forgot to watch their own engines, and their lines froze! So our plane had to go get a replacement line. That shows how fraught with difficulties flying in the Arctic can be.

As we flew over Mould Bay, we finally saw what looked to be a decent site for a landing field. We made a landing on a lake nearby, and found the terrain suitable for our base. It was time to radio Hubbard for the bulldozer. When the plane carrying the small "Cat" landed, it made an abrupt stop in the deep snow. The dozer broke loose of its chain bindings, and crashed into the wall of the cockpit with a terrifying noise. Fortunately, no one was injured, and there was only minor damage to the plane, but you can believe one very shaken-up pilot emerged when the plane's door was opened! After the plane was gone, and there were only the three of us left there, that wonderful arctic silence descended on us. McKay and Chorney were good arctic mates. The awesome stillness and the knowledge that we might as well be on the moon did not disturb them. In fact, they said they were having a ball! Nonetheless, just for security's sake, the three of us got to work smoothing out the rock-strewn area for the landing site.

We had to make a real airstrip capable of handling somewhat bigger planes carrying materials for the scientific research station. Riding that tiny Cat we felt like a flea trying to clear debris off a white elephant's back. Finally, we radioed for some better equipment. A flying boxcar came over, and dropped us a large, heavy wooden beam to use as a drag. That was our "modern" equipment. While Chorney and I took turns riding on the beam behind the Cat, we bounced and ground our way through the dark across the bleak landscape. Snow kicked up and covered whoever was taking his turn on the beam. What a scene it was: three tiny humans and a little Cat, alone on Prince Patrick Island.

One night, while Chorney and I were in our two-man tent, we heard McKay scream out from his tent. He had knocked over his Coleman stove, and his nylon tent had gone up in a flash of fire. McKay was understandably shaken—but luckily, unhurt—and miraculously, none of the radio equipment in his tent had been damaged. McKay had to squeeze in with us until a replacement tent could be brought in. The job of runway clearing was completed, and when the first cargo plane came roaring down our airstrip, the three of us tried not to swell too much with pride.

From then on the island was transformed quickly. A seemingly never-ending stream of C-54 and C-82 cargo planes came and went. Four new men arrived to swell the camp number to seven, but they were not enough to keep up with the flow of supplies coming in. Two of these men I had worked with before: Shorty Polack, the cook from my Padloping days, and a dozer driver from Crystal Two (whose name somehow escapes me these forty years later). In any case, we quickly erected prefab homes, called Jamesway huts; no more sleeping in tents in minus-forty-degree weather. We had dogs and sleds, a diesel generator, all kinds of food and medical supplies, construction materials, dynamite, and even a generator that made hydrogen for filling meteorological balloons. We had ice saws, and, of all things, an ice cream maker. We had books enough for a decent library. What a radical transformation in such a short period of time.

Then one day, some military men showed up (their names will remain undisclosed). As I watched them direct the construction of even larger airfields, I asked the officer in charge, "Aren't these strips a bit big? You could land the biggest bombers here!" He turned to me, fixed me with a stare, and then said sternly, "Knutsen, you will keep your observations to yourself! Is that clear?" It was. I had just realized what the real purpose of this "scientific station" was: a station capable of handling bombers.

It appeared—and this is only my personal opinion—that some in the military were planning a preemptive strike against Russia. We knew that soon the

Soviets would have the bomb, and it suddenly made frightening sense that we might be planning to strike first, while we still could. I am not making a moral judgment against those who may have been planning a preemptive strike. The Soviets had shown themselves to be as merciless with humanity as the Nazis had been, and I personally thought the sooner the world was rid of the leaders under Stalin, the better. So I have kept my observations about that airstrip to myself all these years until now—now that its possible purpose is no longer relevant.

With the new men on the job, I was able to do some exploring. There were indeed herds of musk oxen and Peary caribou still thriving on the island, which Stef would be glad to hear. There were also a few large arctic wolves. But the site that had the most of these rare and magnificent hunters was Eureka, on Ellesmere Island. Once while I flew there on an inspection tour, our plane flew low over a herd of caribou to get a better look at them, and the frightened animals ran right into an ambush of wolves who seemed to have learned to gather when a plane arrived for a landing! At Prince Patrick, white arctic owls watched us work, and foxes were everywhere. They did not seem to mind us. Of course, we were not killing them. The site of the landing strip had been a main run for the foxes of the island, and seeing this, it brought back memories of trapping in Greenland's east coast. Had it only been ten years before? It seemed like hundreds!

One time, while out skiing with Patrick McKay, we found ourselves in a whiteout. We could not tell which way was up or down. Flickering shadows created strange illusions. McKay suddenly put up his hand and motioned me to be still. "Caribou—down in that valley," he said softly. I peered into the milky world, not sure what valley he was talking about. There were indeed gray forms moving about, and at first they seemed to be in the distance. Finally, I began to laugh. "Those aren't caribou, they're lemmings! And they are only a few feet away!" That's what the weather phenomena of the Arctic does to you.

When I looked around Prince Patrick for archaeological sites—which I never found—I found seams of coal, and pieces from them were found right along the shore. Though oily, they did not burn in my stove. I also found many fossils, but I did not find even a sign that Inuit had ever been there. Prince Patrick had just been too far out of the way, even for them. Toward the end of April, while helping to carry a heavy stove, I broke through the crust on the snow with the whole length of my right leg. I was terribly twisted, and badly wrenched my back. It also felt as if I had strained muscles around my heart as well. Paul

Chorney was the only one who knew I was hurt, and I made him promise not to tell the other men. Eventually, though, I realized I was of no use to anyone, and I needed medical attention.

Difficult as it was to be forced to leave before my thirteen months were up, I radioed Thule for an evacuation plane. Because of the weather, no plane would be able to arrive for a month! Back in 1939, it had taken much less time for the ship carrying the plane to rescue Micard. On May 17, Norway's Day of Independence, I made a sketch of Mould Bay, just as I had done a sketch of the hut we called Krogness on another May 17, twelve years earlier.

When the evacuation plane finally arrived it was the end of May, and it was really annoying to have to leave just as summer was beginning. Not to mention that some young new arrivals thought I was faking injury just to get home. That bit of slander actually followed me back to the States, and I had to produce a doctor's report exonerating my integrity. I couldn't believe it. There are "Jess Tilliers" in every land. But at least the route of my return took me to places I had never seen before, and also to some places I had not seen for years. We passed over the Finlay group of islands, which includes the one named by Stef in 1916 for Gilbert H. Grosvenor, then editor-in-chief of National Geographic Magazine, and of course later president of the National Geographic Society for fifty years. We passed over the immense and interesting ice caps of southern Ellesmere Island, and then arrived at Thule. Finally, I was back in Greenland!

Thule had originally been set up by the great Danes, Knud Rasmussen and Peter Freuchen, as a trading post in 1910. Rasmussen and Freuchen had written interesting accounts of their lives there, living with the Inuit people and following the Inuit way of life that had existed for centuries. Just 910 miles from the North Pole, and with plenty of flat land for an airport, Thule was first suggested for a defensive base in 1942 by Bernt Balchen. By 1948, it was still just a small, Canadian and U.S. meteorological site. But, when I arrived in Thule, it was the largest of the sites in the new defense net we were erecting. Though the sites might seem small for the task of defending North America from attack, it must be remembered that our job was to make bases capable of handling the next, much larger phase of construction.

From Thule, I flew down the coast to the base at Sondrestrom Fjord ("southern stream fjord"), which had been active since the early days of World War II. Set at the end of the fjord, where silt and sand from melting glaciers made wide beaches, the base often had to contend with sandstorms. I know, because I later spent two years there. Talk about true grit.

From Sondrestrom Fjord, we then headed to Narssarssuaq in southern Greenland, where in 1944 I had briefed the commando unit that eventually dislodged the Nazi weather stations on the northeast coast of Greenland. There I met some old friends, including Hans Sievers. Sievers had just finished making an aerial movie of the Arctic from Alaska to Greenland so the planners back in Washington and Ottawa could get a better idea of what we were dealing with. But though he had flown near Prince Patrick, he had not known, nor had his superiors, that I had been there, or that there was a base there when he passed over. That's how secret that station was.

Regarding my suspicions about the landing field on Prince Patrick, soon after my arrival home, it was announced that the Russians had the bomb. The "scientific" crew on the remote island was suddenly called home. We will never know, I assume, but was that because a preemptive strike was now out of the question? At any rate, science had been served. Through films such as Hans Sievers's, and because of the work we had done in such unknown spots as Prince Patrick Island, Ellef Ringnes Island, and Ellesmere Island, the "hidden Arctic" was being revealed as never before. Supply ships were learning the waters of the Arctic islands, and could better supply the bases being established in the area. The base at Narssarssuaq was as modern as any in the States. There were quarters for married couples; wives and children of military personnel strolled the streets. A school bus picked up the kids at every corner, and mothers hung clothes out on the line to dry, just like in any American town.

By 1950, Charles Hubbard, with a Navy/Coast Guard task force, had penetrated Kennedy and Robeson Channels between northern Ellesmere and Greenland. They had then cruised far out into the Arctic Ocean. Man was probing further and further. Charles Hubbard had gone by ship's helicopter to Cape Sheridan, Ellesmere, a place that Robert Peary had reached in 1905 after a perilous struggle by the steel-plated wooden ship, the *Roosevelt*, commanded by Bob Bartlett. Cape Sheridan, less than 525 miles south of the North Pole, had been used as a winter base for Peary's unsuccessful attempt on the Pole in 1906. In 1950, Charles Hubbard found a sealed bottle in a rock cairn that contained handwritten records left by Peary, forty-five years earlier.

PART THREE

CHAPTER TWENTY-ONE

The Cold War in the Arctic (1950–1968)

rriving back in the States after my injury on Prince Patrick Island, I went about the difficult transition from Arctic adventure to normalcy. In April 1949, our second son was born just before I returned from Prince Patrick. But Alice's manic depression had gotten worse. Her mother told me they had a doctor's advice that Alice's problem was medical, and there was nothing we could do except let her have the proper professional treatment. Alice refused, and for a short time things actually did calm down. I began to use my painting-sculpting studio. *National Geographic* asked me to write another article, entitled, "Milestones on My Arctic Journeys," which was published in October 1949.

When my injuries had somewhat healed, I used my knowledge of architecture and building to construct a few homes for friends. It almost seemed like I was making the transition to normalcy without too great of a strain. Unfortunately, soon afterwards, Alice began to suffer more from the effects of her ever-increasing manic depression, an affliction that was little understood in those days. Her mother, her doting brother, and her family doctor all thought she needed professional help, and she was committed to a sanitarium.

A few days later, I got word from Washington again. I was needed in Fort Belvoir, Virginia. My in-laws said they would look after the children, and in that unsettled state of mind, I arrived first in Washington, D.C. I found the town filled with many of my old "arctic rat" friends, including Bernt Balchen, Alan Innes-Taylor, Sverre Strom, Eddie Goodale, Hans Sievers, and many others. We were told we were all to be advisors on a new, top-secret project. The tiny weather base at Thule was to be transformed into a state-of-the-art air bomber site. I mentioned my family problems and was told by Hap Arnold himself that this was a time that needed great personal sacrifice. He said something like, "We are at a critical crossroads in history. Soviet Russia is a gigantic power with great

natural resources. The problem is the Soviet philosophy of life: They want to en-
slave mankind—for man's own good, of course. This is probably the most serious point in the history of man. We have got to stop those fanatical maniacs
before they ruin thousands of years of social evolution!"

What could one say after that?

The nuclear age had cast a pall over the earth. Once Russia had uncovered
the secret of the atomic bomb, the U.S. government knew it was only a matter
of time before America could be threatened by such awesome weaponry. We
knew bombers could reach us via the Arctic; and the rocketry that had been developed during the war, particularly by the Germans, had made such rapid
strides after the war that producing a rocket capable of carrying an atomic bomb
over the Pole from Russia to North America was only a matter of time. America
had suddenly realized that its continent was very vulnerable to its new enemy,
the USSR. My work in the Arctic from 1948 until my retirement in 1969 was
therefore focused around the air defense system General Arnold had envisioned.
This may not sound as exciting or adventuresome as my early work, but what I
was doing now was linked to preserving of our way of life, so don't think that it
didn't involve its share of risk!

For two months, I set to work advising on the construction of buildings for this
great new arctic enterprise. I recommended the use of Inuit technology, since it
was the most tried and true. We designed insulated walls resembling igloos, in that
they utilized insulation filled with air pockets, just as snow blocks did. Working
with engineers on projects as diverse as metallurgy and fuel, it was not surprising
to find that competent metallurgists did not know that some metal products capable of functioning in, say, minus-forty degrees, would shatter like glass under a
blow at minus-fifty degrees. After visiting a sample prefab building designed for filling up weather balloons prior to releasing them outside, I suggested that the very
large doors, needed to take inflated balloons outside, be adapted.

"Make small doors inside the big ones," I said, "so that an operator can step
outside to check the weather without losing all of the hut's heat. Make this door
no more than two and half feet wide, and five high; and the bottom jamb must
be at least a foot above ground level so snow will not blow in so easily," I added.

I went on to make additional suggestions for construction. "The large, roll-
up doors must be changed. The folds in the doors will soon freeze solid and be
unusable. Also, the aluminum siding of the hut will tend to 'sweat' inside, and

then freeze. Make an interior surface of more porous material. All the venting pipes from the buildings must have their caps changed. The existing ones will allow snow to drift in. Use 'hoods' that come down over the sides of the stovepipes or venting pipes," I said, telling them the story of how at Micardbu we had almost died of carbon-monoxide poisoning when the generator exhaust pipe had been clogged by snow.

This sort of thing went on for months. Architects followed me around taking notes, showing no signs of hurt egos. This was a serious endeavor, and there was no time for that kind of nonsense. Parts for planes, for generators, and for buildings had to be designed for the state-of-the-art air bomber site. When the mammoth hangars were put up to withstand severe weather conditions, such as hundred-mile-an-hour frigid winds, it had to be done right the first time.

This was an era of new technology, and the project at Thule spawned a multitude of small industries. Though billions of tax dollars were being spent, even more billions of dollars were being generated in the private sector. And it seemed the whole country was involved in the mammoth project. Newspapers, magazines, and television followed our progress in the North in the same way we now follow the launching of a new space project. It was an immense undertaking, and time was of the essence. The U.S. government did not know then how adept the Soviets were at arctic attack, or whether they already had intercontinental bomber bases in Siberia. At the outbreak of the Korean War, the pace of construction at Thule understandably went into high gear.

An agreement between Denmark and the U.S. was signed on April 27, 1951, which permitted the U.S. to use the facilities in Greenland "in the common defense." But construction had started long before that. My advisory work on the project was actually finished long before that agreement was signed. After the signing, the push really began; it was called "Operation Blue Jay," and involved the Army Corps of Engineers and the Transportation Corps, the Military Air Transport Service, and the 18th Air Force and Tactical Air Command, as well as the Navy Sea Transportation Service, and the Coast Guard. Thousands of civilian workers were hired, mostly from Montana and the Dakotas, as they were accustomed to rugged weather. Even so, they would still find it hard to adjust to minus-fifty degrees, and winds of 125 mph!

The Greenlanders living near North Star Bay at Thule called their village site *Pituffik*, which roughly translated, means "where you tie your dog." Because of the noisy activities of the huge air base, the local hunting grounds became useless, and we transferred the whole village further north to where walrus had found new accommodations. After the relocation, the Inuit took the name Pituffik with them. According to the base's official newsletter at the time, this suited many of the Americans who were soon to make the old site their new home, because Pituffik made them feel like they were "in the doghouse." Many of them had indeed been sent to Thule for reasons that had nothing to do with their suitability or usefulness to the epoch-changing project, and the old name seemed to some to be a way of "rubbing their noses in it."

There has been a lot of flap in the news recently about how the Inuit were "forced" out of their old sites against their will. Though it is true their hunting grounds were ruined due to our Cold War activities, I seem to remember they were glad to be moved to where their game was less disturbed. They may not have been thrilled by the whole thing, but I didn't get the sense that they felt forced to move. Back in the States, many communities also had their tranquility interrupted by the building of new bases from which giant bombers noisily flew in and out, sometimes around the clock. The general sentiment was that dangerous times called for sacrifices to be made. Now that the threat of nuclear war with Russia has waned, it seems easy for Monday-morning quarterbacks to criticize the life-threatening game that the Cold War really was.

The building of Thule was the most ambitious military construction project in history, except perhaps the Great Wall of China. I read this claim in an official brochure, and it appeared to those of us who were there to watch and participate in this project that the claim was no exaggeration. I suppose it was true for that time. We were certainly not in Thule to drive off Inuit walrus. The majority of Danes I knew in those early days of 1950s didn't complain about the American presence in Greenland for "the common good." We had liberated Denmark from the iron fist of the Nazis just ten years earlier, for crying out loud. Most Danes liked us. The United States had made some mistakes, and some Americans were annoying and pushy towards the Danes and Canadians, but most involved worked with a spirit of cooperation that the rest of the world could stand to learn from.

Over a hundred flights of cargo planes brought in the preliminary supplies. Then, a thousand ships brought the vast bulk of the rest, consisting of more than

350,000 tons of construction vehicles, building materials, and other supplies. Even a thousand-foot, prefabricated dock was shipped to the location. Work went on around the clock. More than ten million cubic feet of earth and rock were moved to build a runway that was two hundred feet wide. The runway had to be built over a thick gravel pad that was laid down to prevent the melting of the permafrost underneath it. Six heavy-bomber hangars, three fighter hangars, and a base maintenance hangar were built, as were the barracks we arctic advisors had specially designed.

These "reverse refrigerator" buildings had panels made by sandwiching 3-1/2" fiberglass insulation between two 1/4" plywood panels, then facing it with aluminum or stainless steel. These panels were called "elements," but the workers dubbed them "inclements," as in inclement weather. More than three million "inclements" were used in the construction of the base, which, of course, in reality became a modern city. The 1,212-foot navigational operations tower at Thule was the second-tallest man-made structure in the world at the time. (The Empire State Building, the tallest structure in those days, was 1,472 feet tall.) The project at Thule was completed in September 1952. An old Inuit named Adak attended the opening ceremony, having made the trek to the North Pole with Peary almost a half century before. There, at Thule, the Space Age and the Stone Age had merged in fifty short years.

The Korean Conflict

During the early planning and designing of Operation Blue Jay, I was called back to active duty in the summer of 1950 because of the Korean War. Air Force General Curtis LeMay had set up an "Escape and Evasion School" out in Camp Carson, Colorado, near Colorado Springs. I was sent there to instruct the new breed of fighting men, the Strategic Air Command (SAC) bomber crews.

It is easy, four decades later, to forget the tension of those days. We forget the psychological shock the world was experiencing as it awoke to the awful, destructive, potential power of the just dawning nuclear age. The Korean War was the first war mankind had to face in which both sides had the potential to unleash a nuclear holocaust. There was no end to evidence of the murderous capabilities of the Soviet leadership. They openly threatened to annihilate us.

Reading General LeMay's *National Geographic* article, "Air Force School for Survival," published in May 1953, one gets a very clear picture of the psyche of the times, of the importance of the survival school, and the urgent need of flight crews trained in survival. For nearly five years, General LeMay had headed the nation's striking force of huge strategic bombers. An aggressive and resourceful commander, he developed standard techniques of bombing and formation flying as he led American bombers against both Germans and Japanese. During World War II, he rose from major to major general, and in 1951, when he was only forty-five, he became a four-star general. A graduate of Ohio State University, he held a degree in engineering. Since 1951, he had been a Life Trustee of the National Geographic Society. LeMay wrote:

> The downed airman (and we have had many go down over Red-held Korea) cannot defeat cold and hunger and isolation by sitting on his hands. He must know what to do. He must equip himself mentally and physically to do it. And he must act. There are still, perhaps, a few "realists" around who will shrug off the loss of such crews as merely a part of the normal attrition which afflicts any operating air force. They could not be more mistaken. To the Strategic Air Command, no pilot, no bombardier, no gunner, no crew is expendable. The reason lies embedded in hard fact: SAC's mission is to preserve the peace by presenting to the enemy the constant, poised alternative of total retaliation. So far, we have fulfilled this primary obligation. But our deterrent value in peace, and our destructive potential in war, depend alike upon our readiness to deliver a knockout atomic punch—not in a year or a month or a week, but now. Not with crews we might eventually train, but with the precision teams at our disposal today.
>
> Why are these crews so valuable? Because they are made up of human lives and are irreplaceable. Because each crew, manning its massive bomber, commands more lethal power than a whole fleet of World War II planes loaded with ordinary high explosives. Because years of intensive training are required to raise each crew to performance pitch. The ships themselves are important, yes. But the crews are even more so. During the last war it was possible, and necessary, to send airmen into combat after only eight months of training. Many a crew flew its first mission with barely a score of hours aloft together. Today SAC would rate such a crew as apprentices. They would have to

put in another three months of work and a good 150 hours of flying time to graduate to combat-ready status. To make the first team and to become a lead crew might take them from six months to a year and a half. Nor can even the lead crews rest on their honors. Kept in constant practice, they are never allowed to forget that their individual and group proficiency records come under ceaseless scrutiny. At regular intervals they are checked out on all minute aspects of their job, from gunnery and navigation to ditching and bail-out techniques. They know, too, that a black mark in any one airman's specialty downgrades the whole crew. Accountants have put price tags on these thousands of hours of group flying and group training; they say, for instance, that each B-36 crew represents a $3,000,000 investment. They may be right. But the dollar figures are only half the story. We can replace the plane; it is extremely dubious whether we could, in a crisis, ever be given enough time to replace the crew.

With those serious, carefully chosen words, one can understand the deadly frightening atmosphere of those early days of the Cold War. In that grave spirit, a school for survival training was born at Camp Carson, Colorado.

The problem for SAC flight crews was how to survive off the land, whatever that land may be—tundra, jungle, desert, or mountains. Camp Carson was chosen because it provided training for both desert and arctic conditions. Camp Carson was set on an arid plain, but right in the awesome shadow of the Rocky Mountains, which could get as much as thirty feet of snow in the winter.

The commanding officer was Colonel Dmitrios Stampados. Stampados, a big-game hunter during peacetime, had become in World War II a member of the British Commandos and of the 8th Army's Long Range Desert Group. He had served as an intelligence officer for the Office of Strategic Services, and had operated behind enemy lines in the Balkans and the Far East. He had learned survival techniques the hard way. His second-in-command was Major Burton T. Miller, an outdoorsman and an ordnance expert all his life.

To aid Stampados in his groundbreaking work were Lieutenant Colonel Charles A. K. Innes-Taylor; Per Stoen of the Arctic Indoctrination School at Nome, Alaska; survival expert Major L. E. Dawson; my old Norwegian pals, Sverre Strom and Hans Sievers, who had trapped in Greenland; Major Sergeant

K. E. ("Slim") Moore, a Canadian-trained dog-team handler; Major Sergeant William Ferreira, who escaped three times from German prison camps; and a swarm of volunteers who had seen service with the ski troops and with the 10th Mountain Division in Italy.

Through us were channeled successive classes of SAC airmen who had taken standard survival training at the Air Force base units, using such terrain as the jungle at Ramey, Puerto Rico; the Okefenokee Swamp at Turner, Georgia; and the woodland at Lockbourne, Ohio. They came to Carson, summer and winter, to get really intensive instruction in dealing with the kind of terrain they were most likely to encounter in a major war—the terrain of the North.

Before Sverre Strom left for Colorado, we joked about the time he had signaled Charlie Hubbard's PBY away from rocks in Frobisher Bay, but Hubbard had ended up on one anyway. A few days later, on the day I was to leave for Colorado, I got the bad news that Charlie Hubbard had died in an air crash at Alert, a new station on Ellesmere Island. Some cargo was being parachuted from the plane, and in a freak accident, some shrouds got entangled in the tail flaps, causing the pilot to lose control of the plane.

When I arrived at Camp Carson, I found that Strom had just died as well. He had been hauling a heavy branch for firewood high in the Rockies, and the strain had proven to be too much for his bad heart. Hearing this second piece of bad news was a hard way to start my new assignment. I next heard from my mother-in-law that Alice was having more difficulties, had been rehospitalized, and that the children were unhappy. So I sent for the three oldest, while we found a fine family in Rockport who would take good care of our youngest son. It was a trying time to say the least.

I had also gotten involved with a woman, a civilian who worked for the Air Force. Alice had been the first to file for divorce, which was a relief. Her drinking, which before had been just for enjoyment, had become compulsive. Her mother told me it was a family "curse," but it was really an inherited problem. Many of her family suffered the same effect from alcohol, though not to the degree Alice did. Alice got so out of control even her mother, not to mention the courts, thought she should not have contact with our children. I was learning the meaning of Shakespeare's line: "O what a noble mind is here overthrown!" Having once been so fun-loving and intelligent, Alice was now the opposite. Her family and I did not know what else we could do to help her, and we finally had

Willie's drawing of an Ammassalik Inuit man and woman done in charcoal, colored chalk, and colored pencil.

Willie drew this charcoal sketch of an Inuit hunter in 1941.

Willie took this photo of Knud Rasmussen's old expedition ship, *Sea King*, in Ammassalik in 1940.

Willie takes a photo of the U.S. Coast Guard cutter *Northland* just before he is about to board the ship and leave for America and his new life in 1940.

Willie says his final farewell to his good friend Labb in Torgilsbu, Northeast Greenland, in 1940.

Willie teaches skiing techniques as part of the rescue training program on Mount Katadin, Maine, in 1943.

A portrait of Colonel Bert ("Fish") Hassell, aviation legend and base commander at Goose Bay, Labrador, in 1943.

A photo taken in Fish's quarters at Frobisher Bay while he was away in Goose Bay. In the front row (from left) sits Colonel Merriwether, Alexander Forbes, and Vilhjalmur Stefansson. In the back row (from left) is Willie, Captain Bunting, Lieutenant Franzen, and Captain Ward. This photo was taken during a party that Willie hoped would reunite Bob Bartlett and Stefansson.

Willie's sketch of Bob Bartlett done onboard Bartlett's ship, *Morrissey*, in Frobisher Bay, 1943.

This the photo of the historic meeting of the two dogsled teams in the Soper River Pass, Meta Incognito Peninsula, Baffin Island, 1943. It was a rare occurrence to have two teams meet in such a remote spot, let alone have a party. From right is Roger Pepin, Doug Webster, RCMP, Etuachia, Willie, and the cook.

Etuachia, Willie's main sled driver, being fitted for his kayak.

Etuachia with his family and some friends in Frobisher Bay in 1943.

Willie and Fish Hassel with one of the pigs Hassell brought to
Goose Bay to supplement the poor rations at the base.

The "flying husky" rescue plane logo at Presque Isle, Maine, in 1943.

A plane wreckage in the Mealy Mountains in Goose Bay, 1944. It was impossible to carry the dead crewmen over the rough terrain, so they were buried at the site.

Willie's rescue team at Goose Bay, Labrador, 1944. Front row (from left): Roger Pepin, Schultz, Cletius Barbeau; back row (from left): Gabriel Le Blanc, Willie, and Harley Andersen.

Airbase photo taken to show conditions of "Flying Huskies" in flight. To the left is the famous Eddie Goodale, who had been with Byrd at the South Pole. In the center is Lt. Murray Wiener, and to the right, Tech. Sergeant Klekhinger.

Harley Andersen with Willie's team near the Western Front during the Battle of the Bulge in Hyanges, France, 1944. This team of dogs had been with Richard Byrd in Antarctica.

Willie, Cletius Barbeau, and Sgt. Walters near Verdun, France, in March 1945.

Willie in Goose Bay, 1944. This photo was taken for a recruitment poster but was never used as such.

This was the first mass rescue performed by helicopter in the Arctic. The U.S. Coast Guard Sikorski helicopter carried all eleven Canadian flight crew members out, one at a time. (Image courtesy the National Museum of the United States Air Force)

Rescue helicopter being unloaded back in the United States at Brooklyn Naval Air Station, after the rescue in 1944.

Willie meets Sir Hubert Wilkins in Goose Bay in 1954. Wilkins offered his services to the U.S. Army, which retained him to teach Arctic survival skills to U.S. soldiers.

The Manhattan-sized iceberg airbase T-3, or Fletcher's Island, in 1957. During Willie's command, the airbase was renamed "Willieville International Airport."

A meeting of cultures at Thule, Greenland, 1957. (Photo Herbert O. Johansen, editor of *Popular Science* magazine.)

Willie with team dogs Lady and Tramp, the latest in polar bear warning
technology, on T-3 in 1957. (Photo by Spencer Appolonio, oceanographer).

The new Arctic during the Cold War with BMEWS radar and the DEWLine
radar station in 1958.

French polar explorer Paul-Emil Victor and Willie meet again at Sondrestrom Fjord Base in 1967. They had first met in Ammassalik, Greenland, in 1937 and saw each other often over the next three decades. This was the last time they were together.

Willie (left) with Admiral (retired) Richard Blackburn Black, who became the officer in charge of the U.S. Antarctic programs after Byrd in 1957, and Bernt Balchen (far right), the pilot who flew Byrd over the South Pole. They met in Fairbanks, Alaska, in 1969 at Willie's retirement. Balchen and Willie first met in Oslo in 1938. Fifteen years later, in the United States, they discovered they were cousins.

no choice but to give up. There are medications available today for manic depression, and support groups for those so terribly afflicted, but there weren't in those days. So, we divorced. Alice went back to the hospital for help, and we did not meet again for thirty years. The court order for her to stay away from our children meant she never saw them again for twenty years, not until she beat the disease and the alcoholism.

Regardless of these personal matters, the flight crews were already awaiting me, and there was nothing to do but begin their training. During this period while I trained flight crews in Colorado, and instructors as well, I got the news that I was to be sent to Korea to provide survival training for the Koreans. With no one to look after our children, my parents and sister in Norway said they would care for them. Off went my three oldest—my son, age six, and the two girls, seven and ten—on a grand adventure without their parents. After staying a few days in New York with Gunvor Bull-Teilman in her wonderful artist's studio, they flew off to Norway with newspapers declaring them the "first children to fly intercontinental without parents!" It was quite a sensation. Press photos were taken and used as advertisements to show how safe flying had become.

The transfer to Korea never happened. Instead, I was sent to various sites in the Arctic, usually for advisory purposes. The Canadians, for instance, had their own survival schools, but they would send members of their schools to the States, and vice versa. One such cooperative enterprise was called "Operation Mukluk," located in the Canadian Far North.

For Operation Mukluk, I flew up to Fort Nelson where I met my old pals Norman Bright and Harry Strong, who were working with the Canadians. Also on hand was Hans Sievers. Our job during Operation Mukluk was to test new equipment and materials under arctic conditions. We were flown to Cambridge Bay, on the southwest coast of Victoria Island. Victoria, unknown to the majority of the world, is larger than Ireland, or Corsica.

While in the area, I visited the sunken remains of Amundsen's ship, *Maud*. Amundsen had used the ship in an attempt to drift in the polar ice to the North Pole, but after his mission was unsuccessful, he had sold the ship to the Hudson's Bay Company who used it in the icy waters around Victoria Island. The ship had too deep a draft for the waters there, and had gone aground, where it was abandoned. All recoverable material of the ship that had showed above the waterline (the planking and so on) had been salvaged by the local Inuit. The rest of the ship must surely still be there, well preserved in the icy waters. I have a couple of pieces myself.

We were truly far away from American civilization, but it was a mistake to think the locals still lived like their ancestors did. I remember that Hans Sievers tried to present to some of the Inuit one of those cheap Mickey Mouse watches that are included in survival packs to give to the "natives." The Inuit smiled politely, but showed him their own beautiful, expensive watches. Hans sheepishly realized these natives were not the primitives he thought they were. Meanwhile, Harry was trying to speak pidgin English to a teenager. Harry obviously thought this kid would be interested in "real Eskimo stories" he could identify with, and went on and on in that ridiculous language about hunting as the Inuit might have long before. The youth, whom I knew played guitar, then answered in perfect English, with a British-tinged accent, "How very interesting. My grandfather used to tell the same sort of stories, old chap."

Among the men I trained in that operation was Dr. Donald Stulken, the zoologist who was tremendously interested in the behavior of all animals. Some years later he would train the monkeys used in the first "manned" space flight, and then train America's astronauts. He was new to survival techniques, and jokingly called me "Mother" because of all the help he asked of me. Stulken and the other scientists and "arctic-ologists" who assembled there were part of the all-out drive to increase knowledge about the Arctic.

Bernt Balchen's advice to the United States military chiefs of staff to regard the Arctic as the center of the world seemed to have been taken to heart. All types of tests on human physiology in the Arctic were conducted, as were the effects of cold on various fibers for clothing, and mental fatigue under arctic conditions. This was a new phase in arctic research. Instead of "arctic dashes," scientists were uncovering the real secrets of the North. Men with microscopes were more important than men with hopes for glory. The North Pole had been attained long before. It was an uninteresting spot in a frozen sea. The plants and animals of Greenland were far more interesting. The physics of ice, not the sledding on top of it, was what was now important. Scientists in many fields needed to undergo arctic survival training before taking their research to the fields and oceans.

Besides training our own military men, we also trained crews and personnel from other nations, and even private airline companies. Over the years, I believe some twenty thousand men went through our schools. One of our top sites was at Stead Air Force Base, in the north of Nevada. It had the advantage of being in a desert, while close to the Sierra Nevadas, mountains which in winter were tough and snow-clad enough for any training school. We also trained the newly formed CIA for a while, until they started their own school, headed by then Colonel Alan Innes-Taylor.

Our schools were thorough and tough, and when one man complained of the toughness to his father, a senator, the news media came in. There were public cries of brutality. It was quite a public relations flap until some of the men who had had the training, and had survived in Korea because of it, came to the rescue. And, because of the furor, some British survival trainers came over to see our operations, and were astonished at the commotion. They said their training was far tougher than ours, and needed to be in order to train men for the real horrors of trying to live alone in hostile territory, in all kinds of weather. The British announcement that their training was tougher than the Americans' led to "Operation Moonraker," a test of the best men from both lands.

"Operation Moonraker"

An American team of survival students and teachers were sent to England for Operation Moonraker in 1953. Though I was an old-timer by this point, at the age of forty-one, I and a few young men in my team were driven through Wales in the dark by truck to a lonely country road, and dropped off without being told where we were. The object was to get back to our "side" through farmland that had been alerted to the "enemy" in the area. Thirty thousand British troops were spread out over the land. Farmers and even Boy Scouts were on the lookout for us! I think they stacked the deck against us, but that is the reality in real combat situations.

For ten days we scurried from hedgerow, to forest, to haystack. It rained almost incessantly. We had no food, so we had to live off the land. One night we watched, unobserved, a farmer milking a cow. When he went off to do something, he left his full bucket of fresh milk. One of my men dashed to the bucket and filled our canteens, then dashed back. We stayed in our hiding place long enough to watch the astonished look on the poor man's face when he returned to a half-empty pail! We snatched apples from trees, and once slept in a pig shelter with the animals. Thinking of my "pig farmer" days at Goose Bay, I felt right at home, and the hogs kept us warm. However, we also spent some uncomfortable moments lying in cold bogs to avoid patrols. Finally, we met our "underground contact," who informed us we were safe, and were taken to our headquarters. We had braved the worst, but Operation Moonraker showed that the British training experts had been right about our training; it was not tough enough. Many of our young men in other small groups trying to cross Wales had given up to the "enemy" rather than face the elements. The British survival teams taught those who would have us lighten our rigorous training what some of us already knew: We needed to make the training even more realistic.

After Operation Moonraker, I was given leave to visit my children in Norway where they had gone to live with my parents. I had not been to Norway since I had departed on the *Ringsel* in 1940, and had not seen my children for almost two years. While my parents' apartment in Oslo was nice, it was small, especially since my sister Signy and her daughter were also living there. With no place to house my children, except on the weekends, they had been sent to boarding schools for the past two years; happily, they had nothing but enthusiastic stories to tell me.

I also met with many of my old associates while in Oslo, including Kaare Rodahl, John Gjaever, and Helge Ingstad. Helge, who was already quite famous in Norway, came for dinner at the apartment. His equally famous archaeologist wife, Anne Stine, had been invited, but she said she could not make it. I think the real reason was that Helge used to date my sister just before he married Anne, although my always getting him drunk—against Anne's strict warnings—might have also had something to do with her cancellation. At the dinner, Helge said he was trying to obtain funding for an expedition to search for the Viking site rumored to be in Newfoundland. I reminded him about what I had heard from locals near the northern tip of Newfoundland, and he said, yes, yes, he had heard something like that, but there were so many other rumors he would have to go about the search systematically. And of course, he eventually did.

From Oslo I went to Paris for a reunion with Count Gaston Micard. Gaston talked of going back to the Arctic, "even though I am getting on in years," he said with a laugh. We relived the old adventures, the dreams we fulfilled, and the ones we were still pursuing. When I returned to the warm sands of northern Nevada, I had dreams that Gaston had indeed organized another expedition for us. Soon after arriving back I married the woman I had been seeing for three years, Marion Ralston, from Weston, West Virginia.

Soon, I received new orders: I was to return to Goose Bay, Labrador. I heaved a sigh of relief. The survival schools stateside were important, and I am proud to have been a part of them and the good men who were in them, but I hungered for the North. So, in 1954, now a major and remarried, I sent for my children. We were reunited in Goose Bay. For the first time I had my family with me in the North. Marion and I would have three children together over the years, making a total of seven for me.

Goose Bay had changed a lot. It now had schools, movie theaters, and paved streets. There were also more civilians making their home nearby in a place called Happy Valley. But one did not have to go far before that wilderness, with its famous mosquitoes, swallowed you up. I had my sled dogs to look after as in the old days, although now occasionally I had my children to ride with me. They were able to see the Indians still living (in some ways) as they had for centuries, even though their tents were often made from nylon parachutes.

Together, we traveled on weekends through the wilderness on large, covered snowmobiles where previously my men and I had gone by dogsled, snowshoes, skis, and on foot. My children saw lynx chase hares, and in the summer they saw the rivers full of fish and the meadows full of blueberries—and mosquitoes! The kids were not allowed out in summer without netted headgear, their sleeves rolled down and buttoned, and a liberal dose of "6-12" insect repellent coating their cuffs. In the winter we had snow that covered the first floor, and until snow blowers cleared the roads and a tunnel could be dug out from the front door to the street, we had to exit our home by the second-floor windows. The house was often filled with exciting guests like Bernt Balchen, and the children even got to meet one of my childhood heroes, Sir Hubert Wilkins, who came by to say hello. It was quite an exciting childhood experience for them.

Sir Hubert spent several days at Goose Bay, and I arranged that we be flown over much of Labrador so I could point out features of this land—my backyard— that he was so interested in. I pointed out crash sites, and told him of the early days when we had had to quickly set up rescue operations for the Crimson Route.

"How did you ever get to those sites?" he marveled. It was a good question. It was amazing that we had managed it. I answered, "Pure luck."

Without helicopters and other modern equipment that we had when I returned in 1953, our early efforts seemed crude and primitive. But often the old way with dogs and sleds was still the only way to save lives. We talked about this.

"Planes do not fly well in bad weather, and they have a bad habit of running out of petrol," Sir Hubert said with an ironic smile. In 1927 he had run out of fuel with aviation great, Ben Eielson, and had had to walk seventy miles to an Eskimo village. They had been missing so long everyone had assumed they were dead—everyone but his wife. We agreed dogs were a bit more reliable than planes. The man who had done just about everything at both poles told me he still had one dream left to fulfill: "Willie, I still want to take a submarine to the North Pole!" He would get his wish, though not exactly as he planned, but I am getting ahead of the story. After he had left the base, life for me went back to the business at hand.

In February, one of the Strategic Air Command's huge B-36 bombers crashed in northern Labrador. Speedy rescue was imperative because of the frigid midwinter conditions. But just as in the old days, weather prevented an air search-and-rescue attempt. My rescue team and I had to cover part of the distance on snowshoes. Exhausted as we all were, for forty-eight hours—with only short breaks—I urged the men on, fearing the worst for the downed fliers, some of whom I knew because they had gone through survival training with me at Stead Air Force Base in Nevada two years before.

When we approached the reported position of the crash, with our energies nearly spent, I stepped out into a clearing, and a smile spread across my face. I was looking at a perfectly constructed survival camp. The air crew was comfortably settled into lean-tos and para-tepees (tents made from parachutes). Water boiled over fires. Distress signals had been stamped out in the snow, and signals had been made using parachute panels. The others in my rescue unit were staring at the scene. Finally, one of the air crew spotted us and shouted to me, "What are you doing way the hell out here, Major? Following us around to see if we learned anything?"

In 1954 I was sent to Thule, Greenland, from Goose Bay to be an advisor for a Warner Brothers/Pathe movie called *Survival on the Ice Cap*. During that period, sometimes in one week I would go from Goose Bay to New York to work with Pathe-Warner on casting, then back to Greenland for the shooting, and then down to Florida for the editing. The highlight of the filming came one day when we were returning to camp after a day of shooting. We saw two white foxes playing on a steep, icy hill. Sliding down the slope by sitting on their rumps, like children, each took turns giving the other a push. Unfortunately, we had no cameras with us! I thought of all the fox I had trapped. I had not known they could behave this way. You can believe I was glad I had never trapped furs for profit since my first expedition. Fur for survival is something else.

While at Thule I met my old friend, Paul-Emil Victor, who was head of the French Polar Expedition; he was there doing research on the ice cap. Also, members of the famous Danish "Sirius Patrol," the sled patrol organized during World War II, heard I was in town and arrived for a party. We all had a grand time comparing the rigors of the old days to the new "soft" life of the Arctic. While Paul-Emil Victor and I discussed the old days, around this same time planning for one of the most difficult construction projects in history was getting underway. This would be a far larger and more ambitious project than even Thule had been. It was the Distant Early Warning Line, or, DEWLine, a series of radar stations to be strung out from Cape May in Alaska to Iceland.

Mapping teams traveled more than a million miles and reviewed more than eighty thousand aerial photos as part of site and mapping activities. I was offered an advisory position with this planning stage of the DEWLine, and that would have kept me in the North where I wanted to be, but my wife was pregnant at the time, and the thought of being stationed in the Far North was not exactly appealing to her. Goose Bay had been far enough North for her as it was. Reluctantly I accepted a position at my old survival school back at Stead AFB in Nevada for a year, to train more men for the vast arctic projects. Then in 1956 I was sent to Westover Field, Massachusetts, to teach arctic survival to the crews of the newly developed in-flight refueling planes.

During all this time, although I was stationed in Nevada and Massachusetts, I made many trips back and forth to the North, and watched with amazement as new technologies transformed the Arctic when the building of the DEWLine went into high gear.

This project included the largest commercial airlift operation ever documented, with 45,000 commercial flights in 32 months delivering 120,300 tons over an average distance of 720 miles per flight. Involved were Canadian and U.S. commercial airlines. I don't know who figures these things out, but in an official document I had to read to keep abreast of the developments, I found the following statistics: Seventy-five million gallons of petroleum products were shipped to the Line, enough to fill 9,375 tank cars in a train 65 miles long. Some

43,000,000 gallons of this was shipped in 818,000 drums, which would connect New York to Pittsburgh with a two-foot-wide pipeline. The gravel produced was more than 9,600,000 cubic yards, enough to build two replicas of the Great Pyramid or a road eighteen feet wide and one foot thick from Jacksonville, Florida, to San Diego, California.

Airstrips in the Arctic covered 26,700,000 square feet, or 625 acres. Forty-six thousand tons of steel were used—more than enough for the aircraft supercarrier, the USS *Forrestal*. Eighteen hundred piles were sunk an average depth of 12 feet into permafrost. The generating capacity of the power-generation equipment installed was 155,000 kilowatts per day—enough to supply a city the size of Spokane, Washington. If all 4,650 suppliers employed as few as 350 people each, a total of more than 1,600,000 people worked on DEWLine products. Three construction companies used a total of more than 20,000 people in two and a half years on direct work, though peak numbers actually inside the Arctic at any one time was about 7,500 men. Twenty-two thousand tons of food were shipped in 1,000,000 containers in 32 months; 12 acres of bedsheets; 6 acres of rugs; 3 miles of window shades; 100,000 copies of 600 different manuals were prepared to cover operation and maintenance of the line. Then, of course, there were those thousands of news bulletins and fact sheets, including the one I had had to read.

At this same time it was found that our aviation and radar technology was advancing faster than our arctic-trained personnel. We then trained Seabees for "Operation Hardtop," a test to make landing sites on the ice cap near Thule. They had to brave the harsh terrain while building a 5,600-foot runway. Later, when the project was actually under way, severe winds blew one Jamesway hut apart; the two men sleeping inside got a rude awakening, but the training had left them prepared.

The creation of airstrips on the ice cap was not as easy as one might think. There were certain types of snow and ice more suitable for being built on than others. Science was making great strides in snow, ice, and permafrost research. For example, landing sites were made safer with scientific data on the crystalline structure of snow and ice that could predict its tensile strength. Bernt Balchen's initiative spurred on the first ice landings made in the spring of 1950, when the 10th Air Rescue Squadron used the big twin-engine, ski-equipped G-47s. But soon a more scientific study helped make such landings routine.

Meticulous calculation tables were set up to determine how many days under certain conditions were needed for ice to grow to the required thickness for safe landings; there were tables for fresh water, salt water, turbulent water, and water that was exceedingly calm. Data was collected on the resonance waves caused by taxiing planes or other vehicles that could act like sonic sledgehammers, shattering the ice. Pilots were taught that the telltale cracks around the wheels of craft parked on ice were warning signs, telling them it was time to move the plane. Also, pilots were taught that freshwater ice was more slippery than saltwater ice, and so required more time for stopping once landed. Such scientific minutiae saved many lives and made life easier in the North. International technology and science was moving forward at such a frantic pace that there was barely time for anyone involved to catch their breath. This was the age of science in the Arctic; rugged individualists were already a thing of the past.

CHAPTER TWENTY-TWO

Command of Fletcher's Ice Island, or T-3

I n 1957, eight thousand scientists from eighty-four nations got together for one of history's most ambitious projects: the International Geophysical Year Program. The U.S. IGY Program in the Arctic Basin was called "Project Ice Skate," and required that a scientific station be set up to study the mysteries of this vast, frigid area. I was given the honor of commanding a floating flat ice island called Fletcher's Ice Island, or "T-3" (for Target 3). T-3 was to be the northernmost and remotest scientific station in the project. Drifting in the Arctic Ocean, sometimes to within a hundred miles of the North Pole, Fletcher's Ice Island was larger than Manhattan, though with roughly the same dimensions (nine miles long by four miles wide). It was quite a berg.

It had first been discovered in April 1947 by aircraft radar, which showed a mass of ice much thicker and higher than the pack ice around it. One could not detect that difference with the naked eye from that height. Earlier, there had been two other such masses of ice identified by radar. The first, in 1946, was named T-1 (Target One), and was two hundred square miles of solid ice, with a coast rising twenty to forty feet above the jumbled pack ice. The second sighting was of T-2, and was found to be an astounding three hundred square miles of solid ice. These ice islands later would be labeled "land ice."

In July 1951, meteorologist Joe Fletcher was studying recent aerial photos of the Arctic. He came across a photo of "land ice" near Isachsen Peninsula on Ellef Ringnes Island that looked like T-3; the only problem was, T-3 had last been photographed a thousand nautical miles away! But it was indeed T-3, and the photo proved the berg had traveled that distance in one year. This thrilling discovery led to the exciting idea of establishing a drifting station on T-3 that could travel across the Arctic Ocean studying the unknown Polar Basin. Subsequent exploration during the first landing by Joe Fletcher's party in 1952 showed that T-3 had rocks—and even boulders—weighing tons. They also found caribou antlers on it.

Obviously, it had once been connected to the mainland; what was it doing drifting miles out in the ocean?

It was deduced that the massive island of ice had once been part of the great ice fields created by glaciers on the northwest coast of Ellesmere Island. Ellesmere, close neighbor to northwest Greenland, is the northernmost island of the Canadian Arctic Archipelago. Because its northern tip jutted so far out into the Arctic Ocean, it had been used by early explorers like Robert Peary as a base of operations for attempts on the North Pole. Along the rough west coast of the island, the glaciers that had formed inland scoured the land, picking up boulders and other debris on their slow way to the Arctic Ocean, where they then formed wide deltas of ice that extended from the land, like horizontal icicles, miles out to sea.

Eventually, great hunks broke off, just as any iceberg does; only there at Ellesmere, the bergs were fairly flat—and immense. In the 1950s, one such island came down the east coast of Ellesmere and got stuck in the Kennedy Channel. One end touched Ellesmere, and the other, Greenland. In other words, this hunk of glacial ice was about twenty miles long. It created a colossal dam, with water blasting out from under it on the south side. I wish I had been there to see it, not just hear about it. Generally speaking, though, these monster ice cakes stayed in the Arctic Ocean Basin, and when they did drift out of it, it was by way of the east coast of Greenland.

The submerged Lomonosov Ridge, running from central Siberia to Greenland, and dividing the Arctic Ocean, generally acted as a barrier, keeping most of the ice islands in vast, elliptical orbits. These orbits started near Ellesmere, then went west to the Beaufort Sea above Alaska, then over toward the Siberian Islands, before returning northeastward to come close to the Pole before starting the circuit again. When we arctic men first heard of the discovery of the ice islands, and of the rocks, gravel, antlers, and other glacial detritus strewn all about them, suddenly we realized we had the probable solution to an old arctic puzzle.

Early explorers, especially Peary and Cook, had mentioned seeing land north of the extreme northern tip of Greenland where subsequent exploration showed none existed. Stefansson had told of crossing land north of Banks Island where later none was found. The discovery of the massive ice islands explained the fabled islands of "Fata Morgana" allegedly seen by early explorers between Spitsbergen and northeast Greenland. The Russian Papanin Expedition of 1937 reported seeing an island in that region where a year later, aerial photos taken by Lauge Koch proved there was none. The early explorers had probably seen one of the massive hunks of glacial ice imbedded with boulders and gravel. Later, when other explorers arrived to look for the land, the "land" had drifted miles away. Peary actually reported seeing the calving of massive bergs from the ice shelves on Ellesmere Island in 1909, and may have inadvertently given the first description of the process, as well as the first hint toward the explanation for the "Fata Morgana" islands. Back in Germania Land in 1939, I had secretly hoped to discover one of these "islands," but now, in 1957, I had to be satisfied to live on one instead.

T-3 moved at the rate of one to two miles a day, pushed along by deep currents created by the Coriolis Effect. Though surface ocean currents ran the opposite way, the island was so deep in the water that lower currents which ran the other way were the guiding factor in its movement. Joe Fletcher, writing in *National Geographic*, April 1953, said the written report of the photographic discovery of the ice islands "should rank with the important documents of Arctic Exploration."

The story of Fletcher's three-month stay can also be found in Dr. Kaare Rodahl's books, *North*, and *T-3*, which explore his work with that first landing. (You may remember that Rodahl and I had known each other since 1938 when he had almost gone on the Norwegian-French Expedition.) Rodahl had spent fourteen months, beginning in the summer of 1939, on Clavering Island, and had been a member of the Danish Peary Land Expedition of 1947. Rodahl, who was working with the Americans in the 1950s, wrote of the first landing on T-3:

> Erhardt [the pilot] made a new approach, pulled back on the throttle and let down until the rear end of the skis barely touched the ground and dragged across the surface of the snow. We saw the deep ruts made by the skis, and realized with a shock that the snow was much deeper than we had anticipated. . . . The snow was so deep and the surface so rough that we had serious doubts about being able to make a successful landing. . . . These were exciting moments, for this was the climax of anxiety. If this attempt were to prove a failure, it would mean the end of the expedition; months of strenuous preparations would have been in vain, and our hopes of solving some of the intriguing and fascinating mysteries of the Polar Basin would be shattered.

Their successful landing and the subsequent building of a small research station was the beginning of an exciting adventure for scientists, and as Rodahl said, it was made possible by the progress and knowledge so painfully earned over the years by the early pioneers of the Polar Basin.

After Fletcher's pioneering team's departure from the island, rotating crews staying three to six months occupied the island until May 1954, doing important research under harsh conditions. T-3 was abandoned when it came close enough to weather station Alert on Ellesmere Island to no longer be economically useful for weather information. A year later another scientific team occupied it for four months. But for three years before my scientific team arrived, T-3 had been uninhabited.

Before I had been given the honor of commanding T-3, I received a phone call from one of the enlisted men who had worked with me before. He wanted to know if he could be transferred north with me to T-3. This was before I knew anything about it! Obviously, the "Mukluk Telegraph" worked faster than official channels. The next day, I got a phone call from my old friend Jack Crowell, who was in Washington and had been on the panel that voted for me. Jack informed me of the appointment. I was to go the furthest north of my arctic career.

In Washington I was briefed on T-3, meeting Joe Fletcher, who became a longtime friend. I absorbed everything he could tell me with great interest, as it might mean the difference between the success or failure of my mission. Three years in the Arctic is a long time for a station to be abandoned; we did not know if the old camp was functional, and more to the point, we didn't even know where T-3 was at this point in time.

On the way we stopped at Foxe Main, one of the new DEWLine sites on Baffin Island; "Fish" Hassell was station commander there. He was eager to tell me of his latest plan to improve conditions in the North. It was reminiscent of his porcine project in Goose Bay during the war. He told me, "Each of the lights of the runway runs on batteries which keep freezing up. Willie, what do you think? I had a planeload of fresh horse manure brought up. I thought the heat from the manure would do the trick until we had a better solution." I almost fell over with laughter. He chuckled, "It did the trick all right—for one night, that is. The men forgot to insulate the damn manure. After that we had to contend with horse manure frozen around the runway's batteries."

As the IGY team flew north, along with Jack Crowell and Colonel Lassiter, who was to command Thule, the Russians called over the radio to one of the American sites.

"You looking for T-3?" they asked. And then they gave us its position!

Joe Fletcher had told me that while he was on T-3, a Russian pilot had buzzed the camp and dropped some chocolates. Later, when Joe was in Finland, he ran into the Soviet pilot and they joked about the chocolates. Perhaps this marked the early beginnings of *glasnost*.

It was March, and it was cold and gloomy all the way to Eureka, Nansen Sound, and Ellesmere Island. Five lonely, unheated, uninsulated Gooney Birds flew me and my team through the black expanse above the empty world below. The polar desert area beneath us had been first explored by Norwegian Otto Sverdrup on the 1899 to 1902 expedition. Today, the map of that forbidding place is studded with Norse names: Fosheim Peninsula; Nansen Sound; Stor Island; Slidre Fjord; Skaare Fjord; Mokka Fjord; Hoved Island; and Bjorne Peninsula. For a century the places have been named, but it is still empty of people.

As we flew over that world frozen in time, the droning of the planes' motors made it seem like we were heading to the moon, and I am not using poetic license. The Canadian Arctic comprises something like 600,000 square miles, roughly the size of Alaska. The high arctic Canadian waters include about 70,000 miles of coastline, twice that of the Canadian Pacific and Atlantic regions combined, and over 380,000 square miles (larger than the size of Texas) of continental shelf waters, equivalent to the combined extent of the Atlantic and Pacific waters within Canada's two hundred-mile economic zone. And in all that territory, land and water, there is no one. The fifteen thousand people, mostly Inuit, who are spread out across that large landscape might as well be the *molecules* of a needle in a haystack. These can be sobering thoughts if one is heading toward this empty earthly equivalent of the moon. Soaring high above that barren wasteland fraught with the possibility of danger, near catastrophe came suddenly, not from below, but from within the plane.

We had extra gas tanks on board, and one suddenly cracked from the cold and pressure. The fumes were so bad we had to keep the hatch open, even though it meant a miserably cold flight. Fear of sparks haunted us the whole way, and when we landed safely at Eureka, Ellesmere Island, the frigid, somber landscape looked like heaven.

While refueling by hand-cranked pump at the tiny station, one of the men said, "Hey, there's a dog out here."

"That's no dog," I replied. "That's a wild, white wolf!"

The animals were so unused to humans, they were not afraid to come close. They were looking for musk oxen that stayed near the station for protection.

Flying over Axel Heiberg Island, we saw a fantastic, otherworldly sight. Below us, a huge cloud of bio-fog rushed along the ground. A few heads of musk oxen stuck out from the swirling fog in the front, and a few woolly rumps stuck out from the end of the gray mass. We were definitely in the Arctic. Then the planes passed over Land's End, and we saw the open Arctic Ocean, with its 5,500,000 square miles of unpopulated space.

The day was gloomy at the start. The early March sun barely reached over the horizon during the day, but the skies were clear when the planes finally approached T-3's reported position. We were all looking out the windows, trying to locate the island. There was not much light to see by, and it was a very small spot we were looking for in that vast expanse of ice. But suddenly, there it was. T-3 stood out distinctly from the pack ice. It had a different color and looked solid, while ocean ice was usually a maze of cracks. A small area of open water showed at one end. It was the "wake" of the slowly moving island. As we approached, we thought of the dangers of landing on the irregular, corrugated surface, with all those fuel drums from the old camp scattered here and there, hidden from sight beneath the snow, and snow-covered boulders left from prehistoric times on Ellesmere Island. The plane came closer and our stomachs got tighter. We bounced hard and bounced again. Then the plane made a series of rapid, jarring hops, but it was a safe landing. The mission had begun.

We walked to the old camp along ridges formed when T-3 had been a glacier on Ellesmere. By the time we arrived at the camp, the seven of us were exhausted from the effort. In the gloom there was not much to see of the island, and the camp's huts looked forlorn in their cover of ice and snow. The huts were not just covered by ice, but their interiors were also partially filled with ice and hoarfrost. We had to chop our way in, and over the next several days we chopped more and more to create a home for ourselves. Of course, Fletcher's pioneering party at first had to stay in igloos. Igloos are warm, but there is not much room for a scientific team to move around in.

Our work on the site began immediately and frenetically, for there was much to be done in a short amount of time, under frightfully difficult conditions. As Kaare Rodahl wrote of the 1953 expedition, "Never before on my arctic journeys have I experienced such cold. To keep the tissues alive by thawing the exposed parts at short intervals with our bare hands or with the backs of our mittens, or by jumping vigorously about for greater warmth, was a major occupation which required a great deal of our time. . . . kerosene poured like molasses . . . fuel oil had the consistency of slush ice."

We also got the old vehicles chipped out. The Weasel snowmobile, which had been unused for three years and had been encased in ice when we arrived, started right up after its engine had been thawed by a Herman Nelson heater, and its spark plugs replaced. I gave two visiting scientists, who were idling because of the cold weather, the job of chipping out one of these vehicles. Though competent in their fields, these men had no common sense. They decided to use "science" rather than muscles to free the machine, and so they placed dynamite around the tracks, planning to crack it loose, but they ended up wrecking the damn thing!

Despite these conditions, and the additional interference of powerful, frigid windstorms, we got Project Ice Skate under way. The men in charge of various operations under my gentle guiding hand were Lieutenant Wilde, construction boss; Captain Clement, runway supervisor; Jack Crowell, arctic advisor; and Norman Goldstein, head of scientific work. Our main engineering project was the building of a runway capable of landing the giant C-124s and other large aircraft. There was talk of making a runway long enough for jet bombers or commercial liners to use, in case of an emergency. An interesting problem confronted us when we began to make a runway capable of landing large cargo planes.

Parachutes from old drops had been left where they had fallen, and during the summer season of melting, the parachutes had reflected warmth so that the snow beneath them did not melt as much as the surrounding area. When everything refroze, these patches became small mounds, like hummocks, or moguls. These moguls were solid, blue-greenish in color, and hard as rock when they refroze. I immediately ordered that all parachutes from air drops, old or new, were to be picked up.

We also found the island to be a nightmare of corrugated gullies, cracks, and fissures left from the days when it had been part of a colossal glacier on Ellesmere Island. These had to be filled in, and the most effective method was to heat up snow and crushed ice with a Herman Nelson heater, and then have the men tramp it down into the holes. On some of the other ice islands that had been observed aerially, the surface appeared much smoother than that of T-3. This was assumed to be caused when summer meltwater running in the gullies refroze as the temperatures dropped. Because the other islands were more level, it was assumed they were older than T-3, and that they had had more seasons of melt and freeze to naturally fill in the corrugation that had to be performed manually by the men at T-3.

To help speed progress on the runway, a D-4 bulldozer was successfully para-dropped. Though hydraulic lines of our heavy construction machines often froze and cracked, the work somehow progressed against all odds. In April, Thule radioed to ask if the runway was ready. I said: "Give me twenty-four hours. There is one ice bump left to level." But before I could have this fixed, a C-124 carrying the much-needed grading machine came anyway, taxied beautifully down the runway, hit the bump, and collapsed its nose gear.

A C-124 is a monstrously large plane, and is designed so cargo can be stored in its nose, the doors of which swing up to open. We had to jack up the nose of the plane to get the road grader out. The nose doors were badly damaged, the propellers were damaged beyond repair, and there were rips in the fuselage from the props. The repairs were beyond my crew's abilities, so a special civilian crew was sent for. We had to wait until July when the special repair team had finished similar work in the Antarctic; they had been looking forward to heading home to California, but were sent up to us by helicopter from Thule, the first landing by such a craft at T-3. When the poor guys finally finished the work, the sun had begun melting the runway's surface, preventing a plane from landing to pick them up. We were told the helicopter could not be sent in to pick them up either. Helicopters, we were informed, could only be used in an emergency, and the emergency was over when the C-124 had been repaired. Therefore, the men were stuck on T-3 by a good old military catch-22!

These extra men presented a bit of a problem, in that we didn't think we had enough food supplies for so many. Fortunately, while "chipping" out a new room, I discovered a large stockpile of macaroni left from the last expedition in

1954. The men made droll jokes about "oodles of noodles," but everyone got fed until the runway again froze sufficiently for them to be picked up.

Earlier, on April 5, we received a signal from SAS Airlines Flight 988 on the first nonstop flight from Europe to Tokyo via the polar route. This historic moment has been forgotten in the marvels of the jet age which followed, but for me it is memorable because I had been involved in the dream of transpolar flight since my youth. On April 26, another SAS flight came down low enough for radio contact, and I found myself in the middle of the Arctic Ocean having a conversation with its navigator, Einar-Sverre Pettersen, whom I had first met in northeast Greenland in 1938! He told me he was wearing Alan Innes-Taylor's old flight cap for luck. I asked him to send my greetings to my sister Signy in Oslo. He promised he would, and also jokingly said that on the next flight he'd drop me some Norwegian goat cheese that I was extremely fond of.

He later told me that when he phoned Signy and told her he had been talking to me, she had said rather sternly, as if he had been lying, "That's impossible! My brother is on a floating ice island in the middle of the Arctic Ocean!" Her disbelief was understandable. By the way, Oslo's *Aftenposten* put me back on its front page for their feature story about T-3, although they didn't dedicate a full page to me this time.

During the late summer melting period, after tremendous progress was made on the runway project, a large drainage ditch about eight feet deep was uncovered, hampering the completion of the project. Going to inspect this ditch, the men noticed that meltwater in it was running in the opposite direction from its usual course. The only answer we could come up with was that the island was tilting!

The island may have hit an underwater ridge, or some submerged part of the island could have dropped off, affecting the balance of the whole thing. Fletcher's party had also experienced tilting, but they only noticed it with a very sensitive bubble level and reported it happening during windstorms. But the reason for the noticeable tilting during my command was never discovered. Later, the water began to run in the normal way, but it was an uncomfortable feeling to realize how unstable the Manhattan-sized island home really was.

I once jumped down into the ten-foot-deep, narrow drainage ditch while I was alone, just to learn more about it, then tried to climb the slick, hard walls, but I couldn't make it out. Thinking that there was a possibility, though remote, that the water could change flow and come rushing down the narrow, glassy trough and send me on a fast ride to the Arctic Ocean, I became inspired to get out, and fast. Using my sheath knife, I very quickly cut steps into the hard walls.

When melting became so serious a problem that our runway was literally running away, a solution had to be found. The island had a beautiful feature we called "ice candles"—slender, hollow tubes of ice that stood up to two feet high. These ice growths would cover large areas, and glinted like diamonds when the sun hit them. This visual feast broke the white monotony of island, but the ice candles were also put to practical use. We made dams in the channels by filling parachutes with crushed ice candles. We also made similar dams around the runway to hold in the water for when freeze-up began again. When that time arrived, dumping crushed ice candles into water puddles—or "kettles" as we called them, since some of these "puddles" were quite deep—speeded up the refreezing process. Tons of the ice candles were shoved into water pits big enough to swallow the bulldozers—and sometimes did! And it was not easy getting them out either. Ramps had to be made from crushed ice. There was never a dull moment. An official document in Washington, D.C., referring to messages sent from T-3, would later state that this was the first time a runway had been reported as "running away."

Though summer's thaw produced lakes and pools, drinking water was obtained year-round from an "underground" reservoir of unfrozen water discovered by Fletcher's first party. When pierced by a hot-water drill, the reservoir, under tremendous pressure from the ice around it, at first gushed up like a geyser. We had a snow-melting plant for making water, along with bags of asbestos powder to mix up and make insulation for the holding tank, but the unit was never needed, thanks to that ancient store of water. However, I put the powdered asbestos to use, much as one would plaster of paris, for modeling small sculptures, including a small musk ox I still have today. The deadly effects of breathing asbestos powder were not well known at the time, or I never would have gotten so creative with the stuff.

The island had its own geology and geography. Near an area called Silk Hill, on one edge of the island, a great deal of surface dirt was seen during the summer. On the other end of the island, in a spot we called "Area C," many rocks were found. Some of the rocks were of a very rare type, and through an investigation of the geology of Ellesmere Island, the exact point of T-3's original birthplace was thought to be at Yelverton Bay. Amazingly, by studying the geology of the coastal mouth of Yelverton Bay, the probable positions of Silk Hill and "Area C" were determined, from the time when T-3 was connected to the mainland.

Using carbon-14 dating, the dirt, small bits of wood, and seashells found on T-3 were dated to the Wisconsin Ice Age, some 15,000 years ago. The thick growth of ice, of which T-3 was a remnant, probably began to form about 5,500 years ago. It then drifted northeast along the coast to the vicinity of Ward Hunt Island, off the mouth of Disraeli Bay, about 3,000 years ago. In other words, it had been an ice island for that long.

The highest point, a pile of ice about twenty-five feet higher than the surrounding area on T-3, was nicknamed "Mount Everest." The lowest was Colby Bay, a natural platform close to the sea that was used as a dump site. This platform was not from the glaciers of Ellesmere, but rather formed by frozen salt water. During melting season, all about the island we found fish carcasses that we assumed had been dropped by birds. The waters of the deep Arctic Ocean where we drifted were almost empty of fish, which is why we thought the carcasses dated back to when T-3 was closer to land. Even frozen lemmings had been found by Joe Fletcher's party.

Besides the geological features of the island, there was plenty of fauna to amuse us. We actually saw a few white foxes, and the occasional polar bear. The fox followed the bears like hyenas do lions, to scavenge their kills. One polar bear went along the runway methodically smashing the runway lights! Seals, the polar bear's favorite food, had been spotted by plane many miles out in the Arctic Ocean, but as the fishing was so sparse in the waters around us, so were the numbers of seals, leaving very few for the bears to prey on. The giant carnivores' rare visits to us made us aware of their great migratory treks. One bear was found in Alaska that had ear tags placed by scientists at Spitsbergen, two thousand miles away!

Two snow buntings had made a nest in the C-124 while it was being repaired. They and a few other birds fed themselves from ancient seeds and plants that appeared from the "refrigerator of time" during the thaw. All in all, we were too far out in the Arctic Ocean for many animals to come visiting. But we had two dogs, Lady and Tramp, given to us by the staff at Thule to help warn us against polar bears. Tramp, always thirsty in the dry environment, would jump up and down on iced-over "kettles" to break the ice to get to the water. Then he'd look at us as if to say, "Aren't I clever?" After I had left T-3, my replacement's life was saved from a polar bear by Tramp.

Generally speaking, we had good cooperation from everyone involved at T-3; it was a great group of men. Airman second class James Smith of Oildale, California, spent so many hours behind the wheel of a grader that his back began to act up—so severely that he was almost immobilized. But he got the others to carry him to his driver's seat in the grader every day. That was dedication. Others, like airman first class Roy Glassine of St. Paul, Minnesota, worked so hard that one day I had to send someone out to tell him to quit working—it was minus-sixty degrees Fahrenheit! And staff sergeant Francis Nichols of Beacon, New York, sometimes maintained twenty-four-hour vigils over his radio set to guide incoming planes.

We were a long way from civilization, home, and families. Often planes could not bring us supplies or mail for weeks. No wheeled landings were made during the thaw, and even ski landings were not advised. But we had a radio program, and a newsletter called T-3 Tribune which provided local and world news that was informative, funny, and helped to boost morale. Often, due to poor atmospheric conditions, we were out of radio contact with the rest of the world. On one such occasion, during a heavy melt-off, a rumor was started back in the States that our radio silence meant the T-3 had broken up. My wife received a phone call in West Virginia from reporters of The New York Times, wanting to know how she felt about my disappearance, and probable death! But generally, we were able to maintain close contact with the rest of the world through Thule. I heard immediately when King Haakon died, and sent a message of condolence to Norway from T-3.

Though T-3 did not break up, at times the melting did get bad enough to cause buildings to tilt. A series of drain-off channels were dug to clear water from around buildings and the damaged C-124. One positive factor of the thaw was that the surface snow disappeared, so a better survey of the ice surface of the island could be made.

The scientific work headed by Norman Goldstein, who had been with Joe Fletcher on other occupations of T-3, vastly increased man's knowledge, not just of the Arctic, but of the earth itself. He did gravity measurement and magnetic compass reading, and in general kept track of the island's movement and position. He was also doing submarine topography.

Other scientists on T-3 included biologist Herbert Apollonio from the Woods Hole Oceanographic Institute, who made ocean temperature and salinity tests. Samples taken from sediment cores collected from the seabed helped to reveal the character of that world in the very ancient past. Studies were made of ocean photosynthesis, and levels of chlorophyll, oxygen, nutrients, and plankton. (Apollonio continued his work in the Arctic after leaving T-3 when his tour was up.)

John A. Murray and a man named Volbrecht were meteorologists, staying busy with seemingly endless measurements of solar radiation, winds, temperatures, and airway surface observations. Studies were made of island temperatures, atmospheric temperatures, and that under-ice reservoir formation. Other scientists conducted summer thaw studies, and biological studies of algae and lichens trapped in the ice for ages.

Some scientists analyzed the ambient noise field at low frequencies, which—as it was explained to me—in the Arctic is dominated by sounds resulting from pressure ridging caused by convergences in the surface ice field. These convergences are driven by currents in the ocean and by winds on the surface, and are regulated by the ice's strength and compactness. It all seemed very complicated, but I was assured that an analysis of a long-term series of ambient noise might be a useful tool to begin compiling data that would monitor changes in arctic oceanography.

Other testing involved the carbon-dating of organic debris found on T-3, including caribou antlers. During flora studies, one specimen of lichen appeared to be still living. Subsequent studies showed that the Arctic seabed is littered with boulders from the breaking up of such ice islands as T-3 over the course of thousands of years.

T-3 was the first to pick up signals from *Sputnik One*, the first man-made satellite in space. On a cold October day in 1957, the Soviet Union launched a small satellite into orbit around the earth. Radio Moscow made the announcement: "The first artificial earth satellite in the world has now been created. This first satellite was launched today successfully in the USSR." This was after all "the International Geophysical Year" in the scientific world, and *Sputnik* was an important propaganda victory for the Soviets in their cold war with the United

States. Many people believed the nation that controlled the skies could win any war—and the Soviet Union had reached outer space first.

We were sitting around the radio that day, listening to the coverage, and some of the younger men were genuinely worried. Norman Goldstein said, "They got lucky. I've heard about the one we are about to put in space. The Russian satellite is like a bucket of bolts compared to ours. It's not who comes first, but who comes best. Hell, the Russians can't even make a ballpoint pen that works properly!" I don't know where he got his information, but it cheered the station to no end.

The work went on with renewed vigor. T-3 scientists and those at other Project Ice Skate sites took recordings of the ocean floor, and thereby mapped colossal canyons and soaring, precipitous underwater mountains. They would then chart a path that, a year later, enabled a nuclear sub to reach the Pole!

On August 3, 1958, the nuclear-powered submarine *Nautilus* would successfully maneuver under the ice to the North Pole. Then, on August 12, the submarine *Skate* would not only reach the Pole, but break through the ice and surface there. Sir Hubert Wilkins's dream since 1930 of reaching the Pole by sub would at last become a reality, although he would not be part of the historic surfacing. Wilkins had first tried to accomplish this feat nearly thirty years earlier in a surplus World War I submarine, but the complexities of navigating under the ice without sophisticated sonar equipment had forced him to give up the attempt.

A year before, I had received a memorable radio call on T-3 from Bernt Balchen. He was visiting the scientific ice-floe station "Alfa" off the coast of Alaska. Accompanying him was Sir Hubert Wilkins, and Lowell Thomas, the famous traveler, writer, and television presenter of adventure stories. Balchen said they would try to come over to T-3 to visit me. The U.S. military had said they would fly them—weather permitting—to T-3 for historical reasons.

Balchen then dropped the bombshell that Peter Freuchen had been with the group, but sadly had died of a heart attack a few days earlier while they were waiting for the plane north at Elmendorf Air Force Base, Alaska. Peter Freuchen, the Danish explorer and writer, had been a fixture in the Arctic since the turn of the twentieth century. His books, some of which were made into movies, make good reading for anyone interested in tales of the Arctic in those early days. He was also a winner on the American television game show, *The 64,000 Dollar Question!*

When the time came for the last question on the show, a message was read aloud to him. He was then asked, "Who wrote this and when?" He looked puzzled for a moment, but then brightened and said, "I did!" He had written the note and left it in a cairn on north Ellesmere decades earlier. The note had only recently been found by Americans from a military ship visiting the area, so to have it read aloud to him for the first time in years—and on television, at that—was quite astonishing, especially to Peter. Because of his international fame, we arctic rats wouldn't be the only ones who would miss him.

When at last it came time for me to leave T-3 in October of 1957, I flew to Thule on my way to the States. The first thing I heard was a story concerning the late Peter Freuchen. The Danish wife of a radio operator at an Inuit site was on an American base buying food. She asked why there had been a helicopter that hovered over the Inuit camp and dropped something from the air. She was told that the helicopter was scattering Peter Freuchen's ashes over the colony he had founded with Knud Rasmussen in 1910. She exclaimed, "Oh, so that's who I've got in my eye!" This was particularly funny to those of us who knew Freuchen was a ladies' man, and surely "got in many a girl's eye" in his time.

At Thule, the Danes gave me a big party. Members of the Sirius Sled Patrol once again showed up for a great reunion. It was very poignant for us all, for with Peter Freuchen's passing there were getting to be fewer and fewer of the old-timers left. Indeed, about a year later, Sir Hubert Wilkins died on December 1, 1958, three and a half months after *Skate*'s surfacing at the Pole. On March 17, 1959, the *Skate* returned to the Pole, and there during a moving ceremony, Sir Hubert's ashes were scattered to the wind. He finally made it to the Pole by submarine.

———

Author's Note: On August 19, 1958, the U.S. Department of the Air Force awarded Willie Knutsen the Commendation Medal, and on April 14, 1959, he was nominated for the Legion of Merit, which was accompanied by the following citation, for his work on T-3:

Major Willie Knutsen distinguished himself by exceptionally meritorious conduct in the performance of outstanding service to the United States from 1 June 1957 to 22 October 1957. The success achieved in the establishment of Ice Island T-3 was due in large measure to the initiative and foresight of Major Knutsen in his capacity as Station Commander. The quality of Major Knutsen's leadership under difficult circumstances and his broad knowledge of the Arctic environment resulted in the gratifying success of the United States International Geophysical Year Research. In performing the task of making a runway for support aircraft, it was necessary to use hand tools to smooth the ice, often working around the clock in 50 degrees below zero temperatures. His energetic activities have promoted Arctic research and furthered U.S. knowledge in this vital area and added materially to the world stature of USAF in the field of Polar operation.

Because of such fortitude and devotion to duty on the part of Major Knutsen, the mission was accomplished in a superior manner reflecting great credit upon himself and the United States Air Force.

CHAPTER TWENTY-THREE

The Stone Age Meets the Space Age in the Ice Age

The *Skate's* arrival at the Pole was the climax of a century of polar discovery. And then suddenly, as if a stage set had been changed, two great powers took possession of the Arctic and confronted each other, with atomic submarines carrying nuclear warheads that prowled ceaselessly beneath the ice, while overhead, giant jet planes carrying nuclear arms circled warily in vast, frigid arcs in the most astonishing preventive "cold" war in history. The roles of polar men also changed rapidly. High-technology required highly skilled technicians. Experienced arctic men like me became advisors, overseeing that the lessons of a hundred years of arctic exploration were not forgotten in the pell-mell rush toward technological advance. But not everything went smoothly.

Returning from T-3 to the States for my next assignment, I found I was to be sent to Kansas. I had nothing against Kansas, but there was not even an arctic survival school there. Fortunately this error in assignment was soon corrected, and so in 1958 I was assigned to be the arctic advisor to the Federal Electric Corporation, the International Telephone and Telegraph subsidiary handling the daily operations of the DEWLine. The military headquarters for the DEWLine was Newburgh, New York, but Federal Electric headquarters was in Paramus, New Jersey. So New Jersey became home for my family for the next five years while I scurried back and forth from one end of the DEWLine to the other.

If I had been awed by the construction of Thule, the continuing progress of the DEWLine left me even more speechless. What a colossal enterprise it was! Retired Admiral Richard Cruzen* was in charge at Paramus. He had been to the

---

* Author's Note: After they had worked together a few years, Admiral Cruzen wrote a glowing commendation for Willie. Included in his praise was the fact that Willie—through his advice concerning the construction and running of the DEWLine—had saved the U.S. taxpayers twenty million dollars.

Antarctic with Byrd three times, and was equal in command on those historic missions. We became friends as we worked together with his huge Federal Electric staff operating the most complex communications system in the world at the time. Every summer, huge convoys of ships made trips to resupply the main sites. The convoys operating from the west and the east coasts went as far as the pack ice would let them, until the danger of being trapped by ice prevented further penetration of the central sector, which was then supplied by aircraft. The short summer sea-delivery activity went on twenty-four hours a day in order to make best use of the light provided by the midnight sun. The logistics were obviously enormous, and newer, better computers were the main reason it all went so relatively smoothly.

Long before the public phone system was modernized to what it is today, we had super-advanced communications in the Arctic. I could place a call from Alaska to Greenland and have it sound like a local call. If I made a call home to New Jersey, I would have a perfect connection right up to the crucial moment the call went from the military line to the public—then the static and other noise would begin. We were also already using computers that the public would not see for years.

There were by this time sixty-four stations from Alaska to Iceland. The sites were efficiently run by the U.S. military and Federal Electric, and enjoyed a lot of the comforts of home. But just beyond the radar sites it was still the wild Arctic I first knew. Near DYE-4—the easternmost station on Greenland, set on the island of Kulusuk, about fifteen miles from Ammassalik—an Inuit woman from the village of Kulusuk was attacked by a polar bear. The local men drove it off. Under normal circumstances the woman probably would have died. The sea surrounding the island was choked with icebergs, and to go by dogsled over those ice-jumbled fifteen miles to the hospital at Ammassalik was out of the question. But these were new times for my old stomping grounds. The woman was put in a helicopter, and twelve minutes later she had arrived in Ammassalik, where efficient doctors at the hospital saved her life.

Being that close to Ammassalik, DYE-4 was like a metropolis compared to most of the sites. In northernmost Alaska, and in the Far North of Canada, civilians operated radar sites a hundred miles from each other and from any other human being. Given the arctic conditions, that one hundred miles might as well have been several hundred. To reach populated areas to the south one had to travel five hundred to seven hundred miles, depending on where the site was located. In minus-fifty-degree temperatures during the total blackness of winter-time, being on one of those radar sites was like being on a space station. And then there was all that fun when freezing fogs turned buildings and machinery into ice palaces, and hurricane-force winds hammered at your station for days on end. Mail and supplies could be delayed for weeks because of the weather, entertainment was at a minimum for obvious reasons, and if planes were late, men got tired of watching the same movie over and over.

With these conditions, it is understandable that at times nerves were strained. Personal conflicts could turn dangerous when an angry man wasn't able to just go outside and "walk it off." Later, satellite connections helped the late-mail problem, but you can believe that a psychological profile was part of the hiring process when deciding if a man was fit for such long periods of isola-tion with few companions. There were actually some shootings, but considering the approximately seven thousand men involved in the day-to-day running of the sites, problems were very few. One must not forget that these men also had the nerve-wracking stress of watching, on numerous occasions, Russian Bear air bombers loaded with nuclear bombs appearing uncomfortably close on their radar screens. These enemy bombers were just probing and testing our defense line, but our radar experts—we called them "radicians"—had to sweat it out to the last minute until the Soviet planes turned back from their "fail-safe" line.

Some of the new changes to the Arctic were obviously hazardous to the tra-ditional Inuit way of life. In some remote areas the Inuit had started to rely too heavily on rifles to hunt, and the use of the bow was forgotten. The Inuit in these secluded camps would often find themselves out of expensive cartridges long be-fore winter was over. While visiting the east coast of Baffin Island where DEW station DYE-Main was, I actually had to run a school for a few weeks to retrain young Inuit on how to use a bow, just as their elders had long before taught me. In 1959, on the way to my first tour of the DEWLine, I stopped in at Frobisher Bay. By this time it had become a town, complete with tourists. But my old dog driver, Etuachia, and his wife Susie were still there. They were working at the base hospital. Susie presented me with sealskin mukluks she had made for me. She had taken my foot measurements the last time I had passed through in 1948, and had patiently waited a decade until I showed up again. "I knew you would!" she said through worn-down front teeth. She was probably the last to make muk-luk hide pliable by chewing on the skin.

Despite the technological leaps that were being made in the Arctic during this time, there was still a need for the expertise of the early explorers. For instance, Donald MacMillan, an ice pilot during the days of wooden ships, had received a contract for a small survival school on Greenland for Paine Company engineers who were testing the ice cap for future building project sites. MacMillan's career had started in 1908 when he joined the Peary Polar Expedition. In 1913 he commanded the famous Crocker Land Expedition that lasted four years, and during which he crisscrossed 10,500 miles of the Polar Region.

Once, in the early 1960s when I was home in New Jersey on leave, I met McMillan again at a nearby high school where he was giving a lecture and slide show. We had a grand reunion, talking over our first meeting at Frobisher Bay in 1943, and the time we almost crashed in a plane over the wilds of northern Quebec province. When I asked about his school in Greenland, he told me, "I had a lot of fun teaching those kids." The "kids" were in their thirties, but he was eighty-three!

That same year, both Count Micard and Vilhjalmur Stefansson died. Micard had just written to tell me he could hardly believe I had seven children, and that he had nearly fainted when he'd heard the news. He added that he experienced an almost fatherly pride every time he read of my arctic exploits. It was strange to think that he and Stef were gone. They had meant a great deal to me, and to the Arctic. With both of them gone, it was for me a final signal that it was now a new Arctic.

The Space Age, the old-time explorers, and the Stone Age had all converged, and the mix was a strange one at times. I heard that near the high-tech station of Foxe-5, in Canada, an Inuit with his dog team had fallen through the ice. As he was trying to get out of the water, his dogs attacked and killed him. It was close to what happened to me in Germania Land in 1938, except this man died, and in plain view of a symbol of the Space Age. Of course, Space Age or not, the weather was still a hazard, and always would be. Men could not leave the modern buildings during storms because they would lose their sense of direction just a few feet from the door. Some of the sites were in a terrain that was tough for aircraft landings. DYE-4, near Ammassalik on the east coast of Greenland, had a particularly difficult approach, as the wrecks still littering the site testified. The freezing fog and whiteouts prevalent throughout the Arctic would always be a danger to flyers. And there were still other traditional dangers as well.

While at DYE-Main in 1962, I heard of a trichinosis epidemic among the Inuit on Baffin Island. The source was walrus and seal flesh. A helicopter carrying a doctor who had the serum, plus an Inuit translator named Willie Stefansson, the aircraft's crew, and myself made about six stops at remote Inuit camps. I asked Willie, "Your name is Stefansson?"

"Yeah," he replied. "Vilhjalmur was my grandfather."

I had heard that Stef had fathered an Inuit child in 1906 or so. I was glad to be able to share with Willie some personal stories about his famous grandfather. When the weather turned bad, I went on skis alone to cover fifty miles to the last camp of infected villagers. It was my last real arctic journey.

I was fifty, and not in the best shape, but I soon got into the rhythm of the thing. I was alone for the first time in years, and it seemed a great relief. I had no responsibilities for other men, or even machines. There was the urgency of the mission, but on the trail I had only myself to be concerned with. The snow blew, but it did not feel dangerous. By that time in my career I had learned to sense when it was. The sound of the snow pelting my hood and parka was comforting, and I was damn glad the wind was at my back. I followed the sastrugis, the hard, wind-caused ripples in the snow, knowing that they point windward, the direction I wanted to go. Only three times did I stop to check the compass by flashlight. Each time I was right on course. Enveloped as I was, there was no visual contact with the environment. I had pleasant visions of Inuit beating drums, and northern lights dancing to their beat. In this manner, I was able to pass many hours, thoroughly enjoying my arctic experience. Knowing people might be dying, however, was a sobering thought that spurred me on.

On the way back by plane, we landed at Crystal Three, my old station at Padloping Island. I hadn't been there since the war. The site was abandoned by the Canadian crews, though the buildings were still in good shape. My mural in the bar provided mute testament to the good times we'd enjoyed in this place. Once again, the Inuit had not broken into the buildings to use them. Instead, in winter, they lived in igloos as they had for centuries. The only difference was that the window above the entrance, which traditionally was made of oiled bladder skin, was now plastic. And in the interior, where children were housed in the old days, there were now platforms of plywood, wooden shelves, and other modern aids scrounged from the debris about my old camp. Not far away, space-age technology was being employed—to pick up satellite signals, scan the sky, interpret the vast amounts of information with computers, and beam the information to central headquarters halfway around the world.

Often during my years conducting inspection tours of the DEWLine, I would meet some members of my old crews, men who loved the Arctic and had stayed to do any job that was available. But most of the members of the large new arctic crews were new to the whole experience. Two such men went on the Greenland ice cap without rifles to do tests on ice movement. A polar bear came migrating across the east coast. The men stayed in their tent, and radioed frantically for help while they threw food out to the starving animal until help arrived by air. They should have been instructed that bears did indeed cross the vast ice cap, though it would seem impossible, if not impractical for these animals to do so. A memento of such migrations hangs — or did — on a wall in the bar at the air base at Sondrestrom Fjord. It is a bearskin of the animal killed when it came off the ice cap, hungry from the crossing. Next to the skin hangs the crowbar used by an alert plane mechanic to stun the animal when it came at a naive photographer who tried to get a close shot! At Thule there were also herds of musk oxen that wandered freely about. The men were warned not to antagonize them. The leader of the herd was particularly unafraid of men and machines, and had the run of the base. He was named "Willie," either in my honor or perhaps because the men thought he looked like he was getting too old for the arctic, like me. In any case, one of the men later wrote a children's book called *Willie, the Musk Ox*. I was touched.

I have to mention the now mostly forgotten marvel of modern engineering, the top-secret project called "Century City," a nuclear-powered station built under the ice cap at an elevation of six thousand feet. The nuclear reactor went "critical" in October 1960, but I had seen preliminary work as early as 1954 while serving as technical advisor for the movie, *Survival on the Ice Cap* made by Pathe-Warner. The station was 135 miles from Thule. The original plan was to build it one hundred miles from Thule — hence the name Century City — but the ice slippage there proved too great for the project. There were twenty-one tunnels, and "Main Street" was eleven hundred feet long. Typically, one hundred men lived in the under-ice barracks with hot showers, a gymnasium, an automatic laundry, a modern kitchen, and a hospital. Six thousand tons of equipment were used to make the site, and yet the only signs of Century City were the cylindrical escape shafts, and the red flags marking where culvert tunnels were buried.

The trenches for the tunnels were dug by Peter Miller machines from Switzerland, able to dig a trench that was three hundred feet long, sixteen feet wide, and four feet deep, in just one hour. Three machines were used simultaneously. When the twenty-one trenches were ready, they were covered with metal culvert tops, and they in turn were covered over with snow. Thirty prefabricated plywood buildings were placed within the tunnels, and they contained research labs, dormitories, a mess hall, food storage, a shop for vehicles, utilities, and communications, a dispensary, a chapel, a barbershop, a post office, a library, a theater, clubs for officers and enlisted men, and a laundry. Then there was the little matter of storing the nuclear reactor for heat and power (four hundred tons of piping were used).

When I had seen what modern technology was doing at Camp Century back in 1954, I told some friends, "It won't be long before we go to the moon!" My friends just laughed; but I had seen the changes in the Arctic develop at an ever-increasing speed, and had witnessed them firsthand since 1936, so it was easy to imagine that the next step in technology would take us off the planet. The only problem with Camp Century was that someone forgot that the ice cap moves, and the camp was eventually closed down in 1967. I don't know how much of the camp was abandoned and how much was salvaged, but the nuclear reactor was removed and shipped out of the country.

On the ice cap were two huge, five-story radar buildings called DYE-2 and DYE-3. The last sites to be built as part of the DEWLine, these sites were named for the system that began at Cape Dyer, Baffin Island. DYE-2 was about 150 miles from the large USAF Base at Sondrestrom Fjord, while DYE-3 was situated another hundred miles from that.* Beneath DYE-3 was seven thousand feet of ice. These sites were built thirty-five feet off the ground to allow the powerful winds to pile the snow under, not over the sites. As snow accumulated over the years, the huge buildings were elevated on mammoth screws built into stilts, and metal was added to the supports. The stilts also went thirty-five feet beneath the surface. (When the stilts finally got so tall in the 1980s that the buildings were wobbly, they had to be lowered and moved on tracks to a new,

---

* Author's Note: I worked at DYE-3 for three months in 1965 to earn tuition money for college. This is why I can write about it in some detail.

nearby site. We are talking about moving a five-story building across the snow and ice on tracks!)

Like many of the DEWLine sites, these ice cap sites had private rooms and recreational facilities, including bars—something these remote ice-cap stations truly needed. The flat, hostile snow cap did not lure the men out to go exploring. As far as the eye could see from the fifth floor was a flat white expanse. The "radicians" arrived in suits and with briefcases, did their three-month tour, and left the same way, never seeing anything to speak of that was truly at the core of Greenland. It was the Space Age, after all, and their job was to scan the skies for satellites and rockets.

One day in 1964, at the supposedly top-secret and extremely inaccessible radar station of DYE-2 on the ice cap, the men of the site were startled to hear a knock on the door. It was a man, his wife, and their young daughter. They were crossing the ice cap, and had stopped in for tea! They could have been saboteurs. Despite having the most advanced radar in the world, the station had neglected its own security. Children were now crossing the ice cap! This family had been lucky. I would not recommend this kind of "adventure" to anyone. Quite a few other attempts to cross the ice cap were met with near disaster, and it was only because of mobile radios that such adventurists survived, by calling for rescue when they got into trouble. Finally, the Greenland government made such foolhardy people post a large insurance deposit to pay for rescue operations if they were necessary. My advice to future adventurists is to stick to the coasts. They are much more interesting than the empty ice cap!

The changes, as I keep saying, were astounding, and often amusing. Some newcomers tried to change things. Inuit and station dogs near the radar sites were ordered to be tied up in winter; they didn't want the dogs to run loose. In the spring melt-off, the stench was horrible, so the dogs got to run loose again. At the northernmost point of Alaska, I saw the sixteen-hole latrine at Point Barrow, eight on either side. On any given day, the side facing away from the freezing winds was the one that was used!

In this last phase of my arctic journeys, I traveled again to such places as Amundsen's Gjoa Haven and to new places in the area like Inuvik, and Jenny Lind Island. Jenny Lind was named in 1851 by the Canadian artic explorer John Rae after the famed nineteenth-century Swedish woman then known as the world's sweetest singer.

With the arrival of the radar sites, the native people had been offered their first real alternative to subsistence hunting—a different way to make a living. Most adapted easily. Many were employed during the construction phase, and later, on the completed sites, they held jobs ranging from menial to executive. One Inuit that I knew of at Point Barrow, Alaska, a college graduate, was the supply manager for the radar site. My eldest son, Will, worked under him in 1964. I never thought of Inuit as fragile, helpless left-overs from the ice age. Some ran businesses, and sent their kids to college. Vacations to sunny warm resorts were not unknown to them. Once when I was visiting at Stanford University in California, I rang up the daughter of an Inuit friend of mine back in Greenland who I knew was enrolled there. She arrived to pick me up in a snazzy red convertible. Athletic competitions between the natives around radar sites and the newcomers were often held. Softball, soccer, or basketball matches were usually won by the loclas who had picked up the sports quickly. On weekends, rock bands played at meeting halls. Native women were usually not allowed on the radar sites, but clandestine, romantic meetings, and even large parties, were held in secret. At some of the Canadian sites, the missionaries who visited the local villages nearby tried to prevent the drinking of alcohol, and even dancing, but fun usually won out. I met the traveling chaplains of all faiths. Probably the most colorful was Paul Mauer. He had a little tupilak-selling business going on the side to promote native handicrafts. Tupilaks are carvings in ivory or bone that appear to be part man, part animal, part demon or another spirit. The Inuit used these tupilak in days of old to work sorcery on their enemies, or to attract a wealth of seals and walruses. Now they attracted art lovers, for the carving is incredible to see, and beautifully unique.

The sexual mores of the Inuit were often quite different than those of the newcomers, and I know of a few instances where some of the radar site men awoke in the morning after a late-night village party to find themselves in the company of what they would consider to be very underage females. Part of my job as arctic advisor to the DEWLine involved the settlement of financial claims put in by natives for child support. Yes, it was a very different world from the one I had first visited years ago.

While at a big dinner party at Thule, Norwegian General Odd Bull said to me, "Willie, look at us. We are eating jumbo shrimp from Mexico, steaks from the States, and drinking wine and beer from Europe. Think of what the old-timers—Peary, Amundsen, Sverdrup, Rasmussen, and Freuchen—went through, not far from where we sit." I remembered those "good old days"—the cold, the hunger, and the danger, and I certainly did not mind the new luxuries!

I often met up with Paul-Emil Victor, who was still doing research on the ice cap with his *Expéditions Polaires Françaises*, in 1959, 1963, and 1967. Victor had published many popular books on his work from the Arctic to the Antarctic, including a children's book about the Eskimo of east Greenland. Once, in 1963, when we were in a warm room enjoying drinks, music, and all the comforts of civilization, Victor said to me, "Willie, we are no longer explorers. We are entrepreneurs!" But it was not all wine and roses.

During my stay of 1962 to 1963 at Sondrestrom as a liaison officer, I took an H-27 helicopter flight during the summer with Chief Riggin and Colonel Jung. I was to rendezvous with the state-of-the-art icebreaker, the *Edisto*, down the coast at DYE-1, and sail with her to Kulusuk, near Ammassalik. I was sitting up in the cockpit of the helicopter with the pilot, while the others were down in the belly. On the way over the steep, rugged mountain ranges and plunging glaciers, we received instructions to change course because of a double layer of clouds in front of us that would make flying hazardous. As we passed over a precipitous ridge, the engine stopped! Plummeting down the face of the cliff, the pilot fought to keep control, and struggled with the throttle. The mountainside was coming up fast. The engine caught again, and we moved away from death, but then the engine died again for good. It was like riding in an elevator, with the blades causing a slight drag on our way down. But we were still dropping pretty damn fast, and straight toward boulders as big as houses, deposited, unluckily for us, by glaciers eons ago. We prepared to die.

Then suddenly we saw a small square patch of bog between two mammoth boulders. The pilot, struggling to get us to the safety of the bog, sniffed the air. I smelled it too; it was definitely smoke. The pilot shouted, "I thought I told Jung not to smoke that damn pipe of his!" Then we hit. The pilot had had just enough control to set us down in the soft bog with only a hard thump. We heard a loud explosion from the engine, and the cabin immediately filled with smoke. It was certainly not pipe smoke! I leapt out from the high cockpit, wrenching my ankle badly. Jung badly hurt his back in the landing, but we were otherwise all safe. We were immediately greeted by a horde of mosquitoes. At least that had not changed in the Arctic!

Our position was not dangerous, but the men said they were glad an arctic survival man was with them, just the same. I did find some berries, but they were still hard, so just to demonstrate survival techniques to these "tenderfeet," I went over to where patches of snow still lay and found ripe berries preserved from last season. The lakes nearby were probably full of fish, so we could have had an easy time of it, but our SOS had been picked up in—of all places—Long Island, New York, via satellite! This was brand new to us. Long Island's instant relay to Greenland was picked up by an old friend who was in the air on a practice flight nearby. He soon flew over and dropped us some emergency supplies: two packets of cigarettes. And I had a carton with me to use as gifts for my friends. He took off saying he'd be back with sandwiches. By the end of the day, two helicopters from the *Edisto* came to pick us up. In no time I found myself on the deck of the icebreaker, and Jung and the others were in a hospital being checked for injuries.

The *Edisto* sailed down the coast to Cape Farewell, planning to go up the east coast to Kulusuk. For a while I was on the bridge sharing what knowledge I had with the pilot. When I told him how to go this way and that around bergs, he looked at me strangely. Then I realized I was basing my instruction on the experience I had with the *Ringsel,* and with the old icebreaker *Northland* when I was with "Iceberg" Smith. The pilot then showed me the new method of navigating these waters—he went right through the bergs! That was a lot of fun. Once we tried to split a well-polished, blue-green berg. Instead of cracking, it rolled, and it seemed to me that half the ship came out of the water when it rode up on the berg; new times, new machines.

We had rounded Cape Farewell heading for Kulusuk, still 150 miles away, when we saw mountains on the horizon. I told the captain those were right by Ammassalik, but he said we were too far away to see them. I reminded him of the refraction that occurs in certain climatic conditions which causes land or objects to appear closer than they actually are. I knew the mountains of Ammassalik when I saw them. There is nothing else like them in the world.

"Refraction!" The skipper laughed. "Of course! It happens a lot at sea. I had heard it was special in the Arctic, but this is the first time I've seen it."

In that area, refraction is so powerful that ships have reported seeing the mountains of Iceland 350 miles away. So I suppose it is possible that the early Vikings, climbing the Icelandic mountains on the west coast during the proper atmospheric conditions, would have been able at times to see the mountains of

Greenland, thus knowing land existed there. They could have sailed west certain of finding land, and thus set the stage for the discovery of America, and all the resulting changes through the centuries of exploration that led up to the scientific age.

It was good to be sailing the east coast of Greenland again. I was reveling in my memories. When we finally reached the Ammassalik area, and went ashore at Kulusuk, I met a Greenlander who was a fish and game inspector, and a sort of chief to the Inuit on that still-lonely coast. His name was Motzfeldt, a name that came from the Norwegian settlements of the 1700s. It was astounding to think that his name invoked the long history of the exploration of Greenland from the Viking age to the Space Age.

By 1963, my time in the Artic had gained me many Danish friends, including Prince Knud, brother of the Danish king. The prince used to come quite often to Greenland to fish. He told me that he thought the government would rather have him in Greenland than in Denmark, as he was a bit of a partygoer. We did quite a lot of that ourselves whenever we met. One time he told me the government had passed a law that made sure no matter what happened in the line of succession to the throne, he could never get it. I wasn't sure if he was kidding or not. He then handed me a pack of the Kings cigarettes he always smoked, and said, "Willie, that's as close as I'll ever get!" He was a damn good man, like most Danes. Fortunately for me, they had long before forgiven me for laying claim to Germania Land, and then selling my claim to Norway.

When the *Edisto* landed at Kulusuk, the Danish government generously invited me on a tour of the scenes of my early exploration in northeast Greenland. We were to fly all the way to Peary Land, where we would celebrate the sixtieth birthday of my old friend, Eigil Knuth. Knuth was still exploring Peary Land every summer. I will never forget the kindness and generosity of that invitation by the Danes.

In a Catalina plane, we first flew over Scoresby Sound, and then the fjord system of "the Riviera of the North" where on board the *Quest* in 1937 we had seen the fantastic rainbow and light effects I wrote about earlier. The plane landed at the Mester Vig, scientific station on King Oscar Fjord, for refueling. Built for the military, but now an important geological studies center, the place was packed with young students from England and Scotland. There was a lead mine there found in 1948 by a geologist who had accompanied Louise Boyd at Revet in 1938. It was his work at the mine which later prompted the building of the geological field school there.

Before departing, I visited the old cabin at nearby Antarctic Haven, built in 1930 by my now-famous archaeologist friend, Helge Ingstad. This was the infamous site which had led to the settlement of Scoresby Sound. As this was 1963, Ingstad was busy in Newfoundland uncovering the Viking settlement there. Helge sure had a powerful effect on history. And standing there by the cabin the most powerful emotions came over me as I recalled the time those two starving trappers, who had been snowbound in that hut for so many weeks, had paddled furiously after the *Quest*, hoping we would see them in time and stop to save their lives. So much had happened since then. I was almost overcome with the wonder of how in the world I was still alive.

Coming out of this rather nice trance, I wandered to a camp of about twelve colorful tents set up in a nearby valley. They belonged to an Italian mountain-climbing group, financed by a rich young man who was with them. They were in virgin mountain-climbing territory, and had come prepared. They had hired Danes to carry in the wine and Italian food. I had to shake my head. What was this coast coming to? Actually, I would have like to have joined them if I had had the time.

We landed next at Ella Island and spent the night at Lauge Koch's old station, which the *Quest* had passed in 1937. Then we flew over Franz Josef Fjord, following in reverse almost the same route that Count Micard and the rest of us had sailed with the *Quest* so long before. From the air, the mountains sparkled with color, especially the old "Devil's Castle." In the distance, the glaciers and ice cap gleamed. I saw Myggbukta, which had been abandoned by the last Norwegian trappers in 1962. Much of the coast is now protected in Erik the Red Park, the largest in the world at 193,050 square miles.

The Catalina next flew over Hold with Hope, the coast where the *Quest* was almost crushed. We flew over Spathe's Plateau where Tutein had been killed by the polar bear. I could see Loch Fine in the distance. Just past the northern cliffs of the plateau appeared Eagle's Nest, the eastern end of my old trapping line! We flew across the bay to Clavering Island and right over Cape Mary where Schjelderup had slaughtered walrus, and had also gathered eggs for the world's most expensive omelet in 1937. The Catalina finally landed at Sandodden, near where *En Avant!* (also known as *Ringsel*) had gone aground on a sandbank in 1938, on our way to Germania Land.

Sandodden was now a modern station, and the place where the Sirius Sled Patrol had originated in World War II. We all had a fine dinner with drinks and speeches, and poetry by Colonel Vestenholtz. Then we got a message of a downed plane in south Greenland, and suddenly, I was left there while Vestenholtz and his crew went south to join in the search.

I moved into the old station for a brief stay, just to remember the old days. It was only about a fifteen-minute walk from the new station, but gave me the solitude I needed. Right outside the door was the grave and marker of Eli Knudsen, who had been killed by Herman Ritter's Nazi weather spies. The marker brought back so many memories. Every morning I saluted Eli's grave.

While waiting for the Catalina's return, I went with the Sirius Patrol by motorboat on their rounds as they checked their traps. We stopped at Sachenburg, where Kalle, Labb, and I had hunted musk ox. It was not that far from Revet, home of the now-deceased "King of Revet." And we were not far from where my ship had met Louise Boyd in 1938. At Sachenburg I stayed in the old cabin of my friend, Herman Andresen, from the early Crimson Route days at Frobisher. I still have the coffee mug he had left there. I was able to do some Inuit site digging and visited some sites where I had found the Dorset Culture relics in 1937. I walked to the eider duck nests where Inuit had once gathered eggs and left their traces. I spent eight fantastic days there alone before the plane came back, this time with a new crew of men I knew from Sondrestrom.

We picked up the "reunion" flight from where we had left off. We passed over Little Koldewey Island, and saw the harbor on its northern tip where *En Avant!* had wintered in 1938 and 1939. Then came Denmark's Haven, where Olsen and I had been with Alvin Pedersen, the musk ox expert whose theories of musk oxen behavior were shattered when the animals decided to charge him. Denmark's Haven was now a research station with a runway, but we did not land there. We flew on, over Germania Land.

I hadn't seen this land that I once owned since I flew out with Count Gaston Micard in the little Stinson rescue plane in 1939. What nostalgia to see that magnificent, if harsh, land again. I saw the scientific station Micardbu, which we had so laboriously built as the then northernmost station in the world. The original building had been slightly altered by the Danes, who had won the court battle over who owned that part of Greenland. I had sold my rights in the nick of time! I was told by my flight crew that Micardbu was still usable and weather-tight, the news of which pleased me to no end.

Flying over Thomas Thompson's Ness, I recalled the time in 1939 when Nils Nois had shot the two bears and we then had to feed their four orphans. My photo had become world-famous. I thought of the many sled trips Nils and I had made up and down that still-uninhabited coast. We flew up to Ile de France, and over to Ingolfs Fjord in Peary Land, where we landed. I had finally reached my earliest—and ultimate—geographic goal for the Norwegian-French Expedition.

Count Eigil Knuth and I just had to laugh when we saw each other. It was something about our lives, something that is hard to explain, but for a long time we couldn't stop laughing. We then both chattered on about how amazing it was that we were even still alive, let alone meeting again after all these years, and in this place! We really enjoyed ourselves, and I guess we deserved it.

He had much to tell me about his work. In 1948, Knuth had discovered an ancient culture unique to Greenland that proved to be four thousand years old. An umiak, or women's boat, from around A.D. 1400 had been found far inland, and it was assumed that this proved the Inuit of old had made migrations from the west to east coasts. At 42,000 square miles (nearly the size of Denmark), this area in the northernmost part of Greenland was the largest ice-free area to be found in that country. We did not have time to do much touring about the camp, but the rocky terrain was fairly flat, and the fact that it had been ice-free for centuries had obviously made it a natural migration route for long-vanished Inuit. It was starkly beautiful, and the air was incredibly clear and invigorating to the lungs. Here at the land closest to the North Pole, the sky's vault seemed very close, and the earth and sky seemed to touch. When I was in Greenwich Village in 1940, I had been given that oil sketch of the western end of this area painted in 1893 by Fredrick Stokes. Here I was now, standing on the east end. It was truly an amazing sight and feeling.

After the celebration of Knuth's birthday, he and the other scientists got ready to leave with us, loading their dogs, and their heavy boxes of specimen rocks and equipment. We had to crawl over everything just to get in. One of the plane's crew members told me that one year Knuth had so many rocks, the plane would never have flown, but they did not know how to break the news to the famous arctic researcher. So as boxes of rocks were passed in one door, the crew dumped others out the other side!

On the return flight we went inland. I saw that the ice at Flade Bay, north of Germania Land, still had not melted. It probably never would—for centuries, at least. We went over the Germania Plateau where Olsen and I had seen the snow curtain after we emerged from the blizzard there. I was also thinking of the time Olsen and I almost died in that terrible ice storm. I was peering down at the harsh land which had once been mine, when Eigil came up to me. He put out his hand. We shook hands while at the same time grasping each other's elbows warmly. Neither of us said a thing.

Nearing Clavering Island again, I saw Wordie Glacier, where I had climbed with Captain Brun on my first arctic adventure. We passed over my old, much-loved cabin, Krogness, my home in 1936 and 1937, and then over Loch Fine where the *Quest* had wintered.

And then we headed home.

Afterword

While at Thule in 1952, I was called to the Pentagon in Washington, D.C. There was no explanation given. Back in the Pentagon, I waited for a long time in one of those cavernous corridors until I was called into what looked like an interrogation room; I got a bit nervous. A very serious man who never gave me his name said he was to ask me some questions about a case code-named "Miss Hansen." He then asked me to look at some photos.

"Do you know this ship?" he asked rather roughly.

It looked like the *Quest*! I knew that Captain Schjelderup had another ship that looked like it, but in any case, I was pretty sure it was one or the other, so I said, yes, it belonged to Captain Schjelderup of Norway.

He said, "We understand from Danish authorities that he went along the west coast of Greenland, and illegally killed more than a thousand walrus. What is your opinion of this data?"

"I wouldn't put it past him," I said drily.

But there was more. "Because of this man's slaughter, walrus hunting has been made illegal on Greenland this year," he said. "But this same boat has recently been seen on the west coast of Greenland, and the east coast of Baffin Island, taking supplies, including fuel drums, from our old World War II stations that are now temporarily shut down. Is this man capable of such illegal activities?" he asked.

I assured him the old sea dog was definitely capable of helping himself to whatever was not nailed down. And by nailed down, I told him, I meant anything Schjelderup could not get up with a twelve-foot crowbar.

Despite these allegations, no one was ever really able to prove anything against the old sea pirate, and he eventually died peacefully at his home near Bodø in 1969, at age eighty-nine, surrounded by family and friends.

While I was liaison officer at Sondrestrom in 1967, I helped initiate plans to retrieve "Fish" Hassell's plane, left on the ice cap near Sondrestrom in 1928 when he ran out of fuel and crash-landed during his attempted nonstop flight to

Europe. Ever since Hassell and I first met in Frobisher Bay, Baffin Island, we had talked of finding and retrieving the Stinson, which he had left intact. The plane had been found once during World War II by my friend, Peter Hostmark, who was originally from Norway but was then living in the U.S. When he found Hassell's plane, he had been looking by dogsled for another downed plane. He was unable to report the coordinates, however, and as the ice cap buried and unburied its "treasures" with the wind, the plane was lost again. When I saw Hassell in England during Operation Moonraker in the 1950s, he told me wistfully, "I wish I could get at least a piece of the plane as a memento." Then, in 1967, we got word at Sondrestrom that the Stinson was found again by a pilot who gave us its coordinates. SAS Airlines and Danish officials cooperated with me in trying to devise some way of getting the plane out. Our motto was, "We shall overcome."

At the end of my assignment in Sondrestrom, and nearing my retirement, I heard rumors that I was to be given a position in some office. It was supposed to be an honor. I had only a year or so to go to retirement, but I did not want to spend that time behind a desk! By calling all my friends in high places, I was given command of the Survival Training School in Fairbanks, Alaska, thus assuring me that upon retirement as a lieutenant colonel, I would still be doing what I was cut out for. Also around this time, my second wife and I divorced. I suppose I should have taken my own advice: Arctic explorers should never marry. It is unfair to the wife and children.

While in Fairbanks, in September 1968, I got this cryptic message from Greenland: WE HAVE OVERCOME! Hassell's plane had been retrieved, and then shipped back to his hometown of Rockford, Illinois, the town *The Spirit of Rockford* had been named after. In 1969 I was invited for the "Fish" Hassell Day Celebration in Rockford, but could not make it. Hassell passed away soon after his wish to retrieve his old aircraft had come true.

While at Fairbanks in 1969, by a wonderful coincidence I was able to visit with my old friends, Bernt Balchen and Louise A. Boyd. Our mutual friendship had spanned the course of thirty years. More than eighty years old, Miss Boyd was in Fairbanks to receive an honorary degree from the University of Alaska for her contribution to the North. Bernt and I had been invited to attend the ceremony. I last saw Miss Boyd at her home in Sausalito, California, right after my retirement. I told her I had been offered a job with Disney Studios to advise on nature films. She told me in her gruff manner, "Willie, dammit! You're retired now! You've earned a rest! Go back to painting and sculpting, for crying out loud!" I took her advice. She died in 1972, and Colonel Bernt Balchen died in 1973.

I decided in 1970 that I would see how Norway looked after all the years I'd been away. I first made a stop in New York City to visit The Explorers Club and Gunvor Bull-Teilman. She still had her studio on Washington Square in Greenwich Village. Finally in Oslo, I jumped off the airport bus near our family apartment, and found myself in snow up to my hips. I said to myself, "I've had it with the snow and cold!" and soon after, decided to move to Almunecar, Spain. I still spent summers in Norway, however.

In Norway, I heard that my old pal and partner, Kalle Nicholaisen, had passed away, and that his sons had emigrated to Alaska. I tried to find Eigil Halvorsen, the photographer from the Micard Expedition in 1936 and 1937, but had no success. For the last twenty years, during the summers I have rented a four-hundred-year-old cabin in the mountainous area of Vågå, near Boverdalen, where my mother's family had lived for centuries before my grandfather emigrated to Tromsø—over a hundred years before I came back. I had come full circle, and got back to painting and sculpting scenes and memories from my arctic life, although Spanish scenes kept me busy with the brushes as well when I spent winters there.

When in Oslo I met many times with Helge Ingstad, now world-famous for his discovery (based a wee bit on my suggestion I like to think) of the Viking settlement. We had great times and drank too much beer and aquavit while talking of the good old days. And Anne Stine still scolded me over the phone every time Helge returned home to her not quite as sober as she would have liked. In 1989, on his ninetieth birthday, I sent Helge a copy of that sketch I had done of him back in 1937.

For a while I kept company with my first fiancée, Inger, whom I had not seen since I'd left to join Count Micard after he sent me that life-changing telegram back in 1936. I even met my second near-fiancée, Anita. She and her husband often came to the same watering holes in Oslo that I frequented during my summer visits. When we met, her husband would discreetly leave us two old lovebirds alone to chat about old times.

In 1981 my first wife, Alice, and I had a reunion after not seeing each other for thirty years. She had quit drinking and joined AA, and was now amazingly recovered from her manic depression. She had already reunited with our children a few years before. We met in Almunecar where we had some laughs about the good times and the bad, and she came with me to the Norwegian cabin for three months before returning to her home in Coconut Grove, Florida.

Now, in 1990, a new generation of explorers and scientists inhabits the North. There are paved roads through Lapland where not even a trail existed in the old days, when I trudged and sloshed across the land. There are tourist hotels at Alta, and at Frobisher Bay, on Baffin Island, as well as on Greenland, including a very fine one at the still-remote village of Ammassalik. My old fiefdom of Germania Land, including Micardbu, is now part of the largest park reserve on earth: Erik the Red Park has more land than France and the British Isles combined. Children have crossed the Greenland ice cap with their parents, but the early dream of making the Arctic the home of large cities and economic markets still remains just a dream. I think that is just as well.

To all of the arctic men and women who have been mentioned in this book, and to the many who deserved to be but space would not allow it, the credit goes to establishing a better understanding of the Arctic, and therefore, of our planet.

Author's Afterword

I n May 1988 my retired and aging Arctic explorer father invited me from California to visit him in Spain. As he so eruditely put it, "Get over here and write my goddamn book before I die!" I thought it would take a year; it took five. The tale did, after all, cover thirty-five years of arctic work. He told his stories to me daily as I taped them, and I would transcribe them each night. He had written two *National Geographic* articles, was a member of The Explorers Club, and had won nearly every prize possible for arctic work. Some of the greatest names of arctic exploration had often come to our house for dinner. But this was the first time he would tell his whole story. Even his family had had no idea of the breadth and depth of his experiences.

My father was an American-born citizen, but had been raised in Norway before returning to America at age twenty-eight. I first wrote the manuscript in English, but as chance would have it, while my father and I were summering in Norway, it turned out the Norwegians were eager to read this famous man's exploits, which had never before been revealed. In 1939 he had been the most famous man in Norway. The nation's largest newspaper, *Aftenposten*, had once given him the whole front page! So, the first publication of the book was in Norwegian. A careful translation was made. Editor Morten Vegem and I worked hourly for months to meet the deadline.

On the night of July 14, 1992, at home in his summer mountain cabin in Norway, my father read the second proof, made a few last corrections, and then said, "You boys did a hell of a job! Couldn't have done it better myself!" He then added, laughing, "Did I really do all that?"

The next day, as I stood outside in the early morning light, I saw him raise his curtain in his bedroom. Just moments later I went to bring him breakfast. I found him naked in his chair by the window with the sun shining in on him. He had lived his life with this motto: "If you make plans, and stick to them, the sun will always be on your path." His story had been told. He was gone.

It has been written that "Real exploration has its psychological and spiritual side." This is certainly true, and you will see plenty of both in this book. But true exploration is also, as my father would say, "a hell of a lot of fun" —

just as my father's life was, just as it was to write this book. This English edition, rewritten in 2004, was an equally enjoyable experience. I was able to add a lot of really good material that was not in the first edition. Not only had my father done "all that." He had done a hell of a lot more!

WILL KNUTSEN
Foxhill-on-Vaar
Denmark
December 23, 2004

Index